Luther Martin of Maryland

Luther Martin
OF MARYLAND

PAUL S. CLARKSON

and R. SAMUEL JETT

The Johns Hopkins Press Baltimore and London

To the Bench and Bar of Maryland

Contents

PART II: 1788–1826

Acknowledgments

For a life of George Washington, Thomas Jefferson, or Abraham Lincoln, the writer can mine dozens of biographies, but the facts of Luther Martin's life are not well documented. To gather them from the places in which they are scattered would have been impossible without the cooperation of many people and institutions. We cannot acknowledge them all: however, special thanks must go to the Library of Congress, the Library of the Baltimore Bar, and the Johns Hopkins, Enoch Pratt, Maryland Historical Society, and Peabody libraries for their courteous help over the years. The American Antiquarian Society, the Maryland Hall of Records at Annapolis, and the New York Public Library have kindly permitted us to quote from letters in their possession. Miss Elizabeth Baer, of the John Work Garrett Library at Evergreen House, The Johns Hopkins University, has graciously allowed us to reproduce its miniature of Luther Martin on the page facing the Introduction. We are grateful to Mrs. Miriam N. Janney for her interest and skillful typing of the several drafts of the manuscript. For the patience, encouragement, and help of our wives over the many years during which this work has been in progress, we are particularly grateful. And to the many others not named here who have encouraged, aided, and abetted this biography, our thanks.

Introduction

> It has been our unhappy destiny to witness at this
> bar, within the short space of some ten years gone, the
> extinguishment of many brilliant lights. . . . The fires
> of Martin, Harper, Pinkney, Winder, and Wirt have all
> been quenched . . . ; and with their departed radiance has
> gone many a proud boast of Maryland. These were
> names in their day, to call up the robust glory of our
> little state and to seat it beside the worthiest in the
> realms of intellect.—John Pendleton Kennedy, "A
> Discourse on the Life and Character of William Wirt"

Judges, generals, politicians, and merchants have their memoirs and
their histories by the thousands, but the most fleeting of all fame is that
of the great lawyer. He may make crucial contributions to the drafting
of a constitution under which a government is born and grows great;
through his learning, resourcefulness, and persuasive skill he may argue
and win cases of the most critical importance to his own and later generations, yet though he change the course of history, his memory is
nonetheless "oft interr'd with his bones." His work may constitute an
enduring monument, but the name of its architect is often forgotten.

Luther Martin was such a lawyer, the foremost among the great men
who comprised the American bar during the first half-century of our
nation's history, 1775–1825. Massachusetts had her Webster and her
Rufus Choate; New York her Hamilton, Jay, and Kent; Pennsylvania
her Rawle, Dallas, Lewis, and Ingersoll; Virginia her Randolphs,
Marshall, and Wythe—all stars of the first magnitude in the legal firma-
ment. But at no time in modern history has any state boasted at one
time such a galaxy of legal figures as the Maryland bar possessed during
this period: Luther Martin, William Pinkney, Reverdy Johnson, Roger
B. Taney, Samuel Chase, Jeremiah Townley Chase, Robert Hanson
Harrison, Gabriel Duvall, William Winder, Robert Goodloe Harper,
William Wirt, and Francis Scott Key. For almost two generations the
acknowledged leader of this group was Luther Martin.

No other lawyer in American history has been so pre-eminently at
the head of his profession for so long a period, and no lawyer played a
larger role in the forensic drama of his own times than Luther Martin.
Attorney general of Maryland for thirty years; counsel upon one side or

the other in approximately half of all the cases argued in the appellate courts of Maryland over a span of twenty-five years—his professional record is almost incredible and is certainly unequaled. He was one of the less well known but nonetheless most influential delegates to the Constitutional Convention of 1787, wrote many sections of that great instrument of government, and (what is of even more importance) prevented, by his dogged leadership and stubborn courage, the drafting of a document which would inevitably have been rejected by the states. He was the successful advocate for the defense in the two greatest state trials of our history, the impeachment of Mr. Justice Samuel Chase and the trial of Aaron Burr for treason; was counsel in forty cases before the bar of the United States Supreme Court, some of them of the deepest importance in the development of our constitutional and commercial law; and was the only lawyer in American history for whose pension an annual license tax was levied by the legislature upon all members of the bar of his state.

It seems hardly possible that a man who played such a part in his country's history could be today so much ignored. This "walking *corpus juris*," "Thersites of the Law," "Bulldog of Federalism," champion of small states and little men, protector of the rights of the individual against the tyranny of entrenched political power, Martin was without a peer in learning and ingenuity or in the size and importance of his practice. Yet even his grave is unmarked and unknown today. The reason for this neglect lies in the principles—largely undervalued and misrepresented in his own day—which Luther Martin espoused and in the unpopular persons and causes which he represented so successfully. Thus, for example, he antagonized the delegates to the Constitutional Convention of 1787 from the large states by exposing, denouncing, and ultimately defeating their plan to push through the convention a form of government which would have put all state and local offices and legislation under the thumb and all citizens under the heel of an omnipotent national government. This central government, though styled a "democracy," would have been controlled by the oligarchy of Virginia, Massachusetts, Pennsylvania, and South Carolina, aristocrats who believed themselves the best qualified by nature, pedigree, learning, and wealth to govern the "lower classes" who comprised the rest of the country.

Luther Martin was not a great democrat, and he had none of the seductive but meretricious graces of the demagogue. He opposed and defeated Jefferson and the leaders of his party who sought, once more in the name of "democracy" and with all the entrenched wealth and power of government, to control the judiciary by the expedient device of impeachment of Justice Samuel Chase. He again thwarted the vindictive attempt of that popular and powerful president to convict his defeated opponent Burr of the capital crime of treason by use of the dubious and self-serving testimony of one of the slipperiest scoundrels in

American history—James Wilkinson, an American general widely believed then (and since proved) to be a secret agent of the king of Spain.

A titanic struggle requires titans. Thomas Jefferson was a fighter, and Martin was an antagonist of equal mettle. Jefferson used all the arts and implements of political office to ensure Burr's conviction: executive messages, speeches, and pronouncements, the "stump," the press release, the power of patronage, and the prestige of his high position. Martin had no such resources. His only arenas were the public forum and the courtroom, his only weapons his own talents as an advocate, his only strength the justice of his client's cause. Beyond this, however, Martin often invoked, on behalf of his client, timeless principles of government or of law which all good men would concede or even champion. His clients' causes became the symbols and the sounding boards for the transcending rights of all men: an independent judiciary (the Chase impeachment); a fair trial for the unpopular and politically persecuted (*Ex parte Bollman* and *United States* v. *Burr*); the rights of a sovereign state over its own territorial and fiscal policy (*Fletcher* v. *Peck* and *McCulloch* v. *Maryland*). If Jefferson fought for the common man, Martin fought for justice under law for *all* men. He knew then that under a judiciary subservient to executive or legislative pressure justice is not only blind but moribund.

If in the course of this account the reader comes upon some facts and conclusions which are strange to him, he should remember that for the most part our histories and biographies have been written by advocates of the principles which Martin opposed and by partisans of his enemies. The purpose of this biography is to present the great men and events of Luther Martin's day as they then appeared to him and to give him his long overdue day in the court of public opinion.

Part I: 1748–1788

I

Ancestry and Early Life, 1748–1760

> I am an American born. . . . My ancestors were, and
> most of their descendants have been . . . agriculturists
> or cultivators of the earth. . . . From the moment I could
> walk until I was twelve years of age, my time was em-
> ployed . . . in some manner or other, useful to the family.
> —*Modern Gratitude*

Luther Martin's great-great-great-grandfather was probably Isaac
Martin, who came from the west of England and settled with his brothers Robert and Abraham at Rehoboth, Massachusetts, around 1623.[1]
It is certain that Luther's great-great-grandfather, whether or not he
was the son of this Isaac, was John Martin, who was born in the early
1620s and was one of the early settlers of the Piscataqua River valley
near Dover, now in New Hampshire but then part of Massachusetts.
It was there that he married Esther (sometimes called "Hester" or
"Easter"), the daughter of Thomas Roberts, one of the founders and
later governor of New Hampshire, who had come from Wallaston,
England, in 1623. Presumably, this marriage was celebrated around
1644, since Mary, their first child, was born in 1645. In the course of
time Mary had seven brothers and sisters, all but the last born in the
Piscataqua settlement and all of them given names from the Bible as a
matter of course: John, Joseph, Lydia, Benjamin, Martha, Thomas,
and James.

The Martins did not find life happy in mid-seventeenth-century
Massachusetts: the soil was flinty and thin and the winters were longer
and colder than any experience had prepared them for. But beyond
merely physical inconveniences, they resented the harsh strictures imposed by the joyless Puritan theocracy of Increase Mather. The settlers
of Piscataqua were serious, sober, industrious Christians, mostly of the
Baptist denomination. To them "blue laws" were no myth, but a way
of life being forced upon them. Puritan magistrates imposed punishment, both monetary and corporal, for "pride or levity of behavior,"
for drinking a health (an "idolatrous" vestige of the "libations of the

---

[1] All genealogical references to Luther Martin's forebears are, unless otherwise
noted, from Ora Eugene Monnette, *First Letters of ye Plantations of Piscataway and
Woodbridge Olde East, New Jersey, 1664–1714*.

7

heathens"), for smoking tobacco ("intoxicating and a waste of time"), and for "indecent exposure" if a woman failed to wear sleeves down to her wrists or to cover her "bosom" all the way up to her ears. As for civil rights, only a free man could vote, and only a church member could be a freeman, but no man could join the only church that counted until he had first been examined and accredited by the Puritan elders.[2] Toleration was regarded as "the first born of abominations," and in 1662 Quaker women were stripped to the waist in the dead of winter, drawn at a cart's tail, and publicly whipped through Dover, Hampton, and Salisbury for the offense of coming into the area to hold private meetings.[3]

At the same time, the shrewd Lords-Proprietors of New Jersey were disseminating to other colonies their famous "Concessions and Agreements," a document destined to become the Magna Carta of that province. They promised complete religious freedom (short of breach of the peace), local self-government, and sixty acres of land (at a very nominal quit rent) for every man who came to New Jersey during the year 1666, "armed with a good Muskett boare twelve bulletts to the Pound, with Tenn pounds of powder and Twenty pounds of Bulletts, with bandeleers and match convenient, and with six months provision for his own person."[4] In May of that year emigrants from Newbury, Massachusetts, led by Daniel Pierce and John Pike, settled an area a few miles to the east and across the Raritan River from New Brunswick, naming their new home after their esteemed pastor, the Reverend John Woodbridge. Some months later a body from the Piscataqua settlements, who had undoubtedly been in correspondence with their neighbors from Newbury, also decided to migrate to a more hospitable clime.

Accordingly, late in the fall of 1666, John Martin, Charles Gilman, Hopewell Hull, "with the ancestors of the Dunns, the Dunhams, the Fitz Randolphs, the Mannings, the Bonhams, and other old and respectable families,"[5] left Massachusetts with their families for the settlements of East Jersey. There was a tradition in the Martin family that John was accompanied by his brother James, who moved on to Calvert County, Maryland, and perhaps founded the Maryland branch of the family. The group traveled by boat, taking with them their lares and penates: their beloved pastor and the church records, household goods, firearms, and provisions for six months. After arriving in New Jersey they made their way westward by land from Elizabethtown along the old Indian trails to the north side of the Raritan River, to the cleared site of an Indian village adjoining Woodbridge on the southwest, just across the river from New Brunswick. They named their new home

---

[2] Jeremy Belknap, *The History of New Hampshire*, 1:67.
[3] George Barstow, *The History of New Hampshire, etc.*, p. 74.
[4] William A. Whitehead, ed., *Documents Relating to the Colonial History of the State of New Jersey*, pp. 28ff.
[5] Luther Martin, *Modern Gratitude*, p. 131.

after their old one in New England, Piscataqua (with the accent on the "cat," gradually corrupted to "Piscataway"). Just one week before Christmas, 1666, the Woodbridge settlers deeded one-third of their patent—some forty thousand acres—to the leaders of the newcomers, John Martin, Charles Gilman, Hugh Dun[n], and Hopewell Hull.[6]

Others joined the settlement, which gradually became a populous township. Life in this new environment was still difficult, however. The toil necessary to retrieve farmland from wilderness was incessant, and cash for even simple luxuries was almost unknown. Crops were uncertain, and the Indians were unfriendly.[7] Almost 150 years later Luther Martin described the hardships endured by his pioneering ancestors in his characteristically florid, eighteenth-century speech:

That part of the Jerseys, was at the time, of which I am speaking, to a great degree, an uncultivated wilderness, inhabited by its copper-coloured aborigines. Yet these first settlers had to build their own huts, to hunt the game of the forest, or ensnare the scaly tenants of the water, for their food. They had to conquer those forests by the toil of their limbs, and by the sweat of their brows to compel the earth to yield to them its stores; for to them the savages of the wilderness did not stretch forth the hand of hospitality; to them they pointed not the openings of their wigwams; to them the savages offered not the flesh of the deer or the bear, the raccoon or the opossum to assuage their hunger, nor the skins of those animals on which they might repose their wearied limbs. In fine, those savages of the wilderness, notwithstanding all that unbounded hospitality and philanthropy of which modern philosophers and a modern president have discovered they once were possessed, in so superior a degree as to shame even the most civilized and polished professors of Christianity, never once formed an idea of introducing those their white-coloured, emigrant neighbours, into their families, and inviting them to participate in all the rights and benefits of children. . . .

I am an American born, of the fourth or fifth generation.[8] My ancestors were, and most of their descendants have been, of that class or "sect" of people known as agriculturists or cultivators of the earth, and therefore, as Jefferson tells us, have had the happiness of being in the number of "God's chosen people, *if ever he had any*"—of which that sage philosopher seems to entertain as great doubts, as I sometimes am inclined to have, notwithstanding his high authority, of Indian hospitality.

Those two of my name, who first came to that part of East-Jersey, obtained grants for lands highly valuable and to a very considerable extent, which is now broken into small farms. For they and their descendants have been among those not the least distinguished for their "conscientious desire to direct their energies to the multiplication of the human race and not to its destruction."

For this conscientious discharge of their duty they needed not the opinions, the advice, nor the exhortation of a sceptical philosopher, if any such philosophers were known to them; to those, whose family motto ("Iatium [word should be "Initium"] Sapientiae est Timor Dei") was selected from the

---

[6] William A. Whitehead, *East Jersey under the Proprietary Governments*, p. 42.
[7] Thomas Francis Gordon, *The History of New Jersey from Its Discovery by Europeans to the Adoption of the Federal Constitution*, p. 122ff.
[8] Probably, as we have seen, the sixth.

9

sacred code, the command of their God, particularly when that command was accompanied with a blessing, was sufficient. ("And God blessed them, and God said unto them, be fruitful, and multiply, and replenish the earth." Genesis Chap. 1st, verse 28th.) Numerous yet are the persons who bear my name in New Jersey, —to almost all of whom I am more or less distantly related, —and the descendants from the same family are to be found from the Hudson on the east to the Spanish dominions on the west; in the States of New York, Pennsylvania, Delaware, Maryland, Virginia, North Carolina, Georgia, Kentucky, Tennessee, and the Territory northwest of the Ohio."[9]

John and Esther Martin's fifth child, Benjamin, was born sometime in 1660 and married Margaret Reynolds (or Rennals) on 24 October 1680. He must have been well thought of and widely respected, as he was named as executor, overseer, or witness in a large number of wills of the period.[10] His first child, named Benjamin, lived only a year; a second child was born the following summer and was named Easter, after Benjamin's mother. The third child, again named Benjamin and destined to become Luther's grandfather, was born on 14 November 1685.[11]

Twenty-one years later, at a meeting held in his home, this Benjamin was chosen the first deacon of a new Seventh-Day Baptist church and was so ordained by the "laying on of hands." At about the same time he married a young woman named Slater, whose given name is variously spelled ("Philaterate," "Philerato," "Filoretta," and "Filiratea" are some of its forms). Their eldest child, another Benjamin (the first of eight, and Luther's father), was born on 13 February 1708 or 1709. This Benjamin must have married at a somewhat older age than was customary, since his wife Hannah (whose maiden name is unknown) was not born until 1720.[12] From the will of Luther's grandfather,[13] Benjamin Martin (the husband of Filoretta), and other sources, we know that Benjamin and Hannah had nine children: Athanasius, James, Luther, Jeremiah, Zephaniah, Reuben, Lenox, and two others whose names are not now known, at least one of whom was a sister younger than Luther.

There has been considerable and quite unnecessary disparity in dates given for Luther's birth. Most writers state that he was born in 1744,[14]

---

[9] *Modern Gratitude*, p. 131ff.

[10] See Abstracts of Wills, *New Jersey Archives*, 1st ser., vol. 23; vol. 1 *passim*.

[11] Two years later, on 12 January 1687, Margaret died at the time of Jonathan's birth. Benjamin subsequently married Margaret Ellstone (or Alston), by whom he had two more children, Mary and Peter.

[12] Her gravestone in the old Baptist cemetery at Piscataway, N.J., gives her date of death as 28 November 1797, and her age then as seventy-seven.

[13] Abstracts of Wills, *New Jersey Archives*, 1st ser., 3:216.

[14] See, e.g., Albert G. Beveridge, *The Life of John Marshall*, 3:186, 4:284–85; John Thomas Scharf, *History of Western Maryland*, 1:383; Edward Schley Delaplaine, *Thomas Johnson, Maryland and the Constitution*, p. 427; Max Farrand, *The Fathers of the Constitution*, p. 36; *Evening Post* (New York), 11 July 1826 (obituary of Luther Martin).

but there is no authority for this date. Luther himself stated very precisely that he was eighteen years and a bit more than seven months old when he was graduated from Princeton on 24 September 1766,[15] making his birth date approximately 20 February 1748. His first name was probably suggested to his Protestant parents through the natural association of the two names Luther Martin with that of the great German reformer, Martin Luther.[16]

Luther's childhood was spent working on his father's farm, caring for his younger brothers and sisters, and seizing every educational opportunity that presented itself. Of his childhood, he later recalled: "I was the third of nine children all of whom arrived to years of maturity, and all of whom, except one, are yet living [written in 1802]. From the moment I could walk until I was twelve years of age, my time was employed, except what was devoted to the acquisition of science, in some manner or other, useful to the family. When too young for any thing else, I rocked the cradle of a brother or sister that was younger."[17] His parents recognized his promise and gave him all the rudimentary instruction in letters and figures that they could. When he was twelve they sent him away to school, although they could barely afford the expense involved and the loss of his labor on the farm. Years later he paid them this tribute:

From my parents I received a sound mind and a good constitution. They with unceasing tenderness and zeal laboured to impress me with principles of manly independence, with a spirit of kindness and generosity towards my fellow-creatures, and with reverential love and fear of my God. And as the best security for my performance of my duty in all situations in which I might be placed in life, they deeply impressed on my young mind the sacred truths of the Christian Religion, the belief of which, though at that time principally owing to education, has since been rivetted by the fullest conviction, grounded on a thorough and dispassionate enquiry. Those sacred truths, which, though too often departed from in my practice, have ever remained too deeply engraven on my heart to be effaced by the hand of infidelity, and the belief of which is my boast.

These, with a liberal education, were all the patrimony they could bestow upon me, —a patrimony for which my heart bears towards them a more grateful remembrance than had they bestowed upon me the gold of Peru, or the gems of Golconda.

Through the fond partiality of my paternal grandfather,[18] I was the owner of a small tract of land on South River, not far from New Brunswick. As soon as the laws of my country gave me the power of disposition, I conveyed it to

---

[15] "When I graduated at Princeton, I wanted near five months of being nineteen years of age" (*Modern Gratitude*, p. 135).

[16] This combination is not unique; a Luther Martin appears in New Hampshire *Town Papers* in 1777 (see vols. 12:398, 13:502; see also Index of Marriages, Hall of Records, Annapolis, Md.).

[17] *Modern Gratitude*, p. 132.

[18] See n. 13 *supra*.

my two elder brothers, as a trifling compensation of the additional toil they had experienced, in contributing to the support of a family, the expenses of which had been increased by reason of my education.[19]

In August 1760, when he was thirteen,[20] Luther Martin started his formal education in the grammar school at Princeton, in preparation for entering the institution then known as the College of New Jersey.

[19] *Modern Gratitude*, p. 132.
[20] *Ibid.*, p. 133. His statement that "in September, five *years next after,* I received the honours of the college" (which, as a matter of record, was in 1766) must have meant the fifth September after the September in which he entered, since he had stated that he worked and studied at home until he was twelve, i.e., 1760 (*ibid.*, p. 132).

2

The College of New Jersey, 1760–1766

> In September [1766] . . . I received the honours of
> the college. . . . I took with me from the College a testi-
> monial from the highest authority that, in a class of
> thirty-five, I was the first scholar in the languages, —and
> second to none in the sciences.—*Modern Gratitude*

The College of New Jersey moved from Newark to Princeton late in
1756.[1] The Reverend Aaron Burr, the young college's second president
(and father of the third vice-president of the United States), finally succeeded in raising the money for the land and buildings through lotteries
and substantial donations from the adventurous, the pious, and the
generous from New England to Old England, and even from Scotland
and Ireland.

The town of Princeton was small, consisting of perhaps seventy-five
or eighty houses, but because it was on the "King's Highway," the main
route from Philadelphia to New York, it was a flourishing and growing
community. It boasted a general store and several craftsmen's shops.[2]
The first two college buildings, Nassau Hall and the president's house,
were completed shortly before Martin entered the grammar school in
the summer of 1760. The former, built of stone quarried nearby and
named in honor of King William, was the most imposing university
building of its day: 176 feet long and 54 feet wide, three stories high
above a basement, it had some sixty rooms, including a chapel, library,
dining hall, kitchen, recitation halls, and dormitory rooms that each
accommodated two and in a pinch as many as three students. The elegant hall was 40 feet square, with a neatly finished front gallery.

The cost of attending the College of New Jersey at this time could
hardly have been less than £30 a year: the basic charges were £4 for
tuition, £15 for board, £3 for laundry, £2 for firewood and candles,
and £1 for room rent. This sum was much more cash than most American families saw in a year and meant great sacrifice for Luther's family.

[1] Except where otherwise noted, all references to the curriculum and life at the
College of New Jersey in the 1760s are taken from John Maclean, *History of the Col-
lege of New Jersey, from Its Origin in 1746 to the Commencement of 1854*; Thomas Jefferson
Wertenbaker, *Princeton, 1746–1896*; and Paul Wallace, *Princeton Sketches, the Story of
Nassau Hall*, pp. 5–8ff. *et passim*.

[2] One of the shops belonged to Elias Boudinot, a tinker, tavern owner, silversmith,
and father of a future president of the Continental Congress (see George Adams
Boyd, *Elias Boudinot, Patriot and Statesman*, pp. 12–13).

An observant young English traveler has provided a picture of the college as of a month before Luther entered it:

At this place, there is a handsome school and college for the education of Dissenters; erected upon the plan of those in Scotland. There are about twenty boys in the grammar-school, and sixty in the college: at present there are only two professors, besides the provost; but they intend, as their fund increases, which is yet very small, and does not exceed 2,000 £. currency, to add to this number. The building is extremely convenient, airy, and spacious; and has a chapel and other proper offices. Two students are in each set of apartments, which consists of a large bedroom with a fire-place, and two studies. There is a small collection of books, a few instruments, and some natural curiosities. The expense to a student for room-rent, commons, and tutelage, amounts to 25 £. currency per year. The provost has a salary of 200 £. currency, and the professors 50 £. each. The name of the college is Nassau Hall.[3]

The grammar school which Luther entered was a preparatory school for the college itself. The lower school taught reading, the "graces of a good delivery," the proper pronunciation of English, and "vulgar arithmetic," but, more important, it was there that Luther "began the first Rudiments of the Latin language"[4] and Greek, which were requirements for admission to the college: "None may expect to be admitted into the College but such as being examined by the President and Tutors shall be found able to render Virgil and Tully's[5] Orations into English; and to turn English into true and grammatical Latin; and to be so well acquainted with the Greek as to render any part of the four Evangelists in that language into Latin or English; and to give the grammatical connexion of the words."[6]

Upon entering the college itself, Luther was confronted with a heavy load of daily activities—a collegian of today under such a regimen would consider himself hardly used. "The rising bell" sounded at 5 A.M. It rang again at 6 A.M. for morning prayers, followed by breakfast; the first classes began at 7—recitations in Xenophon's *Cyropedia* or in Watts's *Ontology*. At 8 the freshman class proceeded to the translation of Cicero's orations, and later to other courses in the Greek New Testament, Horace, and Lucian's Dialogues.

In the sophomore year the students were introduced to Homer and Longinus, rhetoric and logic, and the sciences: geography, astronomy, and mathematics. In mathematics "the five common rules of arithmetic, interest, rebate, equation of payments, barter, loss and gain, fellowship, compound-fellowship, the double rule of three, comparative arithmetic, geometrical progression, vulgar and decimal fractions, and the square root" were emphasized.[7]

[3] Andrew Burnaby, *Travels through the Middle Settlements in North America in the Years 1759 and 1760*, ed. Rufus Beckwell Wilson, p. 103.
[4] *Modern Gratitude*, p. 133.
[5] Marcus Tullius Cicero.
[6] Maclean, *History of the College of New Jersey*, 1:259.
[7] *Ibid.*, 1:266–67.

In the junior year natural and moral philosophy, physics, and meta-physics were offered, and for those planning to enter the ministry (probably at least half of the students), the beginnings of Hebrew grammar. When he entered his senior year, Luther could compose in Latin and Greek and could read critically "the most improving parts of the Latin and Greek classics,"[8] including Virgil's *Aeneid* and the Bucolics and Georgics, Horace, Lucian, Xenophon, Homer, and Erasmus.

The college was strong on discipline: no student was permitted to be absent from his room without the permission of the president or a tutor. Tutors and upperclassmen were saluted on sight. Of course, young ladies might not be entertained in the dormitory rooms, nor could the students jump, holler, or "make any boisterous noise in the hallways."[9] One wonders whether these rules were observed to the letter.[10]

Seniors had free access to the college library for research and for such collateral reading as their curiosity and opportunity afforded. The library contained only about thirteen hundred volumes, but among them was the finest of English literature and the classics, as well as some of the most abstruse and ponderous theological treatises ever written. Homer, Xenophon, Aristotle, Horace, Sallust, Plutarch, Caesar, Cicero, Tacitus, and Cato, Bacon, Pope, Locke, Shakespeare, and Dryden, were side by side with such weighty tomes as Bunyan's works, *The Whole Duty of Man*, Cotton Mather's *History of England*, Milton's works, Burnet's *State of the Dead*, and the sermons of such Calvinist worthies as Whitefield, Edwards, Pemberton, Tennent, and Doddridge. Although there were a few volumes of geography, navigation, and physics, the library was markedly weak, even for the time, in science.

"Extracurricular activities" during the last two years consisted of practice two or three times a week in debating, both forsenic and syllogistic. These exercises were supplemented by frequent orations of the students' own composition and by declamations selected "from Cicero, Demosthenes, Livy, and other ancient authors, and from Shakespeare, Milton, Addison, and such illustrious moderns as are best adapted to display the various passions and exemplify the graces of utterance and gesture."[11] These speeches were often delivered before the student body at the regular Sunday evening assembly.

A natural outcome of this regimen was the formation of debating societies. In his junior year Luther joined with Oliver Ellsworth, William Paterson, Robert Ogden, and Tapping Reeve to form the "Well Mean-

---

[8] *Ibid.*
[9] *Ibid.*
[10] Another Princeton scholar recollected in 1770 that the students indulged in "strowing the entries in the night with greasy Feathers; freezing the bell; Ringing it at late Hours of the Night; . . . Parading bad Women . . . Darting Sun-Beams upon the Town-People, Reconoitering Houses in the Town, & ogling Women with the Telescope—Making Squibs, & other frightful compositions with Gun-Powder, & lighting them in the Room of timorous Boys, & new comers" (Philip Vickers Fithian, *Journal & Letters of Philip Vickers Fithian, 1773-1774*, ed. Hunter Dickinson Farish, pp. 253–54).
[11] Maclean, *History of the College of New Jersey*, 1:281.

ing Society." Restricted to "the first young men in point of character and scholarship," it held its meetings in one of the rooms on the top floor of Nassau Hall. A similar and competing fraternity, called the "Plain Dealing Society," was organized at about the same time.[12] However praiseworthy in objectives and accomplishment the two societies may have been at the outset, they were suppressed by the faculty shortly after Martin's graduation because of a "violent and vitriolic pamphlet war." In 1770, however, the members of the Well Meaning Society organized in its place the famous Cliosophic Society, which has continued to this day.[13]

During almost all of Luther's attendance at the College of New Jersey, its president was the Reverend Samuel Finley. Short and stocky in build and ruddy of countenance, he was remarkably sweet in disposition for a mid-eighteenth-century Presbyterian divine. Although he had few of the oratorical graces, his sermons made up in substance what they lacked in form and style, being "calculated to inform the ignorant, to alarm the careless and secure, and to edify and comfort the faithful."[14] His influence upon the later religious, intellectual, and political life of this country through the many "boys" who came under his inspiring and beneficent spell was beyond measure. Dr. Finley, in addition to his other duties, taught Latin, Greek, and Hebrew to the senior class and was beloved by the entire student body. Two months before Martin graduated, he died suddenly in Philadelphia while undergoing medical treatment, on 17 July 1766. Eight seniors, in accordance with his last wish, bore his body to the grave.

Luther's roommate in college was John MacPherson, who was beloved by all who ever knew him. He and Martin "trod together the flowery paths of science from the grammar school through all the classes of the college. We graduated together. About the same age, our pursuits were the same. Few brothers were ever bound together by stronger bonds of affection."[15] Another member of Luther's class was Oliver Ellsworth, one day to hold the positions of attorney general, congressman, and senator from Connecticut. He joined Martin in the drafting of the Constitution at Philadelphia in 1787 and later still, while presiding as its chief justice, heard Martin arguing many cases before the United States Supreme Court. Other classmates were Waightstill Avery, who became attorney general of North Carolina and, with another classmate, Hezekiah Balch, aided in drafting the famous Mecklenberg Resolves; David Howell, professor of natural philosophy at the College of Rhode Island (later Brown University), noted congressman, jurist, pundit, and wit; and Nathaniel Niles, Connecticut and Vermont inventor, metaphysician, philosopher, and jurist. Other men whom Luther knew well as upper- or lowerclassmen who

[12] Jacob N. Beam, *The American Whig Society of Princeton University*, pp. 14ff.
[13] Wertenbaker, *Princeton, 1746–1896*, p. 201. See also George M. Giger, *The Cliosophic Society*; Samuel H. Wandell and Meade Minnegerode, *Aaron Burr*, 1:31.
[14] Maclean, *History of the College of New Jersey*, 1:281.
[15] *Modern Gratitude*, p. 133.

were later famous were William Paterson, Tapping Reeve, Thomas John Claggett, Nathaniel and David Ramsay, Jacob Rush, and Ephraim Brevard.

In August of 1766 Luther and his fellow seniors stood for their final comprehensive examinations. In this public ordeal each student was quizzed orally by a group made up of the trustees, the college officers, and any other "gentlemen of liberal education" who chose or chanced to drop in for the occasion. The questions covered the entire four years of study, with special emphasis on the student's proposed professional field. When this trial was over, the students were invited to dine with the trustees. In place of their usual plain fare, they might have "punch, or ham and green peas"—small enough reward, one might think.

On the last Wednesday of September graduation exercises were held. The Princeton Presbyterian church was crowded with the students' families and friends and with the general public, who came from miles around to attend. To people without education or entertainment, the opportunity to see some of the country's most learned men, in all the color and pageantry of academic gowns and processions, and to hear eloquent speeches on subjects both sacred and profane and erudite disputations in both foreign and familiar tongues was not to be missed. At the call of *"progredimini juvenes!"* the participants in the ceremonies proceeded to the church. After the opening prayer the Reverend Elihu Spencer, presiding in the place of the deceased President Finley, spoke: "Doctors and gentlemen, these young men wish to greet you with an oration." This was the signal for the salutatorian, Waightstill Avery, to welcome the assembly in Latin. Dr. Spencer then announced that "whereas, learned doctors, it is a very worth while thing to carry on a rational argument leading to truth away from falsehood, these young men, about to be initiated, will give you a sample of what they can do." There ensued a series of debates in Latin between various members of the graduating class on such subjects as "Whether Moral as Well as Mathematical Truths Are Capable of Demonstration," "Whether Noah's Flood Was Universal," and "Whether the Liberty of Acting According to the Dictates of Conscience, in Matters Merely Religious, Ought To Be Restrained by Any Human Power."[16] This part of the entertainment was completely incomprehensible to the great majority of the assembly, who nonetheless enjoyed it as thoroughly as audiences always enjoy a mystery. But they were not entirely neglected. Other orators spoke in English on such topics as "Patriotism" and "The Blessings of Peace," in order, as the president explained with some condescension, to illustrate the advantages of the "cultivation of one's native tongue." Late in the day the degrees were awarded. Although he ranked first in his class in languages and sciences, Luther has frequently been misunderstood as saying that he was "graduated with honours." He was close to the top of his class, however.[17]

[16] Maclean, *History of the College of New Jersey*, 1:254, 268.
[17] *Modern Gratitude*, p. 136.

3

School Teacher and Law Student, 1766-1771

> My object, in applying for that [teaching] establish-
> ment was, that it might be to me a temporary support
> during the time, I should find necessary for the acquisi-
> tion of a competent knowledge of the law.—*Modern
> Gratitude*

On 26 September 1766 Luther Martin, with his horse, the "small remains" of his pocket money, and some letters of recommendation, set
forth into the world. He was accompanied by young John Bowden and
a few other intimate friends as far as Philadelphia and then went on
alone to the school of the Reverend Mr. Hunt (or Hunts) near the
Octorara Creek in Cecil County, in northeastern Maryland.[1]

It would be pleasant to be able to state that Martin had been recommended to teach at West Nottingham Academy, also on Octorara
Creek, near Rising Sun in the same part of Cecil County, the institution
founded in 1744 and made justly famous by the Reverend Samuel
Finley.[2] He would hardly have failed to mention that he was recommended to teach at West Nottingham, however, and in fact, the pastor
(and thus, in all likelihood, the schoolmaster) at West Nottingham in
1766 was not Dr. Hunt but the Reverend John Beard.[3] Of Hunt not
much is known. He was, in all likelihood, the Reverend James Hunt,
one of the great eighteenth-century secondary school teachers in colonial America. His school at this time was at Upper Octorara, a few
miles north of West Nottingham. He was the product of a great educational trinity: Samuel Finley, Nottingham Academy, and the College
of New Jersey, He became pastor of a Presbyterian church at Bladens-
burg, Maryland, where he opened a school in 1773. It prospered, and
ten years later he moved it to his farm, "Tusculum," in Montgomery

---

[1] All quotations attributed to Martin in this chapter are from *Modern Gratitude*, pp.
132–62 *passim*.

[2] Alice E. Miller, *Cecil County, Maryland, a Study in Local History*, pp. 142–45; Henry
Gress Hanna, *West Nottingham Academy Bicentennial Historical Sketch*, p. 4. By 1766 this
small school numbered among its graduates two signers of the Declaration of
Independence, two members of the Constitutional Convention of 1787, many members of the Continental, and later the Constitutional, Congress, the first United
States senator from North Carolina, the first elected governor of Maryland, and a
series of doctors, lawyers, and founders and presidents of colleges.

[3] *West Nottingham Catalog of Alumni*, p. 4.

County. It was at Tusculum Academy, under the guidance of the cultured, learned, and philosophical Hunt, that William Wirt was educated.[4]

Hunt received Martin kindly (he may have remembered him as an undergraduate at Princeton, as he received his master's degree there in 1763) but told him that the position of assistant master, which Martin had expected, had been filled only a few days before. Martin's hopes were once more raised, however, when he was informed that a schoolmaster was badly needed at Queen Anne's County Free School at Queenstown, some sixty miles down the peninsula of Maryland's Eastern Shore. The teacher there had recently died, and at Mr. Hunt's Martin met a relative[5] who was planning to go down to Queen Anne's to settle affairs there. They prevailed upon Martin to apply for the position, gave him additional letters of introduction and recommendation, and assured him that he was welcome to return to Upper Octorara if for any reason he should be unsuccessful in Queen Anne's.

Queen Anne's County Free School was an institution with a curious history. Believers in the Free State as the most tolerant of the colonies may be surprised to learn that its public school system had its beginnings in a fund established by its Provincial Assembly from a tax on "Irish Servants, being Papists, to prevent the growth of Popery" in the Province. In 1715 the Maryland Provincial Assembly passed a "tariff act" laying duties upon the importation of Negroes, hard liquors, and Irish servants.[6] The stated purpose of the last-named tax of 20 s. per head was "to prevent too great a number of Irish Papists being imported into this Province," but apparently it was imposed upon all Irish servants whatever their religious faith. Two years later, however, an additional duty of another 20 s. was laid upon the importation of "Irish servants, *being Papists*." The administration of the Oaths of Abjuration and Test was required "for the better Discovery of such Irish Papists,"[7] and anyone refusing to take them was declared by the statute to be *ipso facto* Catholic and subject to the duty. By the former, one was bound not to acknowledge any right in the Pretender to the throne of England; by the latter, one acknowledged one's allegiance to and the supremacy of George III, subscribed to a declaration against Transubstantiation, and promised to receive the Sacrament according to the usage of the Church of England.

[4] Information furnished by J. Paul Slaybaugh, president of Wesley Junior College in Dover, Delaware, and author of *Private (Independent) Secondary Education in Maryland*. See also Bernard Christian Steiner, *History of Education in Maryland*, p. 37; Scharf, *History of Western Maryland*, 1:669, 753; John Pendleton Kennedy, *Memoirs of the Life of William Wirt*, 1:42.

[5] The teacher was John Dehorty, formerly of Cecil County. His relative may have been a young man named Holmes but was more probably William Dehorty, the administrator of his estate (cf. Queen Anne's School Minute Book, p. 209, and *Modern Gratitude*, p. 136).

[6] References to this colonial legislation are from vol. 1 of Thomas Bacon's *Laws of Maryland at Large . . . (1637–1763)*.

[7] *Ibid.*, chap. 36, par. 1713.

Of particular interest is the fact that this enactment declared that the duties collected should "for the Advancement of Learning be applied towards the Encouragement of one Public School in every County within this Province."[8] To clarify and emphasize the purpose of the tax, in 1732 the Assembly repealed it for "Irish servants being Protestants," declaring that "no duty . . . ought to be paid for or upon the importation of any Protestant . . . from the Kingdom of Ireland, or elsewhere, into this Province." The impost of 40 s. per head on Irish Catholics remained.

Meanwhile, in 1723, after a number of abortive efforts, the Assembly passed an "Act for the Encouragement of Learning, and erecting Schools in the several Counties within this Province."[9] This law declared in its Preamble that "preceding Assemblies for some Years past have had much at Heart" the problem of providing for "the liberal and pious Education of the Youth of this Province, and improving their natural Abilities and Acuteness (which seems not inferior to any)."[10] The act divided the funds obtained by the duties equally among the twelve counties of the province, and put each share to the credit of a self-perpetuating Board of Visitors in each county, a public corporation set up to establish and maintain a centrally located school. Each Board of Visitors was authorized to purchase 100 acres or more of land for the school lot and to clear 50 acres of it, which the schoolmaster was permitted to use for planting grain or for pasturage. (He was expressly forbidden to raise any tobacco; perhaps the local planters considered this unfair, or at least unnecessary, competition.)

The Visitors were instructed to encourage "good Schoolmasters, that shall be Members of the Church of England, and of pious and exemplary Lives and Conversations, and capable of Teaching well" the three R's, "the Grammar, good Writing, and the Mathematics."[11] As a prudent afterthought, all the above was required in a schoolmaster only if "such can be conveniently got." He was allowed a stipend of twenty pounds per annum for teaching the "free scholars" appointed by the Visitors and whatever he was able to obtain by individual arrangements with the more affluent parents of other children. No one will be surprised to find on the rolls of the school a large number of scholarship or "foundation" students bearing the surnames of the members of the Board of Visitors.[12]

The Queen Anne's County Free School, established promptly under this act in 1724, had a long but uneven and often turbulent existence.[13]

[8] *Ibid.*
[9] *Ibid.*, chap. 19, par. 1723.
[10] *Ibid.*
[11] *Ibid.*
[12] See, e.g., Frederic Emory, *Queen Anne's County, Maryland, Its Early History, and Development*, p. 246ff.; Queen Anne's School Minute Book, *passim*.
[13] See, generally, Edwin H. Brown, Jr., "First Free School in Queen Anne's County," p. 1ff.; Emory, *Queen Anne's County*, pp. 241–56. For some reason, neither Brown nor Emory mention the anti-Catholic origins of this school legislation.

It may have been a bad omen that the lot purchased by the Visitors, a hundred-acre parcel from Richard Tilghman's tract, was known as "The Forlorn Hope." From the complete specifications, which have been preserved, it must have been a very substantial, even imposing, building,[14] and by the time Martin arrived in Queenstown in October, 1766, a dwelling house, kitchen, and barn had been added.

For reasons not entirely clear, Martin did not receive his appointment as master until the following April. There may have been difficulty in getting enough students together to make it worth while. Apparently, there were also vacancies on the Board of Visitors which had to be filled before an appointment could be confirmed.[15] Martin presumably spent most of this intervening period of six months at his home in New Jersey.[16] The minutes of the Board meeting of 23 April 1767 record that "Mr. Luther Martin is admitted Master of the School for one Year to commence from the Day of the opening the said School after his Qualification, who agrees to keep the same for the Salary of Twenty Pounds Lawful Currency."[17] Despite his youth, Martin was chosen over another applicant on the basis of his letter from Princeton certifying his high marks there.

A week later, he delivered to the Board a Certificate of Qualification, showing that he had taken and subscribed to the Oaths of Abjuration and Test, and the Visitors turned over the school's texts and apparatus to him. Books in those days were neither cheap nor common but were treasured and passed on from master to master like heirlooms; they had to be accounted for by each master at the end of his tenure. The books, equipment, and instruments which Martin received indicate the curriculum:

Molineux's *Dioptricks*	Moxon's *On the Globes*
Greek Celestial Motions	*The Cambridge Dictionary*, Covers
Casewell's *Trigonometry*	off

---

[14] Charles Branch Clark, *The Eastern Shore of Maryland and Virginia*, 2:702; Emory, *Queen Anne's County*, p. 243; Brown, "First Free School," p. 1. The site was on the south side of the road from Queenstown to Chester Mills "near where the road branches off, which leads to Tilghman's Neck." The Visitors hired John Salisbury to build the schoolhouse "35 feet long, 20 feet wide and 10 feet pitch, between the floor and roof proportionable, the walls of good well burnt bricks; well laid in mortar 18 inches up to the water table" (Emory, *Queen Anne's County*, p. 243). The first teacher, David Davis, was appointed on 16 January 1724. Although there were a dozen others in the next forty-two years, the school was frequently closed for long periods for want of a teacher, pupils, or both.

[15] The Board of Visitors then consisted of Robert Lloyd, Edward Tilghman, James Hollyday, Dr. John Smith, Colonel Richard Tilghman, Dr. John Jackson, and the Reverend John Barclay. The last three were replaced in December by the Reverend Samuel Keene, William Hemsley, and a younger Richard Tilghman (Queen Anne's School Minute Book, p. 208).

[16] He later recalled that he was nineteen years old when he moved to Queen Anne's and that he moved to Somerset County in the spring of 1770 after living in Queen Anne's for almost three years (*Modern Gratitude*, pp. 138, 140).

[17] Queen Anne's School Minute Book, p. 209.

Good's *Dialling*	Terence's *Comedies*
Scarborough's *Euclid*	Clark's *Homer* 2 Vol
Gregory's *Astronomy* 2 Vol	Horace
Theodosius's *Spherics*	Ovid's *Metamorphoses*
Mercator's *Chart & Plain Chart*	Virgil 3 Vol
Kennett's *Antiquities*	Dionisus' *Geography*
Sallust	Parson's *Clavis Arithmetico*
Potter's *Antiquities* 2 Vol	Caesar's *Commentaries* 2 Vol
Gordon's *Geographical Grammar*	Lycius' *Florus* 2 Vol
	Wells's *Maps*

Marriner's Compass rectified	A Protracting Scale, Box Wood
The Use of the Triangular Quadrant	Gunter's Quadrant Pear Tree
A Circumferenter with Ball Sockett	A Pair of Globes &ca
A Brass Protractor to the same Radius	Fore & Back staff Box
A Brass Protracting Scale	Cross's & Vanes part lost
Brown's Triangular Quadrant, Box wood	Davis's Quadrant
Gunter's Sector Brass	Box Nocturnal[18]

From April through September classes were held from 7 to 11 A.M. and 1 to 5 P.M.; during the fall and winter they began at 6 and ended at 4. There were two weeks' vacation at Christmas and ten days' vacation at Easter and Whitsuntide. There was no school on Sundays and a half day only on Saturdays from November to May.[19] The Minute Book shows that on one occasion the Visitors caught the students "shooting at marks with Guns." They were warned not to do so again, and Martin was ordered to "pay strict attention during their play time and to punish any who shall be catch'd with Guns contrary to this . . . admonition."[20] The offense does not seen too heinous, in view of the location of the school (well out in the country), the general and necessary familiarity of everyone with firearms at the time, and the recent French and Indian wars. On another occasion during Martin's first year the Visitors observed that the students were "uttering their words in a thick confused manner," but there is no indication that he was blamed for this or, indeed, for any other matter, since his services were retained by the Visitors for three years.[21] During this period he made a few visits to his family in New Jersey and kept up a steady correspondence with his Princeton friends Paterson, MacPherson, and Rush.[22]

At this time Martin began to read law at night in the library of Solomon Wright, whose children he taught in school. Wright was one

---

[18] *Ibid.*, pp. 209–10.
[19] Brown, "First Free School," p. 4.
[20] Queen Anne's School Minute Book, p. 210.
[21] *Ibid.*, p. 211. Brown says that Martin was blamed for these dialectal aberrations, but he is unsupported by the Minute Book and the other sources.
[22] *Modern Gratitude*, p. 138; William Paterson, *Glimpses of Colonial Society, and the Life at Princeton College*, ed. Wayne Jay Mills, pp. 37, 141 ff.

of the most able, active, and civic-minded men in the county.[23] He and his wife took a liking to Martin, and he became a frequent visitor to their home. "From him," Martin later wrote, "I had occasionally the use of such books as I had time to read—by him and his very worthy lady I was during the whole time I remained in that county treated almost as a son."[24]

Martin left Queenstown in 1770 for several reasons. The Visitors paid no part of a master's salary until the end of the school year, a device that was calculated to drive an impecunious teacher into debt, and apparently then, as throughout his later life, Martin could not keep within his budget. By the spring of 1770 he owed money to a number of people (in 1769 he had tried, unsuccessfully, to borrow money through his friend Paterson, who was practicing law in New Jersey.[25]) As he himself later observed. "The profits which I received as master of the free-school were the only funds I enjoyed—from which I had to defray the expences of cloathing, lodging, board, physic, books, travelling and every other incidental charge—I am not *even yet*, and I was not *then*, nor have I *ever* been, an *economist* of any thing but time."[26] According to his account, after talking it over with his friends he decided to stop teaching altogether, to borrow enough money to enable him to devote one year to the study of law, and to pay off his various overdue debts. Accordingly, he left Queen Anne's for Back Creek in Somerset County, where he intended to read law full time under Samuel Wilson, Esq., without the distraction of school teaching. When he returned to Queenstown briefly to settle his affairs, he found five suits pending against him for a total of some £11. With the help of Wright he convinced his creditors that he had no intention of absconding and that he would pay them within a reasonable time, and the suits were struck off the county court docket.[27]

There was gossip in later years that Martin's departure from Queenstown was attended, if not caused, by circumstances other than an ambition to enter the legal profession. The first such charge was published in the course of a "broadside war" between Martin and Robert Lemmon some time after the former was appointed attorney general

[23] A prominent lawyer, he later became a delegate to the Provincial Assembly, and when the Revolution took place, he was appointed clerk at the first county court set up under the new state constitution. He was made chairman of the Queen Anne's County Committee of Correspondence at the convention held on 30 May 1777 (Peter Force, ed., *American Archives—1790–1868*, 1:366), and played a very active part in the prosecution of the Revolutionary war on the Eastern Shore. He was a member of the Maryland state conventions of 1775 and 1776 and was one of the first judges appointed to the Maryland Court of Appeals. His son Robert became both a governor of the state and a United States senator (Emory, *Queen Anne's County, passim*).

[24] *Modern Gratitude*, p. 138.

[25] Paterson, *Glimpses of Colonial Society*, p. 141.

[26] *Modern Gratitude*, p. 139.

[27] These debts were all paid in full by 1775 (*ibid.*, p. 154).

of Maryland in 1778. One of Lemmon's partisans suggested that Martin had been "kicked out" of Queenstown because of "impertinence" to the parent of one of his pupils (presumably a girl).[28] In 1802 the adventurer and soldier of fortune Richard Reynal Keene (in the course of an attempted justification of his elopement with Martin's fifteen-year-old daughter), published an equally suggestive and equally unsupported accusation: "You [Martin] entered into your establishment [the school at Queenstown], but alas! it become [*sic*] *expedient* for you to retire. And thus was forfeited, *not* 'the roof of hospitality' by a *chaste amour*; but the post of honor and of profit by—I blush to state the cause!"[29] One may be sure that Keene would not have hesitated to make public the unsavory particulars, if there were any to be told.

The gossip was embroidered with slightly more detail in 1911, but nothing substantial was added: "He remained for about two years, just when and why he left is not known, because the page which would, and possibly did contain this information, is torn in half and part removed from the [Minute] book. It is said that Martin spent most of his time in drinking and finally left the county because his attention to a daughter of a prominent planter was very objectionable."[30] This passage is remarkable for seeming to say much more that it actually does, and must be scrutinized carefully. First, Martin's ability, character, and behavior were satisfactory enough for his teaching contract to be twice renewed by the Board of Visitors, and he served as master at Queenstown for *three* years;[31] he then went on to teach at other schools on the Eastern Shore for two years more. Second, as the published correspondence of the parties concerned shows,[32] "just when and why" Martin left Queenstown is definitely known: he left about April 1770 in order to study law with Samuel Wilson. Third, the page in the Minute Book which could have contained this information is not "torn in half": the top of the page has been cut out by some person, at some time, for some purpose, all unknown.[33] Fourth, the last sentence may or may not be true but, so far as Keene knew, was hearsay and utterly unsubstantiated. It sounds like an ascription to Martin's youth of some of the weaknesses he developed later in life. Martin himself admitted that he went into debt and was imprudent, but he denied anything more than the "usual foibles and errors of a youthful, generous, unsuspecting heart."[34]

---

[28] Miscellaneous Broadside Volume, p. 23, Maryland Historical Society, Baltimore, Maryland.

[29] "A Letter from Richard Reynal Keene to Luther Martin, Esq.," June 1802, in Miscellaneous Broadside Volume, p. 50; *Modern Gratitude*, pp. 122, 153ff.

[30] Brown, "First Free School," p. 10.

[31] *Modern Gratitude*, p. 140. Probably early in April 1770, as Martin states that he was at Queenstown for almost three years (p. 138).

[32] *Ibid.*, p. 141ff.

[33] It is highly unlikely that any such data were recorded there. The words that remain in the margins indicate that the entries concerned only routine business and administrative matters. The page may have been cut for a spill to light a pipe, for that matter.

[34] *Modern Gratitude*, p. 162.

Furthermore, when Keene published these innuendoes, Martin publicly appealed to the people in Queen Anne's who had known him in his early days to say "whether they ever knew or heard of any instance of my conduct when I lived in Queen-Ann, base or dishonourable— whether they ever knew or heard of any cause for my leaving that county, to state which ought to excite a blush in the cheek of any man."[35] No one—friend or enemy, biographer, scholar, or archivist— has brought forward any explicit charge of serious misconduct on Martin's part during this period.

Martin's character at this time is indicated by his friends, associates, sponsors, and people who extended to him their homes, hospitality, and love. While visiting former college friends at Back Creek Academy,[36] Martin became well acquainted with such prominent Somerset County residents as Levin Gale, William Winder, and Samuel Wilson. Gale, an affluent shipowner and lawyer, had been a judge of the Land Office and a justice of the provincial court. A few years after Martin met him, he was appointed one of the first judges of the General Court under Maryland's first constitution. He and his wife treated Martin like "kind and affectionate parents." (A little later, as "proof of esteem and confidence," they placed their eldest son with Martin for instruction in the law.)[37] William Winder was a justice of the peace for Somerset County, and Wilson, of course, had invited Martin to study law at his home.

While he was in Somerset County Martin met John Leeds Bozman, a twelve-year-old boy attending Back Creek Academy. Young Bozman was bright and curious, and Martin took an interest in him.[38] When his father died in 1767, young John and his mother had gone to live with her father, John Leeds of Talbot County, one of the most accomplished scientists and most neglected figures of the American colonial and Revolutionary period. He was born in Talbot County in 1705 and his Quaker mother was left a widow three years later. He had

[35] *Ibid.*

[36] Martin's friends teaching at Back Creek (later known as Washington) Academy were Ephraim Brevard and Thomas Reese. During the Revolution Ephraim was one of seven Brevard brothers who joined the Continental Army. He served four years as a surgeon to the First North Carolina before he was taken prisoner. In 1780 he was freed and died shortly thereafter as a result of a disease he had contracted while a prisoner. Thomas Reese became a famous Presbyterian divine. He served parishes in both North and South Carolina and became well known for his missionary work among the Negro slaves in his district.

[37] *Modern Gratitude*, p. 152.

[38] Three years later the boy entered the College of Philadelphia, from which he graduated in 1776. After the Revolution he went to London to study law at the Middle Temple. When he returned to the United States he served an apprenticeship in the office of Judge Robert Goldsborough. In 1789 Martin was pleased to appoint him deputy attorney general for Talbot and Caroline counties, a position he held until 1807. Thereafter, Bozman devoted most of his time to legal and historical studies. His *History of Maryland, from its first settlement in 1633 to the Restoration in 1660*, though narrow in scope (it covered only the first generation of the colony), was the first scholarly treatment of the subject. See Samuel A. Harrison, *A Memoir of John Leeds Bozman—The First Historian of Maryland*; E. Alfred Jones, *American Members of the Inns of Court*, pp. 27–28.

no opportunity for any formal or extensive education, but his natural talents were such that he became an outstanding mathematician, astronomer, geodesist, and optician. He was deputy surveyor general for the Eastern Shore and also held, in succession, the posts of justice of the peace, clerk of Talbot County, naval officer for Oxford, treasurer of the Eastern Shore, and His Majesty's Judge of the Provincial Court— this last office exceeded in dignity and importance only by that of the colonial governor. In 1762, when the surveyors Mason and Dixon were instructed to draw their famous line dividing the lands of the Penns and the Calverts, Leeds was appointed by Governor Horatio Sharpe to the commission supervising the work. "He did not think it safe with regard to Lord Baltimore's interest," the Governor said, "to be without him, there being no other person he could procure to assist, whose knowledge of such matters he could rely on."[39] With the advent of the Revolution, Leeds found himself unable to renounce his allegiance to the King, resigned all his official positions, and remained a firm but inactive and unmolested Tory. He died in 1790, honored and respected by all who knew him. The "esteem and friendship" of such a man[40] can therefore be considered a tribute to Martin's character and personality.

Martin had been studying at Wilson's for only a few weeks when he was first asked, then begged, to take the place of another fellow Princetonian, David Ramsay, at Onancock Grammar School, far down the Eastern Shore in Accomack County, Virginia.[41] At first Martin declined, on the grounds that it would interfere with his study for the bar. After a personal interview with Ramsay and the trustees of the school, however, he yielded and, some time in the early summer of 1770, took on the duties of superintendent of the grammar school.

The Onancock school fall vacation came about the middle of October, and Martin used the opportunity to return to Queenstown for his personal belongings. From there he went to Baltimore, where he saw Col. Benjamin Young, the deputy surveyor general of the province. Young offered him the deputy surveyorship of Queen Anne's, which was held by James Emory at that time. Although the position would

---

[39] *Maryland Archives*, 14:126, 313, 334, 556, 568.

[40] The phrase occurs in a letter of 31 August 1770 from Leeds to Martin (*Modern Gratitude*, p. 145).

[41] *Modern Gratitude*, p. 142. Ramsay was a year ahead of Martin at the College of New Jersey, but his brother Nathaniel was in Martin's class. After leaving Onancock, he began the study of medicine and was graduated from the College of Pennsylvania in 1772. He was active in the South Carolina state legislature and in the Continental Congress during the Revolution but is best known for his histories of South Carolina, of the United States, and of the American Revolution. Nathaniel, a life-long friend of Martin's, became a captain in Smallwood's famous Maryland regiment and distinguished himself at the Battle of Long Island and the Battle of Monmouth. At Monmouth he was wounded, left for dead, and captured by the British. After the Revolution he served as United States marshal and as naval officer for Baltimore until his death in 1817.

have been worth at least £100 a year to Martin,[42] and the temptation must have been great, he declined. He would rather starve, as he wrote a friend a few days later, than take bread "from the mouth of a friend."[43] He returned to the Eastern Shore and his school, and taught there until the close of the summer term at the end of August 1771, when he considered himself ready to begin the practice of law.

[42] See Donnell M. Owings, *His Lordship's Patronage—Offices of Profit in Colonial Maryland*, p. 84.

[43] *Modern Gratitude*, p. 146. He wrote to Emory warning him that Young was dissatisfied and telling him that he had refused the position, adding, "I should but ill have requitted [*sic*] the kindness I received from you, while I lived in Queen-Ann had I done otherwise" (24 October 1770, quoted in *Modern Gratitude*, pp. 145–46).

4

Frontier and Hinterland, 1771-1772

> It had been my design whenever I should obtain a
> license [to practice law], to fix my residence some where
> in the upper part of the Northern-Neck, or in parts still
> more westward in Virginia. And, at as early a period
> as possible, to make a tour throughout that part of the
> country to determine on the place.—*Modern Gratitude*

Martin presented himself at Williamsburg, the capital of colonial Virginia, about 1 September 1771 for examination of his qualifications for admission to the practice of law in the courts of that province.[1] John Randolph and George Wythe, two outstanding Virginia lawyers, were his examiners.[2] The Virginia statute then in effect[3] required these two examiners, who were appointed by the judges of the General Court, to test applicants for licensing as attornies in the county courts. In accordance with the practice of the time, the examination was probably oral, directed principally to the applicant's knowledge or ignorance of the law of real property, future interests and contingent remainders, and the more abstruse intricacies of common law and equity pleading.

Martin apparently passed this test without difficulty and was licensed to practice in the county courts throughout Virginia. He returned to the Eastern Shore and on 24 September 1771 qualified as an attorney at law in Accomack County. He continued studying law through the fall and winter and in April 1772 returned to Williamsburg to attend the spring term of the Virginia General Court. This was the appellate tribunal, consisting of the Governor and his council, to which appeals were taken from the county courts in all matters, whether civil, ecclesiastical, or in chancery.

---

[1] Unless otherwise stated, the biographical data in this chapter are from *Modern Gratitude*, pp. 146-54.

[2] Randolph was king's attorney (i.e., attorney general) of the province; four years later he fled to England with his wife and daughters, a conscientious and "unreconstructed" Tory. Wythe was a member of the House of Burgesses and its clerk; in 1764 he wrote the celebrated Remonstrance to the House of Commons against the stamp tax. He became the first signer of the Declaration of Independence from Virginia, a member of the Philadelphia Constitutional Convention of 1787, and high chancellor of Virginia. Jefferson called him "the American Aristides the Just": he was one of the busiest, most erudite, and most able members of the Virginia bar. In 1799 he was elected to the first professorship of law in this country, at the College of William and Mary.

[3] Act of 1 Geo. 3, c. 8, March 1761, 7 Hening's Va. Stat., p. 397.

The General Court met in a room on the first floor of the west wing of the H-shaped, Renaissance-style capitol. It had three round, deeply recessed windows in a semicircular bay behind the dais, dark polished paneling, hand-carved railings, and simple but handsome benches. Thirty years later, Martin remembered hearing John Blair, George Wythe, Patrick Henry, John Tazewell, and Thompson Mason, and he must also have listened to Peyton and John Randolph, Thomas Jefferson, John Marshall, Edmund Pendleton, John Tyler, and Dabney Carr. Some of these men had studied law at the Inns of Court in London, and almost all of them were wealthy aristocrats whose elegant manners and speech Martin must have envied.

Three civil cases from the April 1772 term, reported by Thomas Jefferson, are typical of the litigation of the period:[4] *Robin* v. *Hardaway*, argued by Thompson Mason and Col. James Bland, concerning the status of certain Indians as slaves; *Carter* v. *Webb*, argued by Edmund Pendleton, John Randolph, and the learned George Wythe, concerning a dispute over the right to crops and the increase of slaves and other stock between the executor of a life tenant and the remainderman; and *Herndon* v. *Carr*, a chancery case in which Wythe and Pendleton argued the proper construction of a complicated and ambiguous will.

Martin had had much time in which to ponder his prospects and to consider where he should practice. On the Eastern Shore of Virginia and Maryland there was little business and many lawyers. The bar at Williamsburg, of course, was even more crowded with well-known, experienced veterans, who had long since pre-empted most of the legal business of that rich, prosperous, and litigious region for a radius of many miles. With no local connections of any kind, Martin knew that he could not break into that closed circle on the basis of either his ambition or his ability. Accordingly, he decided to begin his practice in some settlement in the upper part of the northern neck of Virginia or the western part of Virginia, Pennsylvania, or Maryland, closer to the frontier than to the seaboard. He had no knowledge of the country, however, and in the spring of 1772 decided to make an exploratory tour of this wild and sparsely settled area.

Martin left Williamsburg in the company of one of the finest lawyers and most promising young men in the Old Dominion, Thompson Mason, a brother of the great George Mason. Jefferson referred to him as "a meteor whose path cannot be calculated," but his genius unaccountably burnt out young, and he is now remembered only by antiquarians. They rode west along the James River Road to Richmond, turned north to Fredericksburg, and then northwest along the Winchester Road to Mason's home in Loudon County. Martin stayed there for a few days, and then continued on by himself. He next stopped at the Berkeley County home of Col. Samuel Washington, the President's brother. During his ten days there Colonel Washington introduced him

[4] 2 Va. R. 109ff.

to other gentlemen of the county. One of them, a General Stevens, gave Martin letters of introduction to Colonel Frazer of Bedford County and to Lord Fairfax and his nephew, Col. Thomas Bryan Martin (apparently no relation), who had been George Washington's colleague in the House of Burgesses a dozen years earlier. With Colonel Martin he went on to the Colonel's home near Winchester, in Frederick County. Although Lord Fairfax was not at home, it was agreed that if Martin decided to settle in that area of Virginia he would be given the appointment of surveyor for one of the counties when a vacancy occurred.

He continued to travel northwest, across the Backbone Range of the Alleghenies, to Old Town, where he had an appointment with George Brent at the home of Col. Thomas Cresap, one of the most colorful men in the American colonies. Cresap was a famous Indian fighter, trader, explorer, road builder, land speculator, and politician. Though he was over seventy, he continued to carry on most of these activities.[5] His house and trading post, constructed like a fort, was fifteen miles east of Cumberland on the north side of the Potomac River, about five miles above the juncture of the North and South Branch. His youngest son Michael, then about thirty, had also built his home and trading post nearby.[6] This little settlement was on the old Indian trail used by the Iroquois on their expeditions against the Cherokees, their traditional enemies to the south. The Cresaps were well known to almost every Indian and white man on the frontier, from Canada to the Carolinas. Thomas Cresap customarily kept a pot of meat stew simmering for chance Indian visitors, and because of this generosity he was called "Big Spoon."

This little settlement has been pictured thus:

The two Cresaps were distinguished among the hardy frontiersmen for courage, intelligence and skill in Indian warfare; they were always on the alert, and their timely warnings saved many of their neighbors from massacre. Their block-house, which was strong enough to resist the savages, served as a place of refuge in case of expected invasion, and as a rendezvous for the settlers in more peaceful times, where they met to hear and tell the news, to try their

---

[5] *Dictionary of American Biography*, s.v. "Cresap, Thomas"; Kenneth P. Bailey, *Thomas Cresap, Maryland Frontiersman, passim.*

[6] Michael Cresap was born around 1742. In the summer of 1764 he married Mary Whitehead at St. Paul's Episcopal Church in Philadelphia. Their eldest child, Maria, was probably born around 1766, since her younger sister, Elizabeth, was born in 1768; on his visit Martin probably paid little attention to this small girl of six or seven. When word of Lexington and Concord reached Maryland, Michael Cresap was called upon to raise a company of volunteer militiamen from Frederick County. His "formidable Company of upwards of 130 men, from the mountains and backwoods, painted like Indians, armed with tomahawks and rifles and dressed in hunting shirts and mocassins" marched almost eight hundred miles from the Ohio River. Like the Indians, they "seemed to walk light and easy, and not with less spirit than at the first hour of their march" ("Extract of a letter to a Gentleman in Philadelphia," dated Fredericktown, Md., 1 August 1775, in Thomas Balch, ed., *Papers relating chiefly to the Maryland Line during the Revolution*, p. 5).

skill as marksmen, or engage in friendly trials of strength or dexterity, and at night, seated around a huge log fire, they would tell adventures of war or of the chase; and if by good luck any of the company possessed a fiddle or jewsharp, and had the cunning to awaken its harmony, the evening wound up hilariously with a dance.[7]

The Cresaps belonged to the same breed of men as Christopher Gist, Conrad Weiser, George Croghan, and Daniel Boone—physically powerful, mentally acute, intrepid and resourceful. Cresap and his eldest son Daniel were associated with the Washingtons (George, Lawrence, and Augustine), the Mercers, the Lees, the Hanburys, and many other Virginia gentry in the formation of the Ohio Company of Virginia.[8]

After staying with the Cresaps for a few days, Martin and Brent went on by way of Braddock's Road. Some twenty years earlier Thomas Cresap and a friendly Indian (it was named for the latter, "Nemacolin's Trail") had blazed and cut it out of the forest from Fort Cumberland to Red Stone (now near Brownsville, Pennsylvania) on the Monongahela, sixty miles across the most rugged kind of country.

Martin stayed for over three weeks at Fort Pitt and nearby Red Stone, where he met the "king of the traders," George Croghan.[9] On his return he stopped again to visit the friendly Cresaps, then followed the Potomac for another day's ride to the east to Berkeley Springs, a famous and fashionable spa. He stayed at the Springs for about six weeks and then, as the season was almost over, reluctantly started home. He stopped again at Thompson Mason's home in Loudon County and then continued down the Potomac River to Great Falls—one of the great scenic beauties of colonial America and a sight that he never forgot—and Alexandria. He crossed into Maryland and went east over the Patuxent to visit the Rev. John Thomas Claggett, a college friend whom he had met at Berkeley Springs, at All Saints Parish in Calvert County. He recrossed the Potomac at Hooe's Ferry (near Dahlgren, Virginia), then an important junction on the old Post Road from Virginia to points north through southern Maryland, made brief calls on people he had met at the Springs, and stayed for almost two weeks with the family of John Augustine Washington (George's brother, who

---

[7] Scharf, *History of Western Maryland*, 1:469–70.

[8] Kenneth P. Bailey, *The Ohio Company of Virginia and the Westward Movement: A Chapter in the History of the Colonial Frontier, passim*; Douglass Southall Freeman, *George Washington*, 1:235ff.

[9] Croghan was a rough and ready frontiersman who had been Sir William Johnson's deputy to the Indians of the Ohio River and Great Lakes area. He had assisted General Forbes in the capture of Fort Duquesne in 1758 and was with Colonel Bouquet at the occupation of Detroit in 1760. A year or two before Martin met him, while on his way out to open up the Illinois country for settlement by the English, Croghan was captured and tomahawked, but survived. In his time he explored, acquired, bartered, and sold hundreds of thousands of acres of land on the western frontier.

had died some years earlier) at its Westmoreland County home on the Potomac, at the mouth of Nominy Creek.[10] The elder Washingtons showed him a "parental affection" for which he was always grateful. From Nominy Martin went on down the peninsula to Chesapeake-on-the-Bay, in Northumberland County, where he met another former Princeton classmate, Dr. John Armstrong (son of Gen. John Armstrong, hero of Kittanning and captor of the Indian chief Jacob). Two or three weeks later, as soon as a boat was available to cross the bay to the Virginia Eastern Shore, Martin returned home, arriving there early in November 1772.

"Perhaps no six months of my life," he later wrote, "ever bestowed upon me more pure and rational pleasure while passing, or when past, on reflection." It was his first vacation and one of the few that he ever had in his life's relentless round of clients, cases, courts, and arguments. He had traveled almost a thousand miles, much of it alone and over the roughest terrain. He had met as many varieties of people as there were in America, from affluent planters, living in feudal luxury off their fertile soil and the sweat of their slaves, to hardy, self-reliant frontiersmen like the Cresaps, hewing and hacking homes and farms for themselves and their families out of the wilderness. He had made the acquaintance of many of the most influential people in the area and had seen at first hand the political problems of the colonies and their citizens. He was thus prepared for his part in the coming struggle for independence and, later, for self-government.

[10] Years later, when his hostess's ten-year-old son Bushrod, a small, dark-skinned, fox-faced boy, had become a justice of the United States Supreme Court, Martin argued dozens of cases before him.

5

Attorney at Law and Revolutionary Patriot, 1772–1778

> From that time I made my residence in Somerset [County] and regularly attended the courts . . . , until the interruption of business, which took place in the early part of the Revolution. . . . From that period, until the courts of justice were again opened, I was engaged in a variety of pursuits, some professional, and some of a different nature.—*Modern Gratitude*

When Martin returned to the Eastern Shore, he found that fate had solved his problem for him. During his six-month absence the three most active lawyers in the area, John Murray, George Handy, and Littleton Dennis, died.[1] Accordingly, he set up practice, in November of 1772, in the two Eastern Shore counties of Virginia (Accomack and Northampton) in which he was qualified and licensed and shortly after was admitted to the bar in the neighboring Maryland counties of Somerset and Worcester. Most of his early cases, however, were in the Virginia courts.

When he began practicing law he was deeply in debt.[2] He had earned only a nominal stipend during his years of teaching, had borrowed to buy his law library, and owed money for what he later called "youthful extravagancies." We can only guess at the last, but no doubt some substantial proportion represented funds for his journey. Almost at once his legal career was lucrative and successful. Within two years his income was "nearly or quite equal to a thousand pounds a year, with every prospect of encrease."[3]

His sobriety, judgment, and experience were so well esteemed that when he established his residence in Somerset County, the trustees of Back Creek Academy made him one of their number.[4] While he was engaged in cases in Virginia in the fall of 1774, quite without his knowledge he was elected a member of the Somerset County Committee of

[1] *Modern Gratitude*, p. 150.
[2] "A Friend to Justice" [Luther Martin], "Queries, addressed to Robert Lemmon, Esq.," p. 21, Miscellaneous Broadside Volume, Maryland Historical Society, Baltimore, Md.
[3] *Modern Gratitude*, p. 150.
[4] *Ibid.*, p. 151.

Observation and also a delegate from Somerset to the convention to be held at Annapolis. Early in November the Maryland delegates to the first Continental Congress at Philadelphia (Matthew Tilghman, Thomas Johnson, William Paca, and Samuel Chase) called this provincial meeting of deputies from all the counties to meet later that month to consider the resolutions and recommendations of the Congress to the colonies.[5]

On 21 November the meeting took place. Some fifty-seven delegates were present, but a number of counties had not had time to select their deputies, and the convention therefore adjourned until 25 November. A report on the proceedings of the Continental Congress was approved, and a resolution was adopted "inviolably to observe, and carry into execution" the Articles of Association that had been signed by the delegates to the Congress a month earlier.[6] The recommendation was made that "during the present time of public calamity, balls be discontinued," and, after resolving that a request be made to the absent counties to send deputies to the convention, the meeting adjourned until 8 December.

On that date eighty-five deputies, representing all the counties, convened, Martin among them. The proceedings of the Continental Congress were again reported, considered, and "*unanimously* approved." In the next four days a wide range of resolutions was adopted, not all unanimously: methods "to increase our flocks of sheep" and to "increase the manufacture of linen and cotton" were approved; action to prevent cornering the market and profiteering in scarce commodities was taken; lawyers were enjoined from prosecuting suits on behalf of violators of the Articles of Association; support of the resistance of Massachusetts Bay, or any other colony, to forcible execution of "the late acts of Parliament" was pledged. The organization of a "well-regulated militia" that would "relieve the mother country from any expense in their protection and defense and obviate the pretence of taxing them on that account, (and render it unnecessary to keep any standing army [ever dangerous to liberty] in this province)" was, not surprisingly, approved unanimously. County committees were authorized to raise ten thousand pounds for the purchase of arms and ammunition.[7]

A Committee of Correspondence was set up, consisting of Matthew Tilghman, John Hall, Samuel Chase, Thomas Johnson, William Paca, Charles Carroll of Carrollton, and Charles Carroll, Barrister, the first five of whom, with Robert Goldsborough and Thomas Stone, were named to represent Maryland at the next Continental Congress. All were besought to put away all former differences about religion and politics and all private quarrels of every kind so that the opposition of

---

[5] See *Proceedings of the conventions of the Province of Maryland Held at the City of Annapolis, in 1774, 1775, & 1776*, pp. 6-10; John Archer Silver, *The Provisional Government of Maryland (1774-1777)*, pp. 11-14.

[6] See *Journals of the American Congress* for 20 October 1774.

[7] *Ibid.*

all to the "settled plan of the British administration to enslave America" would be strengthened. The convention ended with the solemn declaration, "We entreat, we conjure every man, by his duty to God, his country, and his posterity, cordially to unite in defence of our common rights and liberties." The next convention was scheduled for 24 April 1775.[8]

Some months later at the convention, during the summer, a resolution was passed which in effect closed the king's courts.[9] With a few exceptions, no new suits could be filed, and pending litigation was "frozen" until new state courts should be established. No executions were allowed even on judgments already obtained unless special permission was first obtained from the local county Committee of Observation. For practical purposes, this resolution limited executions to Tory-owned property. More important, however, was the fact that for the time being it virtually put lawyers out of work. As Martin later recalled, "The revolutionary measures, then thought necessary to be adopted, and which received my assent, not only in a great degree cut me off from future business, but also deprived me of the benefits arising from the suits, in which I was then employed, by putting a stop to the completion of those suits."[10] However, the new state criminal courts (from necessity, perhaps) were organized before the new state civil courts, and Martin appeared regularly in court at Williamsburg as counsel for people accused of a wide variety of crimes. Out of thirty-one such cases, he obtained twenty-nine acquittals. In one case, his client, who was prosecuted for murder, was convicted of manslaughter, and in another case he procured an arrest of judgment against a former slave of George Washington, "Captain" Davis, who had been convicted of treason.

Despite the fact that throughout the Revolution the Tories made up a "disaffected majority" of the populace of Somerset and Worcester counties, Martin was among the first and the most vocal of those who espoused independence from Great Britain. When the news of the Battle of Lexington arrived, he immediately expressed his "abhorrence of being any longer connected with a nation whose rulers had thus inhumanly stained their hands with the blood of their innocent subjects, because they would not tamely give up those rights and privileges, which they inherited from heaven as their unalienable birthright."[11] On 10 January 1776 Thomas Paine's pamphlet *Common Sense* was published and inspired the colonists with the belief that political independence was not only theoretically just but was actually attainable if they had the courage to fight for it. Within three months over a hundred thousand copies had been distributed throughout the colonies. The

[8] See *Proceedings of the conventions*, p. 15 *et passim*.
[9] *Maryland Archives*, 11:31.
[10] *Modern Gratitude*, p. 150.
[11] "Queries, addressed to Robert Lemmon."

first copy ever seen in Somerset County—indeed, perhaps in all Maryland—was obtained and circulated by Martin, at great personal risk but with highly satisfactory results in rallying the revolutionary minority there.

One of Martin's closest friendships was formed at this time. Samuel Chase, that revolutionary firebrand who played the role in Maryland that Samuel Adams did in Massachusetts,[12] was a native of Somerset County, and doubtless Martin first met him there. They agreed on both the philosophy and the tactics of opposition to Great Britain, as they did on most political matters for a third of a century. Chase was about eight years older than Martin, a leader of the Sons of Liberty, one of the original members of the Maryland Committee of Correspondence, and one of the state's most active delegates to the Continental Congress. When the Maryland convention late in June reversed its earlier instructions to its delegation in Congress and authorized it to vote for the Resolution of Independence on 2 July 1776, Chase's zeal and ardor, and his genius at organizing and articulating grass-roots opinion (which was far in advance of its "leaders") was largely responsible. Although his labors in Maryland prevented him from being in Congress to vote for the Resolution and Declaration of Independence early in July, the following month he became one of the famous fifty-six signers.

In the fall of 1776, Gen. Sir William Howe invaded New Jersey to destroy Washington's small and ragged army.[13] On 30 November Howe and his brother, Admiral Lord Howe, issued a joint proclamation offering a full pardon and protection of his property to anyone who would swear before a British officer to "remain in a peaceable Obedience to His Majesty and not take up arms, nor encourage Others to take up arms" against the king's forces. In return for this act of submission, the colonist would receive a "protection paper." This paper proved to be more of a snare than safeguard, however. The British soldiers, many of them impressed from the prisons and slums of London, and their Hessian allies simply ignored these certificates and raided and pillaged Tory and Whig alike. Completely out of control, they looted homes and farms, burned houses and barns, and emptied the countryside of horses and cattle. Sir William's foragers occasionally gave "receipts" for the cattle taken; more often, the soldiers took the farmer's wagons as well in order to carry off their loot. From time to time women were attacked, and fine homes, like Dr. John Witherspoon's "Tusculum" and Richard Stockton's "Morven," were plundered of their libraries and furniture. In Princeton even the books and scientific equipment of the college were destroyed.

[12] See *Dictionary of American Biography*, 4:34ff.
[13] Alfred Hoyt Bill, *The Campaign of Princeton, 1776–1777*, pp. 31ff.; Lynn Montross, *Rag, Tag and Bobtail*, pp. 163ff.

Much of the fighting took place in the vicinity of New Brunswick and the Raritan River. On 19 June 1777 the forces of Nathanael Greene, Daniel Morgan, and Anthony Wayne chased the British through Piscataway, the home of Martin's family and most of his relatives. The Redcoats fled to Perth Amboy, burning houses and barns as they went.[14] In addition to reading the reports in the newspapers,[15] Martin probably received accounts of these atrocities and depredations from his family.

When General Howe decided to attack Philadelphia from the head of the Chesapeake Bay in the summer of 1777,[16] he naturally wished to allay the fears of the populace that the fate of the New Jersey colonists was about to be visited upon them. Accordingly, he published in the *Maryland Gazette* and had scattered broadside a "Declaration to the inhabitants of Pennsylvania, the Lower Counties on Delaware, and the Counties on the Eastern Shore of Maryland" that "in order to remove any groundless apprehensions which may have been raised, of their suffering by depredations of the army under his command: He [Howe] hath issued the strictest orders to the troops, for the preservation of regularity and good discipline; and has signified, that the most exemplary punishment shall be inflicted upon those who shall dare to plunder property, or molest the persons of any of his Majesty's WELL DISPOSED SUBJECTS." Urging those who had joined the Continental Army to see the error of their ways, Howe promised "a free and general pardon to all such officers and private men, as shall voluntarily come and surrender themselves, to any detachment of his Majesty's forces."[17]

Martin's answer, published on the same page of the *Gazette*, demonstrated the style, as yet unpolished and heavy-handed, for which he was to become famous: he met his enemy on the latter's own ground and used his adversary's own language to reduce his argument to an absurdity. "How very good it is in him," Martin wrote,

to promise protection to men at a distance from his camp; or, to use his own words, those who "remain peaceably in their usual place of abode."— And for the better encouragement of His MAJESTY'S WELL DISPOSED SUBJECTS, . . . he issues particular and strict orders to his soldiers, "Not to dare to plunder their property." But how is he to distinguish in a strange country between Whig and Tory? His soldiers, notwithstanding their extensive practice in the Jersies, have not yet learnt to discriminate. All is fish that comes in their net. . . . But he would have those on the other side of the Atlantic believe, that he is already

---

[14] Christopher Ward, *The War of the Revolution*, 1:326–27. Note also letters 11 and 12, pp. 44 and 46, in *Letters from America 1773–1780*, written by a Scottish officer in the British army, Sir James Murray, dated "Piscataway (N.J.), May 30th (1777)" and "Head of Elke, Maryland, Sept. 1st, 1777."

[15] See the reports of New Jersey atrocities in (Dunlap's) *Maryland Gazette* for 24 December 1776, 14, 21, and 24 January, 8 July, *et seq.*, 1777.

[16] Ward, *War of the Revolution*, 1:336ff.; Willard M. Wallace, *Appeal to Arms: A Military History of the American Revolution*, pp. 134ff.

[17] (Dunlap's) *Maryland Gazette* (Baltimore), 9 September 1777.

in actual possession of Pennsylvania, the Lower Counties on Delaware, and the Counties of Maryland on the Eastern Shore of Chesapeake Bay. Men who only listen to the tales of Ministry will hardly believe after reading his piece, that so doughty a Proclamation retailer commands little more than six miles of all the territory he enumerates; and that he dare not shew himself in the open country, but keeps cowardly sculking along shore.

We have now our cruel and deceitful enemy upon our own ground. Now therefore, is the time to appease the shades of our brethren for the British cruelties which they have suffered, so contrary to the laws of nations and the practice of war, under cover of vile protections, and insidious proclamations. He who does not feel pity for his starved, butchered, and plundered country-men is a base coward, and no man: And he who is not NOW FOUND, READY and WILLING, to seek revenge in the field, is an enemy to virtue and freedom, a foe to humanity, and the FRIEND of GENERAL HOWE.

As was the custom in addresses to the public upon whatever subject, Martin closed with an apposite classical quotation—in this case, from Pope's translation of the *Iliad*:

> These ills shall cease, whene'er by Jove's decree
> We crown the bowl to heav'n and liberty;
> While the proud foe his frustrate triumphs mourns,
> And Greece indignant thro' her seas returns.[18]

On the same day General Howe's proclamation also appeared in Goddard's *Maryland Journal*, this time followed by an affidavit of one Francis Alexander

that he was eye-witness to several brutal ravages committed by the merciless troops of the tyrant of Great-Britain, on their late landing on the Head of Elk; that he particularly saw one of them, in the presence of divers others, ravish, or attempt violently to effect a rape on the person of a young woman of spotless character, living at his house, notwithstanding her cries and resist-ance to the contrary, at the same time making use of severe menaces, in case of refusal; and sundry other acts of barbarity he saw there perpetrated, shocking to humanity, and which cry aloud for vengeance.[19]

This account inspired Martin to a further denunciation of Howe, his "humble ADDRESS of the Inhabitants of Pennsylvania, the Lower Coun-ties on Delaware, and the Counties on the Eastern Shore of Maryland, to his Excellency Sir WILLIAM HOWE, &c. &c.":

Your Excellency, having in the course of your voyage from New-York frequently appeared off our coasts with your numerous fleet, upon your arrival at the Head of Elk, exulted no doubt in the flattering idea that, unable to support, even the distant view of your force, filled with the most abject terrour [*sic*] and dismay, we had fled from our homes and enbosomed ourselves in woods and morasses, there to lie concealed 'till your vengeance should pass over, lest in the severity of your displeasure we should be utterly consumed;

---

[18] *Ibid.* This would suggest that Martin was in Baltimore at this time.
[19] *Maryland Journal*, 9 September 1777.

and hence, actuated solely by that humanity which moves your Excellency so sincerely to "regret those calamities to which many of his Majesty's faithful subjects are still exposed by the continuance of rebellion," although your Excellency most confidently assured your royal Master and the British nation this rebellion should long e'er now be totally suppressed by the immortal prowess of your victorious arms, your Excellency hath been graciously pleased, and who can sufficiently admire the unparalleled condescension, to issue your declaration, calling us forth from those retreats to which you supposed us driven by our fears, and kindly inviting us to our forsaken habitations, holding forth to us terms of domestic security and protection. . . .

These reflections had inclined us to believe, that if there was any security for our persons or property, on the part of your Excellency or army, it must arise, not from your Excellency's orders, which have been so often disregarded, but from some wonderful conversion, some sudden change of the tempers and dispositions of your soldiers, since they were driven from the Jersies; but the conduct of some of them, even while your "strictest orders" must have been yet ringing in their ears, hath completed our conviction, and dispelled every remainder of doubt, when an unhappy woman, of unblemished character, notwithstanding her cries, her prayers, and resistance, was compelled by one of those monsters, whom your Excellency hath the honour to command, to become the unhappy instrument to gratify his impetuous lust, in the presence of numbers of his fellow barbarians, while Heaven looked down on the detested scene, and only restrained its vengeance that by delaying the stroke it might fall with redoubled *weight!*

Happy foretaste of that security and protection which your Excellency tells us is extended to all the inhabitants! . . .

But perhaps this unfortunate woman was not one of his "Majesty's well-disposed subjects," and, upon a review of your Excellency's declaration, we observe it is only their property and persons you have made criminal to plunder or molest. . . . Since it will be of no service to us whether we approve or disapprove the opposition adopted in America, whenever your soldiers shall have an inclination to our houses for shelter, our flocks and herds for food, or our wives, daughters, or sisters, for the gratification of their lust, they will have no more to do than to determine that we, this or that one of us, as the case may be, are not in the number of "his Majesty's *well-disposed* subjects," and immediately all that we have becomes their rightful prey, and that with your Excellency's full approbation.[20]

Since the Baltimore newspapers had no Eastern Shore circulation, Martin had a large number of copies of his addresses to General Howe printed at his own expense. Regardless of the danger involved, he took them to the Eastern Shore and personally distributed throughout the "disaffected areas," where they had "salutary consequences" in stiffening the opposition to Howe.[21]

While the courts were closed and his professional business disrupted, Martin busied himself in various other ways. One of his projects was the homely, laborious, but necessary business of manufacturing salt.

[20] *Ibid.*
[21] *Genuine Information*, p. 152.

Before the Revolution most of the salt used in the colonies was imported. When the war cut off this supply, the states and the Continental Congress adopted many measures to encourage salt production. Early in the war the Annapolis convention appropriated money for the construction of salt works on the Maryland coast,[22] in addition to offering bounties on salt imports. There was so much hoarding, chiseling, and speculation in the commodity, however, that the convention attempted to fix the price to circumvent the "avaricious ill designing men . . . extorting from the people a most exorbitant price therefor."[23] Salt had become so scarce on the Eastern Shore by the fall of 1776 that the residents of Dorchester County seized a local planter's hoard, and the price of a bushel rose from 7s. 6d. in the summer of 1776 to £15 by January 1778. Many people on the Eastern Shore lost their enthusiasm for the revolutionary cause because they believed that they were being allotted an unfairly low proportion of what salt was available.[24] On 12 August 1777 Charles Carroll of Carrollton wrote to Benjamin Franklin in Paris the following "interesting circumstances":

> One of the greatest distresses we have yet felt is the want of salt, but I hope we shall not be in so great want of that essential article for the future as we have been. A bushel of salt some months ago was sold at Baltimore Town for £ 9. Necessity is said to be the mother of invention; it surely is of industry among a people. Many private persons on our sea-coasts and bays, are now making salt to supply themselves and neighbors; these private and the public salt-works together, will in a few months, I hope, yield a tolerable supply to our people, and at pretty reasonable rates compared with those which have obtained for some time past. Perhaps the private saltmakers may afford to sell salt at 30/ per bushel; the undertakers of the public saltworks in this State are under contracts to sell what salt they make at 5/.[25]

Virginia not only made the importation and distribution of salt a state monopoly but set up sea water evaporation plants on the coast in an attempt at large-scale production,[26] and on 1 March 1778 Luther Martin was in Accomack County, "very busily engaged in directions to artificers who were employed in the erection of works for manufacturing salt."[27] It was there that a messenger from the governor's council found Martin and, to his great surprise and gratification, delivered to him Maryland's commission as attorney general.

[22] (Dunlap's) *Maryland Gazette* (Baltimore), 19 June 1776.

[23] *Ibid.*, 13 July 1776, postscript.

[24] *Maryland Archives*, 12:466, 469; Lewis Cecil Gray, *History of Agriculture in the Southern United States to 1860*, 2:584ff.; Emory, *Queen Anne's County*, p. 299. See generally (Dunlap's) *Maryland Gazette* (Baltimore) for 21 and 28 November 1775; 9 January, 4 and 19 June, 13 and 30 July, and 24 September 1776.

[25] Kate Mason Rowland, *The Life of Charles Carroll of Carrollton, 1737–1832*, 1:209–10.

[26] State of Virginia, *Official Letters of the Governors*, letters of Patrick Henry, 1:17, 26, 41–42, 159, 285; letters of Thomas Jefferson, 1:80, 276. See also Virginia ordinance for the erection of salt works in (Dunlap's) *Maryland Gazette* for 13 July 1776.

[27] *Modern Gratitude*, p. 152.

6

Attorney General and Light Dragoon, 1778-1783

> On the eleventh of February in the year of our Lord, one thousand seven hundred and seventy eight, is dated the commission by which I have holden to this time [1802] the office of Attorney General of this state. . . .
>
> There was a period of considerable duration, throughout which, not only myself, but many others acting in the same manner, did not lay down one night on their beds, without the hazard of waking on board a British armed ship, or in the other world.—*Modern Gratitude*

It is usually said that Martin owed his appointment to the office of attorney general to Samuel Chase,[1] and this may be in some measure true. However, sometime in 1777 Martin wrote to Gov. Thomas Johnson requesting the appointment in place of Matthew Tilghman, who had resigned. He offered to render any other service if the position had already been filled or if "the Preference of Some other person will be conducive to the good of the State,"[2] but the state council appointed Benjamin Galloway instead. Galloway declined the office, and the council ruefully noted that "the Gentlemen of the Bar have shown great Backwardness to undertake" the position.[3] The reason was not hard to find: the outlook for the colonies was anything but bright, and courage as well as patriotism was required to accept such a position in the spotlight.

Though dated 11 February 1778, it was not until a week later that the council sent Martin's commission as attorney general to him "with the hope that the Appointment of Mr. Galloway who has resigned, will not alter your former Resolution, which, we hope and have no Doubt, was formed from a Desire of contributing to the Public Service."[4] The adventures of this paper before it actually came to Martin's hands indicate the precarious nature of Chesapeake Bay navigation in those days:

[1] See *Dictionary of American Biography*, s.v. "Martin, Luther"; Beveridge, *Life of John Marshall*, 3:186n; John B. Cutting to Jefferson, in Farrand, *Records of the Federal Convention*, 3:339.

[2] Red Book no. 4, pt. 3, no. 140 (XXI, 15), p. 21, in *Calendar of Maryland State Papers, No. 4, the Red Books*, p. 21.

[3] *Maryland Archives*, 16:504, Council to Justices, 17 February 1778.

[4] *Ibid.*, p. 507.

it was given to a Mr. Waggaman, a Somerset County neighbor of Martin's, who was leaving Annapolis for the Eastern Shore by water "with a fair wind" at his back. On his way Waggaman was captured by a British ship, which was immediately retaken by the American *Dolphin*. The commission was then missent to Baltimore, and a duplicate was sent off to Martin with instructions to proceed to Talbot County to prosecute a number of Tories being held there for treason.

On 2 March Martin wrote the council that he had received his commission and esteemed it "the greatest happiness" to accept and serve in the office.[5] He went to Talbot and on 9 March qualified before the Eastern Shore Court of Oyer and Terminer and Gaol Delivery.[6] After gathering together the evidence for the trial, Martin set off for the chaotic lower Eastern Shore, where there was open warfare between patriots and Tories, and murder, arson, and kidnaping were commonplaces.

It is now generally realized that the American Revolution of 1775–83 was also a civil war. People who had been friends and neighbors for years suddenly found themselves fighting, pillaging, and killing each other. It has been pointed out that Martin's own county of Somerset was a hotbed of Toryism throughout the war. In the spring of 1778 a Maryland Loyalist regiment, numbering some 336 men, was formed on the Eastern Shore and, because of the lack of either a state or national navy, was able to leave Annimessex Island and join the British. It fought with them throughout the remainder of the war.[7] The county militia was frequently called out to suppress Tory uprisings, but with little success, as few persons could be entrusted with arms because of possible Tory sympathies.[8] Finally, the governor's council was forced to send state militia into Somerset, with artillerymen, field pieces, and armed galleys. Such measures, however, were only temporarily successful.[9] Less than three weeks after he assumed office, Martin reported in detail to Governor Johnson the bitter dissension among the residents of Princess Anne in Somerset County and in the neighboring areas of Maryland, Delaware, and Virginia:

Sir

It is with real Pain, I inform your Excellency that the disaffected Inhabitants of this County [Somerset], joined as I have reason to believe by many of the Inhabitants of Sussex [County, Delaware], who have fled from their homes to avoid falling into the hands of some of our Troops who are stationed there, have arrived to so daring a Height of Insolence and Villainy that there appears

[5] Red Book no. 4, pt. 3, no. 146 (XXI, 16), p. 23.
[6] *Ibid.*, no. 1526 (XIX, 53), p. 241.
[7] *Maryland Archives*, 21:89, 106–7. Among the officers of this regiment was Philip Barton Key, uncle of Francis Scott Key, who became a distinguished lawyer, judge, and member of Congress from Maryland (see *Dictionary of American Biography*, 10:363).
[8] *Maryland Archives*, 16:538–39.
[9] See Beverly W. Bond, Jr., *State Government in Maryland, 1777–1781*, pp. 96ff.

but very little Security for the Lives or property of any person who from political or other reasons are obnoxious to them.

Several Boats loaded with Tobacco, Wheat Flower [sic] &c have been taken away from Pocomoke, Jones Creek, Wicomico &c and that very recently: Bodies of armed Men have within these few nights past been seen passing and repassing in the County. Persons in the low part of it particularly one John Sterling, a Defecter, are openly and avowedly enlisting Men and sending them aboard of the Ships. But the [ir] Conduct last night is yet more alarming— a party amou[nting] to sixteen in number commanded by Sterling made an attack upon the house of Mr. David Wilson of Monocan a capt. of the Militia whose zeal and activity had distinguished him—they shot through the Door and badly wounded him, though it is hoped not mortally, in the shoulder, and took away his arms—Wm Winder Son Esq a Mr Venables and one or two more were in their beds in the House at the time—Sterling told them they were his Prisoners and ordered them to get ready to go with him and in the mean time placed Guards at the Doors and out Houses but Mr Venables jumping out of an upper Window was fortunate enough to escape unperceived, which when they discovered, apprehensive that the Neighbourhood would be alarmed they decamped hastily leaving their Prisoners behind—This happened about three in the morning.

Near about the same time another smaller party headed by Isaac Costin, as 'tis said, went to Capt. John Williams about eight miles lower with the same Intent but Mr. Williams and a Gentleman who was with him having got notice in time were prepared to receive them upon which they departed. Whether any others met with the same Treatment I have not yet heard.

The Militia Officers are calling some of the Militia out upon the Occasion but I am apprehensive it will be but of little lasting Utility—Should the disaffected be too weak to resist they will make their Escape by water, there being no armed Boats to prevent them, and as soon as they shall learn the Militia are disbanded they will return back to cause fresh Disturbance [and] those of the Militia who shall have shewn them[sel]ves most active against them will probably be the first objects of their Violence.

I would submit it to your Excellency whether it would not be much more likely to secure the Peace of this place if a company of a hundred Men or there abouts, one half of which to be horse, under proper Officers were to be embodied and taken into constant pay and Stationed in this County. The Expence of which in all Probability would not be much more considerable than what will attend the frequent calling the Militia into actual Duty, while the real Service of such Company constantly embodied, and consequently a constant Check upon the disaffected[,] would be infinitely greater[;] at the same time I presume their superior Strictness of Discipline would be in some degree a Security against those Outrages of which there has been too much reason to complain in Cases where the Militia have an actual duty and which serve rather to exasperate than intimidate—If beside such a Company a galley or armed Boat of some kind was to be stationed in Annamessex[,] where I am told she might be very safe as to the Ships, in order to cutt [sic] off the Communication between the Disaffected and the Shipping[,] we should soon, I flatter myself, be in peace and Safety, and the Principal offenders be brought to Justice, of which at present there is so little prospect that the Sheriff does not dare go to Annamessex to summon witnesses against the criminals who await their Trial at the Special Court, and so[me o]f the most material Witnesses live in that Neighbourhood which I fear will prevent a Possibility of proceeding against them at the Adjournment without manifest Injustice to the State.

Should it be judged expedient to embody a Company to be stationed here I would beg leave to inform your Excellency that Mr William Jones a Nephew of Samuel Wilson Esq and of the Gentleman last Night wounded, a young Gentleman who has served this last Campaign with Credit in the office of first Lieutenant in one of the Sixteen Regiments and has or expects to leave the Army in Consequence of the Reduction of those Regiments[,] would with Pleasure act in the Service of this State in the office of first Lieutenant of Horse if any should be raised or, if no Horse, in the foot—He is a Youth of a good family and independent Fortune, possessed of Zeal for the Cause of his Country, and endowed with resolution sufficient to execute his duty.

I remain with the greatest respect
your Excellency's most devoted humble Servant
LUTHER MARTIN
Princess Anne, March ye 18th 1778.[10]

It was insurrectionists arrested during uprisings in Somerset and Worcester counties and elsewhere in 1777[11] whom Martin was instructed to prosecute in Talbot County. They had been imprisoned there for lack of adequate prisons in other counties, and perhaps also to keep them from being released upon writs of habeas corpus by judges in their home counties. To check the Tory depredations, particularly on the Eastern Shore, the Maryland General Assembly in 1777 decreed the death penalty for any person levying war against either the state or the Continental Congress.[12] Of the persons prosecuted by Martin for high treason during the Revolution, John Tims was one of the first to receive this penalty in its most extreme form. His indictment charged that in April 1778 he led an insurrection of one hundred people armed with "swords, clubs, bayonets and other weapons." In September of 1778 he was tried before Judges William Paca, Nicholas Thomas, and Alexander Contee Hanson, and convicted. The sentence was strictly in accordance with English common law: "that John Tims be carried back to the Place from whence he came and from thence be drawn to the Place of Execution and be there hanged by the Neck, and cut down alive, and that his Entrails be taken out and burnt before his face and his head cut off and his Body divided into four Quarters and his Head and Quarters disposed of at the Pleasure of the State."[13] It is not known whether Tims's innocence was later established, whether there were "extenuating circumstances,"[14] or whether the barbarity of the sentence

[10] Original letter is deposited in the State Archives, Hall of Records, Annapolis, Maryland.

[11] *Maryland Archives*, 16:vii; Emory, *Queen Anne's County*, p. 300ff. See "The Humble Petition of the Loyalists in Somersett-Worchester Countys"; Scharf, *History of Maryland*, 2:386.

[12] Bond, *State Government in Maryland*, p. 94.

[13] In the Minute Book of the General Court of Maryland, Hall of Records, Annapolis, Maryland.

[14] See William Paca to Gov. Thomas Johnson, 23 September 1778, Maryland Historical Society, Baltimore, Maryland.

was too much for the sensibilities of the governor and council; at any rate, he was pardoned on 20 March 1779.

On 29 June 1781, the state council wrote Martin that it was thought "highly necessary that you should attend the Special Court to be held at Frederick Town on the 10 July next for the Trial of a Number of State Prisoners."[15] The background of this trial provides one of the most intriguing stories of espionage and counterespionage in our history. One of the many uncoordinated strategic plans of the British in late 1780 called for General Leslie to invade Virginia, making contact with a second British force moving southeast from the British forts at Pittsburgh and Detroit. The purpose of this maneuver was not only to split the colonies in two but also to release large numbers of British prisoners who were confined in the principal American prison camps, located in the area between Frederick, Maryland, and Winchester, Virginia. These forces were to be enlarged and aided by the enlistment of Tories from both western Maryland and the Eastern Shore.

To this end, in February 1781 Sir Henry Clinton issued a commission to the British governor of New Jersey, William Franklin (natural son of Benjamin Franklin) and a number of other leading Loyalists, including Robert Alexander of Maryland, to set up an organization known as the "Associated Loyalists of America." They were authorized to employ "such of his majesty's faithful subjects in North America as may be willing to associate under their direction, for the purpose of annoying the sea coasts of the revolted provinces and distressing their trade, either in cooperation with his majesty's land and sea forces, or by making diversions in their favor when they are carrying on operations in other parts."[16]

Large numbers of Tories all over the country were recruited into this organization. Their plan for the invasion of western Maryland and the release of the British prisoners failed, however, when the scheme became known to the revolutionary authorities, who arrested all the ringleaders of the plot simultaneously. Tradition has it that the discovery came about in a bizarre way. A British messenger from the west was instructed to deliver documents containing plans, names of conspirators, and other details to a British spy disguised as an American soldier. They were to meet at a certain place and time in the town of Frederick. The messenger arrived a little early and delivered the papers to a real officer in the revolutionary army who, by sheer chance, happened to be standing at the designated place when he arrived. Another account suggests that the conspiracy was discovered through some clever counterespio-

---

[15] *Maryland Archives*, 45:490.

[16] Scharf, *History of Western Maryland*, 1:142ff. See also T. J. C. Williams, *History of Frederick County*, 1:96ff.; Dorothy Mackay Quynn, "The Loyalist Plot in Frederick," p. 201ff.; William B. Willcox, *The American Rebellion—Sir Henry Clinton's Narrative*, pp. 192–93, 237–38; Carl Van Doren, *Secret History of the American Revolution*, pp. 236–37, 406–7; Janet Bassett Johnson, *Robert Alexander, Maryland Loyalist*, pp. 111–14.

nage on the part of a Captain Orendorff, who allowed himself to be recruited into the organization and, when he had found out the names of the chief organizers by intercepting the aforementioned message, arranged for their arrest that night by agents of the Frederick Committee of Safety.[17]

The conspirators were prosecuted before a special court consisting of Judges Alexander Contee Hanson, James Johnson, and Upton Sheredine. Their names were Peter Sussman, Nicholas Andrews, John George Graves, Yost Plecker (or "Bleaker"), Casper Fritchie (or "Frietschie"),[18] Adam Graves, and Henry Shell. Four others, named Newcomer, Kelly, Tinkles, and Parks, seem to have been somewhat less seriously implicated.

Apparently fearful that the blue-ribbon jury selected for the occasion might fail to return true bills against men whom they had known as friends and neighbors, Judge Hanson charged the jurors as follows:

GENTLEMEN OF THE GRAND JURY,

You are convened to execute a Trust of the last importance to your Country. . . .

. . . You are only to inquire after Treasons, Misprisons of Treason, Insurrections, and other high and dangerous Misdemeanors, committed in any County on the Western Shore. —A considerable Number of Persons, charged with an unnatural Conspiracy, to assist our Enemies in subverting the Liberties of America, are confined to the Gaols, and, on this melancholy Occasion, the Governor and Council, at the Request of the House of Delegates, have thought proper to appoint this special Court. . . .

I cannot suspect that you, Gentlemen, who have been selected for your Spirit, Intelligence, and Patriotism will, by an unpardonable Neglect of Duty, or an ill-judged Tenderness to the Lives of Traitors, encourage the Perpetration of the most atrocious Crimes. Those strong and decisive Feelings, which actuate the bosoms of honest Whigs, will prompt you to a zealous Discharge of your Duty. . . .

After all I have said, I would not be understood to favour any unreasonable Prejudices. —In all your Deliberations, attend carefully to the Directions contained in the Oath you have just taken. —You will present every Man for whose Accusation you shall have strong probable Grounds; but, in Favour of Innocence, you will disregard unmeaning popular Clamours. —It cannot surely be necessary to remark, that the extravagant Surmises of intemperate Zeal, or the Suggestions of artful Malice, have frequently subjected an innocent Man to the Expence, the Disgrace, and the Terrours of a Criminal Prosecution.[19]

The grand jury returned indictments. When the trial took place, however, the accused apparently refused to believe the seriousness of their predicament and conducted themselves throughout as if the pro-

[17] Quynn, "The Loyalist Plot," p. 203ff.
[18] Whose son married Whittier's heroine, Barbara Frietchie.
[19] *Maryland Journal & Baltimore Advertiser*, 7 August 1781.

ceedings were a great joke. When the jury brought in a verdict of guilty, however, Judge Hanson ordered the prisoners to stand, and delivered the following sentence:

It has been suggested to the Court, that, notwithstanding your Guilt has been ascertained by the Decision of an impartial Jury, you consider the Proceedings against you as nothing more than a solemn Mockery, and have adopted the vain Idea propagated by the Enemies of this Country, that she dare not punish her unnatural Subjects for engaging in the Service of Great-Britain. —From the strange insensibility you have heretofore discovered, I was indeed to conclude that you were labouring under a Delusion, which might prove fatal to your Prospects of Happiness hereafter[;] I think it my Duty therefore to explain to you your real Situation. —The Crime you have been convicted of, upon the fullest and most clearest Testimony, is of such a Nature, that you cannot, ought not to look for Pardon. —Had it pleased Heaven to permit the full Execution of your unnatural Designs, the Miseries to be experienced by your devoted Country would have been dreadful, even in the Contemplation! The Ends of public Justice, the Dictates of Policy, and the Feelings of Humanity all require, that you should exhibit an awful Example to your Fellow-Subjects; and the Dignity of the State, with every Thing that can interest the Heart of Man, calls aloud for your Punishment.

If the Consideration of approaching Fate can inspire proper Sentiments, you will pour forth your Thanks to that watchful Providence, which has arrested you at an early Stage of Guilt; and you will employ the short Time you have to live, in endeavouring, by sincere Penitence, to obtain Pardon from that Almighty Being, who is to sit in Judgment upon you, upon me, and upon all Mankind.

I must now perform the painful Task of denouncing the terrible Punishment ordained for High-Treason.

You, Peter Susman, Nicholas Andrews, John George Graves, Adam Graves, Henry Shell, Yost Plecker, and Casper Fritchie, and each of you, attend to your Sentence!

You shall be carried to the Gaol of Frederick County, and thence be drawn to the gallows of Frederick-Town, and be hanged thereon; you shall be cut down to the Earth alive, and your Entrails shall be taken out, and burnt while you are yet alive; your Head shall be cut off; your Body shall be divided into four Parts, and your Head and Quarters shall be placed where His Excellency the Governor shall appoint. —So Lord have Mercy upon your poor Souls!"[20]

One has difficulty today in understanding how the correspondent who reported these proceedings to the Baltimore *Journal* could conclude that "the Sentiments contained in the Charge and Sentence, bespeak a Maturity of judgment, a Dignity of Soul, and a *Humanity of the Heart, that would do Honour to any Court of Justice in the Universe.*" Because of Martin's army service, he did not reach Frederick until after the prisoners had been tried and convicted, a special prosecuting attorney having been appointed for the occasion. The Frederick County community was

[20] *Ibid.*

bitterly—and evenly—divided as to whether the prisoners' sentences should be carried out to the letter. As a result of Martin's intervention with Governor Lee, the state of Maryland refused to carry out this barbarous punishment. On 9 August the sentence was commuted, the sheriff being ordered to take the condemned from prison on or before 22 August and "them safely convey to the Gallows in the County aforesaid, the common Place of Execution of Malefactors, . . . there . . . to hang by the Neck on the said Gallows until they are dead, forbearing to execute any other part of the said Sentence."[21] Actually, only three of the seven condemned men—Fritchie, Plecker, and Sussman—were hanged.[22] The other four were apparently released upon condition that they "volunteer" for military service.

One occasional lucrative source of income for Martin during this period was the field of admiralty practice. Of course, with the separation of the colonies from their mother country, His Majesty's admiralty courts went out of business even before the adoption of the Declaration of Independence and of the various state constitutions. By a resolution of 25 May 1776 the Maryland convention established its own admiralty court.[23] Although not all the Admiralty Court records for this period have survived, they have been preserved for some scores of cases covering the years 1778 to 1789.[24] Martin appeared as counsel either on behalf of the libellant or of an intervening claimant in sixteen cases. Most of these were libels to have a captured ship, owned by British nationals, declared a prize of war and, together with her cargo, furniture, tackle, etc., forfeited and sold for the benefit of her captors and the state.

Despite the fact that the Maryland convention resolution established the Court of Admiralty of the State of Maryland to try "captures and seizures" only, with no civil jurisdiction apparently intended or conferred, Martin filed libels in some half-dozen cases for wages, under situations typical then (and since) in such actions, apparently without any jurisdictional objection. In other cases, in his capacity of attorney general he represented the interests of the state in various admiralty proceedings, and it seems incongruous to us today to find the governor's council directing the judge of the Admiralty Court to reverse his decision on grounds of state policy as decided by that council.[25]

[21] Executive Papers, Hall of Records, Annapolis, Maryland; Quynn, "The Loyalist Plot," p. 208. See also papers on the Frederick Town Plot at the Maryland Historical Society, Baltimore.

[22] *Maryland Journal & Baltimore Advertiser*, 28 August 1781. There is a tradition in Frederick County that Fritchie was unjustly convicted and that his wife rode all night to get a reprieve from General Washington, which she obtained; she then rode back home, arriving just too late to prevent her husband's execution. There is apparently no historical basis for this story.

[23] *Proceedings of the conventions*, pp. 154–55.

[24] See Records of Revolutionary Court of Admiralty in Maryland, Hall of Records, Annapolis, Maryland, *passim*.

[25] *Maryland Archives*, 21:239, 250–51 (letter of 16 November 1778 concerning the *Friendship*).

Years later Martin recalled that he was retained "in one or two important *appeals* to the Congress of the United States" in admiralty matters.[26] This reflects an interesting phase of the history of the Continental Congress before and under the Articles of Confederation. By a resolution of 25 November 1775[27] the Congress ordained that each state should establish its own admiralty courts, appeals from the decrees of which might be taken to a committee of members of the Congress— much like the House of Lords committee which hears appealed cases.[28] Martin represented a number of clients before such committees. The first appears to have been an appeal early in 1777 from the decree of the Court of Admiralty for the State of Rhode Island on the libel in the case of *Job Pierce* vs. *The Brig Phoenix*. The appeal having, "by mistake, been heard and determined by a different committee from that appointed to hear the same" and a petition being filed by Martin and John Darrell, the judgment was set aside and the appeal referred to the standing committee for hearing and determining appeals.[29]

Another appealed case, *David Fossett* vs. *The Sloop Jane*,[30] discloses the hectic and uncertain state of seafaring during the Revolution. In the Maryland Court of Admiralty held at Baltimore before Judge Benjamin Nicholson on 3 March 1779 Martin appeared on behalf of the libellant, Fossett. The latter alleged that, with the help of his slaves, he had taken possession of, captured, and beached the sloop *Jane* on Sinepuxent Bay, along the Atlantic coast of Worcester County. The *Jane*, armed with some eight guns and loaded with rum, sugar, and salt, had been captured by the *Experiment*, a privateer fitted out by Tory merchants and adventurters of New York City to prey on American shipping, off Ocracoke Bar, North Carolina. She was manned by a prize crew from the *Experiment* when recaptured by Fossett. He asked that the *Jane*, with her cargo, guns, and tackle, be condemned as an enemy prize and sold for his benefit.

Some thirty other claimants intervened (through their counsel, Jeremiah Townley Chase), claiming an equal share with Fossett for helping him take possession of the prize. Their attempt to horn in on Fossett's capture was apparent, and their claims were dismissed. However, another intervention by Joseph Foster, John Smith, and John Rogers (through Richard Ridgely, their proctor) had more substance. They alleged that they were the actual owners of the *Jane* and asked that they be awarded the ship and its cargo (or the proceeds of the sale), subject to payment of such salvage to Fossett as the court should decree.

---

[26] *Modern Gratitude*, pp. 150–51.

[27] *Journals of the Continental Congress*, 3:373–74, 7:75 (30 January 1777).

[28] See J. Bancroft Davis, "Federal Courts prior to Adoption of the Constitution," 131 U.S., App.

[29] *Journals of the Continental Congress*, 7:13, 30, 79ff.

[30] "The Revolutionary War Prize Cases (Records of the Court of Appeals in Cases of Capture), 1776–87," Microfilm EG 267, Roll 6, Case 48, National Archives, Washington, D.C.

To this claim, Martin countered that the owners were subjects of George III, and hence, as enemy aliens, not entitled to their property. On this question the parties were at issue, and much testimony was presented by each side. Judge Nicholson decided that the owners were subjects of the King of Denmark and decreed that one-half the proceeds of the sale of the ship and cargo should go to the owners and the other half to Fossett, in lieu of salvage. Both parties appealed from this decree to the Continental Congress. The case was argued by Martin (and presumably by Ridgely for the owners) before Ezra L'Hommedieu of New York and William Ellery of Rhode Island, who then constituted the committee to hear admiralty appeals. On 18 January 1780, after due deliberation, they decided that both appeals should be dismissed, with the costs ($1,170) divided between the two parties.

At about the same time, Martin was counsel for Harman Courter and the officers and crews of some half dozen brigs and schooners which had captured the brigantine *Pitt*.[31] This complex case involved capture, recapture, beaching of the ship to avoid re-recapture, salvaging of the cargo, etc. The Admiralty Court of Maryland had awarded the libellants the entire proceeds of the sale of the ship and cargo (some £95,000). Upon rehearing and the adduction of additional evidence, one-half of the proceeds was remanded to the owners. The libellants appealed from this decree to the Continental Congress, which cut down their award still further, to one-eighth of the sum. In still another case, the records of which have not been preserved,[32] Martin represented one Jonas Ingram of Williamsburg, whose ship had apparently been decreed confiscated by the Virginia Court of Admiralty. Upon appeal to the Congress Martin obtained a reversal and later attended court with Ingram and saw his property restored to him.

In recounting the final and most exciting episode in this chapter of Luther Martin's life, we must recall a session of the Continental Congress on 2 March 1778. Because the Continental army possessed no cavalry, the Congress adopted the following resolution:

Whereas, it is essential to the operations of the army during the next campaign that the most vigorous measures should forthwith be adopted for forming a body of horse, upon such principles as are most likely to advance the public interest and the honor of the officers and men who compose the same; and whereas, in times of public danger, when the lives, liberties, and property of a free people are threatened by a foreign and barbarous enemy, it is the duty of those, who enjoy in a peculiar degree the gifts of fortune, and of a cultivated understanding, to stand forth in a disinterested manner in defence of their country, and by a laudable example to rouse and animate their countrymen to deeds worthy of their brave ancestors, and of the sacred cause of freedom:

Resolved, That it be earnestly recommended to the young gentlemen of property and spirit, in the states of New Hampshire, Massachusetts Bay, Rhode

---

[31] Microfilm EG 267, Roll 8, Case 63, National Archives, Washington, D.C.
[32] *Modern Gratitude*, pp. 150–51.

Island, Connecticut, New York, New Jersey, Pensylvania [sic], Delaware, Maryland, Virginia, and North Carolina[33] forthwith to constitute, within their respective states, a troop or troops of light cavalry, to serve at their own expense (except in the article of provisions for themselves and forage for their horses,) until the 31 December next:

That each troop, so to be raised, consist of not less than twenty, nor more than 60 rank and file; that they have a right to choose their own officers, who shall receive continental commissions; and that they rendezvous at the main army on the first day of May next, or at an earlier period if possible. . . .

That every horse which shall be killed, and every horse and all arms and accoutrements, which shall be taken by the enemy in action, shall be paid for by the United States; the value to be ascertained under the direction of the Commander in Chief; and all booty taken from the enemy shall belong to the troop by whom it shall be taken.[34]

It was further recommended that such gentlemen procure their own "Necessaries and Accoutrements," from boots and spurs to sword and "carbine, fusee, or short blunderbuss." A report in the hand of Delegate William Duer of New York suggested by way of postscript that "should Congress adopt this Plan, the sooner it is published in the Papers the better, as Numbers of Young Men of Spirit will immediately set about Equipping themselves in the different States."[35]

The shrewdness of this prediction was demonstrated in Maryland, where response to publication of the resolution was immediate and enthusiastic.[36] Troops of light horse were organized in Baltimore, Annapolis, Frederick, and Kent County.[37] A year later the small but rapidly growing town of Baltimore could boast that "a Number of alert young Gentlemen, of this Town, handsomely accoutred and mounted on noble Steeds, richly caparisoned, have joined General [Andrew] Buchanan's Troops to act as a Corps of Light Dragoons, as long as their Country shall appear to need their personal Services in the Field."[38]

Just when Martin joined this outfit or how much service he and his fellow dragoons actually performed is not known. In the appraisal of the horses belonging to the troop, thirty-six members are listed, and forty-one horses are briefly described and valued. Luther Martin was credited with one of the more valuable horses, a six-year old "Bay Stalion," appraised at a hundred pounds.[39]

Toward the end of May 1781 Lafayette's little army in Virginia appeared to be in full retreat toward Maryland, with Lord Charles

[33] Why this resolution did not extend to South Carolina and Georgia as well is not apparent.

[34] Journals of the Continental Congress, 1774–1789, 10:213ff.

[35] Ibid.

[36] (Dunlap's) Maryland Gazette (Baltimore), 14 April 1778.

[37] Scharf, History of Western Maryland, 2:450; Maryland Archives, 45:459–60.

[38] Maryland Journal & Baltimore Advertiser, 25 May 1779.

[39] Maryland Archives, 45:485; Red Book no. 30, letter 91, 25 June 1881; J. Alexis Shriver, Lafayette in Harford County, pp. 99–100. According to this source the Frederick troop contained some twenty-seven members and twenty-nine horses.

Cornwallis in full pursuit. The Congress, fearing an imminent invasion of the Eastern Shore, ordered the removal of all public stores, cattle, and other provisions from that area. The governor and council called for an immediate and complete state of defense. General Washington wrote Gov. Thomas Sim Lee advising him that the Congress, by a resolution of 31 May, had called upon Maryland for two battalions of infantry and a corps of sixty-four dragoons for three months of service.[40] Governor Lee promptly mustered out the militia and alerted the cavalry. As it happened, Cornwallis was not bound for Maryland, and when Gen. Anthony Wayne's Pennsylvania troops met with Lafayette's meager forces on 10 June, the latter could face about and engage Cornwallis on more nearly equal terms.[41]

What Lafayette lacked above all was cavalry. The British dragoons under Lt. Col. Banastre Tarleton and Simcoe literally rode rings around him. Lafayette's cavalry at that time, led by Lt. Col. John Francis Mercer, consisted of only some sixty men whose efficiency was low because they were constantly overworked, overmatched, and underhorsed.[42] It was, accordingly, with high elation that the young French commander heard that Maryland cavalry had been dispatched to his aid. When they had not reached him by 25 June, however, he wrote to Governor Lee:

I have been for some time past flattered with accounts of an approaching succour in cavalry from your State, but their not joining me, makes me fear lest they should be prevented by some obstacle that had not been foreseen. If it is to be removed by the Executive, I pray your Excellency to give such orders for this purpose as may effect it with as much expedition as possible. Where an Army consists chiefly in Militia, a large and good cavalry is of the last importance. It is our misfortune that ours is chiefly in militia, and that the enemy's cavalry renders every effort of ours that may produce an equality, a primary object. With an Army of this description, and without cavalry to oppose to the enemy, you can easily conceive his advantages.[43]

Even if one had horsemen, it was almost impossible to procure horses for them. As Lafayette wrote Washington, "Nothing but a treaty of alliance with the negroes can find out dragoon horses, and it is by those means the ennemy [sic] have got a formidable cavalry."[44]

On 14 June 1781 Luther Martin and his fellow troopers of the Baltimore Light Dragoons ("an elegant Corps consisting of 50 respectable gentlemen") under the command of Capt. Nicholas Ruxton

[40] *Ibid.*, pp. 92–95; Brown Book no. 1, letter 41, 7 June 1781, in *Calendar of Maryland State Papers, No. 3, The Brown Books*; Red Book no. 5, letter 108, 11 June 1781.

[41] Charlemagne Tower, *The Marquis de La Fayette in the American Revolution*, 2:328.

[42] The roster of Lafayette's army as of 3 July 1781 included militia and "60 very bad" cavalry (*ibid.*, pp. 354–55). See also General Weedon to Captain Moore, in Balch, *The Maryland Line during the Revolution*, p. 156.

[43] Brown Book no. 7, letter 66, 25 June 1781, reprinted in Shriver, *Lafayette in Harford County*, p. 102.

[44] *The Letters of LaFayette to Washington, 1777–1779*, p. 209.

Moore, left Baltimore for Georgetown on the Potomac. There they joined forces with the troop from Frederick and crossed over into Virginia on 18 June.[45] By slow stages they reached Fredericksburg on or about 3 July, and finally joined Lafayette's forces on the evening of 6 July, just too late to take part in the almost disastrous engagement at Green Spring Farms.[46]

When he reached Fredericksburg, Martin was handed an urgent letter from Governor Lee requiring him to proceed at once to Frederick, Maryland, for the trial of Sussman, Andrews, Graves, and the others for treason. When he was able to see Captain Moore the following day, Moore denied his application for leave. Martin reported the circumstances to Governor Lee in a latter dated 4 July:

As he [Moore] had no *Orders* from your Excellency and the Council to give me a furlow and as he found a Disposition in some of the Troop to be disatisfied if I had leave of absence he thought himself under a Necessity of not granting me leave of Absence. —I have no Inclination at present to determine how far I should be justifiable after your Excellencys Letter to go to Frederick Town without permission from my Officer. Your Excellency & the Council, I am sure[,] will suggest sufficient excuses from the Punctilios of a Soldier for my not taking that Measure however justifiable it might be. —Altho' I had no sort of *Inclination* for a Tour of Duty to the Southward yet it was ever my wish that if it should be thought necessary we might undertake [it] with Chearfulness and Alacrity.

I have no wish to be exempted either from the fatigue[47] or Danger to which the others of the Troop may be exposed unless my Absence should be thought necessary, in which Case a Direction from your Excellency and the Council to Capt. Moore to give me leave to proceed [to] Frederick Town will be productive of that Permission.[48]

Just when Martin finally obtained his leave and left for Frederick Town is not known. When he finally got permission to go and reached Frederick, the prisoners had already been tried, convicted, and sentenced.

After the battle at Green Spring on 6 July hostilities quieted down for several weeks. Lafayette assigned the Maryland dragoons to the command of Gen. Daniel Morgan, and on 16 July he dispatched a motley outfit made up of Wayne's Pennsylvania Continentals, Morgan's riflemen from the backwoods of western Virginia, and Moore's gentleman cavalry to the south side of the James River to intercept a possible movement by Tarleton or Cornwallis in that direction.[49]

[45] *Maryland Journal & Baltimore Advertiser*, 19 June 1781, p. 4; Weedon to Lafayette, 18 June 1781, in Balch, *The Maryland Line during the Revolution*, p. 158.
[46] *Maryland Journal & Baltimore Advertiser*, 17 July 1781.
[47] Contemporary accounts of this campaign report that the summer of 1781 was extremely hot, and that both troops and horses suffered severe discomfort (see, e.g., Tower, *The Marquis de La Fayette*, 2:353–54 *et passim*).
[48] Martin to Gov. Thomas Sim Lee, Emmet Collection, New York Public Library, New York City.
[49] Lafayette to Morgan, in James Graham, *The Life of General Daniel Morgan of the Virginia Line*, p. 389.

Lafayette's orders to Morgan regarding the Maryland volunteer dragoons were as follows:

I beg leave to recommend the [Maryland volunteers] to your attention. Most of them are men of fortune, who make great sacrifices to serve their country. You will not, therefore, put them upon duties of orderlies, or the common camp duties which can be as well performed by the Continental horse. In everything else you will find them [to] answer your expectations. As they are only to be subject to your orders, when you have accomplished the objects mentioned in my letter of yesterday,[50] or when it is decided that Tarleton intends southerly and is beyond the reach of being struck, you will be good enough to order their return to head-quarters. It is my wish to dismiss them the moment it is in my power.[51]

Tarleton, as it happened, did not head for the Carolinas but, after a fortnight of sporadic raids, rejoined Cornwallis' main army at Portsmouth.[52] Thereupon, the Baltimore Light Dragoons, having received the thanks of Lafayette, Morgan, and Governor Nelson of Virginia, were discharged from duty. After some seven weeks of duty they arrived back in Baltimore on 4 August.[53]

Apparently, the next assembly of the Baltimore Light Dragoons was its last. On 8 September General Washington and his staff passed through Baltimore en route to Yorktown to capture, with the aid of the French fleet and army, General Cornwallis and his forces. When Washington reached the northern limits of the city, he was met by Captain Moore and his troop and escorted to the Fountain Inn, where he was formally received by a distinguished group of citizens. He survived the welcoming oratory and proceeded on his journey the following morning.[54]

During the last five years of the Revolution Martin, as attorney general, traveled constantly from one end of the state to the other, on both sides of the Chesapeake, on a variety of business: libeling vessels caught smuggling arms and food to the enemy; pressing claims for money and property owed to the state; prosecuting loyalists for arson, treason, and lesser offenses; and, of course, handling the hundreds of more ordinary violations of the criminal law.[55] Although this activity was much less remunerative than his private practice would have been, he came to know the leading citizens in every county, advised state officials on matters of high policy and great moment, and acquired a reputation for patriotism, honesty, industry and capacity, and legal acumen that made him the most respected, as well as the best-known, lawyer in Maryland.

[50] Lafayette to Wayne, 15 July 1781, in Tower, *The Marquis de La Fayette*, 2:372.
[51] Graham, *Life of General Morgan*, p. 389.
[52] Louis Gottschalk, *La Fayette and the Close of the American Revolution*, pp. 275–76; Robert D. Bass, *The Green Dragoon*, pp. 181–82.
[53] *Maryland Journal & Baltimore Advertiser*, 7 August 1781.
[54] Matthew Page Andrews, *The Fountain Inn Diary* (New York: Richard R. Smith, 1948), pp. 16–19; *Maryland Journal & Baltimore Advertiser*, 11 September 1781.
[55] *Maryland Archives*, 16:537–38; 21:199–200, 228–29, 235, 239, 250–51; 43:105, 417–19; 45:14, 130, 178, 326, 490, 594; 47:7, 254; 48:63, 69–70, 234.

7

Background for Philadelphia, 1783-1787

Since the revolution I have constantly attended the general courts on the Western and Eastern Shores of Maryland, and the civil and criminal courts of Baltimore County. . . . I believe I speak moderately, when I say that I have attended on behalf of the State, at least five thousand criminal trials in that court.—Martin, in Charles Evans, *Report of the Trial of the Honorable Samuel Chase*

The story told by Fiske[,] . . . one of stagnation, ineptitude, bankruptcy, corruption, and disintegration[,] . . . is at worst false and at best grossly distorted. . . . We have too long ignored the fact that thoroughly patriotic Americans during the 1780's did not believe there was chaos and emphatically denied that their supposed rescuers were patriotic.—Merrill Jensen, *The New Nation*

When he was appointed attorney general, Martin decided to make Baltimore his home.[1] In 1778 Baltimore Town was picturesque and small but mushrooming.[2] Its streets were unpaved—"the muddiest I ever saw," according to Continental Congressman John Adams[3]—in part because of the constant stream of wagons and baggage trains passing through the town, which had already attracted all the trade of southern Pennsylvania, the area south of the Susquehanna, and most of the trade of western Virginia and western Maryland, all the way to Pittsburgh.

Daniel Grant's Fountain Inn, located on Light Street between Market (now Baltimore) Street and Elliot's Wharf (now Redwood Street), was perhaps the best known of the city's many famous hotels. It was built at a cost of ten thousand dollars and contained a capacious ballroom, sumptuous hairdressing parlors, and stabling for eighty horses. Baltimore harbor was large, safe, and strategically placed almost in the middle of Maryland, near a part of Virginia and Pennsylvania, be-

---

[1] *Modern Gratitude*, p. 152.

[2] This description of Baltimore during the revolutionary period and immediately thereafter is taken from Raphael Semmes, *Baltimore as Seen by Visitors, 1783–1860*; Annie Middleton Sioussat, *Old Baltimore*; Andrews, *The Fountain Inn Diary*; Robert Gilmor, "Recollections of Baltimore," p. 233ff.

[3] Diary, in *Works*, 2:434.

tween the Delaware, Susquehanna, and Potomac Rivers, and nearer the mountains than any other coastal city. It swarmed with packets and clippers, many of them built on its shores, employed not only in trade with the colonies but in the highly profitable running of the French and British blockades of the West Indies with cargoes of flour, corn, timber, and tobacco. There was a boom in real estate near the harbor, and some locations already rented for as much as a guinea a year per square foot. Much of this property, of course, had been owned by Tories, and for four years, despite the recommendation of the Congress,[4] had been protected from confiscation by the wealthy and conservative land-holders in the Maryland Senate, who considered all property—even that belonging to the enemy—sacrosanct.[5] Finally, and belatedly, in 1780 the state ordered "all property belonging to British citizens within the state, debts only excepted" seized and confiscated.[6] The first property auctioned off consisted of valuable sites in downtown Baltimore, which were bought by prosperous merchants and professional people. Martin bought four lots, located on the east side of Charles Street between Baltimore and Lombard Streets, for some £2,360. In partnership with Samuel and Jeremiah Townley Chase and Capt. Charles Ridgely, he also bought up lots on Whetstone's Point (now called Locust Point, the site of Fort McHenry), which had been part of the extensive holdings of the Principio Company, operators of one of the oldest ironworks on this continent.[7]

After the capitulation of Cornwallis at Yorktown, Baltimore began to grow in population, size, and business activity even more rapidly than before. By the mid-1780s the city had almost two thousand houses and over a thousand shops. Market (Baltimore) Street, which every spring and autumn had been waist-deep in mud and virtually impassable—in 1841 an elderly merchant recalled that sixty years earlier he had seen a Continental army drummer boy and his pony almost drown in a mud-hole at Market and North streets when the troops marched south through the city—was paved, lighted, and widened in 1784. A board of port wardens was established to regulate the construction and repair of wharves and to impose duties on vessels entering and clearing the port to meet the cost of these improvements. In the same year a subscription was raised by a number of prominent citizens to tunnel Calvert Street under the old courthouse, which sat on a small hill near the harbor. Parks and market sites were established, and Messrs. Hallam and Henry opened the first resident theater in America.

[4] *Journals of the Continental Congress*, 9:971.
[5] Philip A. Crowl, *Maryland during and after the Revolution: A Political and Economic Study*, chap. 2 *passim*. The ultraconservative constitution of the Maryland Senate is discussed below.
[6] Kilty, *Laws*, Oct. Sess., 1780, ch. 45.
[7] In October 1781, at the request of one of the commissioners, Martin personally delivered the down payment on these lots, £373 14s. 3d., in specie, to Governor Lee (*Maryland Archives*, 47:517).

One day shortly after the close of the war, Martin heard that a young lady bearing the surname Cresap was visiting in Baltimore.[8] He called on her to see whether by chance she were related to the Cresaps who had treated him so kindly eleven years before on his trip through western Maryland. He was pleased and surprised to find that she was Maria, the daughter of Capt. Michael Cresap, who had been a little girl at that time. She was now a lovely young woman of seventeen or eighteen and was returning to her home from Philadelphia, where she had attended Miss Brodeau's finishing school.

Acquaintance ripened into romance, and the couple were married on Christmas Day, 1783, somewhere outside Baltimore. They returned to Baltimore to live[9] (their first residence is not known, but many of their married years were spent in the old William Fell mansion on Hempstead Hill, now the site of The Johns Hopkins Hospital), and had three daughters in close succession. Although the order is uncertain, it is probable that Juliet was the eldest, since she was the first to be married, and that as early as 1799. The next two children were named Maria, after their mother, and Eleonora. (Eleonora was presumably the youngest, as she was only fifteen in 1801, at the time of her elopement with Richard Reynal Keene.[10]) At least two other children died in early childhood: one (sex and name unknown) was buried on 29 September 1789, and Eliza Sophia was born on 10 July 1791, christened on 2 October, and buried on 28 December 1792.

Martin's law practice, which he had resumed after the war, grew rapidly in size and scope, and he continued in office as attorney general.[11] He had become known as a successful lawyer from the lowlands of the Eastern Shore to the mountains of western Maryland, and even far beyond the borders of the state. Before long, his practice was one of the largest and most successful in the history of the American bar. Accordingly, it may be in order to outline briefly the Maryland judicial system at this period and to describe its bench and bar.[12]

Before 1776 there were county courts of limited jurisdiction; a general court for trial of most civil cases at law, called the Provincial Court;

[8] *Modern Gratitude*, p. 148.
[9] *Maryland Gazette* (Baltimore), 16 January 1784.
[10] Juliet was married in New York City on 9 May 1799 to Hector Scott, a merchant of that city; Maria married Ens. Lawrence Keene on 8 April 1808; Eleonora married Richard Reynal Keene (not related to Lawrence Keene) in New York City on 27 January 1802. See also "Register of Births, Marriages and Deaths in St. Paul's Parish, Baltimore," 1:238, 260, 331, 336, Maryland Historical Society, Baltimore, Maryland.
[11] In 1805 Martin stated that he had appeared in over five thousand criminal cases in the Baltimore County court alone (Charles Evans, *Report of the Trial of the Honorable Samuel Chase*, p. 187). He also tried, on behalf of the state, thousands of criminal prosecutions in other counties, apart from his public and private actions in the fields of attachment, real estate, bills and notes, wills, and many other branches of civil law.
[12] See Carroll T. Bond, *The Court of Appeals of Maryland, a History*, chaps. 2 and 3, pp. 22–98, *passim*.

a Court of Chancery, presided over by the chancellor for cases in equity; a Court of Admiralty for the trial of maritime cases; and a Court of Appeals, consisting of the governor and council. An appeal could be made from the Court of Appeals to the Committee of the Privy Council for Appeals in England, which upon occasion declared acts of legislation void as beyond the powers of a colony's charter or in violation of fundamental English law, and thus laid the foundation for the later nullifying of acts of Congress (and of state legislatures) as "unconstitutional" by the United States Supreme Court under the Constitution of 1787.[13]

The first Maryland Constitution (1776) retained the colonial judicial organization almost intact, merely changing the name "Provincial Court" to "General Court." Until 1805 the latter sat at Annapolis and at Easton on the Eastern Shore. This and the Chancery Court were by far the most important state courts of the period. Not unnaturally, many more cases were tried before these tribunals than were heard by the Court of Appeals. The opinions of its judges were carefully, often fully, reported, whereas the Court of Appeals filed relatively few opinions in explanation of its upholding or reversal of the lower courts. Oddly enough, during this period the annual salary of the chancellor ranged from $1,600 to $2,733.33 and that of a General Court judge was $1,333.33, compared with $533.33 for a member of the Court of Appeals.[14]

The Court of Appeals consisted of five judges elected by joint ballot of the two houses of the Maryland General Assembly. It sat in the old Revenue Office, located on the second floor of the State House at Annapolis. Each judge sat at his own desk on a dais raised about two feet above the floor, faced by tables and chairs for counsel. Behind them, in the wall directly opposite the judges, was a fireplace fed by four-foot logs, which heated the room, and, upon occasion on a cold, damp winter day, the court joined counsel in front of the fireplace and there heard the argument of the cases on the docket. Warming their backs and hands, the judges punctuated their questions and comments with occasional expectorations of tobacco juice into the blazing logs (a habit that persists even today among the bench and bar of this tobacco-growing state).

The first Maryland Court of Appeals, appointed 12 December 1778, was made up of Benjamin Rumsey as chief judge and Benjamin Mackall IV, Thomas Jones, James Murray, and Solomon Wright, Martin's former patron and law teacher from Queen Anne's County on the Eastern Shore. All these men were able lawyers, but what was more

---

[13] A. H. Kelly and W. A. Harbison, *The American Constitution, Its Origins and Development*, p. 51ff.; and cf. Winthrop v. Letchmere (Privy Council, 1728), in Eugene Wambaugh, *A Selection of Cases on Constitutional Law*, p. 7, with Marbury v. Madison, 1 Cranch. (U.S.) 137 (1803).

[14] Increased to $833.33 in 1797 and to $1,000 in 1799 (Bond, *The Court of Appeals of Maryland*, pp. 67–68, 77; see also The Chancellor's Case, 1 Bland's Ch. 595ff.).

important was that they were also owners of large tidewater farms, which gave them sufficient income to permit them to accept a judicial appointment with a salary hardly more than nominal. All the judges had been vigorously engaged in the prosecution of the war as members of councils of safety and of the state constitutional convention, procuring supplies for the troops and helping in other ways. Because of this activity the court did not hear argument on any cases until 12 May 1783, when matters continued from the colonial court of governor and council were considered; indeed, the same docket book was used, later cases being entered immediately following the old, with the only hiatus the lapse in time.

The General Court of this period was probably the greatest trial court in the history of the American judiciary. Its chief judge was Robert Hanson Harrison, the ablest of four able men ultimately appointed from this court to the United States Supreme Court.[15] Harrison had been President Washington's military private secretary for the first six years of the Revolution, and Washington urged him to accept the appointment for the sake of his "friends and fellow citizens, anxious for the respect of the Court."[16] That tribunal was then held in relatively low esteem, however,[17] and though the appointment was confirmed, Harrison declined in favor of his existing position which, at that time, was more exalted and more convenient to his home in Charles County. He refused to reconsider even when Alexander Hamilton wrote him that "we want men like you. They are rare at all times."[18] During the same period he also declined an appointment as chancellor of Maryland because it would have required him to move to Annapolis, although in 1790 the stately, sophisticated Maryland capital was even more attractive than Washington.[19]

It was before these judges that Luther Martin resumed his practice. His earliest reported case is *Webster* v. *Hall*,[20] a typical action of ejectment from Harford County involving a common recovery to "dock" (or rid) a tract of land named "Goldsmith's Rest" of its entailment.[21] The principal issue was the validity of a married woman's acknowledgment of a deed which did not specifically state that it was made "out of the hearing of her husband." Counsel for the plaintiff were Samuel Chase, Jeremiah Townley Chase (Samuel's first cousin once removed), and

---

[15] The others were Thomas Johnson, Samuel Chase, and Gabriel Duvall. Curiously, no member of the Maryland Court of Appeals has ever been appointed to the Supreme Court.

[16] Charles Warren, *The Supreme Court in United States History*, 1:42.

[17] It will be remembered that John Jay, the first chief justice, resigned in 1794 to become special ambassador to England and that Justice John Rutledge resigned, after having been absent from every session of the Court for two years, to become chief justice in his own state of South Carolina.

[18] Bond, *The Court of Appeals of Maryland*, p. 89.

[19] *Ibid.*, p. 67.

[20] *Maryland Reports*, 2 Harris and McHenry 19.

[21] Martin was admitted to practice there in March 1779 (Walter W. Preston, *History of Harford County, Maryland*, p. 75).

Luther Martin. They won their case before the General Court at its 1782 October term and on appeal before the Court of Appeals at its May term in 1786. Martin does not appear to have argued the case orally before the General Court (at that time composed of Chief Judge Robert Hanson Harrison, Nicholas Thomas, and Alexander Contee Hanson), and the report does not show who argued the case in the Court of Appeals. However, the copious citation of such varied and exotic authorities as Bacon's *Abridgement*, Sheppard's *Touchstone*, and Viney's *Baron and Feme* (not to mention *Coke on Littleton*, Plowden's *Elizabethan Reports*, and statutes of 34 and 38 Hen. 8) are clues to Martin's preparation of the case. It was altogether typical of him that he should have expended such a wealth of learning and exhaustive research upon a comparatively unimportant case involving so insignificant and apparently obvious a point of law.

Kelly v. *Greenfield* is interesting today not so much for the abstruse and anachronistic problems it raised regarding the Maryland proprietors' rights in case of adverse possession and escheat as for a statement made by Martin in the course of his argument before the General Court. "It is not necessary," he said, "that a dignified subject should have [the] privilege [of *nullum tempus*], though the State of Maryland, *independent and sovereign*, has all the privileges of sovereignty."[22] This was the position taken by all the states and by most of their citizens under the Articles of Confederation. It epitomized Martin's position in the Constitutional Convention less than two years later and foreshadows the difficulties attending both the drafting and the ratification of the Constitution there adopted.

That Martin's distrust of Tories did not automatically and immediately die out with the cessation of hostilities is illustrated by one of his next reported cases.[23] Samuel Johnston, a resident and prothonotary of York, Pennsylvania, had lost his office because he refused to take the oath of allegiance to that commonwealth. He moved to Maryland, where he lived quietly until the war was over. In August of 1784 he applied to the Baltimore County court for admission to the bar as an attorney. Martin, as attorney general, objected that Johnston was not a fit person to be admitted to the bar under the Act of 1783, ch. 17, dealing with the qualification and admission to the bar of solicitors and attorneys. Johnston insisted, however, that his previous reluctance to take oaths of allegiance was due to his feeling that he should not renounce his fealty to the king of Great Britain until a treaty of peace had been formally concluded. The Baltimore County court was apparently willing to let bygones be bygones and admitted him, but Martin was not satisfied. He entered an appeal which was dismissed by the General Court, after a very able argument by Johnston that no

[22] *Maryland Reports*, 2 Harris and McHenry 121. Cf. the language of Samuel Chase in Ware v. Hylton (1796), 3 Dall. (U.S.) 199, p. 224.
[23] State of Maryland v. Johnston (1786), 2 Harris and McHenry 160.

appeal lay as a matter of law. Nothing daunted, and with typical resourcefulness (and stubbornness), Martin sued out a writ of certiorari for the removal of the proceedings to the General Court, to which they were transmitted in May 1785. There, after the customary leisurely practice of those days, the case was "struck off" a year later. Martin was a good loser, however. Throughout most of his life he was too busy trying cases to waste time nursing grudges over minor matters. He and Johnston soon became reconciled and before long were sitting together on the same side of the counsel table at the Baltimore County court and the Court of Appeals.[24]

At this time and for many years thereafter the great bulk of litigation involved title to real estate. The old land records and cases perpetuate the names given to the early homes and farms of the state, reflecting the hopes and fears, the romances and judgments, of their first owners: "Cold Comfort," "Bold Venture," "King's Neglect," "Contention," "Betty's Dowry," "Hobson's Choice," "Kelly's Fortune," "Cockey's Folly," "Turville's Struggle," "Isaac's Chance," "Judith's Garden," "David's Fancy." Some are more mysterious: "Trammel's Conoy Islands" (in landlocked Frederick County), "The Silent Cyphers of Africa," "Long Guile," "Davis' Pharsalia," "The Number of Four," "The Case Is Altered," "Custom of London," "Petticoat's Loose," "Park's Death Knot," and "Widow's Delight Enlarged."[25]

Early in 1784 the governor and council sought Martin's advice in regard to the activities of Sir Robert Eden, Maryland's last colonial governor. After the treaty of 1783 Eden returned to Maryland as the agent of Henry Harford, the last proprietor, to obtain either recognition or compensation for Harford's confiscated property. Although Eden was a popular figure, he went too far, and in Harford's name issued patents to vacant lands which Harford claimed. Martin was asked to investigate and advise whether the state should prosecute Eden not only for fraud but also for treason.[26] The matter was apparently dropped, and Eden died on 3 September 1784.

Martin received state-wide recognition later the same year, when he was elected a member of the Maryland delegation to the Continental Congress. The Senate nominated James McHenry, Gen. William Smallwood, Col. Carvill Hall, Col. Nathaniel Ramsey, Nicholas Carroll, and William Hemsley. The House of Delegates named Gustavus Scott, Rinaldo Johnson, Nicholas Rogers, Thomas Sim Lee, Thomas Stone, Richard Ridgely, and Samuel Chase. On 4 December in the Senate the ballots were deposited in the ballot box, which was sealed and given to the tellers of both houses. After a private conference they reported that William Smallwood, Samuel Chase, James McHenry, Thomas Johnson, Gustavus Scott, and Richard Ridgely had

---

[24] See, e.g., Moale v. Tyson (1790), 2 Harris and McHenry 387, 398.
[25] Taken from 1 and 2 Harris and McHenry, *passim.*
[26] *Maryland Archives*, 48:517.

the majority of the votes.[27] However, Smallwood, Johnson, and Ridgely declined to serve, and the procedure of bicameral nomination and election by the Senate was again followed. This time John Henry, William Hindman, and Luther Martin were named.[28] It is apparent that Martin's election to this office was purely honorary. His other duties, both public and private, obviously precluded his serving, and Henry, Hindman, and McHenry were the only delegates who went to Philadelphia. Martin received no salary or other emolument from his election, since delegates were paid only per diem of attendance, but it was proof of his rising reputation throughout the state.

During the Revolution and under the Articles of Confederation, Maryland statesmen made contributions that were unique, critical, and decisive. On 7 June 1776 the Continental Congress appointed one committee to draft a resolution proclaiming the independence of the thirteen American colonies. It named another committee to draw a "form of confederation" under which the states would become one nation. The first committee's resolution was agreed to by twelve states (New York abstaining) on 2 July, followed two days later by the adoption of the Declaration of Independence. The Articles of Confederation, the product of the labors of the second committee, were not agreed upon by Congress and submitted to the states until 15 November 1777. Within fifteen months twelve states had subscribed to the Articles, but they required unanimous adoption and could not go into effect until John Hanson and Daniel Carroll finally affixed their signatures on behalf of Maryland on 1 March 1781.

The delay was caused by the inability of the states to agree on the ownership and future control of the country lying west of the Appalachians, an area that stretched all the way west to the islands of the Pacific.[29] Massachusetts, Connecticut, New York, Virginia, North Carolina, and Georgia all claimed (some speciously, some with considerable authority) extensive parts of this area. New Hampshire, Rhode Island, New Jersey, Pennsylvania, Delaware, Maryland, and South Carolina had no basis whatever for pretensions to this valuable and inviting territory. Of this group, the most vehement and the most persistent antagonist to the claimants was Maryland. There were many reasons for this opposition, not all of them based upon pure statesmanship and "national vision," in the high-sounding phrases of the group. The claimants planned to use these lands to pay their troops, as well as for other wartime expenses. It seemed unfair to the seven states without

[27] See *Votes and Proceedings*, Nov. Sess., 1784, pp. 8-18, *passim*.

[28] Oddly enough, the delegates' credentials presented to the Continental Congress the following February were dated 4 December, two weeks before Martin, Henry, and Hindman were in fact nominated and agreed upon (*Journals of the Continental Congress*, 28:47-48).

[29] See generally Herbert Baxter Adams, *Maryland's Influence upon Land Cessions to the United States, passim*; Merrill Jensen, *The Articles of Confederation*, pp. 120-24, 159-60, 197, *et passim*; Clarence W. Alford, *The Mississippi Valley in British Politics*, 1:87-89, 93-101, 314-23, *et passim*.

charter claims to the territory that they should have to bankrupt their treasuries and citizens to free the colonies from Great Britain, all for the benefit of six other states. Worse yet, after the war the states with western lands could use them to lower their tax rates and to drain other states of their populations, while their citizens were busily setting up highly speculative land companies to stake out large tracts west of the mountains, which they hoped to sell later at a great profit.[30] These projects were bound to conflict with the claims to the western lands of such families as the Washingtons, the Masons, and the Lees, who through special legislation, surveys, patents, speculation in militia bonuses, and the like professed to have pre-empted hundreds of thousands of acres of what Washington boasted to be "the cream of the country—the first choice of it."[31]

Maryland's official position, proclaimed loudly and persistently, was that "the back lands, . . . if secured by the blood and treasure of all, ought in reason, justice, and policy, to be considered a common stock, to be parcelled out by the Congress into free, convenient, and independent Governments, as the wisdom of that body shall hereafter direct."[32] In this policy Maryland was adamant (despite the temporary victory of the landed states in preserving their claims in the ninth article of confederation) and steadfastly refused to sign the Articles until her position had been accepted.

The larger states were the first to ratify, and one by one the others followed. By the beginning of 1779 all had ratified except "our Froward Sister M[aryland] and her little Crooked Neighbour" Delaware.[33] Delaware capitulated early in 1779. When Maryland remained obdurate, the Continental Congress resolved, on 10 October 1780, that the western lands should be "formed into distinct republican States, which shall become members of the federal Union, and have the same rights of sovereignty, freedom and independence as the other States."[34] Thereupon, New York, Connecticut, and Virginia formally yielded their

[30] For example, many prominent Marylanders like Samuel Chase, Daniel of St. Thomas Jenifer, Charles Carroll of Carrollton, William Paca, and Thomas Johnson were members of the Indiana, Illinois-Wabash, Ohio, and other speculative land companies (see Thomas Perkins Abernethy, *Western Lands and the American Revolution*, pp. 171, 365; Kathryn Sullivan, *Maryland and France 1774–1789*, pp. 97, 99; Crowl, *Maryland during and after the Revolution*, p. 114). Cf. Franklin's efforts on behalf of the Vandalia-Walpole Company (Jensen, *The Articles of Confederation*, pp. 152, 209, 212, 233).

[31] Freeman, *George Washington*, 3:300.

[32] Jensen, *The Articles of Confederation*, pp. 156–57. Samuel Chase, William Paca, Charles Carroll, and other Maryland leaders desired to except from the "common stock" lands already granted or surveyed to or for private persons before the beginning of the Revolutionary War. The fact that this would have left intact the lands of their Illinois-Wabash Company takes much of the bloom off this high-sounding statement of principle (see Abernethy, *Western Lands*, p. 239; Sullivan, *Maryland and France*, p. 97; Sister Mary Virginia Geiger, *Daniel Carroll, a Framer of the Constitution*, p. 87).

[33] William Whipple to Josiah Bartlett, 3 January 1779, in Edmund Cody Burnett, ed., *Letters of Members of the Continental Congress*, 4:5–6.

[34] *Journals of the Continental Congress*, 18:15.

claims to these lands (not, however, without certain important reserva-
tions). At this point Maryland appealed to the French minister, La
Luzerne, for naval assistance to prevent Benedict Arnold from invading
the Chesapeake Bay. He at first demurred but then suggested that
Maryland sign the Articles and thus consolidate the strength of the
colonies in their struggle against England.[35] Jenifer in the Senate and
Thomas Johnson, Samuel Chase, and others in the House of Delegates
who had been dragging their heels over ratification finally took the
hint, "rose above their principles," and voted for ratification late in
January 1781, despite a Virginia proviso denying their land-company
claims. On the issue of the western lands, more than any other, originated the split between the "nationalists" and the "states-righters," between "the haves" and "the have-nots," which was carried over from
the Continental Congress to the Constitutional Convention of 1787
(and which, indeed, still persists). It was with the latter group that
Martin vigorously aligned himself during the first half of his public life.

Maryland's next contribution toward union was the so-called
Potomac Convention or Mount Vernon Compact. By its charter, Maryland's boundary along the Potomac extends to the south bank of the
river, not merely to the middle of the stream. After the Revolution
Maryland as a sovereign state threatened to close the river to Virginia
traffic, except upon her own terms, and Virginia in retaliation threatened to close the mouth of the Chesapeake Bay to Maryland. The two
states then decided to settle their differences, if possible, by treaty, despite the provision of the sixth article of confederation that "no two or
more States shall enter into any treaty . . . between them, without the
consent of the . . . congress." Accordingly, Alexander Henderson and
George Mason, two of Virginia's four appointed commissioners, met
with Samuel Chase, Daniel of St. Thomas Jenifer, and Thomas Stone
at Alexandria in March of 1785.[36] George Washington (though not a
commissioner), dropped in on the conference by accident (or design)
and invited the members to adjourn to Mount Vernon. There a treaty
between the two states was drafted, which allowed free access to both
bodies of water to citizens of both states and provided for other mutual
commercial and economic improvements.[37] The advantages of this
compact soon became apparent to other states, especially Pennsylvania
and Delaware, and in November Maryland invited these two to join in
a convention looking toward the extension of its terms to them also. At
James Madison's instigation, however, the Virginia legislature instead

[35] Sullivan, *Maryland and France*, pp. 98–103; Abernethy, *Western Lands*, p. 245.
[36] See, generally, Kate Mason Rowland, *The Life of George Mason*, 2:81ff.
[37] Gov. Patrick Henry forgot to notify Madison and Edmund Randolph, the
other two Virginia commissioners, of the date set by Maryland (Irving Brant,
James Madison, 2:375ff.). Not having a copy of the Virginia resolution authorizing
the conference, the Maryland delegates did not realize that there was not a quorum
of Virginia commissioners present or that the Virginians lacked authority to make
concessions with regard to the Chesapeake Bay (George Mason to Madison, 9
August 1785, in Rowland, *Life of George Mason*, 2:72, 83ff.; 12 Hening's Stat. 50–55).

invited all thirteen states to send delegates to Annapolis the following year.

The agenda of this conference was limited to the consideration of "a uniform system" for the improvement of commerce and trade among the states. Regarded in the light of its immediate accomplishments, the Annapolis convention of September 1786 would seem to have been a failure.[38] Delegates attended from only five states—New York, New Jersey, Pennsylvania, Delaware, and Virginia. Four states (Connecticut, Maryland, South Carolina, and Georgia) did not send delegates, and those dispatched from the remaining four (New Hampshire, Massachusetts, Rhode Island, and North Carolina) did not arrive in Annapolis while the convention was in session.[39]

Maryland refused to send delegates, even though the convention was meeting in the Senate chamber of its own State House, ostensibly for fear of belittling Congress in the eyes of foreign powers.[40] If this excuse seems flimsy, it had some basis in fact. Louis-Guillaume Otto, the French chargé d'affaires, sent a secret report from New York to the Comte de Vergennes, minister of foreign affairs, in Paris. Otto's sources of information were reliable, and he drew remarkably canny deductions from the facts provided him.[41] He pointed out to Vergennes that the merchant-propertied-creditor classes desired a general overhauling of the government but that it was difficult for them to drum up sufficient popular support to bring about changes which necessarily would spread the base and facilitate the collection of taxes, prevent the watering down of debts by the issuance of paper money, and at the same time effectuate the collection of obligations and the execution of judgments in hard money. Otto then outlined the strategy which would have to be used to misrepresent the country's condition and needs—propaganda so artfully promoted by the one group and so widely believed by the other that it continues to distort most of the histories of this period.[42] Obviously in sympathy with the objectives of these men of property,

[38] Detailed accounts of the Annapolis convention are found in Broadus Mitchell, *Alexander Hamilton*, 1:356ff.; Brant, *James Madison*, 2:375ff. Most of the source material is in the Emmet Collection, New York Public Library.

[39] For the action of various states in sending delegates, see Burnett, *Letters of Members of the Congress*, 8:389–90n. Although they had known for months that the meeting was set for 4 September, the Massachusetts commissioners did not arrive in New York until the seventh and did not leave for Annapolis until the eleventh (Massachusetts commissioners to New York commissioners, 10 September 1786, in *Works of Alexander Hamilton*, ed. John C. Hamilton, 1:432). They did not reach Wilmington until the sixteenth. The convention broke up on 14 September, even though those assembled knew that the other commissioners would arrive shortly (Hugh Williamson to Governor Caswell, 27 October 1786, in *North Carolina State Records*, 18:772).

[40] *Votes and Proceedings*, Nov. Sess., 1785, pp. 77, 88.

[41] Cf. his inside information about the secret transactions of the 1787 Constitutional Convention (Farrand, *Records of the Federal Convention*, 3:39ff.).

[42] See Merrill Jensen, *The New Nation, a History of the United States during the Confederation, 1781–1789*, pp. xii–xiv, Pt. 3 *et passim*; *The Massachusetts Sentinel*, 22 August 1787, reprinted in R. W. Leopold and A. S. Link, *Problems in American History*, p. 120ff.

Otto explained their motives and maneuvers and described the men behind them in a letter that has been strangely neglected and that is of such particular importance for both the Annapolis and the Philadelphia conventions that it is given here at some length:

My Lord: . . .

The people are not ignorant that the natural consequences of an increase of power in the government would be a regular collection of taxes, a strict administration of justice, extraordinary duties on imports, rigorous execution against debtors—in short, a marked preponderance of rich men and of large proprietors. . . .

Although there are no nobles in America, there is a class of men denominated "gentlemen," who, by reason of their wealth, their talents, their education, their families, or the offices they hold, aspire to a pre-eminence which the people refuse to grant them; . . . moreover, they are creditors, and therefore interested in strengthening the government, and watching over the execution of the laws.

These men generally pay very heavy taxes, while the small proprietors escape the vigilance of the collectors.

. . . The attempt, my lord, has been in vain, by pamphlets and other publications, to spread notions of justice and integrity, and to deprive the people of a freedom which they have so misused. By proposing a new organization of the federal government all minds would have been revolted; circumstances ruinous to the commerce of America have happily arisen to furnish the reformers with a pretext for introducing innovations.

They represented to the people that the American name had become opprobrious among all the nations of Europe; that the flag of the United States was everywhere exposed to insults and annoyance; the husbandman, no longer able to export his produce freely, would soon be reduced to extreme want; . . . and that congress, not having the necessary powers, it was essential to form a general assembly instructed to present to congress the plan for its adoption, and to point out the means of carrying it into execution.

The people, generally discontented with the obstacles in the way of commerce, and scarcely suspecting the secret motives of their opponents, ardently embraced this measure, and appointed commissioners, who were to assemble at Annapolis, in the beginning of September.

The authors of this proposition had no hope, nor even desire, to see the success of this assembly of commissioners, which was only intended to prepare a question much more important than that of commerce. The measures were so well taken that at the end of September no more than five states were represented at Annapolis, and the commissioners from the northern states tarried several days at New York, in order to retard their arrival.

The states which assembled, after having waited nearly three weeks, separated under the pretext that they were not in sufficient numbers to enter on business, and, to justify this dissolution, they addressed to the different legislatures and to congress a report, the translation of which I have the honor to enclose to you.[43]

---

[43] Written 10 October 1786, translated in George Bancroft, *History of the Formation of the Constitution of the United States of America*, 2:399ff.; Leopold and Link, *Problems in American History*, pp. 102ff.

This address to Congress and the states, largely the handiwork of Hamilton, called for delegates to be sent to a new convention in Philadelphia the following May to consider not merely the problems of commerce but also "such further provisions as shall appear to them necessary to render the Constitution [i.e., the Articles] . . . adequate to the exigencies of the Union." As Otto described this document,[44] it employed "an infinity of circumlocutions and ambiguous phrases to show . . . the impossibility of taking into consideration a general plan of commerce . . . , without at the same time touching upon other objects closely connected with the prosperity and national importance of the United States."[45] In the language of Madison's biographer, the recommendations were "thickly and softly gloved."[46] At any rate, it was thus that the Constitutional Convention in Philadelphia came into being.

In the winter and spring of 1787 the Maryland general assembly undertook the task of naming delegates, and the selection proved unexpectedly difficult. One feature of the postwar depression was the agitation for the issuance of paper money, and many commentators on the period have suggested that but for this hot political and economic issue Maryland would have been represented at the convention by men of greater state and national prominence. In any event, it is almost certain that Luther Martin would not have been named a delegate had the paper money fight not been in progress.

Paper money was not a new problem in Maryland. Bills authorizing its issue had been introduced in the House of Delegates as early as 1727. The first emission was authorized in 1733, and a sinking fund from "duties on liquors, negroes, and Irish servants"[47] was provided. This issue was ultimately redeemed without loss to the public, as was another authorized in 1769. At the beginning of the Revolutionary War paper money virtually disappeared, but in 1780 and 1781 Maryland authorized further issuances totaling about a million dollars. To compound these fiscal problems, the Continental Congress also authorized paper money and assigned a quota for redemption to each state.[48]

When the war ended, there was a brief period of false prosperity. British merchants supplied citizens of the new nation with goods and extended new credit gladly. Before long, however, they demanded payment for these sales as well as settlement of old accounts. Congress passed a law requiring that all obligations due states be paid within six years, and the tax collectors were importunate. Interest rates ran as high as 25 and 30 per cent, and Charles Carroll of Carrollton was

[44] For the text of the report of the Annapolis convention, see John Mabry Mathews and Clarence A. Berdahl, *Documents and Readings in American Government*, pp. 37ff.

[45] Quoted in Bancroft, *Formation of the Constitution*, 2:399, 401.

[46] Brant, *James Madison*, 2:387.

[47] It will be remembered that these items were also taxed in the same period to finance the establishment of the first public schools in Maryland (see pp. 19–20).

[48] See, generally, Kathryn L. Behrens, *Paper Money in Maryland, 1727–1789*, chaps. 1–7 *passim*.

quoted as saying that under the circumstances it was unsafe to lend any money at all. Debtors' properties were being foreclosed all over Maryland, and there was much distress and unrest. A mob forced the Charles County court to suspend all civil suits for the collection of British debts, and a group in Harford County prevented bidding on land being sold at a sheriffs' execution sale.[49] Similar conditions in Massachusetts led to Shays' Rebellion, accounts of which alarmed creditors everywhere. In Rhode Island the paper money party won the elections and authorized issues of paper money which later depreciated almost to nothing. The president of Princeton, John Witherspoon, reported that in New Jersey "we constantly saw . . . creditors running away from their debtors, and debtors pursuing them in triumph and paying them without mercy."[50]

In Maryland a group of inhabitants of the Western Shore addressed a petition to the governor and council requesting a special session of the legislature to authorize the issuance of paper money. The Baltimore newspapers of the period were filled with articles favoring the issue, and late in 1786, under the leadership of Samuel Chase and William Paca, the House of Delegates, acting in the belief that they were responding to the popular demand, passed a bill calling for the issuance of bills of credit to the amount of £350,000. The Senate, led by Charles Carroll of Carrollton, rejected this bill unanimously, using in its message the arguments that economists always make against fiat money.[51]

Under the Maryland constitution of 1776 the Senate was probably the most ultraconservative body of legislative Bourbons in American history. Senators were not elected directly by the voters but by a group of "senatorial electors" (the prototypes of the later presidential electoral college), themselves elected, who were required to have the same property qualifications as members of the House of Delegates—an estate in freehold of at least five hundred pounds. The senators were required to have a minimum estate of a thousand pounds. The Maryland Senate of this period has been called a politically irresponsible oligarchy of lawyers, merchants, and landowners interested primarily and principally in the protection of their own property. "Leadership in the House of Delegates, seats in the Senate and the Governor's council, and of course the governorship itself were all monopolized by this clique who admitted no interlopers."[52]

Samuel Chase attacked Carroll, claiming that as a creditor he was opposed to legislation that would permit the debtor to repay money

---

[49] Crowl, *Maryland during and after the Revolution*, pp. 73ff., 92–100.
[50] Quoted in Wilfred Ellsworth Binkley and Malcolm Charles Moos, *A Grammar of American Politics*, p. 30.
[51] See, generally, Crowl, *Maryland during and after the Revolution*, chap. 4 *passim*; Behrens, *Paper Money in Maryland*, chap. 8 *passim*.
[52] Crowl, *Maryland during and after the Revolution*, pp. 31ff. The property qualification for governor was five thousand pounds. See also Philip A. Crowl, "Antifederalism in Maryland, 1787–1788," pp. 451ff.

loans in paper and thus relieve himself of a high interest rate. He further accused Carroll of lending money unsparingly to senators opposed to the bill. Chase, of course, was not without a pressing interest in paper money himself, as he had invested heavily in confiscated property and had other speculative commitments that required a ready supply of cash. Other bills passed by the House of Delegates for debtor relief were similarly rejected summarily by the Senate. It was at the height of this stalemate, in an atmosphere of great tension, that the General Assembly was called upon to name the delegates to the convention.

In December of 1786 the Maryland lower house agreed to send delegates, and the Senate willingly agreed. The impression was that Maryland would select her delegates promptly. On 20 January 1787, however, the General Assembly adjourned for an election to decide the issue of paper money and to determine whether the voters were permitted under the constitution to instruct their senators on legislative matters. As a result of this election, held early in 1787, and of the widespread opposition expressed in popular assemblies and by grand juries from Frederick to Talbot counties, the paper money movement bogged down. The personalities and economic attitudes involved, however, continued to affect Maryland politics and influenced the appointment of the Maryland delegates to the Constitutional Convention.[53]

When the General Assembly reconvened in the spring, the House of delegates nominated John Henry, Charles Carroll of Carrollton, Gen. William Smallwood, Robert Hanson Harrison, James McHenry, Thomas Sim Lee, Daniel of St. Thomas Jenifer, George Gale, Alexander Contee Hanson, and Robert Goldsborough. To this list of aristocrats the Senate added the names of Thomas Johnson, William Paca, Samuel Chase, and Thomas Stone. During the course of the next month, of over a dozen persons suggested by one house or the other, almost all declined to serve. The reasons for this reluctance are in most instances not stated. Thomas Stone's name, for example, was dropped because he could not attend because of unspecified peculiar circumstances. Chase and Paca probably declined in the hope of reviving their paper money bill if the opportunity offered itself. It is equally likely that the fear of this very possibility caused most of the others nominated to decline the honor. As a contemporary summed it up, "Mr. Chase having just before menaced the Senate for rejecting a wide emission of paper money—and appealed to the people against them— they had joined in that general issue—and cou'd not venture to relinquish to a violent and headstrong party their active influence in the Senate as well as the lower house. . . . Those gentlemen, therefore remained at home."[54]

---

[53] For details of the legislative action appointing the Maryland delegates, see *Votes and Proceedings*, Apr. Sess., 1787, *passim;* Geiger, *Daniel Carroll*, pp. 122ff.; Crowl, *Maryland during and after the Revolution*, pp. 109–10.

[54] John B. Cutting to Thomas Jefferson, 11 July 1788, in Farrand, *Records of the Federal Convention*, 3:339.

By 23 May (the convention had been scheduled to begin on 14 May), only two delegates had been agreed upon, James McHenry and Daniel of St. Thomas Jenifer. The House of Delegates thereupon nominated Luther Martin, Daniel Carroll, and John Francis Mercer. The Senate, weary of the protracted disagreement and fearful of losing a quorum of its members and thus sending no delegates to Philadelphia, capitulated. It declined to add further nominations and proposed that the five men "be appointed and authorised on behalf of this State to meet with such Deputies as may be appointed and authorised by any other of the United States to assemble . . . at Philadelphia."[55] On 26 May the assembly did so.

Without the paper money issue the Maryland delegation would doubtless have been composed entirely of members of the old Senate aristocracy. As it turned out, the delegates' backgrounds and philosophies of government varied widely. Jenifer, a Charles County planter and owner of a beautiful estate near Port Tobacco called "Stepney," had been on the colonial governor's council, served as president of the Maryland Council of Safety throughout the Revolution, and was intendant of the revenue and financial agent for the state, as well as a member of the Continental Congress. He was a sociable bachelor of sixty-four, a good friend of George Washington. Daniel Carroll, fifty-six years old, was also a large landowner in Montgomery County. His background and economic attitudes were the same as those of his distant relative Charles Carroll of Carrollton, whose first cousin he married. He was a member of the Senate and before the Revolution had served on the council of state and had represented Maryland in the Continental Congress. He and Jenifer were the only native Marylanders among the delegates. James McHenry was born in northern Ireland and came to this country in 1772. His family became wealthy as importers and merchants in Baltimore, and he became financially independent in 1782 at the age of twenty-eight, on the death of his father. After studying medicine and surgery under Dr. Benjamin Rush in Philadelphia, he joined the Continental army at Cambridge, Massachusetts, as a surgeon. He was taken prisoner and released soon after. He then became General Washington's secretary, and later aide to General Lafayette. After the Revolution he was elected to the Maryland Senate, then to the Continental Congress, and was a state senator at the time of his appointment to the Philadelphia convention. He later became President Washington's secretary of war.[56] John Francis Mercer was a Virginian by birth. He moved to Maryland in 1785, after his marriage to Sophia Sprigg, heiress to an estate called "Cedar Park," in

[55] *Votes and Proceedings*, Apr. Sess., 1787.

[56] William Pierce's unflattering description of him as "a very respectable young man . . . of specious talents with nothing of genius to improve them" (quoted in Farrand, *Records of the Federal Convention*, 3:93) is both superficial and inaccurate. Pierce could not have known McHenry at all well, as they were in Philadelphia together for only two days, 31 May and 1 June (*ibid.*, p. 589).

Anne Arundel County. He was just twenty-eight years old and had held no political office in Maryland. He and Martin had in common, among other things, their cavalry service against Cornwallis during the hot summer of 1781.

In view of the economic motives and interests often attributed to the drafters and ratifiers of the constitution written at Philadelphia in the summer of 1787,[57] it is instructive to remind ourselves of the economic background and political beliefs of one of those drafters, Luther Martin. Born and raised in an agrarian environment of hard work and little money, he taught school and studied law on twenty pounds a year. Although his first few years of legal practice were highly successful, the Revolution closed off this source of income almost entirely and reduced him to tutoring and manual labor.

After the war he risked over three thousand pounds speculating in confiscated Tory real estate, paying a small amount down and giving his bond to pay the rest at a later date.[58] In 1787 he still owed the state some six hundred pounds on this debt. This pecuniary interest would thus incline him to oppose a national constitution which forbade the issuance of state bills of credit and paper money. On the other hand, at this time he owned more than three thousands dollars' worth of public securities, the value of which might well increase to 100 per cent of face value under a vigorous, solvent national government. This pecuniary interest would incline him to favor a constitution that set up a strong central government capable of fiscal stability. It is obvious that these financial commitments substantially cancel each other out, and it will be seen in the narrative that follows that Martin's position at the convention on matters economic was influenced far more by his family background and environment and by his personal convictions than by his own relatively small investments, or those of his friends. Economically speaking, he was a free agent.

[57] See Charles A. Beard, *An Economic Interpretation of the Constitution of the United States, passim.* For recent critiques of this work and its supporting data, see Forrest McDonald, *We, the People*; R. E. Brown, *Charles Beard and the Constitution.*

[58] See p. 56 above; Crowl, *Maryland during and after the Revolution*, pp. 42ff., 128; Crowl, "Antifederalism in Maryland," p. 466ff.

8

The Constitutional Convention:
1. The Virginia Conspiracy, March–8 June 1787

> The framers of the Constitution ignored the purposes
> for which they were delegated; they acted without any
> authority whatever; and the document, which the war-
> ring factions finally evolved from their quarrels and
> discussions, was revolutionary.—Albert G. Beveridge,
> *The Life of John Marshall*

> The formation of the Constitution has been dealt with
> almost exclusively from the Federalist point of view. . . .
> Thus the struggle has been generally represented as one
> between the good and the wise, on the one hand, and the
> foolish and the ignorant on the other. Federalist orators
> have been represented as wise and farseeing patriots,
> Antifederalists as "demagogues." This view is unhistor-
> ical and unfair.—R. L. Schuyler, *The Constitution of the
> United States*

If James Madison is truly "the father of the Constitution," at birth his
"child" did not have the form and appearance that he had dreamed
and planned for it during its period of gestation. It was ultimately
shaped by non-Madisonian prenatal influences, among the most important of which was that of Luther Martin.

Madison had been a serious student of history, ancient and modern,
for much of his life, and for a year or more before the Constitutional
Convention met he had been reading extensively in French as well as
English books (many of them specially bought and sent him by Jefferson, from Paris) on government and political science.[1] As a result of this
reading, and with the impending convention in mind, he analyzed
the state of the nation in his famous *Vices of the Political System of the
United States.*[2]

In March 1787, just after Madison's thirty-sixth birthday, Gov.
Edmund Randolph wrote his fellow Virginian (then sitting in the Continental Congress in New York) about the work of the approaching

[1] Brant, *James Madison*, 2:409ff.
[2] James Madison, *Writings*, ed. Gaillard Hunt, 2:361ff.

convention. Randolph's thoughts obviously did not run in the same direction as Madison's but were more nearly representative of what most of the country was thinking—"that the alterations should be grafted on the old Confederation. . . . That the points of power to be granted be detached from each other, as to permit a State to reject one part, without mutilating the whole."[3]

This approach, apart from its general impracticality, would never do for Madison, who wanted "alterations" of a radically different order. On 8 April he replied to Randolph, ambiguously "agreeing" with him that "it will be well to retain as much as possible of the old Confederation," and then proceeded to "just hint the ideas that have occurred, leaving explanations for our interview." Among more general observations were the following specific hints:

Let the national government be armed with a positive and complete authority in all cases where uniform measures are necessary, as in trade, &c., &c. . . .

Let it have a negative, in all cases whatsoever, on the Legislative acts of the States, as the King of Great Britain heretofore had. . . .[4]

. . . The Legislative department may be divided into two branches. One of them to be chosen every _____ years by the Legislatures or the people at large; the other to consist of a more select number. . . . Perhaps the negative on the State laws may be most conveniently lodged in this branch. A Council of Revision may be superadded, including the great ministerial officers.

. . . The northern States will be reconciled to [representation by population instead of the same number of votes for each state] by the *actual* superiority of their populousness; the Southern by their *expected* superiority on this point. This principle established, the repugnance of the large States to part with power will in a great degree subside, and the smaller States must ultimately yield to the predominant will.[5]

As his most recent and eulogistic biographer has summed up Madison's scheme, "these vices [of government under the Articles] add up even more strikingly to a need to bring the states under the thumb—or *the fist*—of a federal constitution."[6] Washington and McClurg were as nationally minded as Madison, and after the Virginia delegation had had ten days of afternoon "indoctrination" sessions in Philadelphia,[7]

---

[3] Quoted in Charles Warren, *The Making of the Constitution*, p. 48.

[4] Cf. Madison's proposal to Jefferson on 18 March 1787 "to arm the federal head with a negative in all cases whatsoever on the local Legislatures" (*ibid.*, pp. 326–27). He made a similar proposal to Washington on 18 April (*ibid.*, pp. 344, 346).

[5] Madison, *Writings*, 2:336ff.

[6] Brant, *James Madison*, 3:412. It is an ironical twist of fate that, just as Martin later became a strong nationalist, Madison became an anti-nationalist, excoriating Marshall's broad interpretation of national powers under the Constitution. During the 1830s, under the "needling" of southern students and states'-righters, Madison disavowed the plain import of his plan and the explicit statements made in his writings during this period (which were unavailable to his critics at the time) in support of even stronger powers in the national government (*ibid.*, p. 417; Farrand, *Records of the Federal Convention*, 3:473, 516, 531, *et passim*).

[7] Farrand, *Records of the Federal Convention*, 3:23.

Randolph, Mason,[8] and Wythe were ready to support Madison's revolutionary Virginia Plan, at least for the time being.

On 14 May 1787 the convention to amend the Articles of Confederation opened at the State House (old Independence Hall) in Philadelphia.[9] George Washington, who arrived the day before "amidst the acclamation of the people," the booming of cannon, and the ringing of bells, noted in his diary: "This being the day appointed for the meeting of the Convention such members of it as were in town assembled at the State House, where it was found that two States only were represented, viz., Virginia and Pennsylvania. Agreed to meet again tomorrow at 11 o'clock."[10] Delegates from Delaware and North Carolina arrived the next day, but it was not until 25 May that most of the delegates had arrived and the convention could get down to business. The delay was no doubt irksome, and served to "sour the temper of the punctual members, who do not like to idle away their time,"[11] but it was not altogether the fault of the delegates. Connecticut did not appoint a delegation until 14 May; New Jersey until 18 May; Maryland named four out of her five on 26 May; New Hampshire appointed hers on 27 June; and Rhode Island never appointed any at all.[12] To these dates must be added at least a day for each twenty miles a delegate had to travel to Philadelphia.

James McHenry, the only one to accept of the Maryland delegates originally appointed by the legislature, did so on 1 May,[13] and left shortly thereafter, arriving at Philadelphia about 14 May.[14] For two weeks he absented himself from the preliminary meetings of other delegates and waited for the others not knowing who they would be or when they would appear. On 28 May McHenry attended the convention for the first time, and from then until 1 June, when he received word from home that his brother was dangerously ill, he made careful notes of the proceedings. On that date he left at once for Baltimore and did not return to the convention until 6 August.[15]

In Philadelphia the other delegates passed the time attending meetings of the Society of the Cincinnati, visiting and taking tea with old friends, and attending lectures by a lady "in reduced circumstances," illustrated by such readings from Milton, Shakespeare, Thomson, and

---

[8] "The last [Mason], I am informed, is renouncing his errors on the subject of the Confederation, and means to take an active part in the amendment of it" (Madison to Jefferson, 23 April 1787, in *The Papers of Thomas Jefferson*, ed. Julian P. Boyd, 11:310).

[9] Farrand, *Records of the Federal Convention*, 3:20. Unless otherwise stated, the narrative of events at the convention is derived from Madison's notes, as reprinted in Farrand.

[10] Quoted in Warren, *Making of the Constitution*, pp. 101–2.

[11] Washington, Diary, 20 May 1787, in Farrand, *Records of the Federal Convention*, 3:22.

[12] *Ibid.*, pp. 559ff.

[13] *Votes and Proceedings*, 1 May 1787.

[14] Bernard Christian Steiner, *The Life and Correspondence of James McHenry*, p. 99.

[15] Farrand, *Records of the Federal Convention*, 1:14–75 *passim*.

Pope "as have a tendency to improve the heart and enlarge the understanding." The delegates were in good company, as the audience was reported to be "composed of gentlemen of the learned professions, ladies of the most elevated rank and fortune, as well as a number of eminent citizens who introduced their wives and daughters into a society where nothing could be heard but the beauties of poetical genius, selected with care and an anxiety to convey general satisfaction."[16]

Every afternoon the Virginia delegates met at three o'clock for two or three hours of discussion of "the great subject of our mission,"[17] the formulation of a tentative draft or outline of a new constitution to replace the old Articles and the strategy to be used to obtain support for it—this in spite of the fact that the convention had been called "for the *sole* and *express purpose of revising the Articles of Confederation, and reporting to Congress and the several Legislatures such alterations and provisions therein.*"[18]

The Virginia delegation, therefore, was engaged in a bold conspiracy to bring about the adoption of a new form of national government. It went far beyond the intent of the legislatures of the states which appointed the delegates and the authorization of the congressional resolution. Such an action was beyond the powers granted the delegates by the various state legislatures: only very limited authority had been granted to the representatives of Massachusetts, Connecticut, New York, and Delaware, while other states were more generous; no state, however, not even Virginia, had authorized the drafting of a new constitution.[19]

Although this conspiracy may well have proved, in the light of subsequent history, to have been benign, necessary, and wise, it was nonetheless a conspiracy. That it should have surprised, even shocked, many delegates, like Luther Martin, to whom it was suddenly presented almost as a *fait accompli* is perfectly understandable. This fact, however, has been overlooked by most modern historians because they have written their accounts from the vantage point of the "Monday morning quarterback," rather than from that of the participants. As Richard Henry Lee later observed, "had the idea of a total change [abandoning the Articles of Confederation] been stated, probably no State would have appointed members to the Convention."[20]

On Friday, 25 May, a sufficient number of delegations (New York, New Jersey, Pennsylvania, Delaware, Virginia, North Carolina, and

---

[16] *Pennsylvania Packet* and *Pennsylvania Herald*, 16 May 1787; Warren, *Making of the Constitution*, pp. 106–7.

[17] Mason to his son, 20 May 1787, in Farrand, *Records of the Federal Convention*, 3:23.

[18] Resolution of the Congress, 21 February 1787.

[19] See Farrand, *Records of the Federal Convention*, 3:559–86 *passim*. The "revision of the *Federal Constitution*" authorized by the state-enabling resolutions referred, of course, to the Articles of Confederation, the only "constitution" then in existence to be "revised."

[20] "Letters of a Federal Farmer," October 1787, in Warren, *Making of the Constitution*, p. 148.

South Carolina) and individual delegates (from Massachusetts and Georgia) had convened to proceed with the organization of the convention. George Washington was unanimously elected as its presiding officer. He made a modest speech of acceptance, Maj. William Jackson was elected secretary of the body, and doorkeepers were appointed.

Next the deputies' credentials were read, and Madison states that it was "noticed" by those then present (if it has been too seldom since) that the Delaware delegates "were prohibited from changing the Article in the Confederation establishing an equality of votes among the States." Apparently he considered this as an inconsequential obstacle in the way of the large-state juggernaut that he was about to start rolling. Mason commented to his son on this obstruction to the Virginia Plan, and added somewhat naïvely that "no other State . . . hath restrained its deputies on any subject."[21] This was not the last to be heard upon this vital and basic subject, however.

A committee of three was appointed to prepare "standing rules & orders" to govern the proceedings; it was composed of George Wythe of Virginia (before whom Martin had taken his examinations for the bar in 1770),[22] Alexander Hamilton of New York, and Charles Pinckney of South Carolina.[23] It was probably no accident that all three were strong advocates of a new constitution and favored a strong central government, with a consequent depletion of the powers of the separate states. It is not surprising that the rules this committee drew up and submitted favored the plans of Madison and his fellow Virginians, aided by large-state sympathizers in the Pennsylvania, South Carolina, and Massachusetts delegations.

Upon reconvening on Monday, several new delegates from Massachusetts, Connecticut, and Delaware reported and took their seats. Maryland was also represented, for the first time, in the person of James McHenry. His credentials were read to the assembly.[24] These credentials are important, for they set forth explicitly both the powers and the obligations of the Maryland deputies as the representatives of that state. They were given the power to "join with" the other delegates "in considering such Alterations and further provisions as may be necessary to render the Federal Constitution," i.e., the Articles of

---

[21] Farrand, *Records of the Federal Convention*, 3:574–75; George Mason to his son, 27 May 1787, in *ibid.*, p. 28.

[22] Wythe left the convention on 4 June 1787 and resigned on 16 June, "being called home by the serious declension of his lady's health" (Madison to Jefferson, 6 June 1787, in *ibid.*, pp. 35, 590).

[23] To be distinguished from Charles Coatesworth Pinckney, who noted early and often that the Convention was acting *ultra vires* even in considering the Virginia plan (*ibid.*, 1:33–34, 39ff., *passim*).

[24] See *ibid.*, 3:586. McHenry's credentials have not been preserved. Undoubtedly they contained, in addition to his own name, the names of Charles Carroll of Carrollton, Robert Hanson Harrison, Thomas Sim Lee, and Thomas H. Stone; these four were not replaced by Daniel of St. Thomas Jenifer, Daniel Carroll, John Francis Mercer, and Luther Martin until 26 May, by which time McHenry had already arrived in Philadelphia.

Confederation,[25] "adequate to the Exigencies of the Union"; each delegate had "full Power to represent" the State of Maryland collectively or singly, if only one delegate was in attendance. The Maryland delegates were also charged with the duty "to report the Proceedings of said Convention, and any Act agreed to therein, to the next session of the General Assembly" of Maryland.[26]

The rules committee next reported its proposed rules of order. In addition to such procedures as the reading of the previous day's minutes, orders of the day, the making of motions, questions of adjournment, and the like, there were others submitted of a much more controversial and vital nature. The first rule read: "A House, to do business, shall consist of the Deputies of not less than seven States; and all questions shall be decided by the greater number of these which shall be fully represented."[27] The Articles of Confederation permitted no amendment without the unanimous consent of all thirteen states. This was one of the major defects of the Articles and one of the principal obstructions to the existence of a strong nation which could act promptly and effectively in domestic and international affairs. This rule, however, went to the opposite extreme in providing for revision of the Articles, the basis of the existing government, which had been set up by thirteen then sovereign and independent states, not by the unanimous consent of all thirteen nor even by a majority of seven, but by a majority of those states present and "fully represented."[28] On 28 May, the day on which this rule was proposed, there were nine states present; thus the vote of only five was required for revision. As there were never more than eleven states present at the convention on any given day, a vote of more than six states was never required on any matter of revision of the Articles.

This rule had been under consideration by the Virginia and Pennsylvania delegates even before the convention opened on 25 May. Madison notes that Gouverneur and Robert Morris of Pennsylvania were in favor of insisting that the large states have some sort of proportionately larger vote than the small states in the convention. The Virginia delegation perceived, however, that such a proposal would meet violent resistance from the delegates of the small states and that,

[25] See n. 19 above. Not only was this the sole possible meaning at that time but was so understood by everyone.

[26] The delegates from Connecticut, New York, and North Carolina were similarly "directed" to report the Philadelphia proceedings to their respective state legislatures. It is highly doubtful, moreover, if *any* of the states sending delegates (except, perhaps, Virginia) anticipated that the proceedings were to be kept secret either from the state legislatures or from the public generally.

[27] *Ibid.*, 1:8.

[28] This rule was later construed by Nathaniel Gorham of Massachusetts, chairman of the Convention committee of the whole, to mean a majority of states present, and not to count ties within delegations. Thus on 1 June, and many times later, "there being 5 ays, 4 noes, 1 divided," or "5 ays, 4 noes, 2 divided," Gorham ruled "that it was an affirmative vote" by "the greater number" of states represented which, obviously and arithmetically, it was not (*ibid.*, p. 69 *et passim*).

if adopted, it would probably cause them to go home, leaving the Virginians and their plan high and dry, and without a quorum of states to pass it. As Madison later observed, it would be much more difficult to get the small states to agree "to disarm themselves of the right [of an equal vote] & thereby throw themselves on the mercy of the large States" at the outset, than it would be to "prevail" upon them "in the course of the deliberations" to do just that "for the sake of an effective Government." For these reasons the Virginians "discountenanced & stifled" the proposal of the Pennsylvanians and adopted as a compromise the rule of revision by a majority of the states present and voting at the Convention.[29]

Upon the adoption of the rules as submitted,[30] Pierce Butler, a delegate from South Carolina,[31] moved that "the house provide . . . against licentious publications of their proceedings." This motion was referred to the rules committee. It reported back the next day, 29 May "that no copy be taken of any entry on the journal during the sitting of the House without leave of the House. That members only be permitted to inspect the Journal. *That nothing spoken in the House be printed, or otherwise published or communicated without leave.*"[32]

The adoption of this rule was not an afterthought, as it might first appear. The large states generally, and Virginia in particular, knew that their project would never be adopted if its radical and unauthorized nature were made public. It is now obvious that the acceptance of this rule by the convention was a part of their plan from the beginning. Butler did not offer the rule until 28 May, and it was not adopted until the next day, but on 27 May George Mason wrote to his son back in Virginia: "It is expected our doors will be shut, and communications upon the business of the Convention be forbidden during its sitting. This I think myself a proper precaution to prevent mistakes and misrepresentations until the business shall have been completed."[33]

Even the careful Madison, in his enthusiasm, noted on 28 May, "The Rule restraining members from communicating the proceedings of the Convention &c. was agreed to nem. con."[34] He later struck out this entry and pasted over it a copy of the original rules made from Jackson's journal. A week later he wrote to Jefferson: "It was thought expedient

---

[29] *Ibid.*, pp. 10–11.

[30] Except for the rejection of one rule, which called for the yeas and nays to be entered in the minutes upon demand. However, as both Jackson and Madison kept detailed records of the vote of each state on every issue, the rejected motion must undoubtedly have been aimed at recording the votes of individual members of each delegation.

[31] Then a member of the large-state bloc.

[32] Under this strange rule Martin was later prohibited from making a copy of the constitution in its tentative draft state for his own study while the committee on detail was revising and rewriting it for final consideration. See Chapter 14, p. 122, below.

[33] Quoted in *ibid.*, 3:28. See also Rowland, *Life of George Mason*, 2:104.

[34] I.e., in regard to disapproving the proposed rule for recording yeas and nays. Quoted in Farrand, *Records of the Federal Convention*, 1:10–11.

... to establish some rules of caution, which will *for no short time* restrain even a confidential communication of our proceeding."[35]

This admission coincides with Martin's later observation that a "veil was interposed between our proceedings and the Public, in my opinion, for the most dangerous of purposes, and which was never designed by the advocates of the system to be drawn aside, or if it was, not till it should be too late for any beneficial purpose."[36] The real reason for this "rule of secrecy," Madison admitted years later, was that the Virginia conspiracy could never have succeeded if the debates had been public.[37]

Thus a curtain of secrecy was imposed upon the proceedings of the most important political gathering in American history. No newspaper reporters, no visitors of any kind, for any purpose, were allowed. No member of the convention was permitted to discuss what Mason was fond of referring to as "the business" with the leading men, much less with the constituents, of his own state.

Of this enforced silence upon the subject of the greatest possible concern to the people, Martin later observed to the Maryland General Assembly:

Before I arrived,[38] a number of rules had been adopted to regulate the proceedings of the convention, by one of which, seven States might proceed to business, and consequently, four States, the majority of that number, might eventually have agreed upon a system, which was to affect the whole Union. *By another, the doors were to be shut, and the whole proceedings were to be kept secret;*[39] and so far did this rule extend, that we were thereby prevented from corresponding with gentlemen in the different States upon the subjects under our discussion; a circumstance, Sir, which, I confess, I greatly regretted. I had no idea, that all the wisdom, integrity, and virtue of this State, or of the others, were centred in the convention. I wished to have corresponded freely and confidentially with eminent political characters in my own and other States; not implicitly to be dictated to by them, but to give their sentiments due weight and consideration.[40]

For once in his life Martin was in agreement with Thomas Jefferson, who wrote from Paris to John Adams in London: "I am sorry they began their deliberations by so abominable a precedent as that of tying up the tongues of their members. Nothing can justify this example but the innocence of their intentions, & ignorance of the value of public discussions."[41] Madison had written Jefferson about the rule of secrecy[42]

---

[35] Letter of 6 June 1787, in *ibid.*, 3:35.

[36] *Maryland Journal*, 18 March 1788; Farrand, *Records of the Federal Convention*, 3:283.

[37] Quoted in Herbert Baxter Adams, ed., *Life and Writings of Jared Sparks*, 1:590.

[38] I.e., on 9 June, three days after his appointment was confirmed by the general assembly.

[39] Italics in original.

[40] *Genuine Information*; Farrand, *Records of the Federal Convention*, 3:173.

[41] Letter of 30 August 1787, in Farrand, *Records of the Federal Convention*, 3:76.

[42] *Ibid.*, pp. 35, 60.

and Jefferson's concern over the "innocence" of Madison's intentions was natural. It is certain that it was confined to the delegates from the smaller states, who had not been admitted to the pre-convention councils of Virginia and Pennsylvania and whose most vigorous spokesmen, such as Martin, Lansing, and Sherman, were not present when the rule was imposed.

Once adopted, the rule was (with a few notable exceptions) rigorously enforced: two doorkeepers, whose wages were paid by the Virginia delegation,[43] were "planted without and within—to prevent any person from approaching near—who appear to be very alert in the performance of their duty."[44] Whenever one of the delegates opened a door to enter or leave, debate was immediately stopped lest some word be heard outside.[45] At the conclusion of deliberations, upon instructions of General Washington, Secretary Jackson, after "burning all the loose scraps of paper which belong to the Convention," turned his Journal, meager as it was, over to him.[46] Even this document was not made public for more than thirty years.

The exceptions to the enforcement of the rule are highly significant. It was apparently invoked by the bloc of large states against the delegates from the small states. No objection seems to have been made, or even considered, when Madison placed a table in front of all the other delegates and from this point of vantage, took full notes of the proceedings.[47] He had free access to the Secretary's journal and was allowed to copy from it such parts as he pleased into his own notes, a privilege denied to others, including Martin. Madison took his notes away with him to his own lodgings outside the convention hall to make a complete fair copy. There was nothing wrong with this—the country, indeed the world, will always be in Madison's debt for his notes, in spite of the fact that they were incomplete, colored by his own attitude on all questions, and constantly amended by him over the next fifty years.[48] The point is that detailed note-taking and access to the official journal was limited to Madison. Others took notes, to be sure—among them

---

[43] These stipends were later either repaid to Virginia or paid again by the Congress (*ibid.*, 3:74). Secretary Jackson's salary was also paid by Virginia (*ibid.*, 4:76–77).

[44] Farrand, *Framing of the Constitution*, p. 58. This "alertness" is a lost trait on the part of legislative doorkeepers.

[45] Warren, *Making of the Constitution*, p. 138. See also Farrand, *Records of the Federal Convention*, 3:86.

[46] William Jackson to George Washington in Farrand, *Records of the Federal Convention*, 3:82. The papers thus destroyed undoubtedly included Charles Pinckney's outline of a plan of government, submitted to the convention at the same time as the Virginia Plan and never seen again after the convention was over.

[47] *Ibid.*, 1:xvi; Warren, *Making of the Constitution*, pp. 126–27.

[48] It is the judgment of the most famous commentator on this, one of the greatest of all recorded debates on government, that Madison's notes, "as supplemented by the other very irregular notes" revealed in the passage of time, comprise only "a fairly accurate and complete account of the proceedings" (Farrand, *Framing of the Constitution*, p. 60; cf. the more detailed account in his *Records of the Federal Convention*, 1:xvi–xix).

Yates, Lansing, McHenry, Martin, Paterson, King, and Hamilton—but they had to be brief, were taken surreptitiously, and were officially frowned upon and were not published for at least a generation (Jackson's journal was published by authorization of Congress in 1819). Madison, however, had no compunction about using his notes later, on whatever occasions he deemed expedient—he even lent them to persons who were not delegates to the convention but were in his political and social circle.[49]

More than this, while delegates from New Hampshire, Connecticut, New York, New Jersey, Delaware, and Maryland rarely and in small degree violated the rule of secrecy which they felt honor bound to observe, volumes 3 and 4 of Farrand's monumental *Records of the Federal Convention of 1787* give letter after letter from the Virginia, Pennsylvania, Massachusetts, and Carolina delegates to friends outside the hallowed precincts in which they pay lip service to the rule binding them to silence and then go on to discuss, sometimes in specific detail, the day-to-day proceedings or to outline their position, aims, and progress more generally, while deprecating those of their opponents.[50]

These are matters of which Martin could not possibly have had any knowledge at the time, but they buttress his position that the small states generally, and his own state in particular were the victims of a well-planned and well-executed conspiracy. That he was able to thwart it in its most extreme form, and to reduce it, as we shall see, to a government of limited national powers, is a tribute to his sagacity, his perseverance, and his eloquence.

On the morning of Tuesday, 29 May 1787, Edmund Randolph opened "the main business" of the convention. With typical shrewdness Madison had persuaded Randolph to introduce the Virginia Plan.[51] The governor of Virginia, thirty-four years old (and looking even younger), tall, handsome, and a clever speaker and debater, made an excellent front man for Madison's plan. "I regret that it should fall to me, rather than to those of longer standing in life and political experience," Randolph began, with a bow in the directions of Washington and Benjamin Franklin, "to open the great subject of our mission. But, as the Convention originated with Virginia, and as my colleagues supposed that some proposition would be expected from us, they have

---

[49] Farrand, *Records of the Federal Convention*, 1:354; 3–372, 381, 416, 417, 475.
[50] See especially 3:32, 48–49, 54–55, 60, 63, 65, 67, 72, 73, 77; 4:63. See also Warren, *Making of the Constitution*, pp. 233, 373–75; Henry Knox to Washington, 14 August 1787, Washington Papers, vol. 239, p. 2, Library of Congress, Washington, D.C.; Otto to Foreign Office, Paris, 10 June 1787, in Farrand, *Records of the Federal Convention*, 3:39–47; Warren, *Making of the Constitution*, pp. 204–7; Burnett, *Letters of Members of the Congress*, 8:607, 611, 623–24, 630; *Documentary History of the Constitution of the United States of America, 1787–1870*, 4:236, 244, 264, 270, 273ff.
[51] It was for similar strategic reasons (i.e., to avoid creating the personal animosity and suspicion which he tended to arouse in others) that Madison persuaded Tyler to introduce the resolution for the Annapolis convention in the Virginia legislature (Brant, *James Madison*, 3:380–82).

imposed this task upon me."[52] Then followed "a long speech in which he pointed out the various defects in the federal system,[53] the necessity of transforming it into a national efficient government, . . . concluding sundry propositions as the outlines of a proper form."[54] The voice was the voice of Randolph, but the words were the words of Madison.

The fifteen "sundry propositions" were so broad, so startling, and so far advanced beyond what any delegates (except those from Virginia and perhaps Pennsylvania) had expected or even considered that it was resolved to sleep on them overnight and to consider them the next day sitting as a committee of the whole house. Although no doubt pleased by the direction in which matters had been headed at the outset, Alexander Hamilton, more practical than the scholarly Madison, sensed that the small states would have to be persuaded to swallow this medicine before they realized the full nature of what was afoot. As noted by McHenry, Hamilton believed that there should be "a necessary and preliminary inquiry to the propositions from Virginia whether the United States were susceptible of one government, or required a separate existence connected only by leagues offensive and defensive and treaties of commerce."[55]

The next morning Nathaniel Gorham of Massachusetts, another member of the large-state, nationalist bloc, was elected chairman of the committee of the whole, and Washington took his seat with the Virginia delegation on the floor. For the next ten days the convention, sitting in committee, proceeded to debate and vote upon the Randolph and other resolutions, which provided the raw material of a new Constitution.[56]

[52] Madison's notes, quoted in Farrand, *Records of the Federal Convention*, 1:18.
[53] *Ibid.* As used in this period, "federal" meant a confederated system, as under the Articles. It was only later that it came to be used to connote a strong central or "national" government, as espoused by the Federalist Party.
[54] Madison's footnote (later stricken), quoted in *ibid.*, 3:18n.
[55] Quoted in *ibid.*, 1:27.
[56] As most of the deliberations of the convention for the vital first five weeks took place in committee, presided over by Nathaniel Gorham, Washington's part in the convention was not nearly as "aloof" as it is represented.

9

The Constitutional Convention:
2. Adoption of the Virginia Resolutions, 9-13 June 1787

The object of *Virginia*, and *other large States*, to *increase their power* and *influence over the others*, did not escape observation; the subject, however, was discussed with great coolness.—*Genuine Information*

From 30 May through 8 June the convention, sitting as a committee of the whole, had postponed many delicate problems, over which it later split violently and all but irreconcilably. However, despite repeated remonstrances by delegates from Delaware, Massachusetts, New York, and South Carolina that it exceeded their powers and those of the convention itself, it had tentatively agreed to the following proposition:

that a *national* Government ought to be established consisting of supreme Legislative, Executive, and Judicial departments;

that the National Legislature should have two branches, and power to legislate on matters as to which the States were "individually incompetent" [whatever that might prove to mean];

that the National Legislature should have power "to negative all laws passed by the separate States contravening, in the opinion of the National Legislature, the [new] "Articles of Union," or treaties thereafter adopted;[1]

that there be a national executive of one man, to be chosen by Congress, having a term of office of seven years, and having power to make appointments (not otherwise provided for) unfettered by the concurrence of any other body;

that a federal judiciary with inferior courts be established.[2]

At this point in the proceedings, on 9 June, Martin took his seat. He found himself one of two Maryland delegates (McHenry had left the

[1] It is interesting to note that Jefferson, replying to Madison's letter of 18 March 1787, acknowledged that the federal courts would and should have power to declare state laws unconstitutional (letter of 20 June 1787, in *Papers of Jefferson*, 11:480ff.). He cited, as an illustration, a state court's disallowing the collection of a debt by a British creditor, despite the treaty authorizing it, and a federal court's "setting all to rights." See Dulaney v. Wells, 3 Harris and McHenry (Md.) 20 (1790), and Ware v. Hylton, 3 Dall. (3 U.S.) 199 (1796). Cf. also Jefferson to Madison, 15 March 1789, in *ibid.*, 14:659.

[2] Farrand, *Records of the Federal Convention*, 1:129-73 passim.

convention for Baltimore on 1 June;[3] Daniel of St. Thomas Jenifer, the other Maryland delegate, had arrived at the convention on 2 June).[4] Martin's behavior upon his arrival was described a year later by Oliver Ellsworth, a delegate from Connecticut and Martin's classmate at Princeton, in these terms:

> The day you took your seat must be long remembered by those who were present; nor will it be possible for you to forget the astonishment your behaviour almost instantaneously produced. You had scarcely time to read the propositions which had been agreed to after the fullest investigation, when, without requesting information, or to be let into the reasons of the adoption of what you might not approve, you opened against them in a speech which held during two days, and which might have continued two months, but for those marks of fatigue and disgust you saw strongly expressed on whichever side of the house you turned your mortified eyes.[5]

Ellsworth had his reasons for this furious attack. In 1788 he was carrying on a bitter newspaper debate with Elbridge Gerry of Massachusetts.[6] Martin wrote a public letter in defense of Gerry,[7] which so angered Ellsworth that he responded in the terms quoted above. Perhaps he did not take careful notes; perhaps he was not endowed with a good memory; perhaps he was forced, in support of a bad case, to substitute vituperation for facts. Whatever the reason, Martin's and Gerry's notes and statements and the records of every person present which have been preserved—those of Jackson, Madison, Yates, King, Paterson, Hamilton,[8] and even the recently discovered account of John Lansing, Jr.[9]—are agreed that, except for making one brief motion and perhaps seconding another,[10] Martin did not speak in the convention for the first ten days of his attendance. His first speech of any length was delivered on 27 June. Martin's reply to Ellsworth's charges will be discussed below; however, it should be noted that when he first took his seat, he was silent in disbelief at what he heard.

After Gerry's motion that the national executive be elected by the executives of the states had been voted down, the Convention proceeded to take up Madison's proposal *"that the equality of suffrage estab-*

[3] *Ibid.*, p. 75.

[4] He impressed William Pierce, one of the delegates from Georgia, as follows: "Mr. Jenifer is a Gentleman of fortune . . . ; —he is always in good humour. . . . He sits silent in the Senate, and seems to be conscious that he is no politician. From his long continuance in single life, no doubt but he has made the vow of celibacy. He speaks warmly of the Ladies, notwithstanding" (*ibid.*, 3:93).

[5] *Maryland Journal*, 29 February 1788; Farrand, *Records of the Federal Convention*, 3:271.

[6] See Farrand, *Records of the Federal Convention*, 3:170, 239.

[7] See *Maryland Journal*, 18 January 1788; Farrand, *Records of the Federal Convention*, 3:259.

[8] See Farrand, *Records of the Federal Convention*, 1:174–324 *passim*.

[9] See Joseph Reece Strayer, *The Delegate from New York*, pp. 41–70.

[10] Farrand, *Records of the Federal Convention*, 1:194, 203, 223. Farrand does not indicate whether this seconding was by Alexander Martin of North Carolina or by Luther Martin.

*lished by the articles of Confederation ought not to prevail in the national Legis-
lature, and that an equitable ratio of representation ought to be substituted.*"[11]

Madison originally moved this resolution on 30 May and noted with surprising naïveté that the revolutionary proposal was well received and would have been agreed to but for the reminder from the Delaware delegates that they were prevented by their instructions from agreeing to "any change in the rule of [equal] suffrage." However, ten days later it was clear that approval of his motion was no longer general.[12]

William Paterson of New Jersey, Martin's classmate at Princeton, rose to his feet and, in a speech that lasted several hours,[13] attacked this proposal logically, earnestly, even at times bitterly. "The proposition for a proportional representation," Paterson began, "strikes at the very existence of the lesser States. But before examining this question on its merits, let us first consider the nature, structure, and powers of this Convention. We are convened in pursuance of an Act of the Congress. The recitals of this act are contained in the commissions of several States here represented, particularly that of Massachusetts, which I ask that the Secretary do now read."[14]

As Secretary Jackson read, "a convention . . . for the sole and express purpose of revising the Articles of Confederation," Martin looked again at his own credentials: "to join . . . in considering such alterations and further Provisions as may be necessary to render the Federal Constitution [the Articles] adequate to the Exigencies of the Union." It had never occurred to him that his authorization was in any wise different, or intended to be different, from the purposes expressed in the Resolution of Congress as adopted by Massachusetts and other states.

Paterson continued:

By these, as well as the credentials of every State, the proper basis of our authority, and of the proceedings of the Convention, is the revision and alteration of the Articles of Confederation in such part as they appear to be defective. We must stay within these limits, or we shall rightly be charged by our constituents with usurpation of powers which they did not give us.

But the Commissions under which we act are not only the measure of our power; they also show the sentiments of the States as to what may properly be the subject of our deliberation. The idea of a national government, as contradistinguished from a federal one, never entered the mind of any of them; and to the public mind we must accomodate our proceedings. We have no power to go beyond the federal scheme, and if we had, the people are not ripe for any other. We must follow the people; the people will not follow us.

A confederacy, sir, supposes sovereignty in the members composing it, and sovereignty supposes equality.[15]

[11] *Ibid.*, pp. 36–37, 176.
[12] *Ibid.*, p. 37.
[13] It is conceivable that Ellsworth confused this speech with Martin's first one along the same lines, made on 27 June.
[14] *Ibid.*, p. 177ff. Cf. similar language in the New York and Connecticut commissions (*ibid.*, 3:579, 584, 585).
[15] *Ibid.*, 1:177ff.

Thereupon James Wilson of Pennsylvania, the most consistent democrat at the convention, at once observed that numbers was the best basis for representation. Pennsylvania, by reason of population, rightfully had twelve votes to New Jersey's five: "Shall New Jersey have the same right or influence in the councils of the nation with Pennsylvania? I say no. It is unjust! . . . The gentleman from New Jersey is candid in declaring his opinion; I commend him for it; I am equally so. I say again I never will confederate on his principles."[16]

This was the first of many crises at the convention. The outlook for agreement was black, and many delegates expected that the next meeting would be the last. That evening Martin obtained a copy of the Virginia resolutions to study over the weekend and was "not a little surprised at the system brought forward."[17] He arranged to meet Secretary Jackson at the convention quarters on Sunday and there examined the journal of the proceedings. It was, of course, utterly useless in reconstructing the debate or the arguments which had been brought forward in support of the proposals, and Martin therefore went to see various delegates who had made notes of the arguments that had taken place before his arrival. "I applied to history for what lights it could afford me," he later reported,

and I procured everything the most valuable I could find in Philadelphia on the subject of governments in general, and on the American revolution and governments in particular. I devoted my whole time and attention to the business in which we were engaged, and made use of all the opportunities I had, and abilities I possessed, conscientiously to decide what part I ought to adopt in the discharge of that sacred duty I owed my country, in the exercise of the trust you [the people of Maryland] had reposed in me. I attended the Convention many days without taking any share in the debates, listening in silence to the eloquence of others, and offering no other proof that I possessed the power of speech, than giving my yea or nay when a question was taken, and notwithstanding my propensity to "endless garrulity," should have been extremely happy if I could have continued that line of conduct, without making a sacrifice of your rights and political happiness."[18]

On Monday, 11 June, Roger Sherman rose to address the convention. Sherman typified in his person most of the outstanding Yankee characteristics. Speaking with a New England twang, a stranger to polite manners ("as badly calculated to appear in such Company as a chestnut-burr is for an eye-stone"[19]), with a bearing of Hogarthian awkwardness, he was as John Adams said, a typical old Puritan, honest but shrewd, hard-headed, and stubborn. Apprenticed to a shoemaker at ten, he had been by turns a surveyor, a mathematician, a computer of almanacs, a pamphleteer, a lawyer, a legislator, and a judge—and in

[16] *Ibid.*, p. 183.
[17] *Ibid.*, 3:277, 283.
[18] *Ibid.*
[19] Silas Deane to his wife, 25 August 1773, in Roger Sherman Boardman, *Roger Sherman, Signer and Statesman*, p. 115.

all these occupations he had read widely and thought deeply. His left hand clenched into a fist, the wrist nervously grasped with his right hand, he proposed that the lower house of the national legislature should have proportional representation and that in the senate each state should have an equal vote.

King and Wilson, however, cleverly broke the proposition up into sections, and after balloting on each the large states won a clear-cut, if temporary, victory. On the first ballot the convention voted seven to three that "the right of suffrage in the first branch [the lower house] . . . ought not to be according to the rule established in the articles of Confederation, but according to some equitable ratio of representation." On this vote Maryland was evenly divided: Martin, sensing what the large-state bloc intended, was opposed, but Jenifer concurred on principle. Connecticut, in accordance with its plan, naturally voted yes.

Next, in order to ensure that the southern states would oppose the second and more critical section of the resolution, Wilson and Charles Pinckney moved to incorporate in it the "three-fifths rule" (adopted by the Continental Congress in levying contributions upon the several states, by which five slaves counted as three whites). Despite Gerry's objection that slaves, having no civil rights, should no more be counted in the South than cattle and horses in the North, this amendment was adopted by a vote of nine to two. Here, in order to give Maryland, with its many slaves, as large a representation as possible (under the first part of the resolution, already adopted), Martin and Jenifer both voted "aye."[20]

Sherman and Ellsworth then moved that each state should have a single vote in the second branch (i.e., the Senate). Here, Sherman, to his sorrow, violated his own cardinal rule of parliamentary tactics: "When you are in a minority, talk; when you are in a majority, vote."[21] The Connecticut group had apparently failed to make a canvass of all the state delegations over the weekend, and with little further debate the large states defeated the motion on a close but decisive six-to-five vote. Martin and Jenifer, voting together, cast Maryland's vote with the minority—Connecticut, New York, New Jersey, and Delaware. The large states then clinched their advantage: Wilson's motion, seconded by Hamilton, that "the ratio of representation [be] the same in the second as in the first branch" was adopted six to five, with the same states voting in the affirmative. The large states thus won the first battle, outvoting and out-maneuvering the small-state group.

The rest of the day's proceedings were anticlimactic: Martin, supported by Sherman and Gerry, endeavored to abolish the requirement that state officers take an oath to support the new constitution. His motion lost by the same close margin as before.

[20] For Martin's position on the subject of the institution of slavery, see below, pp. 127ff.
[21] Farrand, *Records of the Federal Convention*, 1:203.

Thus the first phase of the work of the great convention ended with the adoption, without substantial modification, of the Virginia resolutions. These provided for a national government with extremely broad powers "to legislate in all cases to which the separate States are incompetent" (whatever these might later be determined to be) and to veto any state law "contravening *in the opinion of the National Legislature*" the new constitution; further, control over the election and removal of the chief executive and the appointment of both the supreme and inferior national judicial tribunals, as well as all executive and legislative appointees, was vested in three states (Virginia, Pennsylvania, and Massachusetts) of the heretofore independent thirteen.

Martin's sober and honest observations of the part played in the promulgation of the Virginia plan by two of our greatest national heroes made him highly unpopular, both at the time and later. In his report to the Maryland legislature the following year, he said:

On this occasion the House will recollect, that the convention was resolved into a committee of the whole; of this committee Mr. Gorham was chairman. The honorable Mr. Washington was then on the floor, in the same situation with the other members of the convention at large, to oppose any system he thought injurious, or to propose any alterations or amendments he thought beneficial. To these propositions, so reported by the committee, no opposition was given by that illustrious personage, or by the President of the State of Pennsylvania [Franklin]. They both appeared cordially to approve them, and to give them their hearty concurrence; yet this system I am confident, Mr. Speaker, there is not a member in this House would advocate, or who would hesitate one moment in saying it ought to be rejected. I mention this circumstance, in compliance with the duty I owe this honorable body, not with a view to lessen those exalted characters, but to show how far the greatest and best men may be led to adopt very improper measures through error in judgment, State influence, or by other causes, and to show that it is our duty not to suffer our eyes to be so far dazzled by the splendor of names, as to run blindfolded into what may be our destruction.

Mr. Speaker, I revere those illustrious personages as much as any man here. No man has a higher sense of the important services they have rendered this country. No member of the convention went there more disposed to pay a deference to their opinions; but I should little have deserved the trust this State reposed in me, if I could have sacrificed its dearest interests to my complaisance for their sentiments.[22]

To hold that Washington, Madison, Franklin, Rufus King, and the others were wrong is not to say that they were wicked. Their states had a preponderance of the population, the property, and (they would have been the first to agree) the brains of the country. Accordingly, in their eyes it was only just that they should have the preponderance of power and control over the offices of government.

[22] *Genuine Information*, in *ibid.*, 3:178.

Martin described to the legislature the Virginia plan, as approved on 13 June, as follows:

Having this inequality *in each branch* of the legislature, it must be evident, Sir, that *they would make what laws they pleased, however injurious or disagreeable to other States;* and that *they would always prevent the other States from making any laws, however necessary and proper, if not agreeable to the views of those three States.* They were not only, Sir, by this system, to have such an undue superiority in making laws and regulations for the Union, but to have the same superiority in the *appointment* of the *President,* the *judges,* and all *other officers* of government. . . . This President, and these judges, so appointed, we may be morally certain would be citizens of one of those three States; and the President, as appointed by them, and a citizen of one of them, would espouse their interests and their views, when they came in competition with the views and interests of the other States. This President, so appointed by the three large States, and so unduly under their influence, was to have a negative upon every law that should be passed, which, if negatived by him, was not to take effect unless assented to by two-thirds of each branch of the legislature, a provision which deprived ten States of even the faintest shadow of liberty; for if they, by a miraculous unanimity, having all their members present, should outvote the other three and pass a law contrary to their wishes, those three large States need only procure the President to negative it, and thereby prevent a possibility of its ever taking effect, because the representatives of those three States would amount to much more than one third (almost one half) of the representatives in each branch. And, Sir, this government, so organized, with all this undue superiority in those three large States, was, as you see, to have a power of negativing the laws passed by every State legislature in the Union. Whether, therefore, laws passed by the legislature of Maryland, New York, Connecticut, Georgia, or of any other of the ten States, for the regulation of their internal police, should take effect and be carried into execution, was to depend on the good pleasure of the representatives of Virginia, Pennsylvania, and Massachusetts.

This system of slavery, which bound hand and foot ten States in the Union, and placed them at the mercy of the other three, and under the most abject and servile subjection to them, was approved by a majority of the members of the convention, and reported by the Committee.[23]

That this cleverly planned, smoothly engineered, and almost successful grab for power failed was due to the opposition of men like Martin, Paterson, and Sherman, with whom historians have dealt neither as extensively nor as kindly as with Washington, Madison, Franklin, Hamilton, Wilson, Rutledge, and the other nationalists. To them our country owes a debt as yet hardly recognized. But for them the large-state bloc would have set up a system under which the country would either have been at the mercy of this three-state concentration of power, or would have split into two or more nations, with disastrous consequences to the growth and development of the republic.

[23] *Ibid.,* pp. 177–78.

10

The Constitutional Convention:
3. Rejection of the New Jersey Resolutions,
14-26 June 1787

> Accordingly, while those [Virginia] resolves were the
> subject of discussion in the committee of the whole House,
> a number of members, who disapproved them, were pre-
> paring *another system*, such as *they thought more conducive to
> the happiness and welfare of the States.—Genuine Information*

As the convention progressed and the Virginia resolutions were taken
up one by one and, in substance, agreed to, largely by the same combination of big-state votes, the smaller states became increasingly aware
of their cumulative effect and of their predicament in the proposed new
national government. Accordingly, on 14 June 1787, on the motion of
Paterson, the convention adjourned to allow the small-state bloc to
present an alternative plan government. This motion was seconded by
Randolph, since it was apparent to the Virginians that they could
never muster more than a bare majority (seven) of the thirteen states in
support of their revolutionary and unauthorized scheme. The plan was
filed on the next day, and the convention again adjourned to permit
both sides to consider the two proposals.

The drafting of a plan of government "purely federal, and contradistinguished from the reported [Virginia] plan" was undertaken by
members of the Connecticut, New York, New Jersey, and Delaware
delegations, with whom Martin joined.[1] They proceeded on the premise
that an improvement of the federal system under the Articles of Confederation would be preferable to the oligarchic national government of
the Virginia plan; that this type of government, if so improved, was
desired and expected by the great majority of Americans; and that it
was the only form of government contemplated or permissible under
the resolution of Congress and the powers given to the delegates by the
enabling resolutions of the states.[2]

[1] *Genuine Information,* in Farrand, *Records of the Federal Convention,* 3:178–79; *ibid.,*
1:242.
[2] "A Convention . . . *for the sole and express purpose of revising the Articles of Confederation . . . as shall . . . render the federal constitution adequate to exigencies of Government
& the preservation of the Union*" (resolution of the Congress, 21 February 1787).

The plan of this group for improving the federal government by revising the Articles was explained thus by Martin:

they were for taking our present *federal system* as the basis of their proceedings, and, as far as experience had shown us that there were defects, to remedy those defects; as far as experience had shown that other powers were necessary to the federal government, to give those powers. They considered this the object for which they were sent by their States, and what their States expected from them; they urged that if, after doing this, experience should show that there still were defects in the system (as no doubt there would be), the same good sense that induced this convention to be called, would cause the States when they found it necessary, to call another; and if that convention should act with the same moderation, the members of it would proceed to correct such errors and defects as experience should have brought to light. That, by proceeding in this train, we should have a prospect at length of obtaining as perfect a system of federal government as the nature of things would admit.[3]

The number of states and delegates participating in the drawing of resolutions alternative to those of Virginia's, and the apparent growth of organization, harmony, and *esprit de corps* within this group, gave Madison much concern. "The eagourness," he wrote, "displayed by the Members opposed to a Natl. Govt. . . . began now to produce serious anxiety for the result of the convention.—Mr. Dickenson said to Mr. Madison you see the consequence of pushing things too far."

On Saturday, 16 June, the convention proceeded to debate these "New Jersey resolutions," proffered and read on behalf of the small-state group by William Paterson, in the committee of the whole house. They may be briefly summarized as follows. The first set forth a theory of revision of the government as diametrically opposed to Madison's as it was specifically and pointedly within the language of the resolution of Congress calling the convention: "1. Resd. that the *articles of Confederation ought to be so revised*, corrected & enlarged, as to *render the federal Constitution adequate to the exigencies of Government, & the preservation* of the Union." The second resolution continued in office the unicameral Congress of the Confederation (in contrast to the Virginia plan's bicameral legislature), leaving each state an equal vote, but giving the Congress additional powers: (1) to raise revenue by levying duties on imports, by documentary stamps, and by postage; (2) to regulate interstate and foreign commerce; and (3) to enforce such laws by suits and prosecutions in the state courts, with an appeal to the federal courts. The third resolution provided for the raising of additional federal revenue by assessments based upon state population (incorporating the "three-fifths rule") and for the collection of these taxes from delinquent states.

[3] *Genuine Information*, in Farrand, *Records of the Federal Convention*, 3:179–80 (italics in original).

Any thoughtful comparison of these last two resolutions with the sixth Virginia resolution[4] will show the obvious superiority, at this stage of proceedings, of the former: specific legislative areas and powers were granted by the New Jersey plan, as compared with the vague, nebulous powers given Congress "to legislate in all cases to which the separate States are incompetent; or in which the harmony of the U.S. may be interrupted by . . . individual legislation" and "to negative all laws passed by the several States contravening *in the opinion of the National Legislature* the articles of Union" of the Virginia resolution.

The fourth New Jersey resolution provided for a plural executive "removable by Congress on application by a majority of the Executives of the several States." The ninth Virginia resolution provided for a single executive "removable on impeachment and conviction of malpractice or neglect of duty"—however that might be construed. The other provisions concerning the federal executive were similar in both plans.

The fifth New Jersey resolution (together with the second) established a federal supreme court, "to be appointed by the Executive," with clearly defined original jurisdiction "on all impeachments of federal officers" and with appellate jurisdiction from state courts "in all cases touching the rights of Ambassadors, . . . captures from an enemy, . . . piracies and felonies on the high seas, . . . in which foreigners may be interested, in the construction of treaties" or involving "Acts for the regulation of trade, or the collection of the federal Revenue." In contrast, the eleventh, twelfth, and thirteenth Virginia resolutions called for a national "supreme tribunal" to be appointed by the Senate, with "inferior Tribunals" appointed by the "Natl. Legislature"; the jurisdiction of these courts was to extend "to all cases which respect the collection of the Natl. revenue, impeachments of any Natl. Officers, *and questions which involve the national peace & harmony.*" The style, verbose but lucid, the thorough exposition, and the use of old-fashioned legalisms (e.g., "appeal in the dernier resort" for "appellate jurisdiction") are certain indications of Martin's hand in the drafting.

The sixth New Jersey resolution (similar to Article VI of the Constitution as finally adopted) was also Martin's handiwork.[5] It provided that all acts of Congress made under the Articles as revised and all ratified treaties "shall be the supreme law of the States, . . . and that the Judiciary of the several States shall be bound thereby . . . , anything in the respective laws of the Individual States to the contrary notwithstanding." It further authorized the federal executive "to enforce and compel an obedience to such Acts" and treaties by "the power of the Confederated States, or so much thereof as may be necessary." This resolution gave the Articles the power to function effectively: it provided legal sanctions for ensuring obedience and conformity to the supreme, federal law. Compare the weak, precatory, and ineffective

[4] *Ibid.*, 1:236.
[5] See below, pp. 114ff.

eighteenth Virginia resolution that "the Legislative, Executive & Judiciary powers within the several States *ought to be bound by oath to support the articles of Union.*"

The remaining resolutions are not of sufficient importance to require detailed discussion. Analysis of the two plans shows that the New Jersey resolutions (except for their still debatable theories of government) offered a much more carefully formulated, more inclusive, and more definite framework on which to draft the new Constitution than did Madison's more famous Virginia resolutions, and it is equally clear that, had they been adopted by the committee of the whole for consideration by the convention, they could have been improved and enlarged in purpose, scope, and form quite as easily as were the Virginia resolutions during the three months of debate and compromise that followed.

It has been noted by many competent historians[6] that, had the New Jersey resolutions been presented to the convention early in its deliberations, they would probably have been improved, expanded upon, and adopted. That an opposite theory of government was agreed upon is the result, more than anything else, of the political sagacity of its exponents, who organized themselves and had a plan ready for discussion. For the entire Monday, 18 June, Hamilton expounded his plan of government, based upon the British system, which was "the best in the world." With an "Executive for life" and a Senate "to serve during good behavior," he went as far as he dared toward recommending a king and a House of Lords (he referred to the House of Representatives as "Commons"). It cannot be denied that Hamilton's "benevolent monarchy" was the best of its kind ever devised.

It was apparently decided that night that Madison should "close" for the large states. His speech occupied most of the next day and was one of the longest of the convention. It was logical, learned, and frequently disingenuous: for example, he denounced as violations of the Articles of Confederation both the Mt. Vernon Compact,[7] for both the instigation and the ratification of which by Virginia he privately took credit,[8] and the quelling of Shays' Rebellion by the Massachusetts militia, an action of which he also privately approved.[9] When he took his seat, the committee, wearied by listening to him and to Hamilton for almost two full days, tabled the New Jersey resolutions and voted seven to three to adopt the Randolph plan as the basis for its deliberations. Massachusetts, Connecticut, Pennsylvania, Virginia, North and South Carolina, and Georgia voted in favor; New York, New Jersey, and Delaware were opposed. Jenifer voted aye and Martin no, splitting the Maryland vote.

---

[6] E.g., Farrand, *Framing of the Constitution*, p. 89; Arthur Taylor Prescott, *Drafting the Federal Constitution*, p. 60; Warren, *Making of the Constitution*, p. 221.

[7] See above, pp. 64ff.

[8] Brant, *James Madison*, 2:375–76 and nn.

[9] *Ibid.*, pp. 400–2.

Martin's later account of this debate and the alignment of the various groups—Hamiltonians (monarchists), the large-state power bloc, and the small-state confederationists—on the final vote are revealing:

These propositions were referred to a committee of the whole House; unfortunately the New Hampshire delegation had not yet arrived, and the sickness of a relation of the honorable Mr. McHenry obliged him still to be absent; a circumstance, Sir, which I consider much to be regretted, as Maryland thereby was represented by only two delegates, and they unhappily differed very widely in their sentiments.

The result of the reference of the last propositions to a committee was a speedy and hasty determination to reject them. I doubt not, Sir, to those who consider them with attention, so sudden a rejection will appear surprising; but it may be proper to inform you that, on our meeting in the Convention, it was soon found there were among us three parties, of very different sentiments and views.

One party, whose object and wish it was to abolish and annihilate all State governments, and to bring forward one general government, over this extensive continent, of a monarchical nature, under certain restrictions and limitations. . . .

The second party was not for the abolition of the State governments, nor for the introduction of a monarchical government under any form; but they wished to establish such a system as could give their own States undue power and influence in the government over the other States.

A third party was what I considered truly federal and republican; this party was nearly equal in number with the other two, and was composed of the delegations from Connecticut, New York, New Jersey, Delaware, and in part from Maryland; also of some individuals from other representations. This party, Sir, were for proceeding upon terms of *federal equality*. . . .

But, Sir, the favorers of monarchy, and those who wished the total abolition of State governments, well knowing, that a government founded on *truly federal principles*, the basis of which were the *thirteen State governments, preserved in full force and energy*, would be destructive of their views; and knowing they were too weak in numbers openly to bring forward their system; conscious also that the people of America would reject it if proposed to them,—joined their interest with that party, who wished a system, giving *particular States* the *power* and *influence over the others*, procuring in return mutual sacrifices from them, in giving the government *great* and *undefined powers* as to its *legislature* and *executive;* well knowing, that, by *departing from a federal system*, they paved the way for their favorite object, the *destruction of the State governments*, and the *introduction of monarchy*. . . . From these different sentiments, and from this combination of interest, *I apprehend*, Sir, proceeded the fate of what was called the Jersey resolutions, and the report made by the committee of the whole House.[10]

The New Jersey resolutions thus disposed of, the committee then proceeded to take up the first Randolph resolution, "that a National Government ought to be established, consisting of a supreme Legislative, Executive & Judiciary." In response to the assertions of Wilson, Hamilton, and King that the states were not "sovereigns" but mere

[10] *Genuine Information*, in Farrand, *Records of the Federal Convention*, 3:179–81 (italics in original).

political subdivisions of the nation, Martin stated his basic belief, to which he adhered throughout his career:

> When the States threw off their allegiance to Great Britain, they became independent of her, and assumed a state of nature towards each other. They would have remained in that state until this time but for their confederation. . . . When they thus united for mutual defence, they did so on principles of equality and perfect reciprocity. They now meet again on the same footing. And if a dissolution of the confederation should take place, the States will resume their original rights and sovereignties.[11]

The next day the convention took some of the sting (but none of the substance) out of the previous day's work by striking out the word "national" and substituting "the United States" throughout the Virginia resolutions before it. As Martin later observed in his speech to the Maryland legislature. "Afterwards the word '*national*' was struck out by them, because they thought the *word* might tend to alarm; and although, *now*, they who advocate the system pretend to call themselves *federalists*, in convention the distinction was quite the reverse; those who *opposed* the system were *there* considered and styled the *federal party*, those who advocated it, the *antifederal*." In a conciliatory gesture, Martin continued that even though he considered the system proposed "a system of slavery" he conceded that he had used "expressions perhaps rather harsh." If a unicameral body was considered "dangerous, divide them into two then, *so long as both bodies continued to represent the States.*[12]

At the end of his notes on this speech Madison wrote, "This was the substance of a very long speech." He later struck out this observation, which was obviously not true.[13] He may have confused it with Martin's long discussion of 27 and 28 June; if so, these notes could not have been written until over a week later, after that speech. Scores of other much more serious (and often demonstrably inaccurate) "corrections," alterations, and additions, made over a period of fifty years, based on his own recollection and supplemented by Jackson's unreliable journal and the notes of Yates and others (which Madison publicly attacked but privately used himself), raise a serious question as to the accuracy of his record.[14] Very late in life, when he was over eighty years old, Madison described his course of action in reporting the proceedings as follows:

> I noted in terms legible & in abbreviations & marks intelligible to myself what was read from the Chair or spoken by the members; and losing not a mo-

---

[11] *Ibid.*, 1:324, 329.

[12] *Genuine Information*, in *ibid.*, 3:195; see also *ibid.*, 1:347.

[13] Yates's and Madison's notes of this speech are each less than four hundred words long.

[14] See *ibid.*, 1:xvi–xix *et passim*. Madison's biographer, Brant, condones this "doctoring" (Brant's term): "However, looking forward to publication after his death, Madison undertook to revise his notes. Here was a test of honesty—to let the record stand, with the certainty that it would someday rise to shatter his reputation for consistency and undermine the constitutional base of his fight against the money power in Congress, or doctor it and escape the consequences. . . . The notes stand as an impressive example of integrity and impartiality, in the face of powerful motives for suppression" (*James Madison*, 3:22).

ment unnecessarily between the adjournment & reassembling of the Convention, I was enabled to write out my daily notes during the Seesion [*sic*] or within a few finishing days after its close in the extent and form preserved in my own hand on my files.

In the labor and correctness of this I was not a little aided by practice, and by a familiarity with the style and train of observation and reasoning which characterized the principal speakers. . . .

It may be proper to remark, that, with a very few exceptions the speeches were neither furnished, nor revised, nor sanctioned, by the speakers, but written out from my notes, aided by the freshness of my recollections.[15]

It is obvious that those "few finishing days" must have been much more elastic than he later recalled and that the "freshness" of his "recollections" must have been similarly variable. The meticulous and skillful editing of scholars like Farrand, Tansill, and others[16] have considerably modified Jefferson's characteristically enthusiastic but inaccurate description of Madison's notes as "taken down with . . . exactness beyond comprehension,"[17] and the modern historian may join in the opinion of Fisher Ames, spoken on the floor of Congress on 21 September 1791, that he "was not disposed to pay implicit deference to that gentleman's [Madison's] exposition" of the Constitution.[18]

Although Madison accused Yates of having "committed gross errors in his desultory notes,"[19] for the short period of Yates's attendance at the convention, they were often more detailed than Madison's own, and at least as accurate. Moreover, in spite of this accusation, the great Virginian corrected and expanded his own notes from those of Yates in some fifty places without any indication of his indebtedness, and made about the same number of corrections for this period from Jackson's journal.[20] He acknowledged graciously, in regard to the notes, that it was only normal and human that "the attention of the note taker w[oul]d naturally be warped, as far at least as, an upright mind could be warped, to an unfavorable understanding of what was said in opposition to the prejudices felt,"[21] and upon occasion he even used the portion of Yates's notes which he was at the time damning in letters to his friends as "palpable misstatement."[22] Yates left the convention on or shortly after 5 July, and one cannot tell now how many mistakes of

[15] I.e., somewhere in the mid-1830s (Farrand, *Records of the Federal Convention*, 3:550).
[16] *Ibid.*, vols. 1–4 *passim*; Charles C. Tansill, ed., *Documents Illustrative of the Formation of the Union of the American States*; Warren, *Making of the Constitution*; *Documentary History of the United States Constitution*, vols. 1–3 *passim*.
[17] Jefferson to John Adams, 10 August 1815, in Farrand, *Records of the Federal Convention*, 3:421.
[18] Quoted in Warren, *Making of the Constitution*, p. 793.
[19] Madison to James Robertson, 27 March 1830, in Farrand, *Records of the Federal Convention*, 3:497.
[20] *Ibid.*, vol. 1 *passim*.
[21] Madison to Joseph Gales, 26 August 1821, in *ibid.*, 3:447.
[22] *Ibid.*, p. 446.

commission and omission still remain uncorrected in Madison's notes for lack of another record for the last ten weeks of the convention.

In the next week the convention debated matters relating to the Congress under the new constitution—qualifications, length of term in each branch, eligibility for re-election, etc. While there were disagreements, the discussion was relatively free of rancor. Madison "apprehended the greatest danger is from the encroachment of the states on the national government"[23] and continued to insist on his scheme of giving Congress a veto power over all state laws. This comparative calm preceded the storm which broke over the convention on 27 June.

[23] *Ibid.*, 1:356, 363.

II

The Constitutional Convention:
4. Deadlock, 27 June–2 July 1787

[Martin] was a great, although an excessively voluble,
orator, and the world lost a great oration, for Madison
gives only a fragment of it.—James M. Beck, *The Constitution of the United States*

The Library of Congress until recently possessed an eight-page auto-
graph outline of a speech in the convention, dating from this general
period of its deliberations. Although some doubt has been raised as to
its authorship, with one expert in the field arguing that it was by Roger
Sherman, there can be no doubt that it was written by Luther Martin.[1]
It begins, "I have preserved a respectful silence during the debates of
the Committee of the whole house." This statement would apply to
Martin (who had made one brief motion, perhaps seconded another,
and had made one short statement of his position in committee). Sherman, however, spoke some three dozen times during the same period.
The language, moreover, could be used only by a delegate from one of
the middle states, particularly from Maryland: "at the Eastward
Slavery is not acknowledged, with us it exists in a certain qualified
manner, at the Southward in its full extent."[2] This outline contains a
forthright exposition of Martin's known attitude toward a government
by confederation, toward the Virginia resolutions compared with the
New Jersey resolutions, of the latent schemes for a monarchy, and
other matters. More than that, its handwriting, its style and wording,
its headlong accumulation of facts, its torrential flow of thought, its
vigorous, honest earthiness all indicate Martin's authorship.

It has been suggested that this document related to the short statement Martin made on 19 June 1787. This suggestion appears to be incorrect. On that date the convention was sitting in the committee of the
whole house,[3] the presiding officer of which (Gorham) was properly

[1] Farrand, *Records of the Federal Convention*, 4:20–28. Donald H. Mugridge,
Farrand, and the Library of Congress all attribute it to Martin. When the present
authors attempted in 1956 and again in 1968 to examine this document, it could not
be located either at the Library of Congress or at the National Archives.
[2] *Ibid.*, p. 21.
[3] *Ibid.*, 1:313.

denominated "chairman." This outline begins, however, with the words "Mr. President," which would apply to George Washington, who presided over the assembly when it sat in convention. Martin was precise in matters of detail, was a strict observer of protocol,[4] and would never have confused these two different modes of address.

Although Martin did not follow this outline exactly in convention, it was undoubtedly prepared in advance of his memorable speech of 27 and 28 June. Most of the facts and arguments set out in the earlier outline are expounded at length there.

On Wednesday, 27 June, the Convention met, with Washington in the chair, to consider the sixth of the Virginia resolutions, which defined the powers of the national legislature. John Rutledge, however, moved to postpone that problem in order to take up the seventh and eighth resolutions, which declared that the states should not have equality of representation in the new national congress but that in both the lower and upper houses representation should be in proportion to population. This move caught the small-state bloc somewhat unprepared, but it decided that the issue might just as well be joined at once. Accordingly, in the words of James M. Beck, "They brought up their heaviest artillery in the person of Luther Martin of Maryland, who then was, as he afterwards remained for another generation, the foremost advocate of the American Bar."[5]

Both Madison and Yates comment on the length of Martin's speech.[6] He did not follow his outline—indeed, he may not even have had it with him that morning. Moreover, he was fighting for time: the vote in the committee of the whole had been a narrow, six-to-five victory for the large-state, nationalist bloc. The delegation from the small state of New Hampshire had not been heard from but was expected daily. Of even more immediate concern than that, the four-man delegation from New Jersey was depleted by sickness and did not have the three-man quorum required by its credentials for voting.[7] Martin, however, undertook to lead the first charge in a battle that was to rage for three weeks and then finally to end in a draw. The result was a structure which, although it was bitterly opposed, would commend itself to enough members for adoption. "The pending question," Martin began,

relating to the proposed inequality of representation in the first branch, is important, and I have already expressed my sentiments on the subject.

---

[4] E.g., Martin begins his speech to the Maryland state legislature "Mr. Speaker," since that body was presided over by the speaker of the House of Delegates, just as in the Chase trial, he regularly addressed as "Mr. President" the vice-president, who was (and is) presiding officer, or president, of the United States Senate.

[5] *The Constitution of the United States: Yesterday, Today and Tomorrow*, p. 102.

[6] Farrand, *Records of the Federal Convention*, 1:437, 439. Such "diffuseness" was not confined to Martin: Madison made a characteristic error and inserted at this point a motion made by Lansing on the next day. He latter corrected this mistake on the basis of Yates's notes and Jackson's journal.

[7] *Ibid.*, 1:445, 3:563.

It is my opinion that the General Government was formed for the protection of the States, and not the reverse, as others now contend. . . .

We are now proceeding in forming a general government as if there were no State governments at all. The States, however, must approve what we do here, or you will have no government at all. If we are to have a *federal* government, we have no need of a legislature of two houses. The history of mankind doth not furnish an instance, from its earliest period to the present time of a federal government constituted of two distinct branches. . . . Even the celebrated Mr. Adams, who, the reviewers have justly observed, appears to be as fond of checks and balances as Lord Chesterfield was of the Graces, even he declares that a council consisting of one branch has always been found sufficient in a federal government.[8]

The failure of the Articles of Confederation[9]—weak, contemptibly weak as has been the Continental Congress thereunder—has been chiefly due to the heaviness of public and private debts, and the great waste of property during the war.

Martin then discussed the theory of political equality among individuals and states, reading passages from the treatises (which Madison was fond of quoting) of Locke, Vattel, Lord Summers, Rutherford, and Dr. Joseph Priestly in support of his views. "Thus," he continued,

have I traveled with the most respectable authorities, all of which prove the equality of independent States. Unequal confederacies always result in a loss of liberty. And this would also be true under the Virginia Plan.

There will be about ninety seats in the first branch of the new Legislature. Of this number, Virginia will have 16 votes, Massachusetts 14, and Pennsylvania 12—in all 42. These three States can do as they please unless there should be a miraculous Union of the other ten: the former need to win over but one other to make them complete masters of the rest. Where then will be the safety and independency of the other nine?

Let us pursue this subject yet farther: the executive is to be appointed by the national Legislature, and from him flows the appointment of all your officers—civil, military, and judicial, and there is and will continue to be a natural predilection and partiality for men from their own States. The Executive is also to have a negative upon all State laws. The States, however, particularly the smaller ones, will *never* allow a negative to be exercised over their laws. Suppose, however, that ten States should, by some miracle, solidly combine to pass a law. The Executive may then negative it, and it will thereupon be totally lost, because those ten States cannot amount to two thirds of the Legislature. . . .[10]

It is now claimed that equality of suffrage under the Articles of Confederation was originally agreed to on principles of necessity or expediency. The contrary,

---

[8] A reference to John Adams' then recent and well-known work, *A Defense of the Constitutions of Government of the United States of America*.

[9] Cf. Outline, in *ibid.*, 4:21-22.

[10] As just one illustration of the deficiency of Madison's notes, it may be observed that he omits most of the remainder of Martin's speech on this day. Yates (see *ibid.*, 1:441) and Lansing (see Strayer, *The Delegate from New York*, pp. 88-89) had no difficulty in following or embarrassment in recording it.

however, is true: it was adopted on the principles of *the rights of men* and *the rights of States*, which were then well known, although now they seem to be forgotten.

Here Martin showed, from the journals of the Continental Congress, that when the committee which drafted the Articles reported them to the Congress only Virginia opposed a system of voting based upon equality of the states, and her suggestions were rejected almost unanimously. Even after the Articles were submitted to the states for ratification, almost every state proposed some amendments, but not one, not even Virginia, suggested any change in the first article, which secured state equality. Martin hammered home the point:

This is the most convincing proof that equality of the States was agreed upon, not from necessity, but upon a full conviction that according to the principles of free governments, the States had a right to that equality of suffrage.

It was the smaller States that yielded up rights, not the large States. They gave up their claims to the unappropriated lands with the tenderness of the mother recorded by Solomon: they sacrificed affection for the preservation of others.

It has also been alleged that equality of suffrage in our federal government is the poisonous source from which flows all our misfortunes. But this, also, is not the fact. The truth is that equality of suffrage has never been complained of by the States as a defect in our federal system. Can any of you produce one single instance where a bad measure has been adopted, or where a good measure has failed, in consequence of the States having an equal vote? On the contrary, all our evils have flowed from the *want of power* in the federal head.[11] Let the right of suffrage in the States be altered in any manner whatever, if no greater powers be given to the government, the same inconveniences will continue.

I would not trust a government organized upon the plan, now reported out, for all the slaves of the Carolinas or the horses and oxen of Massachusetts![12] What are called "human feelings" in this instance are no more than the feelings of ambition and the lust for power![13]

Martin had been talking for more than three hours. The day had become increasingly hot, and it was now midafternoon. Reluctantly, he told the convention that he was "too much exhausted to finish his remarks" that day.

The feeling that the argument of one's opponent is interminable and that one is unhappily abiding its course is not limited to lawyers. Thus, Madison ruefully noted, Martin reminded the House that he would continue his speech on the resolutions on the following day. Most modern historians of the convention have called Martin's oration a

[11] Cf. Outline, in Farrand, *Records of the Federal Convention*, 4:23. Cf. Paterson's notes, in *ibid.*, 3:443.

[12] A reference to Gerry's observation on the "three-fifths rule" made on 11 June, two days after Martin took his seat in the convention (see above, p. 87). Cf. Martin's *Genuine Information*, in *ibid.*, p. 198.

[13] This speech is taken from Madison's, Yates's, and Martin's reports in *ibid.*, 1:437–41, 3:181ff.

"boring," "inopportune," and "fatiguing" harangue.[14] These judgments are based almost entirely on statements by Ellsworth and Pierce,
which are examined in Appendix A to this volume. The night of
Martin's speech, however, Dr. William Samuel Johnson wrote to his
son: "I can only tell you that much information and eloquence has
been displayed in the introductory speeches, and that we have hitherto
preserved great temperance, candor, and moderation in debate, and
evinced much solicitude for the public weal. Yet, as was to be expected,
there is great diversity of sentiment, which renders it impossible to
determine what will be the result of our deliberations."[15]

The following day Martin once more took the floor. "It has been
said," he began,

that under a federal system, a minority would govern a majority. But under
the Virginia Plan, a minority would *tax* a majority. In a federal government, a
majority of States must and ought to tax. . . .

If the large States have the same interests as the smaller States, as has here
been urged, there can be no danger in giving each an equal vote; and if the
interests of all the States are not the same, the inequality of suffrage would be
dangerous to the small States.

Is there any ambitious State who is preparing to enslave the others, and
raise itself to consequence on the ruin of others? Or is there any such ambitious
individual? We do not apprehend it to be the case. But suppose it to be true: it
becomes the more necessary that we should sacredly guard against a system
which might enable those ambitious views to be carried into effect, even under
the sanction of the Constitution and government.

Turning toward the Virginia delegation, he then reminded them:

We have lost the idea of the limited powers with which we are here entrusted.
You say that the people, not the State legislatures, will be called upon to approve what we do here. But the legislatures must first approve: by them, according to your own plan, the new constitution must be laid before the people. And
how will such a government, as you propose, operate over so many great States?
Wherever new settlements have been formed in large States, the people always
and immediately want to shake off their dependency. Why? Because the government is too remote for their own good. The people want their government to be
nearer home. Happiness is preferable to the Splendors of a national Government. . . .

At the beginning of our troubles with Great Britain, the smaller States were
attempted to be cajoled into submitting to the views of that nation, lest the
larger States should usurp our rights. We answered them then: "Your present

---

[14] See, e.g., *ibid.*, p. 93; Warren, *Making of the Constitution*, pp. 246–47; A. E.
Smith, *James Madison: Builder*, p. 109. A notable exception is Beck (*Constitution*,
p. 90). Gerry commented that this speech, "if published, would do him [Martin]
great honor" (*New York Journal*, 30 April 1788; Farrand, *Records of the Federal Convention*, 3:299). Madison's biographer, Brant, commented that "it really wasn't such
a bad speech, compared with senatorial filibusters, for in the five-hour talk Madison
found 700 words worth recording" (*James Madison*, 3:82).
[15] Farrand, *Records of the Federal Convention*, 3:49–50; Bancroft, *Formation of the
Constitution*, 3:430.

plan is slavery, which we will not submit to, merely on the remote prospect of a distant evil."

So now, we are threatened that if we do not agree to the system proposed, the large States will confederate by themselves. But the latter are formidable only by the weight of their votes; in case a dissolution of the Union should take place, the smaller States will have nothing to fear from their power.

Speaking slowly, he closed with carefully measured and defiant words:

We will never submit tamely and servilely to a present evil, in dread of a future, which might be imaginary. We are sensible that the eyes of our country and the world are upon us. We shall not labor under the imputation that *we* are unwilling to form a strong and energetic federal government. We shall, instead, publish the system which we approve, as well as the one that we oppose. And we shall leave it to the country, and to the world at large, to judge between us as to who best understands the rights of free men and free States, and who best has advocated them. And to the same tribunal we will submit: who should be answerable for the consequences which may arise to the Union from the Convention breaking up, without proposing any system to their constituents?[16]

Whatever the pejorative observations of Ellsworth, Pierce, and more recent commenters, both the small-state and large-state factions at that time acknowledged the critical weight and effectiveness of Martin's effort. The former group decided to capitalize on it at once. As soon as Martin took his seat, Lansing of New York and Dayton of New Jersey moved to amend the report of the committee of the whole house so as to provide for equality of representation—the same wedge that had split the convention for a month. On the other hand, the nationalist bloc felt constrained to put forward their best orators to answer Martin: Madison spoke the better part of the day and was ably followed by Wilson. The former, with a lack of tact and judgment amazing for one of his reputed acumen, continued to insist on his scheme for giving Congress "the negative on State laws proposed," which would make the national government "an essential branch of the State Legislatures." He admonished the small-state delegates that their "true policy . . . therefore lies in promoting those principles and that form of Government which will most approximate the States to the condition of Counties."[17] Small wonder that Hamilton, in despair mingled with disgust, left the convention the next evening to return to New York.

On 26 June, the night before Martin's great speech, in conference with Paterson, Yates, Sherman, and others of the small-state group, he promised to blow the Virginians and their crowd out of their trenches with the barrage he planned for the next day. While he did not quite succeed in routing his enemies, he did silence enough of their batteries to produce the deadlock that was the turning point of the convention.

[16] Farrand, *Records of the Federal Convention*, 1:444ff., 453ff.; *Genuine Information*, in *ibid.*, 3:187.
[17] *Ibid.*, 1:447.

Sensing that the bitter impasse at which the delegates now found themselves might disrupt the convention, Dr. Franklin, dressed drably in his customary gray homespun, the color of cold gravy, rose slowly to his feet and made his famous plea that the convention humbly apply "to the Father of lights to illuminate our understandings." "I therefore beg leave to move," he earnestly concluded, "that henceforth prayers imploring the assistance of Heaven, and its blessings on our deliberations, be held in this Assembly every morning before we proceed to business, and that one or more of the Clergy of this City be requested to Officiate in that service."[18]

The motion was discussed but never put to a vote, and the assembly adjourned for the day. There has been much comment on this episode. A number of reasons have been given for the convention's refusal to adopt this proposal: it was feared that the public might get some idea of the dissention within the convention, that the Quaker populace might be offended, or that there might be difficulty choosing a minister acceptable to all the denominations represented by the various delegates. It is certain, however, that it was *not* because most of the delegates were Protestants,[19] for many such, including Washington, Sherman, and Johnson, daily invoked the aid of God upon their labors in their prayers, diaries, and letters. The real reason, of course, was prosaic: the convention had no funds to pay a preacher.[20]

The next day, Friday, after extensive remarks by Johnson, Gorham, Read, Madison,[21] Hamilton, and Gerry to the effect that the convention should draft a new constitution for a national government unburdened by "sovereign States," Martin rose and drily observed that once, not so long since, the terms *"Sovereign & independent States"* were quite familiar and well understood, in spite of the fact that they had suddenly become "so strange & obscure." He then read to the assembly the second Article of Confederation which so described the states.

The crucial vote followed, and the large-state bloc voted down the small-state motion for equality in the lower house, six to four. By the same vote, the seventh Virginia resolution for proportionate representation was adopted. The states lined up as they had in the committee of the whole on 11 June;[22] over two weeks of exhaustive debate had produced only bitterness and suspicion.

[18] *Ibid.*, p. 451ff.
[19] As naïvely suggested by Sister Mary Virginia Geiger in *Daniel Carroll*, p. 130, n. 47.
[20] Williamson, in Farrand, *Records of the Federal Convention*, 1:452.
[21] Madison, according to Yates (quoted in *ibid.*, p. 471), thought that "the states ought to be placed under the control of the general government—at least as much so as they formerly were under the king and British parliament." Madison never denied saying this but later went through a good many circumlocutions to explain it away (see *ibid.*, 3:516ff., 521ff.).
[22] For the motion, Connecticut, New York, New Jersey, and Delaware; against, Massachusetts, Pennsylvania, Virginia, North Carolina, South Carolina, Georgia; divided, Maryland.

At this time Georgia, with about eighty thousand residents, was one of the smallest states in population. Delaware had about sixty thousand, and even "little Rhody" had almost seventy thousand people.[23] New Hampshire had well over a hundred thousand and New Jersey, almost two hundred thousand. It seems strange, therefore, to find Georgia lining up with the large states on this vital issue, and Martin's explanation was undoubtedly correct:

It may be thought surprising, Sir, that Georgia, a State *now small* and comparatively *trifling* in the Union, should advocate this system of *unequal representation*, giving up her *present* equality in the federal government, and sinking herself almost to total insignificance in the scale; but, Sir, it must be considered, that Georgia has the *most extensive* territory in the Union, being *larger* than the *whole island of Great Britain*, and *thirty* times as large as *Connecticut*. This system being designed to *preserve to the States their whole territory unbroken*, and to prevent the erection of new States within the territory of any of them, Georgia looked forward *when*, her *population* being increased in some measure *proportioned* to her *territory*, she should *rise* in the scale, and *give law* to the *other States*, and hence we found the delegation of Georgia warmly advocating the proposition of giving the States unequal representation.[24]

The convention next proceeded to take up the problem of representation in the upper branch of the national legislature. For the third time a Connecticut delegate proposed that "the rule of suffrage in the 2d. branch be the same with that established by the articles of confederation,"—that is, each state was to have an equal vote in the senate. Ellsworth stated that "he was not in general a half-way man" but that, so far as he was concerned, the convention would have to adopt this compromise or disband. Abraham Baldwin, of the Georgia delegation, was a native of Connecticut who had recently moved to Georgia. He was only thirty-two, a graduate of Yale, had been a chaplain in the Revolutionary Army and a member of the Continental Congress, and was now a practicing attorney. On this day he announced his opposition to Ellsworth's motion, which is interesting in view of its aftermath.

The rest of Friday and all of Saturday were spent recapitulating the arguments which had split the convention for a month. Madison, in one of his frequent tactless indiscretions, accused Connecticut of failure to comply with the requisitions imposed on it by the Congress under the Articles. Ellsworth was quick to retort that the muster rolls would show that Connecticut (which had less than a third the population of Virginia) had put more men in the field of battle during the Revolution

---

[23] According to the first census of 1790. Compare the estimates published in the *Pennsylvania Packet* for 11 December 1786 (in Warren, *Making of the Constitution*, pp. 217, 287). It may also be noted that the Constitution gave Georgia and New Hampshire only three representatives apiece in the first congress (Rhode Island was given only one).

[24] *Genuine Information*, in Farrand, *Records of the Federal Convention*, 3:187.

than the Old Dominion and had impoverished herself in support of the war.[25]

Gunning Bedford of Delaware next picked up the cudgels for the small states. He warned the convention that if the large states abandoned or attempted to "crush the smaller states" there would be "foreign powers who will take us by the hand."[26] With this threat ringing the ears of the delegates, the convention adjourned over the weekend.

On 2 July, a warm Monday morning, the convention reassembled after, as Martin observed, "a fortnight, perhaps more . . . spent in the discussion of this business, during which we were on the verge of dissolution, scarce held together by the strength of an hair, though the public papers were announcing our extreme unanimity."[27] No one had anything further to say—indeed, there was nothing left to be said on the matter, and the convention proceeded to an immediate vote on Ellsworth's motion for equality of representation in the senate. This was the most critical single vote of the entire convention.

There was no reason to believe that the result of the vote would differ from previous ballots. However, over the weekend the Connecticut delegation had done some proselytizing of Abraham Baldwin, one of the two Georgia delegates present at the time; and the jovial Daniel of St. Thomas Jenifer of Maryland, who had been regularly canceling Martin's vote on almost every roll call for the past weeks, was absent. The reason for Jenifer's absence is a mystery. So far as is known, he never gave any explanation, and Martin, rarely reticent on any subject, never vouchsafed any information on the matter. It is quite possible that he persuaded Jenifer to absent himself for this ballot so that Maryland's vote would be counted with those of the other small states, without Jenifer having to actually vote with them.

Confident of their time-tested majority, the nationalist group offered no delay, and the roll of the states was called on the resolution for equality of representation in the second branch of the new bicameral legislature. Beginning at the north, Massachusetts (New Hampshire being absent) voted no; Connecticut, New York, and New Jersey voted aye; Pennsylvania no, and Delaware aye—all as expected. The Virginians had their first shock when Martin voted aye for Maryland. They were reassured when Virginia and North and South Carolina voted no. Suddenly, however, and quite against the nationalists' expectations, Georgia reported that she was evenly divided (Houstoun no and Baldwin aye), and hence cast no vote. The result was, to the large-state bloc, a dissappointing five-to-five tie.

Immediately after the tally was announced by Washington, Jenifer walked into the room. Thereupon, Rufus King, "valuing himself," as

[25] *Ibid.*, 1:485-87. Madison neglected to mention this little tiff but added it later when Yates's notes disclosed the omission (cf. *ibid.*, p. 497).

[26] *Ibid.*, p. 501. Madison's notes on this episode are much briefer than Yates's and were, in any event, filled in by him some time after 1818 from Yates's record.

[27] *Genuine Information*, in *ibid.*, 3:190.

Martin expressed it, "to divide the State of Maryland on this question, as he had on the former, requested of the President that the question might be put again." Jenifer, however, gave no support to this move, which, as Martin said, "was too extraordinary in its nature to meet with success." Martin later offered this explanation of Baldwin's *volte-face*: "Georgia had only *two* representatives on the floor, *one* of whom (not, I believe, because he was against the measure, but from a conviction, that we would go home, and thereby dissolve the convention, before we would give up the question) voted also in the negative, by which the State was divided."[28]

To be sure, Ellsworth's motion for equality actually lost by a tie vote. And presumably (though by no means certainly), the arrival of Jenifer would have put over the Virginia resolution (for proportionate representation in the senate) by a vote of five to four, with Maryland and Georgia tied and stalemated. The division was too close, however, for the large states to capitalize on it. They feared that the small states really would carry out their threat to leave the convention. Had they done so, there would have been, at the most, only seven states represented, perhaps only five if Georgia and Maryland abstained.

Accordingly, on the motion of Gen. Charles C. Pinckney, a committee was appointed by ballot, consisting of one member from each delegation, to which the question of representation was to be submitted for the working out of a successful compromise, if possible. That the convention was in the mood for compromise is shown by the personnel thus chosen. For example, Gerry was selected from the Massachusetts delegation instead of the eloquent and outspoken nationalist Rufus King; from Pennsylvania, the wise old middle-of-the-roader Franklin instead of James Wilson; from Maryland, Martin instead of Jenifer; from Virginia, Mason instead of Madison (who was opposed to either committee or compromise); from North Carolina, Davie instead of Spaight; and from Georgia, Baldwin (who had brought about the deadlock) instead of Houstoun.[29]

The committee—Gerry, Ellsworth,[30] Yates, Paterson, Franklin, Bedford, Luther Martin, Mason, Davie, Rutledge, and Baldwin—was "stacked" in favor of compromise and the small states, but this "stacking," be it remembered, was voted by the convention itself in order to prevent its own dissolution. The convention adjourned for three days to give the committee time to deliberate, which gave the delegates a much-needed recess during which they could join in the celebration of the Fourth of July by attendance at church, listening to patriotic orations, and viewing parades and fireworks.[31]

[28] *Ibid.*, p. 188.
[29] *Ibid.*, 1:516.
[30] Actually Sherman substituted on the committee for Ellsworth, "who was kept away by indisposition."
[31] Warren, *Making of the Constitution*, pp. 267ff.

12

The Constitutional Convention:
5. The Connecticut Compromise,
3-16 July 1787

> I believe near a fortnight, perhaps more, was spent
> in the discussion of this business, during which we were
> on the verge of dissolution, scarce held together by the
> strength of an hair.—*Genuine Information*

On 3 July the committee met, probably in the room used by the convention itself.[1] Its sessions "were not of a secret nature, nor were they conducted in a secret manner . . . as to the members of the Convention"[2] and were undoubtedly attended (though not participated in) by other delegates. The members restated their positions and were at first as adamantly divided as the convention had been.[3] Finally, Dr. Franklin moved the following mutually dependent propositions: in the lower branch of the legislature each state was to have one member for every forty thousand inhabitants; all bills for raising or appropriating money and for fixing salaries were to originate in the lower branch, without being amended by the upper branch; and the upper branch was to be composed of an equal number of representatives from each state.

In response to this motion, Martin voiced the objections of the small states:

> To this it was answered, that there was no merit in the proposal; it was only consenting, after they [the large-state bloc] had struggled, to put *both their feet on our necks*, to take *one of them off*, provided we would consent to let them *keep* the *other on;* when they knew at the same time, that they could not put *one foot* on *our necks*, unless *we would consent to it* and that by being permitted to keep on that one foot, they should *afterwards be able to place the other foot on whenever they pleased.*
>
> They were also called on to inform us what security they could give us should we agree to this compromise, that they would *abide* by the plan of government formed upon it, *any longer* tha[n] it *suited their interest*, or they found it *expedient*. "The States have a *right* to an equality of representation. This is *secured to us* by

---

[1] Yates, in Farrand, *Records of the Federal Convention*, 1:522.
[2] Martin, "Reply to the Landholder" (Ellsworth), *Maryland Journal*, 7 March 1788, reprinted in *ibid.*, 3:276, 279.
[3] *Genuine Information*, in *ibid.*, p. 188; Yates, in *ibid.*, 1:522–23.

our present articles of confederation; *we* are in *possession* of this privilege—It is *now* to be *torn from us*—What security can you give us, that, when you get the *power* the *proposed system* will give you, when you have *men* and *money*, that you will not *force from* the States that *equality* of suffrage in the *second branch*, which you *now* deny to be their right, and *only give up* from *absolute necessity*? Will you tell us we ought to trust you because you *now enter into a solemn compact with us*? This you have done *before*, and *now* treat with the *utmost contempt.* —Will you *now* make an appeal to the Supreme Being, and call on him to guarantee your observance of this compact? The *same* you have *formerly done*, for your observance of the articles of confederation, which you are *now violating* in the most wanton manner."

. . . However, the *majority* of the select committee at length agreed to a series of propositions, by way of a compromise . . . upon the *express terms*, that they were *wholly* to be *adopted*, or wholly to be *rejected*: upon this compromise a great number of the members so far engaged themselves, that, if the system was progressed upon agreeable to the terms of compromise, they would lend it their names, by signing it, and would not actively oppose it, if their States should appear inclined to adopt it. —Some, however, in which number was myself, who joined in the report, and agreed to proceed upon those principles, and see *what kind of a system* would *ultimately* be formed upon it, yet reserved to themselves, in the most *explicit manner* the right of *finally* giving a *solemn dissent* to the system if it was thought by them *inconsistent* with the *freedom* and *happiness* of their country. This, Sir, will account why the members of the convention so generally signed their names to the system; not because they thought it a *proper one;* not because they *thoroughly approved*, or were *unanimous* for it; but because they thought it *better* than the system attempted to be forced upon them.[4]

The committee made its report, as above outlined,[5] on Thursday, 5 July. For some eleven days thereafter the convention debated it, in detail and in general. Various sections were turned over to subcommittees for discussion despite the insistence of Martin and others that the report had been decided upon and submitted as a unit. For different reasons Madison spoke against the report at length, and concluded truculently that "these observations would show that he was not only fixed in his opposition to the Report of the Committee, but was prepared for any want that might follow a negative of it."[6] Gouverneur Morris got downright threatening. "This country must be united. If persuasion does not do it," he reminded the smaller States, "the sword will. . . . The scenes of horror attending civil commotion can not be described, and the conclusion of them will be worse than the term of their continuance. The stronger party will then make traytors of the weaker; *and the Gallows & Halter will finish the work of the sword.*"[7] Such language reflected the disappointment of the large-state bloc at the failure of their plan, which had been within an hair's breadth of success.

[4] *Ibid.*, 3:188–89.
[5] Cf. *ibid.*, 1:524.
[6] Madison later deleted from his notes this part of his report of his speech (*ibid.*, p. 529n).
[7] *Ibid.*, p. 530.

The next day the convention adopted the section of the report requiring money bills to originate in the lower house by a margin of five to three. For once, Martin and Jenifer voted together, and Maryland joined with Connecticut, New Jersey, Delaware, and North Carolina against Pennsylvania, Virginia, and South Carolina (Massachusetts, New York, and Georgia were all divided).

The argument as to the amount of each state's representation droned on day after day. On 11 July, however, debate started on the important three-fifths rule. The South Carolina delegation insisted that slaves should be given the same weight as whites, while others, such as Wilson and Paterson, objected that they should not be counted at all. As Martin summarized the argument against the adoption of the rule:

It was urged, that no principle could justify taking *slaves* into computation in *apportioning* the number of *representatives* a State should have in the government. That it involved the absurdity of *increasing* the power of a State in making laws for *freemen* in *proportion* as that State *violated* the rights *of freedom*. That it might be proper to take slaves into consideration when *taxes* were to be apportioned, because it had a tendency to *discourage slavery;* but to take them into account in *giving representation* tended to *encourage* the *slave-trade*, and to make it the *interest* of the States to *continue* that *infamous traffic*. That slaves could not be taken into account as *men* or *citizens*, because they were not admitted to the *rights of citizens*, in the States which adopted or continued slavery. If they were to be taken into account as *property*, it was asked, what peculiar circumstance should render this property (of *all others* the most *odious* in its nature,) entitled to the *high privilege* of conferring *consequence* and *power* in the *government* to its possessors, rather than *any other property?* and why *slaves* should, as property, be taken into account, rather than *horses, cattle, mules*, or any *other species*—and it was observed by an honorable member from Massachusetts, that he considered it as dishonorable and humiliating to enter into compact with the *slaves* of the *Southern States*, as it would be with the *horses* and *mules* of the *Eastern*.[8]

Martin also accused the large states of subterfuge in deliberately according Massachusetts, Pennsylvania, and Virginia a total of only twenty-six representatives in the lower house, so that their strength would not be immediately apparent, knowing that when the first census was taken (a couple of years later) they would have between them approximately thirty-three out of a total of seventy-one members.[9]

The proposal to count blacks equally with whites was defeated seven to three, with only Delaware, South Carolina, and Georgia voting for it.[10] Next the opposite motion, the three-fifths rule, was defeated four to six, with only Connecticut, Virginia, North Carolina, and Georgia in favor. When the results of this ballot were announced, it was North Carolina's turn to claim that "the business was at an end" and to threaten to leave the convention.

This impasse was circumvented by a compromise that was one of the most important of the many adopted at the convention. Because of the

---

[8] *Genuine Information*, in *ibid.*, 3:197.
[9] *Ibid.*, p. 198. Cf. the observation of Read in *ibid.*, p. 601.
[10] *Ibid.*, 1:576.

unforeseen direction that federal taxation came to take, however, it worked out in favor of only one side. It was agreed that direct taxation should be according to representation and that such representation should include "the number of white inhabitants" and three-fifths of "all other people."[11] As it later turned out, the slave states were to benefit from the increased representation provided by their slaves while paying no taxes on their account, as federal taxes were to be indirect and not apportioned among the states according to their population. The very fact that the southern states obtained this concession, however, made equal representation in the senate for all the states a certainty.[12]

The convention spent eight days arguing over the compromise, as a whole as well as section by section. When the delegates assembled on Saturday morning, 14 July, Luther Martin "called for the question on the whole report, including the parts relating to the origination of money bills, and the equality of votes in the 2d. branch." He explained that "he did not like many parts of it." In addition, as everybody now knew, Martin did not like "the inequality of votes in the 1st branch." However, he was willing to go ahead with the compromise in order to see what kind of a government could be framed on it, "rather than do nothing."[13]—nothing, that is, but talk and perhaps disband with the states more divided than when they had assembled.

But the large-state delegates, disappointed over the failure of their plan, took their defeat badly. Wilson asserted that if the delegates' constituents could have voted on the question of equal state representation in the senate, two-thirds of the country would have been found opposed to the plan. This, of course, was a very large "if," and Martin was on safe ground when he denied that any such proportion of the public was opposed to equality of votes. Pinckney then moved that a thirty-six-member senate be fixed, with Virginia having five senators, Massachusetts and Pennsylvania four, and so on down to Rhode Island and Delaware with one each. Madison, as might be expected, thought this a fair compromise. Quite obviously, it was no compromise at all, but the same old inequality in definite instead of indefinite form.

The first thing Monday morning, however, the Connecticut compromise, as reported out by the committee of eleven, was passed by the closest possible vote: Connecticut, New Jersey, Delaware, Maryland, and North Carolina voted aye, Pennsylvania, Virginia, South Carolina, and Georgia "no," and Massachusetts was evenly divided.[14]

[11] *Ibid.*
[12] Cf. Martin's speech on prohibiting or taxing the importation of slaves (*ibid.*, 2:364; *Genuine Information*, in *ibid.*, 3:211, discussed in Chapter 15 below).
[13] *Genuine Information*, in *ibid.*, 3:191–92.
[14] *Ibid.*, 2:15. Warren, whose book is of inestimable value in understanding the proceedings in and surrounding the convention, makes one of his rare errors of fact in recording Virginia as voting for and Maryland against the Connecticut compromise (*Making of the Constitution*, p. 309). The "swing" state here was North Carolina, which had voted consistently with the large-state group, and the "swing" vote in that delegation was William Richardson Davie (see Blackwell P. Robinson, *William R. Davie*, p. 186).

Randolph, who arrived late, was surprised and shocked at the result. He had a different plan and moved an adjournment in order that it might be considered. Thereupon, Paterson, aware that the convention had already greatly exceeded its powers, stated it was time that the delegates rescinded the rule of secrecy and went home to consult their constituents. If Randolph would make his motion one to adjourn *sine die*, he said, he would "second it with all his heart."[15]

The convention adjourned until the next morning, and the large states contemplated the defeat of their plans. They finally, if belatedly, realized that the small states were in earnest and that their only choice was between the compromise and the adjournment of the convention without having drawn up a new constitution. It was therefore decided to give up the fight on equality of representation in both branches and to concentrate on influencing the draft of the remainder of the constitution in their favor.

[15] Farrand, *Records of the Federal Convention*, 2:18.

13

The Constitutional Convention:
6. The Federal Supremacy Clause,
17-18 July 1787

> You [Martin] originated that clause in the Constitu-
> tion. . . . You voted that an appeal should lay to the
> Supreme Judiciary of the United States. . . . These are
> among the greater positive virtues you exhibited in the
> Convention.—"The Landholder" [Oliver Ellsworth]

> Contrary to Martin's intentions, that resolution with
> a single significant change developed into one of the all-
> important articles of the constitution strengthening the
> national government.—Max Farrand, *The Framing of
> the Constitution of the United States*

Martin must have been conscious of the antipathy and antagonism he
had aroused among a large number of delegates at the convention.
Although he was always friendly, hearty, jovial, and even convivial
after hours, when engaged in a political controversy his advocacy was
exhaustive, exhausting, and without quarter. Delegates who had not
prepared their cases thoroughly or were not prepared to meet Martin's
arguments often found themselves unexpectedly overwhelmed where
they had contemplated an easy victory. On such occasions, their comments were apt to be bitter.

The small states' ultimate success, on 16 July, in getting equality of
representation in the senate was in large part the result of Martin's
rallying of their less numerous and illustrious forces in opposition to the
Virginians. From that point on, the convention listened to him with
respect, if without friendliness.

For example, on 17 July the convention took up the problem of what
powers should be given to the new national government. Madison again
spoke at length in support of his favorite idea that the Congress should
have power to "negative all laws passed by the several States."[1] Martin
pointed out the consequences: no law "passed by the legislature of
Maryland, New York, Connecticut, Georgia, or any other of the ten

[1] Farrand, *Records of the Federal Convention*, 2:27.

States, for the regulation of their internal police, should take effect" except at "the good pleasure of the representatives of Virginia, Pennsylvania, and Massachusetts." How could anybody seriously propose, he asked the convention, that "all the laws of the States be sent up to the General Legislature before they shall be permitted to operate?"[2]

The proposition lost decisively by a vote of seven to three. Madison's reputation as the wise, far-sighted, statesman-like father of a great system of government owes much to this outcome, for few more unworkable, short-sighted, divisive, and undemocratic propositions have ever been put forth by a "father" of a constitution. As his most recent biographer has observed, "Most remarkable of all, in so realistic a student of politics, was his failure to realize that if his idea had prevailed, the Constitution would never have been ratified."[3]

Martin then moved the adoption of a resolution that was almost a verbatim copy of the sixth New Jersey resolution, which he had drafted with Paterson and others on 14 June and which had been rejected by the convention five days later.[4] A far greater concession to the larger states than they had ever been willing to make to their smaller sisters, it made possible the drafting of a truly workable, *federal* law. This was the famous federal supremacy clause, perhaps the most vital single cog in the constitutional machine. As adopted unanimously on 17 July, it read:

> The Legislative acts of the United States made by virtue and in pursuance of the articles of Union and all Treaties made and ratified under the authority of the United States shall be the supreme law of the respective States as far as those acts or Treaties shall relate to the said States, or their Citizens and Inhabitants—and that the Judiciaries of the several States shall be bound thereby in their decisions, any thing in the respective laws of the individual States to the contrary notwithstanding.[5]

With what appeared to be slight but which actually were most important changes (which Martin opposed), it became the second paragraph of Article VI of the Constitution as ultimately ratified.[6] Martin has been given too much credit for this final version, which he was the first to disclaim, and his reasons for opposing the changes have been largely ignored. The first ten amendments to the Constitution ultimately removed the danger inherent in this provision as adopted and at the same time indicate the soundness of Martin's position.

[2] *Genuine Information, ibid.,* 3:178.
[3] Brant, *James Madison,* 3:129.
[4] See Farrand, *Records of the Federal Convention,* 1:313, 322, 327.
[5] *Ibid.,* 2:22.
[6] This provision as finally adopted (art. VI, sec. 2) reads: "The Constitution, and the Laws of the United States which shall be made in Pursuance thereof; and all Treaties made, or which shall be made, under the Authority of the United States, shall be the supreme Law of the Land; and the Judges in every State shall be bound thereby, any Thing in the Constitution or Laws of any State to the Contrary notwithstanding."

In February of 1788 Oliver Ellsworth, in a long letter attacking Martin's position and conduct at the Philadelphia assembly, called his originating this clause "among the greater positive virtues you exhibited in the Convention."[7] In his answer three weeks later, Martin gave his reasons for introducing and insisting upon the clause in its original form:

To place this matter in a proper point of view, it will be necessary to state, that as the propositions were reported by the committee of the whole house, a power was given to the general government to negative the laws passed by the state legislatures, a power which I considered as totally inadmissible; in subsitution of this I proposed the following clause, which you will find very materially different from the clause adopted by the Constitution.[8] When this clause was introduced, it was not established that inferior continental courts should be appointed for trial of all questions arising on treaties and on the laws of the general government, and it was my wish and hope that every question of that kind would have been determined in the first instance in the courts of the respective states; had this been the case, the propriety and the necessity that treaties duly made and ratified, and the laws of the general government, should be binding on the state judiciaries which were to decide upon them, must be evident to every capacity, while at the same time, if such treaties or laws were inconsistent with our [state] constitution and bill of rights, the judiciaries of this state would be bound to reject the first and abide by the last, since in the form I introduced the clause, notwithstanding treaties and the laws of the general government were intended to be superior to the laws of our state government, where they should be opposed to each other, yet that they were not proposed nor meant to be superior to our constitution and bill of rights. It was afterwards altered and amended (if it can be called an amendment) to the form in which it stands in the system now published; and as inferior continental, and not state, courts are originally to decide on those questions, it is now worse than useless. For being so altered as to render the treaties and laws made under the federal government superior to our constitution, if the system is adopted it will amount to a total and unconditional surrender to that government, by the citizens of this state, of every right and privilege secured to them by our constitution, and an express compact and stipulation with the general government that it may, at its discretion, make laws in direct violation of those rights.[9]

Thus, with no federal bill of rights incorporated in the constitution as submitted to the states, and the states' constitutional bills of rights inapplicable and subordinate to federal legislation, the citizens would be at the complete mercy of the whims and excesses of the new congress.[10] If the latter were to enact a law interfering with the exercise of religion (or any of the other liberties which we have come to take for granted as

[7] "The Landholder," *Maryland Journal*, for 29 February 1788, in *ibid.*, 3:273.
[8] See n. 6 above.
[9] *Maryland Journal*, 21 March 1788, in *ibid.*, pp. 286–87.
[10] That these fears were not merely theoretical speculations, witness the Alien and Sedition Acts of 1798.

fundamental freedoms), there would have been no law and no court to protect the citizen against its operation. And such a person would not even be tried in a state court, but in a federal court, presided over by a federal judge who was not bound by any federal constitutional bill of rights and who could take no cognizance of a state bill of rights on the defendant's behalf. This potentially tyrannical situation was corrected by the adoption of the federal bill of rights nearly five years later, but, in 1787 there was no probability, much less assurance, of its enactment. It is somewhat startling to find, among all the great statesmen of the period, so few men other than Martin (and none more vehemently than he) expressing solicitude concerning such an important matter.

The importance of this clause as the backbone of our Constitution should not be overlooked: under it the supremacy of the national constitution over any other federal law, treaty, state statute, or state constitutional provision conflicting with it is established. It is the basis for the American "doctrine of *judicial* supremacy," by which it is for the courts to determine whether there is a conflict between the provisions of federal statutes and treaties or state constitutions and laws and the federal Constitution, and, in such a case, to declare the former invalid and inoperative. The necessity as well as the logic of this power in the judiciary was as obvious to Martin and most other members of the convention in 1787 as it was to Chief Justice Marshall and the Supreme Court in 1803.[11]

Four days later, on 21 July, the convention for a second time debated Wilson's proposition that the power of vetoing congressional legislation should be given to the president in association with the Supreme Court.[12] This proposition appeared in the original Virginia resolutions,[13] and had been rejected on 6 June, after Wilson had moved its adoption and Madison had seconded it and argued for it at considerable length. Wilson urged this joint veto power not only because state statutes might be enacted which exceeded the constitutional powers of the legislature but also because they might be undesirable. "Laws may be unjust, may be unwise, may be dangerous, may be destructive," he maintained, "and yet not so unconstitutional as to justify the Judges in refusing to give them effect. Let them have a share in Revisionary power, and they will have an opportunity of taking notice of these characteristics of a law, and of counteracting, by the weight of their opinions the improper views of the Legislature."[14]

Gerry was opposed to this idea, and Martin, as often happened (despite Ellsworth's forgetful or mendacious subsequent recollection[15]),

[11] Cf. Marbury v. Madison, 1 Cranch (5 U.S.) 137 (1803).
[12] Farrand, *Records of the Federal Convention*, 2:73ff.
[13] No. 8 (see *ibid.*, 1:21).
[14] *Ibid.*, 2:73.
[15] See "The Landholder," in *ibid.*, 3:271.

agreed with him. "I consider the association of the Judges with the Executive," Martin told the Convention,

as a dangerous innovation; as well as one which could not produce the particular advantage expected from it. A knowledge of mankind, and of Legislative affairs cannot be presumed to belong in a higher degree to the Judges than to the Legislature. *And as to the Constitutionality of laws, that point will come before the Judges in their proper official character. In this character they have a negative on the laws.* Join them with the Executive in the Revision and they will have a *double* negative. It is necessary that the Supreme Judiciary should have the confidence of the people. This will soon be lost, if they are employed in the task of remonstrating against popular measures of the Legislature. Besides in what mode & proportion are they to vote in the Council of Revision?[16]

Martin expressed the same thought again in his report to the Maryland General Assembly:

By the *third article*, the judicial power of the United States is vested in *one supreme court*, and in such *inferior courts*, as the Congress may from time to time ordain and establish. These courts, and *these only*, will have a right to decide upon the laws of the United States, and all questions arising upon their construction, and in a judicial manner to carry those laws into execution. . . . Whether, therefore, any *laws* or *regulations* of the *Congress*, or any *acts* of its *President* or *other officers*, are *contrary to*, or not *warranted* by the constitution, rests *only* with the judges, who are *appointed* by Congress to *determine;* by whose determinations *every State* must be *bound.*[17]

It is important to note that neither then nor for many years thereafter did anyone contradict this power and duty of the judiciary to declare a legislative act contrary to the basic law of the constitution invalid and hence inoperative.[18] Even Jefferson, who saw the impractical and undemocratic nature of Madison's favorite project, recommended a *judicial* review of the validity of such legislation under the federal constitution. "Would not an appeal from a State Judicature to a Federal Court," he wrote to Madison, "in all cases where the Act of Confederation controuled the question, be as effectual a remedy, and exactly commensurate to the defect?"[19] This letter was written, of course, in 1787; a quarter-century later political expediency impelled him to deny the existence of a similar judicial power to review acts of Congress when the latter came to be controlled by a majority of his party.

[16] *Ibid.*, 2:76–77.
[17] *Ibid.*, 3:220.
[18] Mercer of Maryland and Dickinson of Delaware regretted that the courts had such power but could propose no substitute for it (*ibid.*, 2:298–99). The necessity for such power was conceded by Madison, Mason, Sherman, Gouverneur Morris, Gerry, King, Wilson, Rutledge, and others as well as Martin (see Farrand, *Framing of the Constitution*, p. 157; Warren, *Making of the Constitution*, pp. 332ff.).
[19] Letter of 20 June 1787, in *Papers of Jefferson*, 11:480ff.

On the following day (18 July) the subject of a federal judiciary was resumed. The establishment of a Supreme Court had been agreed to without dissent on 4 June, but Randolph's twelfth resolution ("that the National Legislature be empowered to appoint inferior tribunals") now ran into opposition. Pierce Butler of South Carolina "could see no necessity" for them, since the state courts could handle their business. Sherman and Martin concurred. Although Madison gives only the sketchiest report of the debate on this matter, Martin's account is more explicit:

It was urged that there was occasion for *inferior* courts of the *general government* to be appointed in the different States, and that such ought not to be admitted. That the different *State judiciaries* in the respective States would be *competent to* and *sufficient for*, the cognizance, in the *first instance*, of all cases that should arise under the laws of the general government, which, being by this system made the supreme law of the States, would be binding on the different State judiciaries. That, by giving an *appeal* to the *Supreme* Court of the United States, the *general government* would have a *sufficient* check over their decisions, and security for the enforcing of their laws.[20]

It should be remembered, moreover, that at this time, the powers of Congress had not been either defined or limited; on the contrary, only the day before the national legislature had been given authority as broad as it was nebulous: "to legislate in all cases for the general interests of the Union, and also in those to which the States are separately incompetent, or in which the harmony of the United States may be interrupted by the exercise of individual Legislation." It was on this basis that the next argument developed: as Martin pointed out,[21] the extensive and undefined powers of Congress would give the federal courts jurisdiction over so many fields as to put the state courts virtually out of business. This objection was unquestionably influential with the committee on detail, which, as we shall see, three weeks later presented a constitution limiting Congress to eighteen specific powers, rather than the vague and almost unlimited *omnium gatherum* which it took from the convention floor into the committee room. The bitter disagreement over the question of lower federal courts was finally compromised by passing the buck to the congresses of the future to establish "such inferior tribunals" as they should decide upon.[22]

[20] *Genuine Information*, in Farrand, *Records of the Federal Convention*, 3:206–7.
[21] *Ibid.*
[22] Warren, *Making of the Constitution*, p. 326.

14

The Constitutional Convention:
7. The Executive, 19-26 July 1787

> With the powers that the President is to enjoy, and the interests and influence with which they will be attended, he will be almost absolutely certain of being reelected, from time to time, as long as he lives.—*Genuine Information*

On 17 July the convention had quickly and unanimously agreed that the chief "National Executive" should be "a single person," but it then bogged down for ten days on the problems of his election, eligibility for re-election, and length of term in office. All these factors were so inevitably interdependent, in the eyes of the delegates, that a change in any one factor called for reconsideration and further debate on the others. The upshot was that the convention reversed itself numerous times and then reached a compromise, which was rejected in its turn in the last days of the convention.

On that day Luther Martin moved that "the Executive be chosen by Electors appointed by the several Legislatures of the individual States." Although this was substantially the method finally adopted, and still in effect,[1] on that day "it passed in the negative," only Maryland and Delaware voting for it. The convention then voted for election of the president by Congress.

When the convention proceeded to strike out the provision for the ineligibility of the president for re-election, the seven-year term of office provided for in Randolph's resolution seemed much too long to many delegates. All factions agreed upon Montesquieu's theory of separation of the executive, legislative, and judicial powers. But if the president could be re-elected, and if his election was to be by the Congress (as had been agreed), then he would have to curry and cultivate the favor and votes of the legislators, and the independence of the executive would be lost. On the other hand, if the president could not be re-elected, how could he be kept responsible to the electorate at large? For days, the

---

[1] See Constitution, art. II, sec. 1, par. 2.

convention sought to extricate itself from this dilemma, which Martin's proposition had avoided.

Finally, Dr. McClurg, of Virginia, came up with a motion to give the president a term "during good behavior." It has been suggested that the motion was actually made by McClurg for Madison, who had offered a similar proposal on 1 June.[2] On that former occasion Madison omitted his own proposal in his notes because "if recorded [it] would have required an explanation"[3]—an interesting commentary on the reliability of Madison's account of the convention.

Whatever the reason for making this motion, it was gleefully approved by Gouverneur Morris and Jacob Broom. Madison, however, sensing the general disapproval of the delegates for what amounted to the appointment of a chief executive for life, rose to the defense of Dr. McClurg, whose appointment to the convention he is said to have personally arranged,[4] apparently so that he could use McClurg's vote to cancel out that of the democratic Mason, over whom he had no control. Madison's long and ambiguous disquisition concluded that while the soundness of the proposed plan was questionable, "respect for the mover entitled his proposition to a fair hearing & discussion."[5]

Despite all Madison's later protests that the motion for a life term for the president was made merely as an *extensio ad absurdum* to ensure the executive's independence of the legislature, the proposal was defeated by only two votes, with the Virginia delegation, incidentally, voting in favor. Immediately thereafter, a motion to strike out the seven-year limitation was defeated by the same vote.

On 18 and 19 July, and again five days later, Martin moved that the president be declared ineligible for re-election. Although these motions were not successful, his arguments in support were cogent and vigorous and have been confirmed to a remarkable degree by our political experience:

There was a party who attempted to have the President appointed during good behavior, without any limitation as to time; and, not being able to succeed in that attempt, they then endeavored to have him reeligible without any restraint. It was objected, that the choice of a President to continue in office during good behavior, would be at once rendering our system an elective monarchy; and, that if the President was to be reeligible without any interval of disqualification, it would amount nearly to the same thing. . . .

. . . It was said, that the person who *nominates* will always in reality *appoint*, and that this was giving the President a power and influence, which, together with the other powers bestowed upon him, would place him above all restraint

---

[2] Brant, *James Madison*, 3:105-6.

[3] *Ibid.*, p. 106. Cf. King's notes for 1 June in Farrand, *Records of the Federal Convention*, 1:71. Brant, referring to McClurg as Madison's "stalking horse," notes that "it would be useful to have so strong a nationalist on hand, in case George Mason kicked over the traces" (*James Madison*, 3:18).

[4] *Ibid.*, p. 106; Farrand, *Records of the Federal Convention*, 2:34.

[5] Quoted in Farrand, *Records of the Federal Convention*, 3:35.

or control. In fine, it was urged, that the President, as here constituted, was a king, in everything but the name; that, though he was to be chosen but for a limited time, yet at the expiration of that time, if he is not re-elected, it will depend entirely upon his own moderation whether he will resign that authority with which he had once been invested; that, from his having the appointment of all the variety of officers, in every part of the civil department for the Union, who will be very numerous, in them and their connexions, relations, friends, and dependents, he will have a formidable host, devoted to his interest, and ready to support his ambitious views. . . . That these circumstances, combined together, will enable him, when he pleases, to become a king in *name*, as well as in substance, and establish himself in office not only for his own life, but even, if he chooses, to have that authority perpetuated to his family.[6]

As we know, a number of presidents (e.g., Washington, Jefferson, and Jackson) refused to run for a third term only because of their own belief in the politically healthy and even then well-established principle of rotation of office.

Martin's arguments (characteristically unreported by Madison in his notes), which were strongly supported by Mason, were persuasive, and on 26 July the convention, by a vote of seven to three, again reversed itself and, on the motion of Mason, approved a seven-year term, without re-election, for the president. This provision was subsequently rejected, and a four-year term without limitation on re-election was adopted.[7] Martin's later observation on this reversal was characteristically forthright:

As the propositions were reported by the committee of the whole House, the President was to be chosen for seven years, and not to be eligible at any time after. In the same manner the proposition was agreed to in convention, and so it was reported by the committee of detail, although a variety of attempts were made to alter that part of the system by those who were of a contrary opinion, in which they repeatedly failed; but, Sir, by never losing sight of their object, and choosing a proper time for their purpose, they succeeded at length in obtaining the alteration, which was not made until within the last twelve days before the convention adjourned.[8]

Thus it was that Virginia and Massachusetts secured for their aristocracies the office of the presidency for the first forty years of government under the new constitution.[9]

On 24 July, the convention, with the consideration of the Randolph resolutions approaching an end, appointed a five-man committee on

[6] *Genuine Information*, in *ibid.*, 3:216–18. The Twenty-Third Amendment, adopted 26 February 1951, essentially incorporates the limitations on the president's term of office proposed by Martin.

[7] On 6 September (*ibid.*, 2:525).

[8] *Ibid.*, 3:216.

[9] Of the ten terms between 1789 and 1829, the two Adamses from Massachusetts each served one, and four Virginians—Washington, Jefferson, Madison, and Monroe—were each re-elected. The latter three kept the presidency, with all its perquisites, in the hands of Virginians for twenty-four years.

detail "to report a Constitution conformable to the Resolutions passed by the Convention." This group was composed of Rutledge of South Carolina, Randolph of Virginia, Gorham of Massachusetts, Ellsworth of Connecticut, and Wilson of Pennsylvania, four of the five from the large-state bloc. The following day it was moved that this committee be furnished with copies of the proceedings to use in their deliberations. South Carolina voted against this motion, though it is difficult to imagine how the committee could possibly draft a constitution that would conform to the resolutions of the convention without having a copy of them at hand. Martin then rose to his feet and made a motion, equally reasonable, that the other members of the convention also be permitted to have copies of the resolutions. This motion was defeated by a vote of six to five. Again, it is difficult to understand this refusal. Was debate about the form and powers of the government proposed to be limited to the committee? Why should the convention as a whole blindfold itself to the framework of government which it had tentatively agreed upon? This day's proceedings are recorded only in Madison's notes, and it is characteristic that he did not consider the debate of sufficient interest to be recorded—indeed, it was not until years later that he set down the motions themselves, the outline of which he took from Major Jackson's sketchy and belatedly published journal.

Fortunately, however, Martin offered a possible explanation of this strange behavior to the Maryland legislature. Before the committee on detail adjourned, he recalled,

I moved for liberty to be given to the different members to take *correct copies* of the *propositions*, to which the convention had then agreed, in order that during the recess of the convention, we might have an opportunity of *considering* them, and, if it should be thought that any *alterations* or *amendments* were *necessary*, that we might be *prepared* against the convention met, to bring them forward for discussion. But, Sir, the *same spirit*, which caused *our doors to be shut*, our *proceedings* to be *kept secret,—our journals to be locked up,*—and *every avenue, as far as possible, to be shut* to *public information*, prevailed also in this case; and the proposal, so *reasonable* and *necessary*, was *rejected* by a *majority* of the convention; thereby *precluding even the members themselves from the necessary means of information and deliberation* on the *important business in which they were engaged*.[10]

On 26 July, after reasserting its decision that the president was to be ineligible for re-election, the convention adjourned until Monday, 6 August, in order to give the committee a chance to prepare a draft of the new Constitution.

[10] *Genuine Information*, in *ibid.*, pp. 190–91.

15

The Constitutional Convention:
8. The Slavery Compromise, the Contract Clause,
and the Bill of Rights Rejection,
27 July-4 September 1787

> It ought to be considered that national crimes can only
> be and frequently are punished in this world by national
> punishments; and the continuance of the slave-trade . . .
> ought to be considered as justly exposing us to the dis-
> pleasure and vengeance of Him, . . . who views with equal
> eyes the poor African slave and his American master.
> . . . I was impressed with the necessity of not merely
> attempting to secure a few rights, but of digesting
> and forming a complete bill of rights, including those of
> states and of individuals.—*Genuine Information*

On 6 August, in conformity with its resolution of 26 July, the convention reconvened,[1] but so many members were absent that it adjourned
to the next day after copies of the report of the committee on detail had
been distributed to those present. John Francis Mercer from Maryland
took his seat in the convention for the first time, and James McHenry
was also present for the first time since 1 June.[2] That afternoon,
at McHenry's suggestion, the entire Maryland delegation—Daniel
Carroll, Jenifer, McHenry, Martin, and Mercer—met at Carroll's
lodgings to agree, if possible, on a position so that the delegation could
act together when the convention took up the report.[3]

Mercer asked whether the others thought that Maryland would
accept the proposed system of government. Martin responded that it
would not, that only a compromise had enabled its proponents to push
it as far as they had, and that had Jenifer voted with him from the beginning the situation would have been quite different. Jenifer defended
himself somewhat lamely, and with more anger than accuracy, by
claiming that he had voted with Martin until he was convinced that it
was useless to continue to oppose the new form of government.

[1] Farrand, *Records of the Federal Convention*, 2:176.
[2] *Ibid.*, pp. 177, 190.
[3] *Ibid.*, p. 190ff.

McHenry tried to bypass this dispute by proposing that the Maryland delegation move to postpone consideration of the report until the original question of amending the Articles of Confederation "without altering the sovereignty of suffrage" had been submitted again. If that motion failed, then the delegation would work together, if possible, to amend the report in such a way as to make it more acceptable. However, Carroll, Jenifer, and Mercer did not believe that the Articles were susceptible of the kind of radical revision that was necessary. The delegates came to no agreement and decided to meet the next day to try once more to decide upon a common course of action. Martin announced that he could not attend the meeting because he had to go to New York and would not be back until the following Monday.

As the delegates were about to leave, McHenry noticed Mercer studying a piece of paper containing a list of all the present and past delegates to the convention, with each name marked "for" or "against." In response to McHenry's inquiry, Mercer told him that this was a tally of those in favor of and opposed to some form of monarchy—frequently referred to euphemistically as "high-toned government."[4] Among those in favor listed were Daniel Carroll and some nineteen others. Martin agreed to some of the tallies but questioned the accuracy of others, and McHenry assured him that he had personal knowledge of the feelings of many delegates named and that the remainder were based on better sources of information than Martin's.[5]

Relying in part upon this list, Martin later reported to the Maryland General Assembly that there was at the convention

one party, whose object and wish it was to abolish and annihilate all State governments, and to bring forward one general government, over this extensive continent, of a monarchical nature, under certain restrictions and limitations. Those who openly avowed this sentiment were, it is true, but few; yet it is equally true, Sir, that there was a considerable number, who did not openly avow it, who were by myself, and many others of the convention considered as being in reality favorers of that sentiment; and, acting upon those principles, covertly endeavouring to carry into effect what they well knew openly and avowedly could not be accomplished.[6]

When Martin brought this unsavory and unpopular matter into the open, there were heated denials, some abusive language, and a rash of explanations of what was meant as opposed to what was said.[7] The revelation caused Daniel Carroll to be defeated for Congress the following year, or so he alleged. The denials and explanations are still unconvincing today, and one may safely conclude that McHenry's accusation was in substance correct.[8]

[4] *Ibid.*, pp. 191-92.
[5] *Ibid.*, 3:321.
[6] *Genuine Information, ibid.*, p. 179.
[7] *Ibid.*, p. 319ff.; *Documentary History of the Constitution*, 4:636, 638ff.; Warren, *Making of the Constitution*, p. 441ff.
[8] Farrand, *Framing of the Constitution*, p. 174.

Upon Martin's return to the convention on 13 August, he took a position in favor of the payment of senators by their states instead of by the federal government, opposed the power of Congress to subdue rebellion in a state without the consent of the latter, and (with Gerry's support) argued for some limitation on the size of the national peacetime army.[9]

On Thursday, 16 August, the convention considered that section of the report of the committee on detail which gave Congress the power to borrow money "and emit bills" based on the credit of the United States. Gouverneur Morris moved to strike out the three words "and emit bills," which apparently raised the specter of paper money. Most of the delegates, of course, were closely associated with property-creditor-commercial interests and saw in Morris' motion (coupled with the denial to the states of the power to issue paper money, which was decided, some days later[10]) an opportunity to outlaw such currency forever in the new nation's economy. The emotional impact of this question upon the representatives of wealthy business interests is demonstrated by the observation of the aristocratic George Read of Delaware that these words, "if not struck out, would be as alarming as the mark of the Beast in Revelations [sic]" and by the threat of the wealthy John Langdon of New Hampshire that he "had rather reject the whole plan than retain the three words" ("and emit bills").

There were, however, delegates like Mason and Randolph of Virginia and Mercer and Martin of Maryland—the former men on principle opposed to paper money and the latter two more friendly toward it—who did not think that they should be frightened into prohibiting absolutely and for all time a power which might, on some future occasion, be fiscally indispensable to the government. As Martin later reported this episode,

Against the motion we urged that it would be improper to *deprive* the Congress of that *power;* that it would be a novelty unprecedented to establish a government which should not have such authority; that it was impossible to look forward into futurity so far as to decide that events might not happen that should render the *exercise* of such a *power absolutely* necessary; and that we doubted whether, if a war should take place, it would be *possible* for this country to *defend* itself, without having recourse to *paper credit*, in which case there would be a *necessity* of becoming a *prey* to our *enemies*, or *violating* the *constitution* of our government. . . . But, Sir, a majority of the convention, being wise beyond every event, and being willing to risk any political evil rather than admit the idea of a paper emission in any *possible* event, refused to *trust* this authority to a government to which they were *lavishing* the *most unlimited* powers of *taxation,* and to the *mercy* of which they were willing *blindly* to *trust* the *liberty* and *property* of the *citizens* of *every State* in the Union; and they *erased* that clause from the *system.*[11]

[9] Farrand, *Records of the Federal Convention*, 2:292, 317, 330.
[10] On 28 August (*ibid.*, p. 439).
[11] *Genuine Information, ibid.*, 3:205–6.

Some eighty years later the United States Supreme Court, despite the convention's specific denial of this authority, found that Congress did have the power to issue bills of credit, as well as the power to make them legal tender in payment of debts, under the "elastic clause" in conjunction with the power "to borrow money" which had been granted under the Constitution.[12]

On the following Monday, 20 August, the subject of treason came up for discussion and definition. Envisioning a possible war between the states in which a citizen would be caught between the Scylla of treason against his own state and the Charybdis of treason against the United States, Martin unsuccessfully proposed

that no act or acts done by one or more of the States against the United States, or by any citizen of any one of the United States, under the authority of one or more of the said States, shall be deemed treason, or punished as such; but in case of war being levied by one or more of the States against the United States, the conduct of each party towards the other, and their adherents respectively, shall be regulated by the laws of war and of nations."[13]

Martin later outlined to the people of Maryland his reasons for proposing such an amendment:

By the *principles* of the American revolution, *arbitrary power may* and *ought* to be resisted, even by *arms* if necessary. The time may come, when it shall be the *duty* of a *State*, in order to preserve itself from the oppression of the general government, to have recourse to the sword; in which case, the proposed form of government declares, that the *State* and every of *its citizens* who *act under its authority* are guilty of a direct act of treason;—reducing, by this provision, the different States to this alternative, that they must *tamely* and *passively yield to despotism*, or *their citizens* must *oppose it* at the *hazard* of the *halter* if unsucessful: and reducing the citizens of the State which shall take arms, to a situation in which they must be *exposed* to *punishment, let them act as they will;* since, if they *obey* the authority of their *State government*, they will be *guilty of treason against the United States;* if they *join* the *general government*, they will be *guilty of treason* against *their* own State.[14]

The amendment was not adopted because, as Martin said, it was "too much opposed to the great object of many of the leading members of the convention, which was, by all means to *leave the States* at the *mercy* of the *general government*, since they could not succeed in their *immediate and entire* abolition."[15]

[12] Hepburn v. Griswold, 8 Wall. 602 (1870); Knox v. Lee, 12 Wall. 457 (1871); and Julliard v. Greenman, 110 U.S. 421 (1884). See also brief of Clarkson N. Potter, Esq., in Hepburn v. Griswold. The "elastic clause" is the last paragraph of art. I, sec. 8, empowering Congress "to make all laws which shall be necessary and proper for carrying into Execution the foregoing Powers."
[13] *Genuine Information*, Farrand, *Records of the Federal Convention*, 3:223.
[14] *Ibid.*
[15] *Ibid.*

At about this time, at Gerry's suggestion, a number of delegates who opposed the drift and philosophy of the system then under consideration, on the basis that it tended to destroy the rights and liberties of the states and their citizens, began to meet in the evenings to plan a course of action and to draw up formal amendments which might render the proposed scheme of government "less dangerous."[16] Gerry and Martin, George Mason of Virginia, and delegates from Connecticut, New Jersey, Delaware, South Carolina, and Georgia made up the group.

Most of the next two days were devoted to the question of whether there should be any limitation upon the importation of slaves in the new Constitution.[17] Martin moved to give Congress power to tax or even to prohibit the importation of slaves. This, of course, brought a storm of protest from the southern delegates and from some New Englanders. "Religion and humanity have nothing to do with this question," Rutledge claimed. "Interest alone is the governing principle with nations. . . . If the Northern States consult their interest, they will not oppose the increase of slaves which will increase the commodities of which they will become the carriers."[18] The North Carolina, South Carolina, and Georgia delegates threatened that their states would have no part of a constitution which regulated the institution of slavery. It was finally agreed to refer the matter to a committee—of which Martin was a member—to work out some compromise. On 24 August this committee made its report, which formed the basis for another of the most crucial compromises of the convention. It recommended that Congress be forbidden to prohibit the importation of slaves until 1800 but be allowed to impose a moderate duty upon such imports, that the requirement of a two-thirds vote of each house of Congress for enactment of navigation acts be rescinded, and that federal capitation taxes be levied in accordance with the national census.[19]

This report aroused great debate. Some delegates, like Madison and Sherman, opposed a restrictive tax on slaves on the grounds that it was "wrong to admit in the Constitution the idea that there could be property in men." As Martin caustically observed, "they anxiously sought to avoid the admission of expressions which might be odious to the ears of Americans, though they were willing to admit into their system those *things* which the *expressions* signified."[20] An alliance of southern and New England interests agreed that the South should be permitted to continue its importation of slaves for the time being, and in return the requirement of a two-thirds vote for the enactment of navigation laws was dropped. Martin summarized the vigorous fight

[16] *Ibid.*, p. 282.
[17] *Ibid.*, 2:364.
[18] *Ibid.*
[19] *Ibid.*, p. 400.
[20] *Genuine Information*, in *ibid.*, 3:210.

he, Mason, Wilson, Dickinson, and a few others waged, in characteristically logical fashion:

It was said, that we had just assumed a place among independent nations, in
consequence of our opposition to the attempts of Great Britain to *enslave us*; that
this opposition was grounded upon the preservation of *those rights* to which God
and nature had entitled *us*, not in *particular*, but in *common* with *all the rest of
mankind*; that we had *appealed* to the *Supreme Being* for his *assistance*, as the *God of
freedom*, who could not but *approve* our efforts to preserve the *rights* which he had
thus *imparted to his creatures*; that now, when we scarcely had risen from our *knees*,
from *supplicating* his *aid and protection*, in *forming our government* over a *free people*,
a government formed pretendedly on the *principles* of *liberty* and for its preservation,—in *that* government, to have a provision not only putting it out of *its* power
to *restrain* and *prevent* the *slave-trade*, but *even encouraging that most infamous traffic*, by
giving the *States power* and *influence* in the *Union, in proportion* as they *cruelly and
wantonly sport with the rights of their fellow creatures*, ought to be considered as a
solemn mockery of, and *insult to that God* whose protection we had then implored,
and could not fail to hold us up in *detestation*, and render us *contemptible* to every
true friend of liberty in the world. . . .
   It was urged, that, by this system, we were giving the general government
full and absolute power to regulate commerce, under which general power it
would have a right to *restrain*, or *totally prohibit*, the *slave-trade*; it must, therefore,
appear to the world absurd and disgraceful to the last degree, that we should
except from the exercise of that power, the *only branch* of *commerce* which is *unjusti-
fiable in its nature*, and *contrary* to the rights of *mankind*; that, on the contrary,
we ought *rather to prohibit expressly* in our *constitution*, the *further importation of
slaves*; and to *authorize* the general government, from time to time, to make such
regulations as should be thought most advantageous for the *gradual abolition of
slavery*, and the *emancipation* of the *slaves* which are already in the States: That
slavery is *inconsistent* with the *genius* of *republicanism*, and has a tendency to *destroy*
those *principles* on which it is *supported*, as it *lessens* the *sense* of the *equal rights* of
mankind, and habituates us to *tyranny* and *oppression*.[21]

   The coalition between the southern slave interests and northern
business resulted in an extension of the period in which slaves could be
imported to 1808, the imposition of an import duty of not more than
ten dollars per slave, the passage of the capitation tax provision without
change, and, finally, the dropping of the two-thirds vote requirement
for the enactment of navigation acts.[22] As a result of these compromises
in favor of economic interests, as well as the general drift toward what
he considered an over-powerful central government at the expense of
the states, Martin resolved to fight the adoption of the constitution by
Maryland. He was open and frank about his opposition, and not even
Washington's popularity and esteem affected his decision. When Washington observed to him that it would be a shame if there existed such a
"diversity of sentiment as to cause any members [of the Convention] to
oppose the [proposed] system when they returned to their States," he

[21] *Ibid.*, pp. 210–11.
[22] *Ibid.*, 2:449ff., 453.

replied forthrightly that he "was confident no State in the Union would more readily accede to a proper system of Government than Maryland, but that the system under consideration was of such a nature that I never could recommend it for acceptance, and that I thought the State never ought to adopt it, and expressed my firm belief that it never would."[23]

A few days later, Martin moved to amend the president's power to grant "reprieves and pardons" to permit it after conviction only. Upon Wilson's objection that a "pardon before conviction might be necessary . . . to obtain the testimony of accomplices," Martin withdrew his motion.[24] (This episode had curious repercussions almost twenty years later, when Jefferson pardoned one of Martin's clients, Erich Bollman, before he was convicted of any crime, as part of his scheme to get Aaron Burr, another of Martin's clients, convicted of treason.)

The next day the question of the power of Congress to suspend that great Anglo-Saxon defense against arbitrary imprisonment, the writ of habeas corpus, was debated. Over the protests of Rutledge, Wilson, and Martin, the suspension of the writ was authorized "when in cases of rebellion or invasion the public safety may require it."[25] With great foresight Martin predicted that the power could and would be used to imprison, at places remote from their homes, citizens who opposed acts of the federal government as unconstitutional impositions upon the rights of the states. Martin later summarized these arguments in his report to the Maryland General Assembly:

if we gave this power to the general government, it would be an engine of oppression in its hands; since, whenever a State should oppose its views, however arbitrary and unconstitutional, and refuse submission to them, the general government may declare it to be *an act of rebellion*, and suspending the habeas corpus act, may *seize* upon the persons of those *advocates of freedom*, who have had *virtue* and *resolution* enough to excite the opposition, and may *imprison* them during its pleasure, in the *remotest* part of the Union; so that a citizen of Georgia might be *bastiled* in the furthest part of New Hampshire, . . . cut off from their family, their friends, and their every connexion.[26]

On the same day the convention considered limitations on the power of the states to coin money, to issue bills of credit, to pass *ex post facto* and retrospective laws, or to otherwise interfere with contractual obligations. The first two prohibitions were adopted, although Martin thought it more than sufficient restraint that the states should be denied the power to issue bills of credit without the consent of Congress.[27] On

[23] Letters of Martin, *Maryland Journal*, 18 and 21 March, 1788, in *ibid.*, 3:281, 286.
[24] Monday, 27 August, *ibid.*, 2:426.
[25] *Ibid.*, p. 436.
[26] *Genuine Information, ibid.*, 3:213. Three-quarters of a century later, during the Civil War, many a Marylander was actually imprisoned for the duration in "bastilles" in Boston Harbor (see John A. Marshall, *American Bastille*; *Ex parte Milligan*, 4 Wall. [70 U.S.] 1 [1866]).
[27] *Genuine Information*, Farrand, *Records of the Federal Convention*, 3:214.

12 September the committee on style provided the final version: state laws "impairing the obligation of contracts" were prohibited. George Mason thought such a broad denial of power to the states altogether unwise. "Cases will happen that cannot be foreseen," he insisted, "where some kind of interference will be proper, & essential." With even more vigor, and with characteristic farsightedness, Martin explained his opposition to such restraints:

> I considered, Sir, that there might be times of such *great public calamities and distress*, and of such *extreme scarcity of specie*, as should render it the *duty* of a government, for the *preservation* of even the *most valuable part* of its citizens, in some measure to interfere in their favor by passing laws *totally or partially stopping* the courts of justice, or authorizing the debtor to pay by *instalments*, or by delivering up his property to his creditors at a *reasonable* and *honest* valuation. The times have been such as to render regulations of this kind necessary in most or all of the States to prevent the *wealthy creditor* and the *moneyed* man from *totally* destroying the *poor*, though even *industrious* debtor. *Such times* may *again* arrive.[28]

The accuracy of this prediction was demonstrated during the Great Depression of the 1930s, when, despite the arguments of counsel and the dissenting justices that the convention had deliberately and specifically denied the states such powers, the Supreme Court held that a state must and therefore does have the power to alleviate the plight of debtors by moratorium laws during periods of economic emergency. The dissenting opinion cited the convention debate at length and quoted Martin's exposition of the economic hardship that would result if the state should be denied the power to aid the poor debtor. The four dissenting justices had the intent, the understanding, and the actual decision of the 1787 convention on their side, along with a long list of earlier Supreme Court decisions. The majority of five justices, on the other hand, were persuaded by the arguments Martin adduced on behalf of the many hard-pressed working men—arguments which had failed to move the convention delegates, members of the creditor class.[29] Moved by the force of Martin's argument, the Virginia and Maryland delegations voted against Rutledge's motion for the inclusion of the "obligation of contracts" clause.[30]

The next day the convention debated the admission of new states to the Union. Gouverneur Morris expressed the fear of many of the large states that they would lose not only the land and wealth of their bordering territories, but also the increased representation in Congress which they expected to result from the growth of population in those areas.

---

[28] *Ibid.*, pp. 214–15.

[29] Home Bldg. & Loan Ass'n v. Blaisdell, 290 U.S. 398, 78 L. Ed. 413 (1934) (opinion by Hughes, C. J., Brandeis, Stone, Roberts, and Cardozo, JJ., concurring; dissenting opinion by Sutherland, J., with Van Devanter, McReynolds, and Butler, JJ., concurring).

[30] Maryland, Virginia, and Connecticut voted no; seven states voted aye (Farrand, *Records of the Federal Convention*, 2:440).

Accordingly, he proposed that no new state should be created within the boundaries of any existing state without the consent of its legislature and the Congress.

Martin was on his feet instantly to offer a counterproposal that Congress might establish a new state "if they shall under all the circumstances think it reasonable . . . *without the consent* of the State" of which it was originally a part: "Shall Vermont be reduced by force in favor of the states claiming it? Franklin & the Western country of Virginia [are] in a like situation."[31] It was the old battle between the large states, with even larger "backlands" which they jealously guarded, and the small states with no such territories.[32] From his own travels and talks with the inhabitants of these frontier lands, Martin knew their resentment at being treated as stepchildren by the seaboard states, and he gladly defended their rights:

The hardship, the inconvenience, and the injustice of compelling the inhabitants of those States who may dwell on the western side of the mountains, and along the Ohio and Mississippi rivers, to remain connected with the inhabitants of those States respectively, on the Atlantic side of the mountains, and subject to the same State governments, would be such as would, in my opinion, justify even recourse to arms, to free themselves from, and to shake off, so ignominious a yoke.[33]

It was argued that it was inconsistent with the concept of a free and independent state to divide it without its consent. Martin admitted the logic of the objection, but insisted

that it was not *more inconsistent* with the rights of free and independent States, than that *inequality of suffrage* and *power* which the *large States* had *extorted* from *the others*; and that, if the *smaller States* yielded up *their rights* in *that instance*, they were entitled to demand from the States of extensive territory a *surrender* of their rights in this *instance*; and in a particular manner, as it was *equally necessary* for the true interest and happiness of the *citizens* of *their own States*, as of *the Union*.

Then, with that instinct for the vital weakness in his opponent's position which was to make him the most successful and respected advocate at the American bar for over a quarter of a century, he continued:

But, Sir, although, when the large States demanded *undue* and *improper* sacrifices to be made to their *pride* and *ambition*, they treated the rights of free States with more contempt than ever a British Parliament treated the rights of her colonial establishments; yet, when a *reasonable* and *necessary sacrifice* was asked *from them*, they spurned the idea with ineffable disdain. They *then perfectly under-*

---

[31] *Genuine Information, ibid.,* 3:225, 2:455.

[32] See Chapter 7, pp. 62ff., above.

[33] *Genuine Information,* Farrand, *Records of the Federal Convention,* 3:224ff. Witness West Virginia's winning her independence from Virginia by force of arms in 1862. It was this very feeling which Burr attempted to capitalize upon in 1805 to 1807 (see Thomas Perkins Abernethy, *The Burr Conspiracy,* pp. 3–4).

stood the *full value* and the *sacred obligation* of *State rights*, and at the least attempt to infringe them, *where they were concerned*, they were tremblingly alive, and agonized at every pore.[34]

The debate bitterly continued for the rest of that day and on into the next. John Dickinson of Delaware, John Langdon of New Hampshire, and Daniel Carroll supported Martin and urged that the question be referred to a committee to settle the differences. However, the large states were adamant and voted down this suggestion. They ultimately had their way, and their position became codified in art. VI, sec. 3, of the Constitution.[35]

On Pinkney's motion, the provision that no religious test was ever to be demanded as a qualification for federal office was added. Although Martin strongly favored a guarantee of religious liberty in any bill of rights, he felt that acknowledgment of a belief in God was not too much to require of an officeholder: "there were some members *so unfashionable* as to think, that a *belief of the existence* of a *Deity*, and of a *state of future rewards and punishments*, would be some security for the good conduct of our rulers, and that, in a Christian country, it would be *at least decent* to hold out some distinction between the professors of Christianity and downright infidelity or paganism."[36]

The convention next proceeded to consider the delicate problem of how many states would have to ratify the new constitution for it to supersede the Articles of Confederation.[37] Almost every number from seven through thirteen was advocated by one delegate or another. The Maryland group, of course, argued that adoption must be unanimous by all members of the confederation. For nearly two days this proposal was angrily debated, and when Carroll's and Martin's motion to require the consent of all thirteen states came to a vote, every delegation voted no except Maryland. Maryland then voted with three other states for ratification by ten members, and finally joined the majority (New Hampshire, Massachusetts, Connecticut, New Jersey, Pennsylvania, Delaware, and Georgia) in voting for ratification by nine. Only Virginia and North and South Carolina continued to insist on adoption by a simple majority.

At this point Gouverneur Morris suggested that the convention conclude its deliberations quickly so that a state ratifying body could be called at once by the Pennsylvania legislature, which was just about to convene, before the enemies of the new constitution had a chance to publicize their objections. He added that if there was a delay and the numerous arguments against ratification were all heard, he doubted that the people of Pennsylvania or any other state in the union would adopt it. This constituted a bold admission of Martin's claim that the

[34] Farrand, *Records of the Federal Convention*, 3:225.
[35] *Ibid.*, 2:464.
[36] *Genuine Information, ibid.*, 3:227.
[37] *Ibid.*, 2:468–69, 475–77.

convention was attempting to deceive the general public, and he immediately rose to state that he agreed with Morris and for this very reason,
he argued, popular consideration of the new system ought to be careful,
deliberate, and informed.

Several times during the convention, Martin introduced into the discussion the preservation of specific individual liberties and the possibility of providing the Constitution with a complete Bill of Rights.
Some months later Oliver Ellsworth, using the name "Landholder,"
with typical disregard for the facts, insisted that at the convention Martin had never stated his belief that a bill of rights was a necessary part
of the new constitution.[38] In a public letter of response Martin made his
position clear:

With respect to a bill of rights, had the government been formed upon principles truly federal, as I wished it, . . . there would have been no need of a
bill of rights, as far as related to the rights of individuals, but only as to the
rights of states. But the proposed constitution being intended and empowered
to act not only on states, but also immediately on individuals, it renders
a recognition and a stipulation in favour of the rights both of states and of
men, not only proper, but in my opinion absolutely necessary. I endeavoured
to obtain a restraint on the powers of the general government, as to standing
armies, but it was rejected. It was my wish that the general government should
not have the power of suspending the privilege of the writ of habeas corpus, . . .
but I could not succeed. . . . because the more the system advanced, the more
clearly it appeared to me that the framers of it did not consider that either
states or men had any rights at all, or that they meant to secure the enjoyment
of any to either the one or the other; accordingly, I devoted a part of my time
to the actually preparing and draughting such a bill of rights, and had it in
readiness before I left the Convention, to have it laid before a committee. I
conversed with several members on the subject; they agreed with me on the
propriety of the measure, but at the same time expressed their sentiments that
it would be impossible to procure its adoption if attempted. A very few days
before I left the Convention, I shewed to an honorable member sitting by me
a proposition, which I then had in my hand, couched in the following words;
"Resolved that a committee be appointed to prepare and report a bill of rights,
to be prefixed to the proposed Constitution," and I then would instantly have
moved for the appointment of a committee for that purpose, if he would have
agreed to second the motion, to do which he hesitated, not as I understand from
any objection to the measure, but from a conviction in his own mind that the
motion would be in vain.[39]

Martin added that a delegate from South Carolina, Charles Pinckney,
was also most anxious to have certain civil liberties specifically guaran-
teed by the constitution. His motion, however, was referred to the
committee on detail, from which it never reappeared.[40] During the last
few days of the convention, after Martin, despairing of changing the

[38] *Maryland Journal*, 29 February 1788, *ibid.*, 3:273.
[39] *Maryland Journal*, 21 March 1788, *ibid.*, pp. 390–91.
[40] See proceedings of 20 August 1787, *ibid.*, 2:340ff.

tone or the tenor of the new document, had left Philadelphia, a proposed guarantee of individual liberties (trial by jury and freedom of the press), and a motion by Mason and Gerry for the inclusion of a complete bill of rights were defeated.[41]

It has been suggested that the reason for this inaction lay in the delegates' assumption that there could be no danger because Congress had been granted no power to legislate in the area of civil liberties.[42] At the convention, if Madison's notes are to be considered conclusive, only Sherman expressed alarm.[43] The later protestations of Hamilton[44] and others that a bill of rights was not only unnecessary but dangerous were a poor defense against the public outcry in state after state over this vital omission. These very same spokesmen who, in 1787 and 1788, unctuously poohpoohed the popular fears as imaginary and insubstantial procured the enactment of a "Sedition Act" to imprison or hang anyone who spoke disrespectfully of them a decade later.[45] Apparently, most delegates were either ignorant or unmindful of the implications of the "elastic clause" (art. I, sec. 8), which gave Congress the right to enact all laws that were necessary for the execution of the powers actually granted, or which might ever be held to have been granted, to the federal government. Moreover, the overwhelming majority of delegates were not interested in civil liberties, moratoria for debtors, abolition of slavery, local self-government, or other abstract matters. They had come to Philadelphia to draft a form of government which would be good for business. They wanted freedom of commerce, protection of American industry, a stable, hard-money currency, inviolable contractual (i.e., creditors') rights, and unobstructed importation and exploitation of slaves. George Mason, Patrick Henry, Richard Henry Lee, William Paca, Luther Martin, and thousands of less famous citizens believed that good government required a broader foundation than that of good business, but this was a minority view at the convention, and the Bill of Rights was the price the good-business group was forced to pay to an aroused citizenry the following spring in order to get its system adopted. Even then, many states ratified the Constitution grudgingly and by a very narrow margin.

[41] *Ibid.*, pp. 587-88, 616-18, 628, 633.
[42] Warren, *Making of the Constitution*, p. 506ff.
[43] Farrand, *Records of the Federal Convention*, 2:617-18.
[44] *The Federalist*, No. 81.
[45] See James Morton Smith, *Freedom's Fetters: The Alien and Sedition Laws and American Civil Liberties, passim.*

16

Maryland's Ratification
of the Federal Constitution,
5 September 1787-1 May 1788

> The whole history of mankind proves that so far from
> parting with the powers actually delegated to it, govern-
> ment is constantly encroaching on the small pittance of
> rights reserved by the people to themselves, and gradually
> wresting them out of their hands.—Martin, 28 March
> 1788

> In some states the Antifederalists were in an undoubted
> majority, and, so far as can be determined, they consti-
> tuted nearly if not quite one-half of the American people.
> We should be careful about indicting even half a nation.
> —R. L. Schuyler, *The Constitution of the United States*

> Maryland has acceded to the proposed Constitution by
> a great majority. Chase, Paca, Martin, and Mercer
> opposed it with their utmost vigor and abilities, but with
> decency.—C. Griffin to James Madison, 5 May 1788

Of the seventy-three delegates to the constitutional convention appointed by the states, only fifty-five attended its meetings at Philadelphia for any length of time. Of these, only thirty-nine actually signed
the document on the closing day of the deliberations. About half of the
others, including Gerry of Massachusetts, Lansing and Yates of New
York, Mason and Randolph of Virginia, and Martin and Mercer of
Maryland, were sincerely opposed to the new system of government—
indeed, late in the afternoon of the last working day (15 September),
Randolph, Mason, and Gerry all argued for a second convention to
consider changes and improvements in the constitution just drafted, to
be proposed by the people and the state conventions.[1] The great
majority of the delegates, fearing even greater disagreement at such a
gathering, rejected this proposal out of hand. It had its merits, however,
and was later widely proposed.[2]

[1] Farrand, *Records of the Federal Convention*, 2:631–32.
[2] Warren, *Making of the Constitution*, p. 274ff. See also *Documentary History of the Constitution*, 4:353, 573, 585.

In an effort to represent the constitution as the unanimous product of all the delegates, Gouverneur Morris came up with the ambiguous concluding statement, "Done in Convention by the Unanimous Consent of the States present," and then obtained Franklin's persuasive talents to get it approved on the floor.[3] When Madison returned to New York to resume his seat in the Continental Congress, he found considerable opposition to the draft constitution in that body. It was believed that the convention had gone far beyond its powers to amend the Articles of Confederation and that a bill of rights, lack of which was a fatal defect, should be added by the Congress before the constitution was sent to the states for approval. Madison capitalized upon this sincere and sound but unorganized and diffuse opposition by maneuvering a resolution through the Congress in which that body unanimously washed its hands of the sticky problem and left the decision to the States.[4] This resolution, though it was intended to be noncommittal on the merits of the Philadelphia document, was given the appearance of a unanimous endorsement by the Congress. Washington congratulated Madison on this deception: "This apparent unanimity will have its effect. Not every one has opportunities to peep behind the curtain; and as the multitude are often deceived by externals, the appearance of unanimity in that body on this occasion will be of great importance."[5]

The delegates dispersed from Philadelphia, and one of the most far-ranging, widespread, and important debates in the history of government began. The newspapers published thousands of articles and letters, whose authors ranged from the illustrious to the obscure and anonymous. Citizens took sides freely and volubly. It very soon became apparent in Maryland that the financial and mercantile interests, together with a large part of the population dependent on them, enthusiastically supported the new constitution, as promising a more efficient government, a more stable currency, and protection of new and potentially successful industries.[6]

Late in November, the Maryland House of Delegates began its consideration of the constitution. In accordance with the instructions of the previous spring, it invited the Maryland delegates to report on the proceedings at Philadelphia.[7] Accordingly, on 29 November Carroll, Jenifer, McHenry, and Martin appeared before the House (Mercer ap-

---

[3] Farrand, *Records of the Federal Convention*, 2:663–64.

[4] Madison to Washington, 30 September 1787, in *Documentary History of the Constitution*, 4:307ff.

[5] Washington to Madison, 10 October 1787, in *ibid.*, p. 321. Cf. R. H. Lee to Mason, 1 October 1787, in Burnett, *Letters of Members of the Congress*, 8:652–53.

[6] See the petition of several hundred Baltimore tradesmen, mechanics, etc., to the first Congress, dated 11 April 1789, reprinted in Beard's *Economic Interpretation of the Constitution*, pp. 42–43.

[7] For the report of the convention delegates to the Maryland legislature, see General Assembly, *Votes and Proceedings*, pp. 5, 9ff., *et passim*; Bernard Christian Steiner, "Maryland's Adoption of the Constitution," pp. 22ff., 27ff.

parently did not attend). McHenry had been very reluctant to sign the constitution in Philadelphia but finally decided to give in to Washington's persuasion and do so.[8] He began his address to the Assembly with the reminder that upon concluding its business the convention, "having deposited their proceedings with their Worthy President, [had] by a Resolve prohibited any copy to be taken, under the Idea that nothing but the Constitution thus framed and submitted to the Public could come under their consideration." For that reason, he insisted, he was forced to rely on his memory and could not be as complete and accurate as might be wished. After this disclaimer, he went on to outline the Virginia resolutions submitted to the convention, and then proceeded to discuss each section of the constitution which had evolved out of them. After a sketchy presentation of the powers of each of the three branches of the government, he closed with the remark that "I myself could not approve of it throughout, but I saw no prospect of getting a better—the whole, however, is the result of that spirit of Amity which directed the wishes of all for the general good, and where those Sentiments govern, it will meet, I trust, with a Kind and Cordial reception."[9]

When McHenry took his seat, Martin rose and for the remainder of that day and part of the next gave an account not only of the accomplishment of the convention but of the conflicting philosophies, motives, and arguments on most of the matters considered there.[10] Portions of this long speech have been quoted above in the narrative of the proceedings at Philadelphia. Though seldom read and rarely quoted today, it is an invaluable source of details which Madison was too busy or too selective to include in his notes. Partisan in approach, vehement in tone, it gives a colorful, homely portrayal of many of the leading figures at Philadelphia and suggests the reasons for their positions on each issue raised there.

The Federalists had imposed upon the convention a conspiracy of secrecy. They had locked up its meager journal and ordered all other papers and records burned. However, Martin pointed out an even more significant fact: a larger number of critical changes and innovations had been written into the constitution during the last few days of the convention, when most of the remaining delegates were too weary (as Madison himself noted[11]) to prolong the meeting with further objections and debate. For example, the omnibus "general welfare clause" was

---

[8] Steiner, *James McHenry*, p. 107.

[9] Reported in Farrand, *Records of the Federal Convention*, 3:144ff.

[10] Martin's notes for this great speech are among the John Leeds Bozman Papers at the Library of Congress and are reprinted in *ibid.*, p. 151ff. Shortly after it was delivered, Martin rewrote his remarks, which were then published under the title *The Genuine Information* in the newspapers and in pamphlet form.

[11] "As the final arrangement of it [the mode of electing the president] took place in the latter stage of the Session, it was not exempt from a degree of the hurrying influence produced by fatigue and impatience in all such Bodies" (Madison to George Hay, 23 August 1823, in *ibid.*, p. 458).

added on 4 September;[12] all of the powers of the president (except treaty-making) had been accorded at a time when it was agreed that he should be elected by the Congress and should be ineligible for re-election, while the change to election by an electoral college and the dropping of the clause forbidding his re-election came on 6 September.[13] On 12 September the convention finally voted against inclusion of a bill of rights.[14] The "obligation of contracts" clause, written by the "Committee of Style," was not adopted until 14 September.[15]

After outlining the objectives and necessary consequences of the Virginia plan, Martin described the adoption of the Connecticut Compromise, and added that "soon after this period, the Honorable Mr. *Yates* and Mr. *Lansing*, of New York, left us—they had uniformly opposed the system, and, I *believe*, despairing of getting a *proper one* brought forward, or of *rendering any real service*, they returned no more."[16]

At that point, one of Martin's fellow delegates interrupted him, as he later recalled, "in a manner . . . not the most delicate, to insinuate pretty strongly, that the statement which I had given of the conduct of those gentlemen, and their motives for not returning, were not candid."[17]

It is not known which of Martin's colleagues allowed his Federalist enthusiasm to so overcome his discretion as to make such an accusation, but it was probably McHenry, as Carroll and Jenifer were in Philadelphia when Lansing and Yates left, while McHenry had returned to Baltimore.[18] At any rate, substantiation of Martin's account was not long in appearing, in the form of a joint public letter to Governor Clinton of New York from the two gentlemen in question. They had left Philadelphia, they said, because they believed that the new consitution exceeded the powers of the Convention and was highly prejudicial to the "equal and permanent liberty" of all American citizens, and because they were convinced that to remain would be "fruitless and unavailing."[19]

Martin's discussion of the new Constitution ranged from the powers of the new congress and of the president and the jurisdiction of the new federal courts, the importation of slaves, and the suspension of the writ of habeas corpus to problems of judicial supremacy, treason and civil war, the election and term of office of the chief executive, ratification, and dozens of other topics. His peroration was an odd compound of simple fact and dire predictions regarding the fate of the country if

[12] *Ibid.*, 2:495–97.
[13] *Ibid.*, p. 525.
[14] *Ibid.*, pp. 582–83, 587–88.
[15] *Ibid.*, p. 610.
[16] *Ibid.*, 3:190–91.
[17] Martin to Hon. Thomas Cockey Deye, Speaker of the House of Delegates of Maryland, 27 January 1788, published in the *Maryland Gazette* for 29 January 1788, reprinted in *ibid.*, pp. 269–70.
[18] *Ibid.*, p. 586ff.
[19] Reprinted in *ibid.*, p. 244ff.

the constitution should be ratified. He concluded by predicting "an enormous increase" in the number and value of public offices:

Whether, sir, in this variety of appointments, and in the scramble for them, I might not have as good a prospect to advantage myself as many others, is not for me to say; but this, Sir, I can say with truth, that, so far was I from being influenced in my conduct by interest, or the consideration of office, that I would cheerfully resign the appointment I now hold; I would bind myself never to accept another, either under the general government or that of my own State. I would do more, Sir;—so destructive do I consider the present system to the happiness of my country, I would cheerfully sacrifice that share of property with which Heaven has blessed a life of industry; I would reduce myself to indigence and poverty, and those who are dearer to me than my own existence I would intrust to the care and protection of that Providence, who hath so kindly protected myself, if on *those terms only* I could procure my country to reject those chains which are forged for it.[20]

This important address was only a beginning. Martin continued to make his views on the constitution known. He became a frequent contributor to the flood of newspaper writings on the subject—most written over his signature, although some, especially letters to northern papers, were not.[21] The most informative, as well as the most revealing of his candor, acute intellect, knowledge of history and political science, and potential as an adversary, are those in his controversy with Oliver Ellsworth, "The Landholder." Ellsworth published an extended series of letters in the *Connecticut Courant* in which he addressed himself, from a strongly Federalist point of view, to various aspects of the new constitution. In his eighth letter he accused Gerry of introducing a motion, near the end of the convention, for "the redemption of the old Continental money," of which he asserted that Gerry had hoarded a large sum. The official journal and Madison's notes indicate no such motion. The charge of speculation, moreover, came from a man who himself owned large amounts of Continental securities, and Ellsworth had supported, while Gerry opposed, the constitution which was to give such securities a resurrection of value.

Martin wrote a brief but forthright letter in support of Gerry,[22] to which Ellsworth responded with a letter of over two thousand words accusing Martin not only of excessive "volubility"[23] but of lack of veracity and of having been absent from approximately half of the convention sessions. Martin's response was that the letter demonstrated

[20] *Ibid.*, pp. 231–32.
[21] See *Maryland Journal* and *Maryland Gazette* for December 1788, *passim.* See also *Connecticut Courant* (Hartford) for 5, 12, 19, and 26 November; 3, 10, 17, and 31 December 1787; 3, 10, 17, and 24 March 1788; *American Herald* (Boston), 4 February 1788; *Independent Gazetteer* (Philadelphia), 19 April and 5 May 1788; *New York Journal*, 16 June 1788.
[22] *Maryland Journal*, 18 January 1788, reprinted in Farrand, *Records of the Federal Convention*, 3:259.
[23] See Appendix A to this volume.

"the disingenuity of the Landholder, and that it is very possible to convey a falsehood, or something very much like it, almost in the words of truth."[24] He demolished Ellsworth's charges and innuendoes one by one and challenged any member of the Philadelphia convention to refute him. No one did.

It was this war of letters which made even practiced polemicists wary of crossing swords with Luther Martin in public debate. The same pen name was used in the *Courant* and in the *Maryland Journal*, and the question arose of whether "The Landholder" was one or two persons. To this Martin observed:

Whether the Landholder of the Connecticut Courant, and of the Maryland Journal, is the same person, or different, is not very material; I however incline to the former opinion, as I hope for the honour of human nature, it would be difficult to find more than one individual who could be capable of so total a disregard to the principles of truth and honour. . . . had I not come in for a share of his censure, I confess I should have been both disappointed and mortified. It would have had at least the appearance, that the Landholder had discovered something in my principles, which he considered congenial with his own.[25]

Martin ended by declaring himself "at a loss which most to admire—the depravity of this writer's heart, or the weakness of his head." As Ellsworth's anonymity was increasingly threatened and his accusations seriously challenged, he dropped the lopsided debate.

Using Ellsworth's articles as a springboard, however, Martin addressed four open letters to the citizens of Maryland, to be published in the three weeks before the election of delegates to the convention which was to consider the question of ratification. The mushrooming nature of government, which continually encroaches upon the liberties of the people as it grows unless its area of permissible activity is explicitly limited, has nowhere been better described:

If those, my fellow citizens, to whom the administration of our government was about to be committed, had sufficient wisdom never to err, and sufficient goodness always to consult the true interests of the governed, and if we could have a proper security that their successors should to the end of time be possessed of the same qualifications, it would be impossible that power could be lavished upon them with too liberal a hand. Power absolute and unlimited, united with unerring wisdom and unbounded goodness, is the government of the Deity of the universe. . . . We have no right to expect that our rulers will be more wise, more virtuous, or more perfect than those of other nations have been, or that they will not be equally under the influence of ambition, avarice and all that train of baleful passions, which have so generally proved the curse of our unhappy race. . . . But the advocates of the system tell you that we who oppose it, endeavour to terrify you with mere possibilities which may never be realized,

[24] *Maryland Journal*, 7 March 1788, reprinted in Farrand, *Records of the Federal Convention*, 3:276ff.
[25] *Maryland Journal*, 7 March 1788.

that all our objections consist in saying government may do this, and government may do that. —I will for argument['s] sake admit the justice of this remark, and yet maintain that the objections are insurmountable. I consider it an incontrovertible truth, that whatever by the constitution government even may do, if it relates to the abuse of power by acts tyrannical and oppressive, it some time or other will do. . . . Ascertain the limits of the may with ever so much precision, and let them be as extensive as you please, government will speedily reach their utmost verge; nor will it stop there, but soon will overleap those boundaries, and roam at large into the regions of the may not. Those who tell you the government by this constitution may keep up a standing army, abolish the trial by jury, oppress the citizens of the states by its powers over the militia, destroy the freedom of the press, infringe the liberty of conscience, and do a number of other acts injurious and destructive of your rights, yet that it never will do so; and that you safely may accept such a constitution and be perfectly at ease and secure that your rulers will always be so good, so wise, and so virtuous—such emanations of the Deity—that they will never use their power but for your interest and your happiness, contradict the uniform experience of ages, and betray a total ignorance of human nature, or a total want of ingenuity.[26]

One of the leading Federalist essayists in Maryland was the great judge Alexander Contee Hanson, who used the *nom de plume* "Aristides." Seeking to refute the Antifederalist objections to the broad jurisdiction of the new federal courts, he wrote that under the draft constitution no appeal lay to the federal from state courts. Martin was at some pains to correct this error. He further persisted in asserting that the federal courts could not entertain suits by an individual against a sovereign state. He was wrong again: it was not until the Eleventh Amendment a decade later that this became the case. As Martin observed, if the learned Hanson could not understand the proposed constitution, what chance had the average man?[27]

By March of 1788 six states had ratified the new constitution, the first being Delaware on 7 December 1787. Pennsylvania's early ratification, less than a week later, had been procured by fraudulent, if not criminal, means.[28] Gouverneur Morris's strategy of adjourning the convention so that Pennsylvania could call a ratifying convention before opposition to the constitution was well organized had succeeded, of course.[29] Accordingly, a few days after the convention adjourned, a

[26] *Maryland Journal,* 18, 21, and 28 March, 4 April 1788.

[27] Paul Leicester Ford, ed., *Pamphlets on the Constitution,* p. 217ff.; Steiner, "Maryland's Adoption of the Constitution," p. 22; Martin's "Reply to the Landholder," *Maryland Journal,* 28 March 1788, reprinted in Paul Leicester Ford, ed., *Essays on the Constitution of the United States,* pp. 372–73. Recent accounts of the writings and activities of the Antifederalists will be found in Morton Borden, ed., *The Antifederalist Papers;* Crowl, "Antifederalism in Maryland"; Cecelia M. Kenyon, ed., *The Antifederalists;* McDonald, *We, the People;* Jackson Turner Main, *The Antifederalists, Critics of the Constitution 1781–1788;* Robert Allen Rutland, *The Ordeal of the Constitution: The Antifederalists and the Ratification Struggle of 1787–1788.*

[28] See, generally, John Bach McMaster and Frederick D. Stone, *Pennsylvania and the Federal Constitution, 1787–1788, passim.*

[29] See Chapter 15, p. 132, above.

resolution was introduced in the Pennsylvania Assembly calling for such a convention. In order to delay the proceedings until the people had time to study the new constitution, its opponents absented themselves *en bloc* from the Assembly. Finding themselves without a quorum, citizens favoring the constitution kidnaped a number of members of the opposition, dragged them bodily into the Assembly, and kept them there by force until the resolution was passed.[30]

Ratification by New Jersey, Georgia, and Connecticut followed quickly. The opposition in Massachusetts, however, was more stubborn and almost succeeded.[31] The final vote for ratification was 187 to 168, and the Federalists won only by making two important concessions, one to principle, and one to practical politics: they agreed to recommend a list of amendments amounting to a bill of rights, and they bought Gov. John Hancock's support, and the critical block of votes which he controlled, with the promise that the Bowdoin faction would back him for re-election as governor and for the vice-presidency or even the presidency under the new government. Seduced by such allurements, Hancock's convenient gout, which had kept him absent from the debate, suddenly vanished, and he swung the balance in favor of ratification. The influence of this compromise was crucial: all the seven remaining states except Maryland formally appended similar bill-of-rights amendments as conditions of their ratifications.

One matter of the greatest significance remains a mystery to this day. As has been mentioned, at the Philadelphia convention, later in the Continental Congress, and then in public and private discussion throughout the country, men like Randolph, Mason, Gerry, and Richard Henry Lee made the reasonable suggestion that the draft constitution be debated in the different states, which could propose amendments (such as, but by no means limited to, a bill of rights) to be considered at a second constitutional convention. The Virginia act calling for its ratification convention provided for the expenses of sending delegates to such a second gathering and for discussion of proposed amendments with other state conventions.

On 27 December 1787 this act was sent to the governors of the other states to be submitted to their legislatures. Strangely enough, however, the copy sent to Governor Clinton of New York did not reach him until 7 March 1788. This delay saved the day for the Federalists. The Virginia enactment reached New York too late for the state legislature to act on it. The conclusion is inescapable that "had this action of Virginia been known in time, New York would have responded with an offer of co-operation, and a second general convention would have been inevitable."[32] (This was not the first nor last time that the Federalists

---

[30] McMaster and Stone, *Pennsylvania and the Constitution*, pp. 14–15, 212.
[31] See generally, Samuel Bannister Harding, *The Contest over the Ratification of the Federal Constitution in the State of Massachusetts, passim*.
[32] Edward P. Smith, "The Movement towards a Second Constitutional Convention in 1788," p. 61; *Documentary History of the Constitution*, 4:262, 5:62.

were accused of tampering with the mails and of slowing down or stopping the interstate movement of newspapers containing Anti-federalist intelligence.[33])

At the time of the Maryland elections, early in April, general sentiment throughout the state was strongly in support of the constitution.[34] There were many dissenters, and some violent opposition, however, largely confined to a few areas of the state. The entrenched conservative faction in Anne Arundel County, led by the powerful and wealthy Carrolls and Worthingtons, expected no difficulty in electing their slate, but only a few days before the election, the Antifederalists united under John Francis Mercer, Benjamin Harrison, Jeremiah Townley Chase, and Samuel Chase[35] (the last was hastily chosen to replace Governor Smallwood, who was out of the county and could not be reached in time). After a brief, whirlwind campaign, all four were elected over the Federalist ticket. In Baltimore County, the Antifederalist slate of Charles Ridgely, Charles Ridgely of William, Edward Cockey, and Nathan Cromwell won a decisive victory over a surprised Federalist group led by Gen. John Eager Howard, and Harford County elected not only a solid Antifederalist delegation but perhaps the most distinguished of any: a former governor and signer of the Declaration of Independence, William Paca; Attorney General Luther Martin; a former judge and Revolutionary patriot, John Love; and the young and brilliant William Pinkney (then a clerk in Samuel Chase's law office).[36]

In Baltimore, according to an apparently independent observer, "the election was the most irregular, disorderly, and riotous that ever happened in the town or State."[37] The General Assembly had ruled that all persons could vote who were male, over twenty-one years of age, were possessed of the property qualification of thirty pounds, and had lived in the state for one year. On this basis, there were about 1,050

[33] See, e.g., *Maryland Gazette* (Baltimore) for 8 and 22 April 1788; Wesley E. Rich, *History of the United States Post Office in the Year 1829*, pp. 65–66; Burnett, *Letters of Members of the Congress*, 8:716.

[34] In addition to Steiner, "Maryland's Adoption of the Constitution," see Crowl, *Maryland during and after the Revolution*, p. 111ff.; Crowl, "Antifederalism in Maryland," p. 446ff.; Delaplaine, *Thomas Johnson*, p. 426ff.; Max P. Allen, "William Pinkney's First Public Service," p. 277ff.; *Documentary History of the Constitution*, 4:597ff. *et passim*.

[35] The relationship between these two great jurists is as interesting as it is complicated: Samuel Chase's father, the Reverend Thomas Chase, and Jeremiah Townley Chase's grandfather, the Reverend Richard Chase, were brothers; Samuel and Jeremiah Townley also married sisters, Anne and Hester Baldwin; Samuel and Anne Chase's son, Thomas, married Jeremiah and Hester Townley's daughter, Mathilde (see F. A. Hill, *The Mystery Solved: Facts Relating to Lawrence-Townley-Townley-Chase Marriage and Estate Question*; Crowl, *Maryland during and after the Revolution*, p. 141).

[36] Four delegates were to be elected by each county, with an additional two from Baltimore City and two from Annapolis. There was no requirement that candidates live in the county or city from which they were elected; thus Samuel Chase, a resident of Baltimore, was elected from Anne Arundel, and Luther Martin of Baltimore and William Paca of Queen Anne's County were elected from Harford County.

[37] *Maryland Gazette* (Baltimore), 15 and 22 April 1788.

qualified voters on the assessment lists in Baltimore Town. Almost 700 who qualified did not vote in this election, yet well over 2,000 votes were counted. The Australian (secret) ballot was unknown, of course. The election officials usually opened the polls at a convenient time and place (customarily a tavern) for several days, and the citizens appeared and gave their votes orally. However, at this election the town commissioners, Federalist sympathizers who were also by law judges of elections, refused to take their oath of office as such, and decided to allow any free man over twenty-one, regardless of property or domicile, to vote. The Federalists flooded the polls with hundreds of foreigners, sailors, and other transients, subjects of Great Britain, Ireland, France, and Holland. On the third day of the election, a mob of Federalist thugs, armed with clubs, commandeered the polls and prevented many people, chiefly Germans and other Antifederalists, from voting. Moreover, during the four-day election the commissioners arbitrarily declared the polls open or closed whenever most convenient for Federalist voters and least so for Antifederalists. The total number of votes cast for Federalists McHenry and Coulter was 1920, for Antifederalists Sterrett and McMechen 765. It is evident that while the Federalists might have won an honest election in Baltimore, it would have been by a majority of only three to two, rather than the clearly fraudulent three to one.

Maryland's action was critical. The assent of nine states was required. Six states (Delaware, Pennsylvania, New Jersey, Georgia, Connecticut, and Massachusetts) had already approved. Two (Rhode Island and North Carolina) had postponed or refused ratifying conventions. The Federalists needed three of the remaining five, and the Antifederalists seemed to have the upper hand in New York, Virginia, and perhaps South Carolina as well. Rejection by Maryland would probably have doomed the draft constitution and compelled a second constitutional convention. As Madison wrote to Washington, "The difference between even a postponement and adoption in Maryland may, in the nice balance of parties here, possibly give a fatal advantage to that which opposes the constitution."[38]

The delegates met at Annapolis on 21 April, with such prominent Federalists as Thomas Johnson, Thomas Sim Lee, James McHenry, and Alexander Contee Hanson confronting the equally brilliant Antifederalists Paca, the two Chases, Mercer, Pinkney, and Martin. The Antifederalists had two objectives: to prolong the convention until Richard Henry Lee, George Mason, and Patrick Henry succeeded in defeating ratification by Virginia at its convention, which was to begin shortly;[39] and to recommend additions and amendments to the constitution so numerous and so drastic as to require, if not outright rejec-

[38] Letter of 10 April 1788, *Documentary History of the Constitution*, 4:575.
[39] McHenry to Washington, 20 April 1788, and Washington to Thomas Johnson, 20 April 1788, *ibid.*, p. 581.

tion, at least another convention. In view of the heavy Federalist majority in the convention (sixty-four to twelve), the Antifederalists were not optimistic as to their first goal but felt they had a fair chance, given free and open debate, of achieving the second.

On Monday, the first day, after electing a president, George Plater of St. Mary's County, and appointing a "committee on elections" (*i.e.*, credentials), the convention adjourned, there being fewer than fifty delegates present. On Tuesday the elections committee (composed of four Federalists and one Antifederalist) declared all members duly elected as reported, with the single objection that Baltimore's delegates, McHenry and Coulter, had been elected by fraudulent votes. On Wednesday the constitution was given its first reading. Immediately thereafter, as a result of a Federalist caucus, it was ruled that the convention should not "enter into any resolution upon any particular part of the proposed plan"; a second reading was called for, to be followed by full debate upon the draft as a whole—it was to be ratified or rejected *in toto*. It was also agreed to forego all debate in support of the constitution so that a decision might be reached promptly.[40]

Samuel Chase, Paca, and Martin arrived at Annapolis on Thursday and found their second objective blocked by this resolution. There were two reasons for their delinquent arrival: they had decided upon this delaying tactic in the knowledge that the convention would not proceed to a conclusion in their absence, and Martin was suffering from a severe sore throat and laryngitis, which prevented him from speaking.[41] Samuel Chase opened for the Antifederalists in a speech of some two and a half hours. The convention then adjourned for lunch. In the afternoon the greatly respected William Paca stated that he had "a variety of objections" to the constitution as drafted but that, with the addition of some amendments, which he would propose, he might be able to support it. However, as he had just arrived and was unprepared, he asked permission to address the assembly on Friday morning. Thomas Johnson, Maryland's beloved war governor and acknowledged representative of George Washington, conceded Paca's request to be "candid and reasonable," and the convention adjourned.

When Paca rose to proffer his amendments the next morning, he was immediately forestalled by objections from more than a dozen county and city delegations. Paca attempted to argue that his presentation had been agreed to on Thursday and that he was advancing his amendments not as preconditions for ratification but only as recommendations to the people for adoption following such approval. The Federalist leaders, however, had an overwhelming majority of the votes, and did not mean to see their power dissipated by amendments

[40] Hanson's "Narrative of the Proceedings in Our Late Convention," *ibid.*, p. 650.
[41] For Martin's laryngitis see William Smith in Baltimore to Otho H. Williams in New York, 28 April 1788, "Calendar of the General Otho Holland Williams Papers in the Maryland Historical Society," No. 401, pp. 150–51.

highly debatable at the least and, in many cases, both meritorious and popular. Accordingly, delegate after delegate rose to declare that Paca was out of order, that the question of whether to ratify the constitution as drafted or with amendments had been settled at the polls in favor of the draft, that they had been sent by their constituents to Annapolis to ratify the constitution as drafted, and that they had no authority to consider amendments.

These Federalists who had no difficulty in finding the "authority" to ignore the explicit restrictions placed by the Continental Congress upon the Philadelphia convention now represented themselves as so circumscribed by an unwritten mandate from their constituencies that they could not even discuss amendments for the later consideration of the people. This position is all the more remarkable in view of the fact that the General Assembly had refused to adopt the Senate resolution calling a convention for "assent and ratification" of the constitution and had instead, called for "a convention of the people for their full and free investigation and decision."[42]

With Paca's Antifederalist amendments out of the way, the convention proceeded with its debate on the constitution as presented. Its opponents set forth their arguments earnestly, soberly, and at length. The Federalists, however, "although repeatedly called on, and earnestly requested, to answer the objections, if not just, remained inflexibly silent."[43] They had the votes and participated in the debate only to call repeatedly for the putting of the question.

On Saturday afternoon, the Antifederalists gave up, and the vote was taken. The result was sixty-three for ratification to eleven against. At the last moment, Paca voted with the Federalists on the understanding that his proposed amendments would be given a hearing and a chance for adoption. As George Washington summed up the proceedings, "Mr. [Samuel] Chace [sic], it is said, made a display of all his eloquence—Mr. Mercer discharged his whole artillery of inflamable matter—and Mr. Marten [sic] I know not what—perhaps vehemence— but no converts were made—no, not one."[44]

After the vote, Paca arose and again proffered his amendments. They would not now be binding upon anyone, but he insisted on behalf of himself, his fellow Antifederalists, and their constituents that sooner or later the changes he proposed would have to be made if the liberties and the peace of the country were to be preserved. That even his opponents saw the force of his position is evidenced by the fact that the convention resolved, by a vote of sixty-six to seven, that a committee draw up over the weekend a list of possible alterations for consideration by the convention and, if approved, by the people of the state. The committee consisted of nine Federalists (headed by Judge

[42] See Steiner, "Maryland's Adoption of the Constitution."
[43] Antifederalist Manifesto, *Maryland Journal*, 29 April 1788.
[44] Letter to Madison, 2 May 1788, *Documentary History of the Constitution*, 4:607.

Hanson) and four Antifederalists (Paca, Samuel and J. T. Chase, and Mercer).

Although many federalist members of the convention sided with Thomas Johnson in believing that the recommendation of amendments in the nature of a bill of rights would dissolve the remaining popular opposition to the constitution, there was a small but determined group of Federalists who opposed any amendments, recommendatory or otherwise, as an admission of the weakness of the official Federalist position that the Constitution was perfectly satisfactory as drafted.

By Monday morning the committee had agreed upon thirteen amendments, most of them unanimously, and all by a great majority:

1. Limitation of powers of Congress to those expressly granted in the constitution [later adopted as the Tenth Amendment];

2.-3. Expanded application of the jury system [incorporated in part in the Fifth Amendment and by Federal statute];

4. Establishment of minimum amounts necessary to give lower federal courts jurisdiction in civil suits [now in effect by federal statute];

5. Establishment of concurrent state and federal jurisdiction in matters arising *ex delicto*;

6. Prohibition of federal jurisdiction by fiction or collusion [long since adjudicated and incorporated in federal statute];

7. Prohibition of acceptance of any position of profit by a federal judge during his judicial tenure;

8. Requirement that warrants for search and seizure be explicit and under oath [incorporated in the Fourth Amendment];

9. Limitation of military enlistments to four years during peacetime;

10. Quartering of soldiers in private homes during peacetime without the consent of the owner prohibited [incorporated in the Third Amendment];

11. Limitation of duration of any mutiny bill to four years;

12. Inviolability of the freedom of the press [the language of the Maryland state constitution, adopted in the First Amendment];

13. Limitation of imposition of martial law on the state militia to cases of war, invasion, or rebellion.

The committee voted down some fifteen other amendments, some of them (those assuring freedom of religion and recognition of conscientious objection to bearing arms and that making ineffective any treaty which abrogates a state constitution or bill of rights) of great importance. The majority proposed that the thirteen amendments agreed upon should be reported to the convention. The minority agreed and undertook to support the new government on condition that three of the fifteen rejected amendments also be reported out by the committee. These three provided that state militia not be used within the borders of an adjoining state, that Congress not interfere in the election of its members unless a state fails to act, and that a state may pay to the federal government direct taxes levied on its citizens in a lump sum.

At this point, Judge Hanson insisted that an explanation accompany these amendments emphasizing their unofficial nature. A majority of the committee objected to reporting out the amendments and the explanation proposed by Hanson. While this last-minute argument was going on, the delegates grew restless and several times called upon the committee to return and make its report. Finally, Governor Paca reported to the convention. He read the thirteen amendments accepted and the three rejected and explained that the minority did not insist upon a committee recommendation of the last three proposals, but only that they be placed before the whole body. The minority agreed, he said, to abide by the decision of the convention.

In view of this disagreement, however, a majority of the Federalists decided not to water down their ratification of the constitution by approving any amendments whatsoever. They moved a vote of thanks to the president and immediate adjournment. The last motion was adopted by a vote of forty-seven to twenty-seven. The fifteen delegates who joined with the Antifederalist twelve in opposing adjournment without action on the amendments included Thomas Johnson of Frederick County and fourteen others from nine counties. A certificate of ratification to be forwarded to the Congress was signed by the "virtuous sixty-three," and the convention dispersed.

The Antifederalists were convinced that they had been tricked by Hanson and the others. Even Federalist Thomas Johnson was disappointed. When McHenry complained to Washington that Johnson had allowed his principles to come before "the cause of federalism,"[45] Johnson told Washington, "I was not well pleased at the manner of our breaking up. I thought it to our discredit, and should be better pleased with the constitution with some alterations, but I am far from wishing all that were proposed to take place."[46]

Wild celebration followed immediately throughout the state. The Federalist delegates adjourned to George Mann's tavern for a banquet punctuated by thirteen toasts, each drunk to the booming of thirteen cannon. Following this repast, the wives were allowed to join their husbands in watching a fireworks display paid for by the assessment of a guinea from each convention delegate.[47] The celebration in Baltimore was even more spectacular and protracted. A parade, in which some three thousand persons participated, was described by the *Maryland Journal* as "the most interesting scene ever exhibited in this part of the

[45] Letter of 18 May 1788, *ibid.*, p. 618; cf. Daniel Carroll to Madison, 28 May 1788, *ibid.*, p. 635.
[46] Letter of 10 October 1788, in Steiner, *James McHenry*, pp. 112–13; *Documentary History of the Constitution*, 4:618.
[47] Daniel Carroll to James Madison, 28 April 1788, *Documentary History of the Constitution*, 4:598.

world."[48] The procession began at Philpott's Hill (from that day on known as Federal Hill) under the command of Capt. David Plunkett and Martin's former commanding officer, Capt. Nicholas Ruxton Moore. It marched to Fell's Point and from there through the main streets of the town. Each trade and profession had its banners and floats, which indicated their high hopes for the new government. "No importations, and we shall live," declared the silversmiths and watchmakers, while the blacksmiths' banners pointedly proclaimed that "while Industry prevails, we need no foreign nails." The most unusual float was the "Ship Federalist," fifteen feet long, mounted on wheels and drawn by horses, which was launched in the basin immediately after the celebration, and later sailed to Mt. Vernon and presented to General Washington.[49] The procession circled back to Federal Hill, where a sumptuous feast for four thousand people, arranged by William Goddard, editor of the *Maryland Journal*, and George Salmon, first president of the Bank of Baltimore, was set out on a table reported to be 3,600 feet in circumference. The celebration closed with the customary thirteen toasts accompanied by the usual cannonry.[50]

The twelve Antifederalists comprising the delegations from Anne Arundel, Baltimore, and Harford counties, lost no time in publishing a signed manifesto addressed to the people of Maryland, setting forth in circumstantial detail the proceedings of the ratifying convention and explaining how it happened that the proposed amendments, concurred in by such a large proportion of the delegates, had been neither officially approved nor reported to the electorate in the public press or elsewhere.[51] About a week later, an anonymous communicant (undoubtedly Hanson) announced that this minority address had contained some important misstatements and omissions which would shortly be remedied by the majority. Hanson's illness, the pressure of other business, and the indifference and dispersion of his fellow Federalists prevented the publication of this document. It may be seen in rough draft in the form in which he sent it to James Madison, among the latter's papers.[52] It represents a difference in emphasis and point of view more than a refutation of the facts put forth in the manifesto and, for the most part, confirms the charges of the minority.

Luther Martin's participation in the Maryland convention, while of necessity non-vocal because of his laryngitis, was nonetheless substantial. Despite the large majority of Federalist delegates, it was the Antifederalists who truly represented the people's demand for a bill

---

[48] 9 May 1788. See also John Thomas Scharf, *The Chronicles of Baltimore*, pp. 249–51.
[49] John Thomas Scharf, *History of Baltimore City and County*, p. 116; *Documentary History of the Constitution*, 4:691.
[50] *Maryland Journal*, 8 May 1788.
[51] *Maryland Journal*, 29 April 1788; *Maryland Gazette* (Annapolis), 1 May 1788; *Maryland Gazette* (Baltimore), 6 May 1788; reprinted in *Elliot's Debates*, 2:555–61.
[52] Vol. 15:125ff.; reprinted in *Documentary History of the Constitution*, 4:645ff.

of rights, a demand indicated by the fact that Maryland was the first state to ratify the first ten amendments (in December of 1790) and was the first state to communicate her ratification of them to Congress (in January 1791).

At the time, Luther Martin's part in the drafting and ratification of the constitution may have seemed more obstructive than otherwise. His prophecies of doom and disaster and of the political enslavement of the American people under the new constitution were wildly exaggerated, yet lest he be too readily dismissed as the political Cassandra of his time, the two outstanding attributes of that unhappy creature must be remembered: her prophecies were doomed to disbelief by her contemporaries, and they were doomed to come true. Time has shown him to have been accurate in recognizing many of the weaknesses and loopholes in the constitution as ratified, but his principal contribution was to block Madison's move toward a constitution of such extremely broad national powers that it would unquestionably have failed to be adopted, leaving the country under the Articles, in the very state which the Federalists professed to fear. Having done his best to explain to the citizens of Maryland his view of the issues before them, Martin took his defeat—as does every sound advocate—philosophically and without rancor. He resumed his private life and his neglected professional practice, and from 1788 on, his activities were almost entirely forensic.

Part II: 1788-1826

17

The Calvert Entail and
the British Debt Cases, 1788-1793

> In the cases here reported will appear names of Lawyers who have shed a lustre over the jurisprudence of Maryland.—Preface, 1 Harris and McHenry's Reports

> It is a cursed thing to pay debts—it has ruined many a man.—"Spendall"

Martin's private practice and his duties as attorney general had been laid aside for the Philadelphia and Annapolis conventions, and when he returned from the political wars, he found the accumulation of almost a year demanding his attention. As attorney general, much of his time was devoted to the routine prosecution of criminals on every conceivable variety of charge. Relatively few of these cases went up for hearing before an appellate court.[1] On the other hand, his civil practice was extremely diversified, as illustrated by those of his cases which are set out in the *Maryland Reports* for the period.[2] They are of interest not only as demonstrations of Martin's talents as a legal student and advocate but also as glimpses of the social and economic life of the time.

It must be remembered that until the revolutionary act of 1805,[3] which completely revised Maryland's judiciary system, the major part of all litigation in civil cases (other than that before magistrates) took place at Annapolis.[4] The General Court sat on the Eastern as well as the Western Shore, but the large part of its business came from the latter because of the greater population and commerce there. In addition, the Chancery Court and the Court of Appeals also sat in the State House at Annapolis, to which lawyers, parties, and witnesses all traveled for the hearing of their cases.

[1] However, for instances of such appeals, see State v. Hughes, 2 Harris and McHenry 479 (1790), and State v. Tibbs, 3 Harris and McHenry 83 (1791).
[2] Harris and McHenry, like most private reporters of the period, chose only the more important or interesting cases to report. However, in vol. 2 of their reports, which covers decisions of the General Court and the Court of Appeals from May 1780 to May 1790, of fifty-six cases reported at any length, Martin actively participated as counsel in twenty-three.
[3] Acts of Maryland, 1804, ch. 55, confirmed by Acts of Maryland, 1805, ch. 16.
[4] Bond, *The Court of Appeals of Maryland*, chap. 3, *passim*.

Roger Brooke Taney, when he was a young student reading law in the offices of Jeremiah Townley Chase, one of many great judges to sit on the General Court, has given us a picture of the practice of law in Annapolis shortly before the turn of the century:

This [General] Court had original jurisdiction in all civil cases, throughout the State of Maryland, where the matter in dispute exceeded £1 Maryland currency, ($2.66-⅔), and in criminal cases of the higher grade. It sat twice a year at Annapolis for the Western Shore, and twice at Easton for the Eastern Shore; and jurors from every county of the respective Shores were summoned to attend it. This Court was abolished in 1805, and courts sitting in the several counties substituted in its place. It may now, perhaps, at this day [1854], be a matter of surprise that it was continued so long; for it was exceedingly inconvenient to the suitors who resided in the distant counties to attend it, and the costs of bringing witnesses to Annapolis and Easton, and keeping them there sometimes for weeks together, was oppressive, and often ruinous to the parties. There were no railroads or steamboats at that time, and stages were almost in their infancy in Maryland; and such as had been established were as rough as a road-wagon, and found only between the principal towns, and running then only once or twice a week. Almost everybody came on horseback to Annapolis, except those coming from Baltimore.[5]

Most litigation was ended as well as begun in either the Chancery Court or the General Court, which heard cases in equity and common law, respectively. Despite the fact that relatively few cases were taken to the Court of Appeals, it is clear from Taney's account that, at least until the establishment of local county courts in 1805, there were few courts available to any but the well-to-do.

Martin's practice was quite different from that of the twentieth-century lawyer: he had very little litigation sounding in tort (none, in fact, for negligence), no tax practice, no divorce cases, and few cases involving sales or, indeed, contracts of any kind. Most suits concerned property: bills of exchange and promissory notes, the trial of the title to real estate (by ejectment or otherwise), or the construction of wills as to the disposition of real or personal property, the latter frequently consisting, in part, of slaves.[6] The field of property law was particularly difficult, abounding in the most abstruse and recondite principles and distinctions.[7] Moreover, this was before the days of comprehensive digests and texts like *Corpus Juris* and *American Jurisprudence*, which are now readily accessible to every lawyer. These modern working tools set

[5] Quoted in Samuel Tyler, *Memoir of Roger Brooke Taney, LL.D.*, p. 56ff. See also Chapter 7 above for a general description of the Maryland bench and bar at about this period.

[6] E.g., Reeder v. Cartwright, 2 Harris and McHenry 469 (1790).

[7] See, for example, Griffith v. Ridgely, 2 Harris and McHenry 275 (1790), in which is reported at great length the most learned and subtle argument by all counsel, including Martin, on the law pertaining to lineal warranties of real estate; Martindale v. Troop, 3 Harris and McHenry 244 (1793), concerning adverse possession as against tenants in fee tail; Partridge v. Colegate, 3 Harris and McHenry 339 (1793), on validity of grants of escheated lands.

out the rules of law and their exceptions, with tabulations of the precedents from every jurisdiction recognizing them, and the lawyer today can readily acquire the cases in point without the necessity of working out their underlying reasoning or philosophy. In Martin's day, Blackstone's *Commentaries* and *Coke on Littleton* were the most widely used and accepted texts. Their authority, however, was hardly regarded as "biblical," and their premises, explanatory history, and justifying policy were regularly subject to critical scrutiny.

One of Martin's first cases in the Court of Appeals after his return from the Annapolis ratifying convention was to sustain the annulment by the chancery court of a patent to a tract of land called "Roger's Inspection," alleged to have been procured fraudulently and contrary to the rules of the Land Office.[8] A number of his cases, however, involved much more than the usual "ejectment for Blackacre" and concerned matters of the highest local, national, and even international importance.

In the first group must be placed the famous litigation under the name of *Benedict Calvert's Lessee* v. *Sir Robert Eden et al.*[9] By way of background, it may be explained that from first to last there were six lords Baltimore, all in a direct line of descent and all bearing the surname Calvert, who were the founders and proprietors of colonial Maryland: George, first lord Baltimore; Cecilius, second lord Baltimore; then the first Charles, followed by Benedict; the second Charles; and Frederick, the sixth and last. As often happens, the later Calverts lived off the fame and fortune acquired by the earlier, and made little contribution of their own. The first lords Baltimore had divided large parts of the colony into huge plantations, called manors, generally let out for life or for years by their agents, with yearly rents payable to the proprietors and their heirs.[10] One of these was surveyed and laid out in 1669 and called Anne Arundel Manor after Cecilius Calvert's bride. It comprised some 12,600 acres—almost twenty square miles.

The fifth lord Baltimore had an illegitimate son, known variously as Benedict or Benjamin Calvert or Benedict Swingate.[11] In an effort to provide for him, in 1750 Charles willed this manor "to Benjamin Calvert, Esq., his heirs and assigns forever." The difficulty with this disposition or any other attempt to convey the fee simple title to any of the

---

[8] Smith and Purviance v. State, *ex rel.* Yates, 2 Harris and McHenry 244 (May Term 1788).

[9] General Court, May term, 1789, affirmed by the Court of Appeals in 1792, reported in 2 Harris and McHenry 279–376.

[10] C. P. Gould, *The Land System in Maryland, 1720–1765, passim*; Paul H. Giddens, "Land Policies and Administration in Colonial Maryland, 1753–1769," p. 16off.; James High, "A Facet of Sovereignty: The Proprietary Governor and the Maryland Charter," p. 67ff.

[11] This practice seems to have been not unusual among the Calverts: Cecilius Calvert, brother of the fifth lord Baltimore, also had a natural son (see 2 Harris and McHenry, pp. 350–51). Frederick, sixth and last lord Baltimore, had at least two: the famous Henry Harford, son of Hester Wheland, and a daughter by the same mistress.

Calverts' Maryland property was that it was entailed: by the terms of the controlling deeds and wills, it could not be granted outright in fee simple but could pass only to direct, legitimate descendants ("heirs of the body"). The owner could neither sell nor will the property outright to anyone. In order to avoid this restriction, his legitimate son, Frederick, tried in numerous ways to divest the property of the entail (*i.e.*, to "bar" or "dock" it) so that he might acquire the entire title in the lands and dispose of the fee of them as he pleased. Accordingly, in 1753 he applied to Parliament for such relief by statute, but it was refused. In 1761 he executed a series of conveyances (known as "lease and release") for the same purpose, but apparently had so little faith in their efficacy that he never recorded them in Maryland, as was required.

In 1765, in order to prevent the devolution of Maryland lands to collateral relations, especially to his illegitimate half-brother, and to acquire liquid assets, Frederick Calvert, through his lieutenant governor, Horatio Sharpe, put up for sale some 28,500 acres; shortly thereafter, he offered more than 100,000 additional acres.[12] Two years later, through his counsel in Maryland (which, in all his life, he never visited), Lord Baltimore went through a fictitious but well-recognized form of law suit known as a common recovery.[13] On the strength of such proceedings, which in England would unquestionably have disposed of the entailment and given Frederick the entire title, Anne Arundel Manor was advertised for sale in the *Maryland Gazette*. Some sixty-odd purchasers, one of whom was Sir Robert Eden, bought tracts of various size. To satisfy the buyers' doubts with regard to his fee title (because of his father's devise of the manor to Benedict Calvert) and to render the tract more marketable, Frederick instructed Governor Sharpe to "incert in grants thereof . . . proper engagements and stipulations in our name and behalf . . . to warrant the titles of the lands to be so granted against the said Benedict Calvert" and all persons claiming under him.[14]

In order to settle the title to this great tract, Benedict Calvert brought an action of ejectment in the General Court at the September term, 1772, against the purchasers. The original docket entries, still extant,[15] show that the case was filed in the name of a fictitious "Isaac Lackland," alleged lessee of Benedict Calvert. William Cooke and Thomas Jenings appeared for the plaintiff, and Samuel Chase, Luther Martin,

[12] See "A State of the Sales of His Lordship Manours," Maryland Historical Society, f. 3, State Archives, Hall of Records, Annapolis.

[13] Four years later Frederick died and in his will left the greater part of Maryland to his illegitimate son, Henry Harford. The ensuing lawsuit between Harford and Frederick's elder sister, Louisa Calvert Browning (who by her father's will was left the proprietorship of Maryland in case of Frederick's death without legitimate issue) was rendered moot by the Revolution. It was ultimately decided that the State of Maryland had succeeded to the rights of the proprietor after 4 July 1776 by the Act of Confiscation of 1780, ch. 45.

[14] John Kilty, *The Land-Holder's Assistant and Land-Office Guide*, pp. 243–44.

[15] At the Hall of Records, Annapolis. The case itself is reported in 2 Harris and McHenry 279ff.

and Jeremiah Townley Chase for the defendants. A special verdict setting out all the findings of relevant facts was returned by the jury in 1774. Because of the Revolutionary War, however, the case was not argued in the General Court until the May term of 1789.

Cooke, a native of Prince George's County, had studied law at the Inner Temple in London. After returning to this country, he acquired a substantial practice in Annapolis and became counsel for the crown. With the Revolution, he steadfastly maintained his loyalty to the king and retired to his Prince George's County estate, where he sat out the war.[16] Jenings, as able a lawyer as Cooke, was apparently somewhat less firm in his loyalty to the crown: he aided in drafting a petition to King George III opposing the tax on tea. He was attorney general for the lord proprietor from 1773 to 1776, and it was when he declined the post of attorney general for the new state of Maryland that it was offered to Martin, early in 1778.[17] Later in that year, however, he took the oath of allegiance and became a member of the state Senate. Until his death in 1796, he appeared in most of the important cases before the appellate courts of Maryland.[18]

The argument before Judge Alexander Contee Hanson in the general court, though long and learned, is of only antiquarian interest today. Two major problems were presented: the title of Benedict (or Benjamin) Calvert under his father's will, and the title of Frederick Calvert's grantees, which, in turn, depended upon the efficacy of Frederick's efforts to dock the entail and to acquire the fee simple title to his lands. Cooke and Jenings apparently argued at much greater length for the plaintiff than did Martin and Chase for the defendant. The former were able to convince Judge Hanson first, that on the death of Frederick Calvert without legitimate issue the manor reverted to Charles Calvert, and second, that the latter's devise of this reverter to his illegitimate son Benedict was perfectly effectual *unless* Frederick had been able to bar such reverter by legally ridding the manor of its entailment and thereby acquiring the fee. On this latter point, plaintiff's counsel argued that Lord Baltimore could not effectually suffer a recovery in his own courts because they were staffed with his own appointees as judges and officers. Martin and Chase satisfied Judge Hanson, however, that it had long been settled that a lord Baltimore might sue in his own courts: "if it be not absurd for him to be a plaintiff in his own Courts, it is not absurd for him to be defendant."[19]

Despite the legal learning on both sides, Judge Hanson concluded: "The case before the Court, I apprehend to be far more important on

---

[16] John Bassett Moore, *International Adjudications. Modern Series*, vol. 3, *Arbitration of Claims for Losses and Damages Resulting from Lawful Impediments to the Recovery of Pre-War Debts*, pp. 182–83 (from data supplied Moore by Chief Judge Carroll T. Bond of the Court of Appeals of Maryland).

[17] See Chapter 6 above.

[18] Moore, *Arbitration of Claims*, p. 182.

[19] 2 Harris and McHenry, p. 339.

account of the value of the thing in contest, than difficult of decision."[20] His judgment for Martin's clients (including costs against the plaintiff in "the sum of Fifteen thousand six hundred and ninety one pounds and two fifths of a pound of tobacco") was upheld by the Court of Appeals three years later. This case was the subject of extensive comment by such respected experts on real estate law on both sides of the Atlantic as Daniel Dulany, Francis Hargrave, and John Hall.[21] They all supported the claims of Benjamin Calvert, but the court's decision in favor of Lord Baltimore's purchasers prevailed.

One of the earliest state cases in the country to present a question under the new federal constitution, and certainly the first in Maryland, was *State of Maryland* v. *Sluby*,[22] argued in the General Court in the May term of 1790. The *Baltic Merchant* had put into the port of Baltimore with a cargo of merchandise, only to be confronted with a bill from the State of Maryland for duties in the amount of £352 0s. 8d.[23] Bond was posted for the duties imposed so that the cargo could be landed and disposed of while the litigation took its leisurely course.

Philip Barton Key[24] and Richard Potts argued for the importer that, however valid when enacted, the Maryland statutes imposing the duties were clearly contrary to the provisions of the new federal constitution, and hence inoperative. They maintained that exclusive power to tax imports, in any amount or for any purpose, was given by art. I, sec. 8, to the national Congress.[25] In reply, Martin and Samuel Chase argued that the motive behind these restrictions on state power was to outlaw discrimination among the ports of the country and to "prevent any favorite port from being erected." Since only foreign commerce was involved here, the provision did not apply. Moreover, they pointed out that the wording, "no State *shall*, without the Consent of Congress, lay any Imposts or Duties on Imports," must apply to the enactment of

[20] *Ibid.*, p. 340.
[21] *Ibid.*, pp. 341–76.
[22] *Ibid.*, p. 480.
[23] Pursuant to the Maryland Acts of Assembly of 1784, ch. 84, and of 1785, ch. 76. These were state tariff acts imposing duties on specific items such as wines, tea, sugar, etc., and a flat ad valorem duty on most other items. Duties were also laid on exports, effective until 1 May 1806. In State v. Maxwell, argued before the General Court at Easton on 6 May 1789, Martin maintained that the duties imposed by the former laws applied to imports by land as well as by water. A divided court held, however, that the law imposed duties on the latter only (see *The Maryland Herald & Eastern Shore Intelligencer* for 21 September 1790, p. [2], col. 3).
[24] For Key, see p. 42, n. 7, above.
[25] Art. I, sec. 8, empowers Congress "to lay and collect Taxes, Duties, Imposts, and Excises" with the proviso that "all Duties, Imposts, and Excises shall be uniform throughout the United States" (par. 1); and "to regulate Commerce with foreign nations, and among the several States" (par. 3). Cf. also sec. 10: "No State shall, without the Consent of Congress, lay any Imposts or Duties on Imports or Exports, except what may be absolutely necessary for executing it's [sic] inspection laws; and the net Produce of all Duties and Imposts, laid by any State on Imports or Exports, shall be for the Use of the Treasury of the United States; and all such Laws shall be subject to the Revision and Control of the Congress" (par. 2); "No State shall, without the Consent of Congress, lay any Duty on Tonnage" (par. 3).

future laws and that all state laws "laying duties antecedent to the Constitution of the United States, remained in force until Congress laid duties." They further urged that, in any event, the duties were sustainable under sec. 10(2) as in aid of Maryland's inspection laws.[26] The General Court sustained the state, and the Court of Appeals affirmed, in due course, some two years later.

This case is interesting on several counts. It shows that our federal system of national government was not created "full blown" as we now have it, but developed, and at times erratically. The case could not, of course, stand up as the country's commerce increased, and it was overruled in 1827 by *Brown* v. *Maryland*.[27] Of paramount interest is the attitude of counsel on both sides toward the question of a conflict between a state law and the federal constitution. It was natural for Key and Potts to argue that in such a situation the state law must fall, but it is significant that Martin and Chase also agreed that "all acts inconsistent with the Constitution are null and void. . . . No state can pass a law contrary to this provision of the Constitution."[28] They won by convincing the court that the constitution had no bearing on their case. Martin, as the draftsman of the basic "supremacy clause," was too sound a lawyer and too honest an advocate to argue (as Jefferson and others later found it politically expedient to do[29]) that the states could at their pleasure disregard provisions of the federal constitution applicable to the nation as a whole.

Other litigation raising the issue of federal supremacy, this time in the area of treaties and international law and involving private liability for large amounts of money, soon presented itself. At the outbreak of the American Revolution, thousands of colonists found themselves in debt to British creditors.[30] This situation was particularly critical in such colonies as Maryland and Virginia, whose economy was based on tobacco. Planters there had become accustomed to luxurious living, to pay for which their crops were sold long before they were harvested.[31] Except for the scale of their indebtedness, most large planters of this

---

[26] 2 Harris and McHenry, p. 481, does not mention Chase's first name. However, on 16 June 1790 Martin wrote to Governor Howard setting forth the reasons for his retaining Samuel Chase to argue the case on behalf of the state with him and asking the Governor and his council to make satisfactory remuneration to Samuel Chase for such services (Charles F. Gunther Memorial Collection, Chicago Historical Society, Chicago, Ill.).

[27] Brown vs. Maryland, 12 Wheat. 419.

[28] 2 Harris and McHenry, p. 481. They also conceded that "if the constitution admits of any construction necessarily repugnant to the laws of the state, it is a repeal of them."

[29] Cf. Jefferson's acknowledgment, in this period, of the supremacy of the federal constitution over conflicting state laws (given in Chapter 13, p. 117, above).

[30] The best coverage of the treaties, statutes, and cases involved will be found in Moore, *Arbitration of Claims, passim.*

[31] An excellent survey of this problem in Maryland is contained in Crowl, *Maryland during and after the Revolution,* chap. 3 *passim.* For descriptions of the extravagant living habits of Maryland planters, see William Eddis, *Letters from America, Historical and Descriptive,* pp. 22ff., 27ff., 112ff., *et passim.*

period found themselves, like sharecroppers of a later day, hopelessly and endlessly indebted to, and, for all practical purposes, working for, their British creditors.[32] Many historians have gone so far as to conclude that no small part of the enthusiasm for the independence movement was motivated by the desire of colonial debtors to rid themselves of their obligations.[33]

Apparently, it was Thomas Paine who first suggested in print that the Revolution could be financed by confiscating the property of the Loyalists.[34] As early as 24 June 1776 the Continental Congress declared such property subject to seizure, and the following year it urged the states to confiscate and sell both the real and personal property of the Tories and to invest the proceeds in Continental loan office certificates.[35] But laws to confiscate property—even that of the enemy—were anathema to Maryland's plutocratic state Senate. The House of Delegates passed such measures in 1779 and again in 1780, only to have them rejected by the upper house. At the October session of 1780 the Senate was finally forced (by circumstances not here relevant) to accede to such legislation.[36] With regard to debts owed to British nationals and sympathizers, the General Assembly provided that a debtor could discharge his debt to any creditor who was not a citizen of Maryland or of the United States by paying it into the state treasury on or before 20 March 1781 in depreciated bills of credit at the rate of forty to one. Such a payment was thereby "deemed in law a payment of such creditor or his assignee, and the treasurer's receipt shall be good evidence in the courts of law and equity."[37]

In Maryland the total amount of indebtedness to British creditors was something over five hundred thousand pounds; in Virginia, rather more than four times that amount.[38] Over one-fourth of the Maryland debt[39] was paid off by some sixty-six debtors, in accordance with the act of 1780, through the deposit of Continental bills of credit and other depreciated currency actually worth only a little over £3,600 sterling. When the treaty which closed the Revolutionary War was drawn, however, it contained (largely through the insistence of John Adams[40]) the provision that "creditors on either side shall meet with no lawful im-

[32] See Gray, *History of Agriculture in the Southern United States to 1860*, vol. 1, chap. 17; Charles A. Barker, *The Background of the Revolution in Maryland*, pp. 84ff.

[33] See, e.g., Jensen, *The Articles of Confederation*, pp. 20–28; A. M. Schlesinger, *The Colonial Merchants and the American Revolution, 1763–1776*, pp. 32–39, 134ff., 359–60.

[34] On this subject, see, generally, James Truslow Adams, *Dictionary of American History*, s.v. "Confiscation of Property."

[35] Worthington Chauncey Ford, ed., *Journals of the Continental Congress*, 5:475; *ibid.*, 27 November 1777, 9:971.

[36] Kilty, *Laws*, Oct. Sess., 1780, ch. 45.

[37] *Ibid.*, ch. 5, par. 11.

[38] See Samuel Flagg Bemis, *Jay's Treaty, a Study in Commerce and Diplomacy*, p. 103n; Isaac Harrell, *Loyalism in Virginia*, pp. 26ff.

[39] £144,574 9s. 4½d. See *Maryland Journal* for 11 April 1783. In Virginia about £274,000 of such debts were similarly "paid off." See also *Votes and Proceedings*, Nov. Sess., 1785, 6 March 1786.

[40] Moore, *Arbitration of Claims*, p. 11.

pediment to the recovery of the full value in sterling money, of all *bona fide* debts heretofore contracted."[41] This treaty of peace was ratified by the Continental Congress on 14 January 1784 and was given additional recognition by the subsequent inclusion in the new constitution of the "supremacy clause," the substance of which was, as we have seen, drafted by Luther Martin.[42]

For several years the collection of the debts due British creditors followed an uncertain and hectic course.[43] The Maryland courts in numerous cases recognized the validity and collectability of such debts as did not involve a claim of payment and discharge under the act of 1780.[44] Some two dozen cases invoking this law, tried in the General Court for the Western Shore in its October 1790 term, tested its effect in the light of the subsequent treaty. Two of these, taken up as test cases for the entire group to higher appellate courts, were *Dulany* v. *Wells*[45] and *Clerke* v. *Harwood*.[46]

In the former, the plaintiff, represented by William Cooke, brought an action as administrator of one Thomas Bladen, a British national, to recover on bonds in the amount of £468 11s. 3d., executed on 1 April 1775 by the defendant Wells, with one William Goodwin as surety. Wells pleaded, through his counsel, Martin, that in 1781 Goodwin paid Thomas Harwood, the treasurer of the Western Shore, £11 14s. 4d. in full discharge of the indebtedness under the act of 1780 and exhibited the treasurer's receipt as proof. The argument of counsel before the General Court has not been preserved, but it was doubtless the same as that made later before the Court of Appeals.[47] The General Court, doubtless relying upon the supremacy clause of the Constitution, ruled for the plaintiff, whereupon the defendant promptly appealed to the Court of Appeals.

The argument in the Court of Appeals was thorough, learned, and ingenious.[48] Cooke, citing the standard treatises on government and international law (Grotius, Rutherford, Vattel, Bynkershoek, etc.),

---

[41] *Ibid.*, p. 3.

[42] Art. VI, clause 2. See Chapter 13 above.

[43] See Crowl, *Maryland during and after the Revolution*, pp. 69ff., *passim*.

[44] The United States Supreme Court sustained the efficacy of the treaty to effect the collection of such debts in Georgia v. Brailsford, 2 Dall. 402, 415 (1792); 3 Dall. 1 (1794).

[45] 3 Harris and McHenry 20 (1790). The original entry appears in Docket, Western Shore, October Term, 1788, f. 121, Hall of Records, Annapolis, Md. In the margin appear the initials of counsel: for the plaintiff, W. C. (William Cooke); for the defendant, S. C. (Samuel Chase), L. M. (Luther Martin), R. R. (Richard Ridgely), and D. M. (David McMechen).

[46] Not reported in *Maryland Reports*, but its decision in the United States Supreme Court in 1797 is reported at 3 Dall. 342.

[47] 3 Harris and McHenry, pp. 23–82.

[48] *Ibid.*, p. 23ff. Oddly enough, the report begins with the argument of the three lawyers for the appellee: William Cooke, Philip Barton Key, and Thomas Jenings. Martin, the sole lawyer for the debtor-appellant, apparently wrote out the summary of his argument, which Harris and McHenry printed in their report of the case (*ibid.*, p. 78; see n. 53 below).

maintained at length that the debt had been neither confiscated nor extinguished independent of the state law; that it was neither extinguished nor confiscated by the act of 1780, chap. 5; and that, even if it had been, the treaty was the supreme law of the land and revived the debt. He insisted that the statute merely made the payment to the state an "impediment" to its recovery which the treaty removed, and cited the recent case of *Georgia* v. *Brailsford*[49] as a holding by the United States Supreme Court that an alien creditor had a right, at the termination of war, to sue upon a debt sequestered but not confiscated by a state.

Key's argument was based upon the "state of nature" (a mythical concept as popular then as always) supposed to exist among the citizens of a state upon the secession of part from the whole. He urged that if a state of war worked a confiscation of debts, "millions would have been beggared on such principles in the frequent wars between England, France, Spain and Holland in this century."[50] Jenings closed for the creditor with an able exposition of the effect of the supremacy clause upon the rights and duties of the creditor, the debtor, and the state.

Martin's argument was characteristically vigorous and all-inclusive: he maintained that under accepted international law the debts owed to an enemy alien were as subject to confiscation by belligerent states as his physical property. Discussing the effect of the treaty, he maintained that, even if it were conceded to be the supreme law of the land, it could apply only to the future. To use it to annul rights legally acquired before the adoption of the constitution and the ratification of the treaty would be most unjust and iniquitous. In any event, Martin continued, the debt in question did not come within the purview of art. IV of the treaty but only within art. V, by which Congress was required to "earnestly recommend to the legislatures of the several States to provide for the restitution of all estates, rights, and properties which have been confiscated." This clause was, of course, at most only precatory. He insisted that the binding provisions of art. IV should not be made retroactive unless clearly and necessarily so intended. Martin's argument would not render art. IV nugatory, since it could readily and reasonably be used to require payment of unsatisfied and unconfiscated debts in sterling rather than in paper money. Martin went on to disavow any controlling effect of the then unreported decision in *Brailsford* v. *Georgia*, stating that he had been advised by Mr. Justice James Iredell that the debtors in the case had never paid the debt into the state treasury and that Georgia had enacted no law prior to the treaty confiscating or extinguishing the debt.

At the June term of 1795 the Court of Appeals reversed the judgment of the General Court in this and all similar pending cases, holding good and valid all payments made under the act of 1780. From this determi-

49 See n. 44 above.
50 Moore, *Arbitration of Claims*, p. 185.

nation several Maryland cases were carried to the United States Supreme Court, among them *Court & Co.* v. *Vanbibber*[51] and *Clerke* v. *Harwood.*[52] That tribunal, in the test case from Virginia, *Ware* v. *Hylton,*[53] had sweepingly declared that art. IV of the treaty superseded all state laws and required payment of all valid, subsisting indebtedness to British creditors.

The argument in *Ware* v. *Hylton* is of interest in many respects: it was argued for the debtors by John Marshall and Alexander Campbell. This was Marshall's only appearance as an advocate before the great tribunal over which he later presided for more than thirty years. It is curious that neither Marshall nor Campbell used Martin's argument that the treaty should be given only a prospective construction and application, and the abandonment of this point may have cost the debtors their case. It would have given the Court an opportunity to give effect to both the treaty and the laws attacked. With this exception, the arguments follow Martin's so closely in propositions, details, and authorities cited that the conclusion is inescapable that they had a written outline (or other detailed notes) of Martin's successful argument before the Maryland Court of Appeals.[54] The Supreme Court decision in *Ware* v. *Hylton* would have had far greater political and economic repercussions but for the fact that, as one result of the postwar diplomatic negotiations with Great Britain, the United States a few years later made a lump-sum payment of £600,000 (or some $2,660,-000) to satisfy British creditors for prewar private debts.[55]

---

[51] 3 Harris and McHenry 140, reversed 3 Dall. 199, 342.
[52] See n. 46 above.
[53] 3 Dall. 199 (1796).
[54] Cf. 3 Dall., pp. 210ff., with 3 Harris and McHenry, pp. 64ff.; cf. Moore, *Arbitration of Claims*, pp. 189ff., 202ff.
[55] Samuel Flagg Bemis, *A Diplomatic History of the United States*, p. 103; Thomas A. Bailey, *A Diplomatic History of the American People*, p. 77; Richard B. Morris, *John Jay, The Nation, and the Court*, pp. 73ff.

18

Slave's Counsel and
Supreme Court Advocate, 1794-1796

> It is noteworthy that throughout the eighteenth cen-
> tury, and somewhat beyond, negroes petitioning to be
> declared free commanded the services of some of the best
> lawyers at the bar for their cases, and received the fullest
> measure of care and consideration from the courts.—
> Carroll T. Bond, *The Court of Appeals of Maryland*

> America held no barrister to stand against this "Ther-
> sites of the Law," this "Federal Bulldog," this "Lawyer
> Brandy Bottle," whose attributes exhausted the epithets
> of friend and foe.—Holmes Alexander, *Aaron Burr, the
> Proud Pretender*

At about this time an antislavery society was organized in Baltimore
under the name "The Maryland Society for Promoting the Abolition of
Slavery and the Relief of Free Negroes and Others unlawfully held in
Bondage." This was the first such society in Maryland, the fourth in the
United States, and the sixth in the world.[1] Philip Rogers was elected its
first president, and among other officers elected were "honorary-
counsellors Samuel Chase and Luther Martin." Both Martin and Chase
at this time owned slaves as domestic servants, and it is interesting to
note that art. XII of the society's constitution forbade membership to
slaveowners but authorized the appointment of "persons of legal
knowledge, owners of slaves, as honorary-counsellors." Before long the

---

[1] It was organized on 8 September 1789. See William Frederick Poole, *Anti-
Slavery Opinions before the Year 1800*, pp. 47ff. *et passim*; Thomas W. Griffith, *Sketches of
the Early History of Maryland*, pp. 127–28. Its constitution was published as a pamphlet by William Goddard and James Angell in Baltimore in the same year.
Similar societies were organized elsewhere in the area at about the same time: in
Dover, Delaware, 3 June 1778 (*Baltimore Maryland Gazette*, 18 July 1788); in Caroline County, Maryland (*The Maryland Herald & Eastern Shore Intelligencer*, 14 December 1790); in Chestertown, Maryland, some time before 23 April 1793 (*Apollo or
Chestertown Spy*, 3 May 1810). Cf. *Minutes of the Proceedings of a Convention of Delegates
from the Abolition Societies Established in Different Parts of the United States* (Philadelphia:
Zachariah Poulson, 1794–1801).

society was investigated and censured by a committee of the General Assembly for its active prosecution of petitions for freedom.[2] It thereafter confined itself, outwardly at least, to helping and educating free Negroes, to assisting individual slaves to establish their right to freedom, and to petitions and testimonials to the General Assembly in support of legislative amelioration of the more inhumane aspects of slavery.[3]

Naturally, many of Martin's cases involved slaves or the institution of slavery in one way or another. Under the law of slavery, the owner's advantages were so numerous and powerful as to render futile litigation on the part of a slave.[4] Because a slave was himself property, like a horse or a cow, he could not own any property nor make any legal contract, not even one of marriage. Slaves had no rights as spouse, parent, or child. They had no rights to wages or to the product of their labor. Their food, clothing, and shelter was provided at the pleasure of the owner. If a slave offended his master, the latter could inflict any punishment—even death if he wished.[5] A slave had no civil rights, and could testify in court only against another slave, certainly not against his owner. Moreover, all Negroes were presumed to be slaves, and subject to all the slave's legal handicaps until either descent from a free ancestor or manumission according to law was proved. For many years, in many states, including Maryland, a slave could be kept in bondage contrary to the wishes of his master because of laws making a slave-owner's manumission by deed, will, or other order during his last illness illegal and void.[6]

As attorney general, Martin prosecuted many Negroes for violations of the criminal law. Few of these cases were appealed and still fewer re-

[2] *Report of the Committee of Grievances*; Jeffrey R. Brackett, *The Negro in Maryland*, p. 152.
[3] Brackett, *The Negro in Maryland*, p. 52.
[4] See, generally, William Goodell, *The American Slave Code in Theory and Practice: Its Distinctive Features Shown by Its Statutes, Judicial Decisions, and Illustrative Facts, passim*; J. C. Hurd, *The Law of Freedom and Bondage in the United States, passim*; *Minutes of Proceedings*, 1797, pp. 52ff.
[5] The widespread inhumanity, cruelty, and brutality of slaveowners is one of the best-kept secrets of American history. There were many scores of insurrections and, of course, thousands of escapes and attempted escapes by individuals and groups. See, e.g., Herbert Aptheker, *American Negro Slave Revolts, passim*; William S. Drewry, *Slave Insurrections in Virginia (1830–1865), passim*; Helen Honor Catterall, *Judicial Cases concerning American Slavery and the Negro, passim*; Henrietta Buckmaster, *Let My People Go*, pp. 11–13, 20–23, 39–41, 52–55, 84, 101–2, 191, 195–97, 239, 278; J. C. Furnas, *The Road to Harpers Ferry*, pp. 222–30; Kenneth M. Stampp, *The Peculiar Institution: Slavery in the Ante-Bellum South*, pp. 132–40; William Still, *The Underground Railroad, passim*. For Maryland in particular, see Brackett, *The Negro in Maryland*, pp. 72ff., 78ff., 91ff., 112ff., 117ff., 130ff., 140ff.; [Anon.], *The Suppressed Book about Slavery, passim*, esp. pp. 187ff.
[6] Act of 1752, ch. 1, sec. 3, repealed by Act of 1790, ch. 9. See also Acts of 1796, ch. 57, sec. 13; *Speech of William Pinkney, Esq. in the House of Delegates of Maryland, at their Session in November, 1789* (Philadelphia: Joseph Crukshank, 1790); House of Delegates, State of Maryland, *Journal*, 1789, pp. 9–14; Brackett, *The Negro in Maryland*, pp. 51–52, 57; *Federal Gazette* (Baltimore), 24 April 1797, p. 3, col. 4.

ported.[7] The civil suits in this field were largely of two kinds, those involving slaves as property and as the subject of ownership and transfer of title,[8] and those involving petitions for freedom, in which the right of one person to keep another as his slave was contested. Of the first group, *Fishwick* v. *Sewell* is typical.[9] This was an action to recover the value of certain Negro slaves and a spinet, brought by Martin and Francis Scott Key for the plaintiffs. The defendants were represented by William Pinkney and William Magruder. In her will one Ann Lookerman had made an unusual bequest, "to her niece, Jane Fishwick, the child her negro wench Dido went with, be it boy or girl, to her and her heirs forever." The child was a girl and was named Dinah. The case turned on the validity of a transfer of title made by Jane while she was a minor.

An exciting case was *Mason* v. *Ship Blaireau*,[10] to determine the amounts of money to be awarded a crew who had saved the ship *Le Blaireau* in a daring, difficult, and desperate salvage operation. Even as recounted in the staid and sober opinions of District Judge Winchester, Circuit Judge Samuel Chase, and Chief Justice Marshall, it makes stirring reading. The *Blaireau*, on a voyage from Martinique to Bordeaux laden with a cargo of sugar, was run down by the Spanish sixty-four-gun ship, *St. Julien*. The latter, having more pressing business elsewhere, took off all the *Blaireau's* crew except a stubborn Irishman named Toole and abandoned the derelict to her fate. Another ship, the *Firm*, came to the rescue, however, and put a salvage crew of five men and an apprentice boy aboard. They shifted the cargo, patched the crushed bow with sheets of leather and lead, kept the pumps manned, and sailed the *Blaireau* three thousand miles to Baltimore.

According to several experienced sea captains, it was a "service of great risk and peril, and nearly desperate, and such as they would not have undertaken."[11] One of the salvage crew, which was represented by Martin, was Negro Tom, a slave of a Reverend Mr. Ireland, a former resident of Maryland then living in England. Tom's share, almost a thousand dollars, was retained for the account of his owner as a matter of course. The latter, however, instructed his attorneys to manumit the slave according to the Maryland law and to have him given one-fifth of the salvage award.

---

[7] But see, e.g., *Negro Peter* v. *State*, 4 Harris and McHenry 3 (1797), on the sufficiency of an indictment "that negro Peter . . . one game cock of the value of fifty pounds of tobacco . . . feloniously did steal, take, and carry away." Peter was convicted, and the Frederick County court sentenced him to be whipped on his bare back with ten stripes and to stand in the pillory for five minutes, but the general court reversed the judgment. See also *State* v. *Negro Ben*, 1 Harris and Johnson 99 (1800).

[8] See also *Mulatto Joan* v. *Shields*, 3 Harris and McHenry 7 (1793); *Somerval* v. *Hunt*, 3 Harris and McHenry 113 (1792); *Claggett* v. *Speake*, 4 Harris and McHenry 162 (1798); *Berry's Lessee* v. *Berry*, 1 Harris and Johnson 417 (1803); *Scrivener* v. *Scrivener*, 1 Harris and Johnson 743 (1805).

[9] 5 Harris and Johnson 393 (1818).

[10] 2 Cranch (U.S.) 240 (1804).

[11] *Ibid.*

As for the second type of cases involving slaves, the Maryland statutes authorized a "petition for freedom," whereby one held as a slave might challenge his master's right so to do.[12] Counsel for the petitioner usually acted without a fee (unless one was paid by an antislavery society or a group of Friends) and was further required to pay all the costs of the suit unless the court decided that there was probable cause for bringing the action.[13] It is one of the glories of the Maryland bar that, despite the lack of recompense, the time and labor expended, and the unpopularity of such litigation among "better class" citizens, Negro petitioners rarely failed to recover their legal rights for lack of professional help.[14]

On some such occasions Martin represented the master who asserted title to a Negro;[15] in others he appeared for the slave, as, for example, in *Negro Cato* v. *Howard*.[16] There the petitioner showed that in January 1793 Nathan Harris had sold Cato to Jesse Harris for sixty-five pounds, for a period of seven years. At the end of that time (or sooner, if Jesse so wished), Cato was to be manumitted. Six years later, however, Nathan repossessed Cato and sold him to a third person, one Howard. Hearing this, Jesse made out and had properly recorded formal manumission papers, and Cato brought his petition, Martin appearing for him. The Montgomery County Court ruled against Cato, though upon what grounds it is difficult to see. Martin appealed to the Court of Appeals, which reversed the lower court and ordered Cato set free.

At the insistence of the governor and council of Maryland, Martin went to Philadelphia to attend the United States Supreme Court early in February 1791.[17] The Court had met twice before, in February and again in August of 1790, sitting in the Royal Exchange at the foot of Broad Street in New York City.[18] It did not yet have any cases to hear, and its only business was to adopt certain rules of court. The rule pertaining to the admission of attorneys or counselors to practice before the Court required only that the applicant should have been admitted for at least three years to the supreme court of his own state and be of a good private and professional character. Although Mr. Justice Wilson was not from Maryland, Martin was the attorney general of the state, and he had known him well as a fellow-delegate to the

[12] Act of 1715, ch. 44 (based upon an early act of 1697, ch. 12), amended by Act of 1793, ch. 55, and Act of 1796, ch. 67.

[13] By Act of 1796, ch. 67, sec. 25.

[14] *Negro Franklin* v. *Waters*, 8 Gill 322, 331 (1849). See also Bond, *The Court of Appeals of Maryland*, pp. 74–75.

[15] See, e.g., *Rawlings* v. *Boston*, 3 Harris and McHenry 139 (1793); *Mahoney* v. *Ashton*, 4 Harris and McHenry 63, 210, 295 (1797); *DeFontaine* v. *DeFontaine*, 5 Harris and Johnson 99n (1818). See also Chapter 25 below.

[16] 2 Harris and Johnson 323 (1808).

[17] It was not in Independence Hall, as long supposed, but at the newly built city hall (Warren, *The Supreme Court*, 1:53; Frank Monaghan, *John Jay*, p. 307). The members of the Court present were Chief Justice John Jay and Associate Justices William Cushing, James Iredell, and James Wilson (see *Philadelphia Gazette of the United States*, 9 February 1791, p. 3, col. 3).

[18] Warren, *The Supreme Court*, 1:46ff.

Constitutional Convention, Edmund Randolph, attorney general of the United States and another delegate to the convention, moved Martin's admission to the Supreme Court bar. It will be noted that attorneys and counselors were differentiated, like the English barrister and solicitor. The distinction probably implied no more than differing degrees of experience as a practicing lawyer, however. At any rate, Martin engaged the services of John Caldwell, a Philadelphia lawyer, as an "attorney on the part of the State (in that Court, the Duties of Attorney & Counsel being different)."[19]

The state business which brought Martin to Philadelphia over almost impassable roads in "a peculiarly disagreeable season of the year"[20] was *Vanstophorst* v. *Maryland*,[21] the first case entered upon the dockets of the Supreme Court. This suit, brought by a firm of Dutch bankers as creditors against the State of Maryland, presented the question of whether a sovereign state was subject to suit without its consent. Numerous other cases raised the same issue. In *Chisholm* v. *Georgia*[22] the Supreme Court surprised everyone by answering this question in the affirmative. The result of the decision of course, was the prompt adoption of the Twelfth Amendment by the states.

Martin's fearlessness and colorful and unique talent as an advocate are illustrated by numerous cases during this period. On one occasion he had the entire bench of three judges comprising the Charles County court cited for contempt before the General Court for refusing to honor a writ of certiorari removing a criminal prosecution for murder from the county to the General Court. After hearing argument on behalf of the judges by Chief Justice Michael Jenifer Stone in proper person and by Philip Barton Key on behalf of the other two, the General Court fined Stone "twenty shillings, current money," and each of the associate justices "twenty shillings, current money, and costs." The General Court refused to grant the justices' request for an appeal to the Court of Appeals.[23]

In another case William Pinkney argued, with his usual brilliance and cleverness, for a point that was obviously precluded by the explicit language of a controlling statute. After reviewing the statutory history in perhaps unnecessary detail, step by obvious step, Martin closed his argument, with a glance at Pinkney, by saying with exasperation, "I think it is impossible [that] the smallest doubt should really be entertained on the subject, unless by a person extremely in the habit of doubting on the plainest subjects, or whose interest it is to doubt."[24]

[19] Martin to Gov. Thomas Sim Lee, 3 December 1793, Princeton University Library, Princeton, N.J. See also Charles Warren, *A History of the American Bar*, pp. 87, 113, 242–43.

[20] Martin to Lee, 3 December 1793, Princeton University Library.

[21] Reported at the following term, August 1791 (2 Dall. 401) on a motion for a commission to examine witnesses, but never decided on its merits.

[22] 2 Dall. 419 (1792).

[23] *State* v. *Stone et al.*, 3 Harris and McHenry 115 (1792).

[24] *Johnson* v. *State*, 3 Harris and McHenry 223, 227 (1791).

Kentucky,[10] and, convinced that it would be endangered by the Indians who were determined on war, they intended to put them down once and for all. The plan was to make a raid on one of the Indian villages, called Horsehead Bottom, near the mouth of the Scioto River (now Portsmouth, Ohio).

Clark's group was unable to agree upon anyone among them with the necessary experience and prestige to be their commander. They were unanimous, however, in the conclusion that Michael Cresap was the man. When they sent messengers for him, they found that he was already on his way to confer with them. To their surprise and chagrin, however, Cresap argued against their enterprise and warned them that whether the expedition was a success or a failure, the certain result would be a disastrous conflict between the Indians and the whites.[11] Cresap recommended that the party instead repair to Wheeling for a few weeks to see which way the Indians moved: if they did not go to war, there would still be time to establish the settlement in Kentucky. This plan was at once agreed to.

Accordingly, the group started back up the Ohio toward Wheeling and on the way fell in with a party of Indians led by the Delaware chief Killbuck. They stopped for a long conference with him about the mood of the Indians. Because Killbuck had attempted to kill his father, Thomas Cresap, from ambush on a number of occasions,[12] Michael Cresap was afraid that his temper might get the better of him if he met the chief. He therefore crossed to the other side of the Ohio during the conference.

When Clark's men arrived at Wheeling, the entire countryside, fearful of a general outbreak, began flocking into the town. At this point, Lord Dunmore's agent, Dr. Connolly, sent a message advising the citizens to prepare themselves, for war with the Indians was imminent. This was followed a few days later by a second urgent message to Cresap himself, ordering him to use Clark's group for the protection of settlers along the Ohio until forts could be built. Shortly after Dunmore made a formal proclamation of war and instructed the Virginia militia to protect the white settlers. No more incentive was necessary: the expedition held a council, Indian fashion; at its end they set up a war post and danced around it.[13]

[10] George Rogers Clark to Dr. Samuel Browne, in *Papers*, pp. 6ff.; reprinted in Mayer, *Tah-gah-jute*, p. 149ff.; Jacob, *Michael Cresap*, p. 154ff.; and in Appendix B to this volume. The original is now among the Jefferson Papers, 104:17801-4, Library of Congress, Washington, D.C.

[11] *Ibid.*

[12] For an amusing incident in this connection, see Jacob, *Michael Cresap*, p. 37.

[13] Thwaites and Kellogg, *Dunmore's War*, p. 12; Jacob, *Michael Cresap*, p. 58; Martin to Jefferson, *Porcupine's Gazette*, 8 February 1798, reprinted in Force, *American Archives*, 1:387, 468, 484; James, *George Rogers Clark*, p. 14; Clark, *Papers*, p. 7. Lord Dunmore's proclamation was issued on 25 April (Thwaites and Kellogg, *Dunmore's War*, p. 12; Jacob, *Michael Cresap*, p. 58; Force, *American Archives*, 1:283). There is no evidence anywhere for Brant's gratuitous statement (*James Madison*, 1:437n) that "the dance around a pole [was] led by Cresap." It is far more likely, in view of Cresap's repeated efforts to prevent violence, that the dance was led by Clark, Smith, McDonald, or another hothead.

173

From this point on, the events of this bloody war became increasingly violent and confused. A few days after the killing at Little Beaver Creek Michael Cresap was canoeing upstream on the Ohio near Wheeling and spotted Butler's canoe, paddled by Cherokees. As Cresap approached, the Indians made for the opposite shore. There it was fired on by white men concealed in the bushes along the shore, and the two Indian occupants were killed. The third occupant, a white man named Stephens, jumped into the river and was rescued by Cresap. Under the circumstances, Stephens' suspicions of Cresap's complicity in the affair,[14] despite the latter's denials, were natural. The next day, 27 April, an Indian war party of fourteen or fifteen men in five canoes was seen sneaking down the Ohio behind the screen of an island. Cresap gave chase with an equal number of men and forced the Indians aground some fifteen miles away, near Pipe Creek. In the skirmish that followed one Indian was killed and one or two men on each side were wounded. The Indians' canoes were found to be loaded with ammunition and other articles of war.[15]

At this point John Gibson, a white interpreter (called "Horse-Head" by the Indians because of his sagacity), fell in with Clark's party on the Ohio (near what is now Friendly, West Virginia) and stopped to exchange news. He and two other white traders were on their way down the Ohio from Pittsburgh. Clark and his men told Gibson a wild story about some Shawnees having been killed by whites farther down the river (which Gibson knew to be completely untrue) and, using this as an excuse for the assumption that an Indian uprising was imminent (they were obviously itching for a fight), said that they would kill every Indian they found on the Ohio River. The next day, after Captain Cresap had been sent for, he spent a fruitless hour trying to calm them down. Finding them determined to pick a fight with the Indians, Cresap announced that he would not stay with them but would go across country to Red Stone to avoid the consequences of their folly.[16]

When they returned to Wheeling, the Virginians, for want of anything better to do, resolved to attack the camp of the well-known Mingo Tah-gah-jute, a friend of the white man who had gone so far as to take a white man's name, Logan. The following day, 28 April, the party set out for Yellow Creek, about thirty miles up the river (what is now East Liverpool, Ohio). Once there, it was obvious that the Indian group was on a hunting rather than a scalping expedition, and Clark's men began to feel qualms about their project. Again it was Michael Cresap who persuaded them to turn around and go back to Wheeling. The next day

[14] See Force, *American Archives*, 1:1015–16.

[15] Clark, *Papers*, p. 7; Force, *American Archives*, 1:345; *American Journal of Science*, 31 (January 1837), 11ff.; Jacob, *Michael Cresap*, p. 67.

[16] Deposition of John Gibson, reprinted in Jefferson, *Notes on the State of Virginia*, Appendix 4, pp. 232, 234. Cf. Peregrine Fitzhugh to Jefferson, 20 June 1797, quoting a witness, Col. Francis Deakins, to the effect that most of Clark's crowd were drunk and out of control when he saw them a few days before the Yellow Creek affair (Jefferson Papers, 102:17434–35).

they set out with Cresap for Red Stone, some fifty miles east of Wheeling and seventy-five miles southeast of Yellow Creek.[17]

Michael Cresap's friendly policy toward peaceable Indians was not adopted by all white settlers on the Ohio. On 30 April, one of the most brutal and unnecessary of all the white man's atrocities toward the Indians took place: a group of Indians, including Logan's brother and four other men, Logan's mother, and his sister and her baby, crossed the Ohio near Yellow Creek to visit the post of a trader named Greathouse, perhaps at his invitation. He and two friends, Baker and Sappington, made the Indians drunk on rum and then persuaded some of them to fire at a target, whereupon the white men summoned others from hiding who shot them down in cold blood. The other Indians were tomahawked and Logan's sister was shot without further ado. Her baby was spared because it was half white (its mother was the Indian wife or squaw of the "Horse-Head" Gibson referred to above). Hearing the shots, the rest of the Mingo party, on the other side of the river, jumped into their canoes and crossed, to be greeted by rifle fire from Greathouse and his gang. From their ambush along the east bank they killed and wounded a score of Indians.[18]

Logan may have heard of Clark's abortive expedition to Yellow Creek and may, not unnaturally, have attributed the massacre of his family to Cresap, Clark, and the others. Rumors blaming Cresap for the incident even found their way into the newspapers back in the east,[19] and Logan may have been told about them. Whether this event was the immediate *casus belli* of Lord Dunmore's War is still a matter of debate. Most historians consider the war to have been inevitable, given Dunmore's activities and the deep-seated hostility between the Indians and the whites.[20] At any rate, Logan now went on the warpath against the whites and called on other Indians for aid. He announced to the world that he would not be satisfied with less than ten lives for each of his massacred relatives. Some months later, after a series of savage forays against the white settlers, he returned with thirteen white scalps dripping from his belt and one prisoner.[21]

After the long summer of shooting, pillage, and scalping, participated in by some thousands of Indians and settlers alike, including Michael Cresap (Dunmore gave him a captain's commission in the Virginia

[17] Clark, *Papers*, pp. 7–8; Jacob, *Michael Cresap*, p. 143.
[18] Clark, *Papers*, p. 8; Thwaites and Kellogg, *Dunmore's War*, pp. 9ff.; Withers, *Chronicles*, p. 149.
[19] E.g., Force, *American Archives*, 1:285, 435.
[20] Withers, *Chronicles*, pp. 141–42; Theodore Roosevelt, *The Winning of the West*, vol. 1, chap. 8 *passim*; Mayer, *Tah-gah-jute*, pp. 84ff. Roosevelt, while not minimizing the cruelty of this and other white atrocities, lays the principal blame for the war on the Indians. See Lord Dunmore's listings of Indian atrocities, in Force, *American Archives*, 1:482, 872–73; Mayer, *Tah-gah-jute*, pp. 66ff.; see also Justin Winsor, *Narrative and Critical History of America*, 6:709.
[21] Force, *American Archives*, 1:471, 475, 546; Withers, *Chronicles*, pp. 155–58; Roosevelt, *Winning of the West*, 1:243ff.

militia[22]), the whites, under Col. Andrew Lewis, defeated the Indians at the Battle of Point Pleasant on 10 October 1774. A few days later, Cornstalk and the other Indian chiefs met Lord Dunmore and his staff around a council fire at Camp Charlotte, near Chillicothe on the Scioto, to discuss terms of peace. Observing that Logan was not among them and believing that his presence was necessary to give the treaty sanction, Dunmore dispatched Colonel Gibson to fetch him. Logan refused to come, but sent a message instead which has been preserved as an example of Indian eloquence. Its authorship, origins, and authenticity have been as long disputed as have those of any document in the entire gamut of American literature. In it, Logan attributed the massacre of his relatives to "Col. Cresap." This was the cause of considerable joking and chaffing at Michael Cresap's expense. Clark told him "that he must be a very great man, that the Indians palmed everything that happened on his shoulders." Cresap smiled ruefully and said that he had "an inclination to tomahawk Greathouse for the murder."[23]

It was known by people on the scene then, as it is now by historians and biographers of the period, that Michael Cresap had no part in the sorry event of 30 April,[24] although a few reports, based upon rumor and hearsay, did attribute it to him.[25] His complicity in the killing of the two Indians in Butler's canoe is at least doubtful, and, whoever was to blame, Lord Dunmore's agent had implicitly sanctioned it by declaring that an Indian war was at hand. The death of the single Indian in the

[22] Force, *American Archives*, 1:723; Roosevelt, *Winning of the West*, 1:238ff.

[23] Clark, *Papers*, p. 8.

[24] See Winsor, *History of America*, 6:711; Thwaites and Kellogg, *Dunmore's War*, pp. 12, 14; Clark, *Papers*, pp. 4–5, 8; James, *Michael Cresap*, pp. 15–16; Bakeless, *George Rogers Clark*, pp. 24–28; *The Olden Time Magazine*, 2 (February 1847):54; John Esten Cook, "Logan and Cresap," p. 169ff.; statement of Henry Jolly in *American Journal of Science*, 31 (January 1837):11; Rev. E. B. Raffensperger, "Who Killed the Logan Family?," p. 187ff.; Withers, *Chronicles*, p. 149; Roosevelt, *Winning of the West*, p. 237ff, 289; *Dictionary of American Biography*, s.v. "Cresap, Michael"; statements of John Gibson, Ebenezer Zane, Jacob Newland, John Anderson, and John Sappington, in Jefferson's *Notes*.
  To the same effect are depositions and statements of Benjamin Tomlinson, Thomas Chenowith, and Gen. Daniel Morgan in Luther Martin's letter to Jefferson, published in *Porcupine's Gazette* for 3 March 1798. Jefferson revised his account accordingly, and attributed both the killing of the Indians at Grave Creek (actually Little Beaver Creek) and at Yellow Creek to Cresap and Greathouse. Nathan Schachner's statement (*Thomas Jefferson, A Biography*, pp. 229, 538n) that Brant (*James Madison*, 1:281–91) had "re-examined" the matter and "discovered the confirmation of Jefferson's original account" in "contemporary first-hand evidence . . . that Cresap *was* responsible for the massacre" is without foundation. Brant himself conceded that "Cresap himself did not do it," and the evidence Schachner cites (i.e., Force, *American Archives*, 1:285) is hearsay. Even Jefferson's many apologists have grudgingly conceded his misstatement (see Brant, *James Madison*, 1:281; Dumas Malone, *Jefferson and His Time*, 1:386–87). Most biographers of Jefferson simply ignore this episode of his life (although John Dos Passos [*The Head and Heart of Thomas Jefferson*] states that *Logan* was "murdered by white men on the Ohio").

[25] Force, *American Archives*, 1:285, 435; Dunlop's *Pennsylvania Packet*, 11 July 1774; *Documents Relating to the Colonial History of the State of New York*, pp. viii, 459–63, 471, 477; statements of James Chambers and John Heckewelder, in Jefferson's *Notes*, Appendix 4.

skirmish at Pipe Creek occurred during a gun battle between two groups of equal strength which were avowedly at war with each other. During the six-month course of Dunmore's War, Michael Cresap added to his already great renown as an Indian fighter (this last of the Colonial Indian wars was sometimes known as Cresap's War), but it is hardly fair to call Cresap's actions "murder" and those of Boone, Clark, Kenton, Lewis, McDonald, and other frontiersmen of the period "prowess" or "heroism." As the record shows, Michael Cresap repeatedly and consistently sought to avoid having peaceable Indians killed, whether by himself or by others.[26]

Half a dozen years later,[27] Thomas Jefferson set about to answer a series of questions asked by François Marbois, secretary of the French legation at Philadelphia, about the American states, their geography, climate, flora, fauna, natural history, resources, etc., with particular regard to Virginia. The result was his famous work, *Notes on the State of Virginia*. After some years of intensive but sporadic research and writing, he published it anonymously in Paris in May of 1785,[28] in an edition of two hundred copies intended for private distribution only. Shortly thereafter, French and English editions appeared.[29] The 1785 edition was pirated in Philadelphia in 1788, and the authorized version appeared there in 1794.[30] In talking of minerals, flora, and fauna, Jefferson took issue with a favorite theory of the great French scientist Georges Louis Leclerc, Comte de Buffon. The latter maintained that all animals native to the New World, whether beast or human, were small and degenerate relative to their European counterparts, and that this disparity was the result of the higher temperature and drier atmosphere in Europe than in America.

With admirable zeal and care, Jefferson proceeded to demolish Buffon's theory, from premise to its conclusion, logically, statistically, factually, and scientifically. With regard to the native American Indian, Buffon alleged that he was "feeble, and has small organs of generation; he has neither hair nor beard, and no ardor whatever for his female; . . . he has no vivacity, no activity of mind; . . . they love their parents and children but little; the most intimate of all ties, the

---

[26] The *Dictionary of American Biography* sums up the dispute dispassionately: "Perhaps the final judgment should be that Cresap, whose interest as a settler of new lands would have impelled him to keep the peace with the Indians, was forced to act in defense of his land and of the people who made him their leader, and that in performing this duty he was caught in a snarl of intercolonial politics that has not yet been unraveled."

[27] In the summer or early fall of 1780, not 1781, and indirectly, through Joseph Jones, a Virginia delegate to the Continental Congress, not directly, by letter from Marbois, as Jefferson later recalled (*Papers of Jefferson*, 4:166–67; Paul Leicester Ford, ed., *The Works of Thomas Jefferson*, 1:85). These discrepancies would be irrelevant but for Jefferson's insistence upon the reliability of his memory in the crucial passages of his debate with Martin.

[28] Not 1784, as Jefferson recalled (*Notes*, p. 229). The first printed edition was misdated 1782 on the title page.

[29] Paris: Morellet, 1787; London: Stockdale, 1787.

[30] Prichard and Hall, 1788; Mathew Carey, 1794.

family connection, binds them therefore but loosely together,"[31] and more to the same effect. After discussing the Indian's physical attributes, both hirsute or philoprogenitive, as he had personally observed them from boyhood, Jefferson proceeded to "a just estimate of their genius and mental powers." By way of illustrating the latter, Jefferson cited their "eloquence in council" and "challenge[d] the whole orations of Demosthenes and Cicero, and of any more eminent orator, if Europe has furnished more eminent, to produce a single passage, superior to the speech of Logan, a Mingo chief, to Lord Dunmore, when governor of this State."[32] By way of background, he gave the following account of the affair at Yellow Creek:

> In the spring of the year 1774, a robbery and murder were committed on an inhabitant of the frontiers of Virginia, by two Indians of the Shawanee tribe.[33] The neighbouring whites, according to their custom, undertook to punish this outrage in a summary way. Col. Cresap, a man infamous for the many murders he had committed on those much-injured people,[34] collected a party, and proceeded down the Kanhaway[35] in quest of vengeance. Unfortunately a canoe of women and children, with one man only, was seen coming from the opposite shore, unarmed, and unsuspecting an hostile attack from the whites. Cresap and his party concealed themselves on the bank of the river, and the moment the canoe reached the shore singled out their objects, and, at one fire, killed every person in it. This happened to be the family of Logan, who had long been distinguished as a friend of the whites.[36]

Jefferson then proceeded to tell of Logan's part in Lord Dunmore's War, the eventual defeat of the Indians, and the peace treaty, and then set forth what he identified as Logan's message to Lord Dunmore:

> I appeal to any white man to say, if ever he entered Logan's cabin hungry, and he gave him not meat; if ever he came cold and naked, and he clothed him not. During the course of the last long and bloody war, Logan remained idle in his cabin, an advocate for peace. Such was my love for the whites, that my countrymen pointed as they passed, and said, "Logan is the friend of white men." I had even thought to have lived with you, but for the injuries of one man. Col. Cresap, the last spring, in cold blood, and unprovoked, murdered all the relations of Logan, not even sparing my women and children. There runs

---

[31] Quoted in Jefferson, *Notes*, pp. 58-59.
[32] *Ibid.*, p. 62.
[33] They were Cherokees.
[34] "Col. Cresap" would mean Captain Michael Cresap's father. Assuming, however, that it was intended to mean Michael, he was never, before the publication of the *Notes*, infamous in any sense.
[35] Although the family of Mr. Hog and several white men were killed by Indians on the Kanawha River early in April 1774 (Force, *American Archives*, 1:1015), there were no killings of Indians on that river during this period—only the Ohio River was involved.
[36] *Notes*, p. 274, n. 96. This is the version published by Jefferson in all editions before that of 1800.

not a drop of my blood in the veins of any living creature. This called on me for revenge. I have sought it: I have killed many: I have fully glutted my vengeance. For my country, I rejoice at the beams of peace. But do not harbour a thought that mine is the joy of fear. Logan never felt fear. He will not turn on his heel to save his life. Who is there to mourn for Logan?—Not one.[37]

This two-hundred-word lament had been published in newspapers throughout the colonies in 1775[38] and doubtless would have died there but for Jefferson's resurrection of it. From that source the *Annual Register*, school readers,[39] and history books copied it. The texts varied widely except for the last nine words, which were always unchanged. "Col. Cresap" appears as the villain in these reprints, most of which also included Jefferson's indictment of him.

The Cresap family, who knew that the charge was false, resented Jefferson's libel but had neither the means nor the medium to refute it or to compel Jefferson to substantiate his accusation. A family of backwoodsmen was no match for the famous and respected scholar, author, scientist, and statesman. Their first opportunity came when Maria Cresap's husband, Luther Martin, became famous as a lawyer and polemicist. Michael's nephew, Daniel Cresap, Jr., fought as a lieutenant under his uncle in Lord Dunmore's War, marched with him to Boston in the first months of the Revolution, was captured by the British, and, after many hardships, escaped. In 1794, during the Whiskey Rebellion, he commanded a regiment under Light-Horse Harry Lee and died of the rigors he endured in that campaign shortly after he returned home.[40] On his deathbed he left Martin "a sacred trust, that had he lived he intended to have performed himself, to rescue his family from this unmerited opprobrium."[41]

Accordingly, after Maria's death later in the winter of 1796, Martin undertook to carry out his trust. In the Philadelphia newspapers the next spring there were notices of "Readings and Recitations, Moral, Critical, and Entertaining" to be given at College Hall by the brilliant English actor James Fennell. In addition to selections from Pope, Gray, Shakespeare, and other literary worthies, "The Story of Logan, the Mingo Chief" was to be given. On 30 March 1797 Martin wrote to Fennell about his recitation, sending copies of his letter to the newspapers. In his letter he assumed that the "Col." Cresap referred to was

[37] *Ibid.*, p. 63.
[38] It first appeared in the *Pennsylvania Journal* (Philadelphia) for 1 February (to which it was sent by James Madison), then in the *Virginia Gazette* for 4 February, the *New York Gazette* for 13 February, and the *New York Gazetteer* for 16 February. Neither Madison nor his biographers have revealed the source of his version of the text. He told Bradford, "You must make allowances for the unskilfulness of the interpreters," but the meaning of this admonition remains a mystery.
[39] *Annual Register*, 29 (1787):151; *McGuffey's New Fifth Reader, Eclectic Series*, p. 324.
[40] Joseph Orr Cresap and Bernarr Cresap, *The History of the Cresaps*, p. 295.
[41] Quoted in Luther Martin to James Fennell, printed in *Porcupine's Gazette*, 3 April 1797.

Col. Thomas Cresap of Old Town, who had only recently died at the age of almost a hundred:

> You found that story and speech in Jefferson's Notes on Virginia; you found it related with such an air of authenticity, that it cannot be surprising that you should not suspect it to be *fiction*.
>
> But, Sir, philosophers are pretty much the same, from old Shandy, who in support of a system sacrificed his aunt Dinah, to DeWarville and Condorcet, who for the same purpose would have sacrificed a world.
>
> Mr. Jefferson is a philosopher; he too had his hypothesis to establish, or what is much the same thing, he had the hypothesis of Buffon to overthrow.

After summarizing the life and character of Thomas Cresap, Martin proceeded to his second point, viz., that Logan never delivered any speech such as that reported by Jefferson:

> As to Logan; lightly would I tread over the grave even of the untutored savage, but justice obliges me to say, I am well assured that the Logan *of the wilderness,*— the *real* Logan *of nature*[,] had but little, if any[,] more likeness to the *fictitious* Logan *of Jefferson's notes*, than the brutified Caffree of Africa to the enlightened philosopher of Montecello [*sic*].
>
> In what wilderness mr. Jefferson *culled* this fair flower of *aboriginal* eloquence; whether he has *preserved* it in the same state in which he found it, or by *transplanting* it into a more genial soil, and *exposing* it to a kinder sun, he has given it the *embellishments* of cultivation, I know not.

Martin closed by conceding that he had no authority to prohibit Fennell from the recitation but suggested that in all "propriety and justice" he should advise his audience that it was "at best the ingenious fiction of some philosophic brain," and that "with the poison" he should "dispense the antidote, by reading to them this letter."[42]

About three months later, on 24 June 1797, Martin wrote directly to Jefferson the first of what became a series of eight letters, all of them published in *Porcupine's Gazette*.[43] He waited until the day Congress adjourned, so as not to interrupt the country's business with a private affair and so that Jefferson could have no excuse for not responding. The three questions Martin put to him were: the source from which he acquired Logan's speech; the identity of the person referred to by Logan and Jefferson as "Col. Cresap"; and his evidence for the statement that "Col. Cresap" or any person named Cresap was "infamous for the many murders" of Indians.

Jefferson resorted to a favorite dodge of the cornered politician: he publicly ignored the letter while privately bending every effort to obtain

---

[42] Printed in *Porcupine's Gazette* for 3 April 1797 and doubtless others (italics in original).

[43] They were published on 17 July and 14 December 1797 and on 4, 13, and 20 January, 8 and 14 February, and 3 March 1798.

evidence to support his charges.[44] He, of course, ascribed Martin's motive not to an attempt to restore the character of a brave man, now dead, but entirely to gratification of "party passions." In accordance with this pose, he told his friends that he did not read beyond the first of Martin's letters.[45]

After waiting six months for some response, direct or indirect, from Jefferson, Martin again took up his pen:

> I have waited sufficiently long for your answer; but that you have not thought proper to give me; you have preserved obstinate, stubborn silence. Was I much more your enemy than I am, I could not have wished you to have acted differently; it is precisely the part least honorable to your head or to your heart.
>
> One of two things only with propriety could you have done: either justified your publication, or acknowledged your error.
>
> That the first was not in your power, *I knew*; and for the last, I did not believe you to possess sufficient candor.

Martin warned that he would continue his one-sided correspondence "through the medium of the public papers, until I effect the object I have undertaken, that of effacing from the name of Cresap the stain you have attempted to fix thereon. Whether in so doing I shall sully your own the world will determine."[46]

Gov. John Henry of Maryland asked Martin to call on him to explain the background and basis for the controversy, and as a result of the meeting Henry wrote to Henry Tazewell, a mutual friend, suggesting the possibility that Jefferson unintentionally misstated the facts in his *Notes on Virginia* and saying that he could "see no reason why Mr. Jefferson should not give some speedy assurance directly to Mr. Martin or to some of his friends that the correction shall take place."[47] Tazewell forwarded the letter to Jefferson, who wrote to Henry in the loftiest of terms: if only Martin had written directly to him, instead of to the newspapers, Jefferson would have cooperated with him in every way. The account he gave was merely what "everybody knew" and what he had been told by Lord Dunmore in 1774 at the end of the war. He maintained that "to this moment, I have seen no reason to doubt" the account, this despite the fact that six months earlier he had received a

[44] He had seen Martin's letter to Fennell but did not "desire to enter the field in the newspapers with Mr. Martin" (letter to Peregrine Fitzhugh, 4 June 1797, in Jefferson Papers, 101:17414ff.). In a similar incident, while he was still in Washington's cabinet, he wrote a letter to Philip Mazzei in which he viciously attacked Mazzei's policies. Publicly he denied writing the letter while privately conceding the authorship (see Schachner, *Thomas Jefferson*, p. 577ff.).

[45] E.g., letter to Dr. Samuel Browne, 25 March 1798, Jefferson Papers, 103:17676; letter to James Lewis, Jr., reprinted in E. Millicent Sowerby, *Catalogue of the Library of Thomas Jefferson*, 3:311. In his letter to John Gibson of 21 March 1800 this improbability was further refined to the point where he claimed to have read only the beginning of Martin's first letter.

[46] *Porcupine's Gazette*, 14 December 1797; original in Jefferson Papers, 102:17515ff.

[47] Letter of 24 December 1797, Jefferson Papers, 102:17522ff.

letter from General Gibson stating categorically that Captian Cresap was not present when Logan's relatives were killed.[48] Jefferson did quote Gibson as saying that Logan, in private conversation with him, "gave" him "that speech for Lord Dunmore"; that he "carried it to Lord Dunmore; translated it for him," etc.[49] He then assured Henry that he was making an impartial inquiry into the facts and that he would see that justice was done Cresap and Logan.

According to this story, Logan gave Gibson a message in writing, which Gibson carried himself to Dunmore and then (it being in a foreign language, presumably Indian) translated into English (Jefferson quoted Gibson as saying that he had received the message "from Logan's hand,"[50] not his mouth). The flaws in the tale are two-fold: (1) Gibson very carefully refrained from making any such assertion in his letter; and (2) Logan, as Jefferson well knew,[51] could not write English, and the Indians had no written language, as Jefferson also knew.[52]

Martin continued to detail his charge against Jefferson. In the letter of 4 January he stated that he would prove (1) that neither Thomas Cresap nor Michael Cresap were reputed to be "infamous" Indian murderers, nor did they deserve to be; (2) that no one named Cresap had any share in the death of Logan's family; (3) that Logan's reported speech was not genuine; and (4) that Logan was not a chief. In this and succeeding letters, he demonstrated, and corroborated with documents, that Michael Cresap's fortunes, interests, and activities were directly dependent upon peaceable relations with the Indians and that those who knew him at the time had never accused him of having caused their misfortunes at the hands of the savages. The testimony of people who were at the affair at Yellow Creek, which Martin quoted, was that the killings were caused by the insolence, thievery, and threats of the Indians,[53] and that, in any event, Michael Cresap was neither present nor concerned in any way. As for the peace council at Camp Charlotte, the witnesses agreed that the paper that had been produced and read aloud by General Gibson, purporting to contain the translated message to Lord Dunmore, did not name Michael Cresap or

---

[48] Letter of 17 June 1797, *ibid.*, p. 17428.

[49] Jefferson to Henry, *ibid.*, p. 17528ff.

[50] *Notes*, p. 252; see also Jefferson to Harry Innes, 20 June 1799, Jefferson Papers, 105:18040–41.

[51] Affidavits of Innes and Robinson, in *Notes*, pp. 231–32, 242ff. Logan had a white man write a letter in English for him on another recorded occasion; see Paul A. W. Wallace, *Conrad Weiser*, p. 275.

[52] "Before we condemn the Indians of this continent as wanting genius, we must consider that letters have not yet been introduced among them" (Jefferson, *Notes*, p. 63). Cf. Clark Wissler, *Indians of the U.S.*, p. 293.

[53] Attempts of the white murderers to excuse their crime by the drunken behavior of the Indians ignore the fact that it was they who had purposely gotten the Indians drunk. For accounts which place the blame at least as much at the door of the Indians as of the white men, see Mayer, *Tah-gah-jute*, p. 97ff.; deposition of Joseph Cresap, *Porcupine's Gazette*, 3 March 1798; Withers, *Chronicles*, pp. 113ff.; deposition of John Sappington, Jefferson, *Notes*, pp. 255–57.

any other individual as the killer of his relatives. Martin summarized this evidence as indicating

> that the circumstances you have so minutely detailed, a party of the whites proceeding down the river in quest of vengeance; a canoe of unsuspecting women and children being discovered by them; their concealing themselves on the bank of the river; their singling out their objects as the canoe reached the shore, and killing every person in it, are as little to be depended on as that Mr. Cresap commanded the party, or that the transaction happened on the Kanhawa; in fine, that these circumstances have no other foundation but the fanciful reveries of a philosophical imagination. And as *no children were killed*, I presume they were introduced by you to render the story more pathetic.

His conclusion, which seems perfectly justifiable, was that "in your controversy with the celebrated Buffon, being anxious to support the reputation of your American savage, and having some where picked up the *fictitious* speech of Logan, you thought it might be made useful; . . . and as to the *story*—that you exercised the ingenuity, which I know you to possess, to *form one* that might *suit* the *speech*."

Martin closed each of his first seven letters with the complimentary ending, "with *due* respect." His eighth letter ended: "Here for the present, I *pause*. The future must determine whether any degree of respect whatever, shall be entertained for you, by Your very humble servant, Luther Martin."

Jefferson meanwhile was writing letters to any and all persons who might be of service.[54] Of all his correspondents, General Gibson was the most crucial. On 31 May he asked the general "to give me what information you can on this subject, as well respecting the speech as the facts stated by me," and suggested that Gibson look up a copy of the *Notes* in Pittsburgh "so as to see in what manner the facts are stated."[55] Gibson replied that he had checked Jefferson's text of Logan's speech in the *American Encyclopedia* and found it, "to the best of my recollection, nearly the Substance of Logan's Speech as delivered by him to me, and which I afterward communicated to Lord Dunmore."[56] Whatever Gibson intended by his phrase "nearly the Substance," it did not necessarily mean that Jefferson's version and Gibson's translation were identical, "with only two or three verbal variations of no importance," as Jefferson had put it to Henry. Further, Gibson says Logan "delivered" the speech to him and that he then "communicated" it to Lord Dunmore. These highly ambiguous verbs Jefferson construed as meaning that the

[54] See letters to Peregrine Fitzhugh, 4 June 1797, Jefferson Papers, 101:17414ff.; to John Page, 2 January 1798, *ibid.*, 102:17544; to Mann Page, 2 January 1798, *ibid.*, pp. 17545–46; to Dr. Samuel Browne, 25 March 1798, *ibid.*, 103:17676; to John Heckewelder, 11 April 1798, *ibid.*, p. 17711, etc.

[55] *Ibid.*, 101:17408ff.

[56] Letter of 17 June 1797, *ibid.*, 102:17428. Cf. Clark's comment on Jefferson's version of the speech: "Except a few mistakes in the names of persons, places, etc., the story of Logan, as related by Mr. Jefferson, is substantially true" (letter to Dr. Samuel Browne, 17 June 1798, reprinted in Mayer, *Tah-gah-jute*, p. 149).

speech was written—"from Logan's hand"—and gave the words as Gibson's own.

The statement in Gibson's letter most damning to Jefferson's case, however, was that "Capt. Cresap was not present when Logan's relations were killed." Recognizing this, Jefferson wrote back at once asking Gibson how, if so, could Logan's attribution to Cresap of the slaughter of his entire family be understood. He emphasized that the story circulated by Lord Dunmore "made Cresap the head of the [group?] which destroyed Logan's family," but, he grudgingly conceded, "you must know this best."[57]

Six months passed, and Gibson made no reply, perhaps because Jefferson had not mentioned his own request for a job, which he had included in his letter, perhaps because he was in no hurry to commit to writing an account of his part in such a sticky affair. Jefferson wrote him again on 12 January 1798, and in several letters Gibson again responded evasively, while continuing to press Jefferson for an appointment in the Indian Department.[58] In spite of Jefferson's insistence that "I wish to get *a minute history of the whole transaction*,"[59] he got no satisfaction from Gibson.

Two years later, early in 1800, Gibson wrote Jefferson—this time an unsolicited letter: "I received the enclosed letter from a Mr. Luther Martin of Baltimore requesting me to answer the Queries therein contained.[60] But as I am fully Convinced he is actuated by party Spirit, more than by any other Consideration, I shall not return him answer until I hear from you. In the meantime, permit me to request you to send me a Copy of the last letter I wrote you, when I shall be able to give you a deposition of everything I know concerning it."[61] (One may wonder why Gibson needed to see what he had previously written before he could send Jefferson his present recollections.) He then got down to the *quid pro quo*: "Since I had the honour of addressing my last letter to you, my affairs have Become very much embarrassed. The present prothonotary of Allegeney [*sic*] County is very ill and cannot possibly Survive many days. Permit me, Dear Sir, to Sollicit your Interest with Governor McKean in my Behalf. A single Line from you will Insure me the office, and you may rest assured that nothing shall be wanting on my part to render myself worthy of your recommendation."[62]

Jefferson lost no time in answering this letter. He could not dictate Gibson's affidavit, but he could make every effort to condition his

<hr />

[57] Letter of 24 June 1797, *ibid.*, 88:15288 (Jefferson received Gibson's letter on 22 June).

[58] Letter of 12 January 1798, *ibid.*, 102:17555; Gibson refers to Jefferson's letter of "the 31st ulto.," which has not been located at the Library of Congress or elsewhere.

[59] Letter of 2 February 1798, *ibid.*, p. 17569.

[60] Letter of 13 February 1798, *ibid.*, p. 17575.

[61] The enclosure is not preserved, and the contents of Martin's letter are not known. It is probable that he asked questions about Logan's speech similar to those he asked Benjamin Tomlinson (see *Porcupine's Gazette*, 3 March 1798) and others.

[62] Letter of 14 March 1800, Jefferson Papers, 106:18219ff., reprinted, in part, in Sowerby, *Catalogue of the Library*, 3:313.

"recollection" (at the distance of a quarter of a century) in return for the favor. Accordingly, he set out in specific detail such evidence as he wished to disclose, together with his rationale of it, hoping that Gibson's deposition would generally conform to it. With regard to the prothonotaryship, there were practical difficulties to be overcome. Gibson was clearly hovering over the deathbed of the incumbent like a vulture, impatient to snatch the job and its perquisites. As Jefferson reminded him, "there are delicacies in this business which must be observed," and his approach to Governor McKean must be "indirect in the manner." He assured Gibson, however, that "ancient recollections and a thorough sense of the just grounds on which you have a right to be thought of, give me a sincere wish to serve you." After almost three years of correspondence, during which Jefferson had not been able to get answers to any of his questions, it was natural for him to suspect some chicanery about Logan's speech. Accordingly, for the last time (as the revised edition of his book was about to go to press), Jefferson asked Gibson whether it was genuine, whether it was written, if so, by whom, and in what language. He reminded Gibson that only he could set the record straight.[63]

This time Gibson did respond, in a deposition filled with interesting but irrelevant details of the events leading up to the war. He devoted only a hundred words or so to Logan's message and ignored Jefferson's questions. Again he stated that Capt. Michael Cresap was not present at the massacre, that Logan "delivered" the speech to him, "nearly as related by Mr. Jefferson in his notes," and that he in turn "delivered" it to Lord Dunmore.[64] He further swore to Jefferson that at the time of the peace council he had assured Logan that "it was not Col. Cresap who had murdered his relations"; why then did he preserve this false statement in his transcript of the speech? One may also ask why Gibson, whose own child by Logan's sister was alive and well and who knew that Logan had other surviving relatives, did not emend Logan's statement that not a drop of his blood ran in any living creature.[65] The issues of how "nearly" to Logan's speech was Gibson's translation, and of how "nearly" to Gibson's translation was Jefferson's report of it, remained unanswered. One month later, Gibson was appointed secretary of the Indiana Territory, a post he held for sixteen years thereafter, under Jefferson and Madison.[66]

---

[63] This portion of the letter is omitted in Sowerby.

[64] Letter of 21 March 1800, Jefferson Papers, 106:18226ff., reprinted, in part, in Sowerby, *Catalogue of the Library*, 3:313–14.

[65] It came shortly after 4 April 1800 and is reproduced in Jefferson's *Notes*, pp. 232–34; the original is in the Jefferson Papers, 104:17915, 106:18237.

[66] Gibson raised the child in his own house (see statement of William Huston, Jefferson Papers, 103:17720; *Notes*, pp. 237, 239, 257). Logan's wife and children were not killed at Yellow Creek, nor were his brothers and their families—in fact, Logan met his own death, years later, at the hands of a nephew whose family he had attacked in a fit of insanity (see Wallace, *Conrad Weiser*, pp. 272–76, 429ff., 443; John H. Carter, "Shikellamy," p. 42). Logan's descendants survived well past the middle of the nineteenth century (see Mayer, *Tah-gah-jute*, pp. 139–40).

Jefferson had not been idle during the two years of waiting to hear from Gibson. He wrote to numerous people seeking support for his libel, taking care in each case to set out in detail his theory of the affair and the kind of evidence he was after. He even had his long letter to Governor Henry printed as a pamphlet, which he gave to "particular friends for their satisfaction, & on whom I could rely against the danger of it's [sic] being published." The statements he obtained in this way, reproduced in his Appendix along with Gibson's letter, largely represented second- or third-hand reports, prompted by leading questions and, what was far worse for their evidentiary value, by "leading answers" supplied in advance by Jefferson. As a lawyer, he knew the worthlessness of such testimony, yet blandly presented it as inspired only by a "regard for truth and justice."[67]

When confronted by the testimony of his own chief witness that Cresap had no part in the Yellow Creek affair, Jefferson undertook what in law is called a "departure": he put forth evidence that on other occasions, on another river, under other circumstances, Cresap had killed other Indians. One fact does emerge from the Appendix and other documents: it was widely reported, and in some places believed, that Michael Cresap was the villain of the massacre. Jefferson wrote John Heckewelder, a Moravian missionary to the Indians, for information about it, and Heckewelder responded with a long confidential letter, in which he told of reports current among the Ohio Indians, miles away from the Ohio River, that Cresap had killed Logan's family.[68] This letter is duly reproduced in full in Jefferson's Appendix. Jefferson did include some statements absolving Cresap from complicity in the Logan murders as well, but he was selective in what he included: for example, the fact that Cresap had an iron-clad alibi for the time of the incident is not mentioned, nor is the fact, emphasized by Martin and well known to Jefferson, that Cresap's interest and his personal inclination lay in maintaining peaceable relations with the Indians. A careful examination of the Appendix reveals that he published only those documents which, while absolving Cresap from the Yellow Creek affair, at the same time involved him (in almost every case, by hearsay) with the killing of other Indians at other times.[69] Jefferson asserted that there had been four separate killings of Indians during the spring of 1774 and that Cresap was a principal in some of these. As for Yellow Creek, he brought forth a new suggestion, without any supporting evidence, that perhaps Cresap had "ordered" it. He then edited the published documents (or such parts of them as he had

[67] Letter to Dr. Samuel Browne, 25 March 1798, Jefferson Papers, 103:17676, reprinted, in part, in Sowerby, *Catalogue of the Library*, 3:309.
[68] Letters of 11 April 1798 and 28 April 1798, Jefferson Papers, 103:17711, 17730, 17731-34, 17743.
[69] Statements of John Gibson, Ebenezer Zane, Charles Polke, Judge Henry Innes, John Sappington, and others attributing the murders to Greathouse's party without specifically absolving Cresap (*Notes*, pp. 234, 236, 241-42, 255-57).

chosen to include), identifying each Indian killing mentioned therein as one or another of the four.[70]

As for Logan's speech, Martin was only one of many who suspected[71] that the speech reported was substantially the work of Gibson. It has apparently never been noted before that the opening sentences of Logan's Lament are a direct paraphrase of Matthew 25:35-36. However natural such language might be for a white man, it is highly improbable that it would flow from the lips of an illiterate, non-Christian Indian like Logan. One other speech of Logan's is extant and is of the highest interest for purposes of comparison. It was dictated by Logan to a white captive of his, for delivery to Michael Cresap:

Captain Cresap,

What did you kill my people on Yellow Creek for? The white people killed my kin, at Conestoga, a great while ago; and I thought nothing of that. But you killed my kin again, on Yellow Creek, and took my Cousin Prisoner. Then I thought I must kill too; and I have been three times to war since; but the Indians are not angry; only myself.

Captain John Logan.[72]

July 21st, 1774

Here Logan correctly addresses Cresap as "Captain"; three months later the Logan of Logan's Lament refers to him as "Colonel." There is a curious account that years before Lord Dunmore's War a speech very similar to the Lament was seen, in the handwriting of either Sir William Johnson or his brother Guy, the famous British superintendents of Indian affairs.[73] Whether Gibson had seen or heard this speech, and to what extent it colored his version, will doubtless remain a mystery. In any event, a glance at his florid address to the Indiana territorial legislature some years later[74] will indicate that he was fully capable of translating the bereaved Mingo's heartfelt grievances into the prose immortalized in Jefferson's *Notes*.

[70] In addition to George Rogers Clark's statement, which completely clears Cresap and is not reprinted by either Jefferson or Sowerby, Jefferson omitted other such testimony: see John Page to Jefferson, 26 April 1798, Jefferson Papers, 103: 17735–36; John Anderson to Jefferson, *ibid.*, 106:18199ff.; Dr. Samuel Browne to Jefferson, 4 September 1798, *ibid.*, 104:17861–62, reprinted in part in Sowerby, *Catalogue of the Library*, 3:309–10); Judge Henry Innes to Jefferson, 2 March 1799, *ibid.*, 105:18008–9. Jefferson published only part of the last affidavit in his Appendix and omitted entirely Judge Innes's conclusion that, after extensive inquiry he, believed that the Yellow Creek murder "was committed by a certain Daniel Greathouse & others, in the perpetration of which Cresap had no part, neither was he present." Jefferson mentioned this opinion in his reply to Judge Innes (letter of 20 June 1799, *ibid.*, 105:18040–41, 18046–47).
[71] See *Porcupine's Gazette* for 3 March 1798.
[72] *Notes*, p. 232.
[73] See *The Olden Time Magazine*, 2 (February 1847):54ff.
[74] John Brown Dillon, *A History of Indiana*, p. 408; Logan Esarey, *A History of Indiana*, 1:154ff.

In this connection, one of Jefferson's more interesting suppressions in the Appendix was the last half of John Anderson's certificate,[75] in which the latter, an intimate friend of Gibson, stated that he told Gibson at the time that he suspected that he had written the speech for Logan, to which Gibson made a perfunctory denial. John Page reported to Jefferson[76] that there never had been a meeting between Logan and Gibson in the woods, as Gibson claimed (Jefferson did not record Page's account). Benjamin Tomlinson, who was officer of the guard on the day that Logan's message was read at Camp Charlotte and who stood next to Dunmore and heard everything that went on, swore that it was not Gibson but a man named Simon Girty who was sent to fetch Logan and, that when Girty returned Logan was not with him. "I saw John Gibson on Girty's arrival get up, go out of the circle, and talk with Girty, upon which he, Gibson, went into a tent . . . and after a short space he returned into the circle, drew out of his pocket a piece of clean new paper, on which was written in his own hand writing, a speech for and in the name of Logan." There was no doubt, said Tomlinson, that the speech "originated in, and was composed by John Gibson."[77] Jefferson more than once had the bad luck or bad judgment to rest his case on an unreliable witness.

[75] The first half appears on p. 236 of the *Notes*. The complete statement is in Jefferson Papers, 106:18199, 18201.
[76] Page to Jefferson, 26 April 1798, *ibid.*, 103:17735ff.
[77] *Porcupine's Gazette*, 3 March 1798. Wallace also confirms this account (*Conrad Weiser*, p. 276).

20

Leader of the Bar, 1801-1804

> Nature, I think, intended you for an Attorney-General,
> but, sir, it would require a greater revolution in your sys-
> tem, than ever was effected in France, to make you a
> politician.—Alexander Martin to Luther Martin, 15
> April 1801

> In the enumeration of the great men of the bar, I have
> placed Luther Martin first. He was . . . the acknowledged
> and undisputed head of the profession in Maryland.—
> Roger Brooke Taney, *Autobiography*

In the summer of 1791 President Washington wrote to James McHenry asking his opinion as to the man best qualified to fill the position of Federal district attorney of Maryland. McHenry answered promptly that "Luther Martin is the best qualified man in the state; but, through his politics, is the last person who merits the appointment."[1] Shortly after this, however, Martin, theretofore known as an extreme Antifederalist (and therefore politically unacceptable to Washington and McHenry), became an equally ardent advocate of the nascent Federalist Party, its candidates and its principles.

It was not so much Martin's own political philosophy that had changed as the objectives of the men who organized and led the first political parties in the United States. Generally speaking, the men who had espoused the adoption of the Federal Constitution became the leaders of the Federalist Party during the 1790s, and those who had sought to prevent the adoption of the Constitution became the backbone of the emerging Antifederalist or Democratic-Republican Party. The Republican Party of Martin's day adopted a broadly based, democratic philosophy—indeed, its lineal descendant is the Democratic Party of today. Martin, on the other hand, consistently adhered, both at the Philadelphia convention and throughout his life, to a belief in a republican form of government.

Early in 1801, in a long political controversy carried on in a series of letters in Baltimore newspapers,[2] Martin was accused of "prostitution"

---

[1] Steiner, *James McHenry*, pp. 133-34.
[2] See *American Daily Advertiser* (Baltimore), 21, 24, and 25 March, 11 and 15 April 1801; *Baltimore Telegraph*, 26 March and 1 April 1801; and *Federal Gazette* (Baltimore), 4 and 18 April 1801.

of his principles, of "political depravity and apostacy," and of other less abstract vices. One writer, under the name "Demophilos," suggested that perhaps Martin's extravagant views stemmed from "the fumes of wine." Martin replied to these attacks at his customary length, but with his usual good humor, honesty, and forthrightness. He disdained to enter into "personalities, always best to be avoided" and therefore had "no wish to know whether your beverage is '*wine*' or *small beer*, or whether you write under the inspiration arising from 'the fumes' of either." He pointed out that at the time of the Constitutional Convention and ever since he had been "a friend to the republican system of government"; that when the Constitution was originally submitted it had numerous shortcomings which endangered the liberties of both the states and individuals; that he had believed that the corrections should be made before rather than after ratification; that most of these deficiencies had been corrected by the first ten amendments;[3] that, as so amended, the Constitution had proved to be a workable system of government under which the administrations of Washington and Adams had enacted much wise and beneficial legislation; and that the Republican Party, in opposing the Federalist administrations and in gaining control of the federal government in the election of 1800, had abandoned "true republicanism" in favor of a "mobocracy" under which neither liberties nor property were safe. He decried not merely the inherent weaknesses of democracy but the exploitation of democratic excesses by the leaders of the Republican Party in order to obtain and retain power:

The difference between myself and a great number of the present highest toned democrats consists only in this; we all to the utmost of our abilities, opposed, whether mistakenly or not, the adoption of the constitution, but I have never opposed it since its adoption. While they on the contrary have transferred and continued all that opposition which they made to the constitution, to almost every wise and salutary act of the several administrations under it, and to those administrations having joined with them in the opposition to the adoption of the Constitution. Had I joined with them in opposing & clamouring against these administrations, and those measures, I might yet have been the theme of their panegyric;—I might yet have been a luminary of some magnitude in the system of Democracy; but I must have been despised by myself, and detested by those whom I most esteem.[4]

He had been approached by the early organizers of the Republican Party because of his opposition to the draft constitution, he said, and gave his reasons for declining this invitation.

I *was* at the *time*, when I was a member of the convention, I *am now* and I *unchangeably have been*, a friend to liberty; but it is the temperate, the chastened liberty of a well checked, well constituted republicanism; a liberty, the mild

---

[3] Adopted 15 December 1791.
[4] *American*, 24 March 1801.

rays of which cheer, refresh and invigorate all on whom they shine; a liberty diffusive of social happiness, preservative of peace, quiet and order, and securative of person and property; not the scorching, feverish, convulsive, revolutionizing liberty, or rather licentiousness, of modern democracy.[5]

Martin's political philosophy was more tolerant and sophisticated, than one would expect in an eighteenth-century Federalist:

I am a friend to a republican government and would wish to live myself under such as long as it should be able to give me the protection which is due to every citizen, and to obtain which, we enter into society; but I feel no Quixotish desire of proselyting the world to the republican system; no hatred or contempt for those who live under governments of a different form; nor do I think the man, who believes a republican government the best adapted for all nations, without regard to their habits and manners, and who would wish to compel its adoption in all climes and in all countries, a whit more wise or less cruel, than the tyrant, who took into his head the barbarous whim, by stretching or lopping every individual who came in his way, to reduce them all to the standard of the same bedstead. The man who pretends to expect, by universally republicanising the world, to effect the perfectability of human nature, the perfectability of human reason, and the perfectability of human happiness, or to introduce a millennium on the earth, will ever by me be considered an enthusiastic visionary . . . or a crafty villainous impostor.[6]

Early in 1800 it did not seem possible that John Adams and the other Federalist candidates could lose the presidential election, strongly entrenched as they were by the appointments they had made to thousands of new federal offices and by the numerous state laws limiting the franchise and placing the elective power in the hands of conservative state legislators. By persistent blundering, however, they managed to "snatch defeat from the jaws of victory." In Maryland the Federalists compounded the unpopularity they had gained from the enactment of the Alien and Sedition Acts, the Army bill, and the direct tax law by unsuccessfully attempting to have Maryland's presidential electors selected by the General Assembly rather than by popular election.[7] Arguments by Martin[8] and others that there was no constitutional right to direct election of the electors were beside the point. The voters were sensitive to the fact that the Federalists, in allowing them to choose their President only at third hand, did not trust them to administer their own government.

[5] *Baltimore Telegraph*, 1 April 1801, reprinted in *Federal Gazette* (Baltimore), 7 April 1801.
[6] *Ibid.* See also Martin's letter in the *American*, 11 April 1801, reprinted in the *Federal Gazette*, 18 April 1801. See also the letter signed "An American" (probably Martin), in the *Federal Gazette* for 5 November 1800, describing objectively the contrasting political philosophies of the Federalist and Republican parties.
[7] See, generally, Edward G. Roddy, "Maryland and the Presidential Election of 1800," pp. 244ff. *et passim*.
[8] See letters signed "An American" in the *Federal Gazette* for 8 and 25 September 1800, which have all the marks of Martin's authorship.

Accordingly, in the election of November 1800 Maryland's ten electoral votes were evenly divided: five for Adams and Charles Cotesworth Pinckney, five for Jefferson and Burr. Because of the provisions of the Constitution at that time,[9] Jefferson and Burr each received 73 votes for the presidency in the Electoral College, Adams received 65, and Pinckney 64. Since no single candidate had a majority of the electoral votes, the selection of a president passed automatically to the House of Representatives, to be decided by a roll call of the states, each one having one vote. There being sixteen states, a nine-state majority was required to elect. Because of numerous lame-duck holdovers in Congress, the Federalists thus had the power to prevent the election of Jefferson as President, to elect Aaron Burr, or even to delay the election of any president until after the 4 March 1801 deadline. In the event of such a delay, the Constitution gave Congress authority to elect an interim president until the next election.[10]

Most Federalists, including Martin,[11] greatly preferred Burr to Jefferson, whom they had denounced from one end of the country to the other as a slacker in war, a backstabber in politics, and an atheist in religion. They believed that they could at least "do business" with Burr. Burr unquestionably could have had the office by cooperating with the Federalists, who were able, willing, indeed anxious to give it to him,[12] but they insisted upon certain commitments, which Burr refused to make and publicly declined the offer.[13]

There was no question, of course, as to who had been elected president by the voters, and the Federalists' attempt to keep Thomas Jefferson out of the White House added another item to their long list of political follies. For five days, in thirty-five ballots taken at all hours of the day and night, the vote was monotonously unchanged: New York, New Jersey, Pennsylvania, Virginia, North Carolina, Georgia, Kentucky, and Tennessee were for Jefferson; New Hampshire, Massachussetts, Rhode Island, Connecticut, Delaware, and South Carolina were for Burr; and two, Maryland and Vermont, were divided. There was talk of insurrection and civil war, and it was said that the militia would be called out to support or suppress one faction or another, or even to assassinate Jefferson or Burr, if and when elected.[14]

[9] Art. II, sec. 2, revised after the election of 1800 by the Twelfth Amendment.
[10] Art. II, sec. 5. See opinion to this effect signed "Horatius," probably written by John Marshall, published in the Washington, D.C., *Federalist* for 6 January 1801, reprinted in Beveridge, *Life of John Marshall*, 2:541–42.
[11] See Luther Martin to Alexander Martin, editor of the *American*, 11 April 1801, reprinted in the *Federal Gazette*, 18 April 1801.
[12] See Beveridge, *Life of John Marshall*, 2:539, 545ff.; William O. Lynch, *Fifty Years of Party Warfare*, pp. 103–5; Nathan Schachner, *Aaron Burr, a Biography*, pp. 191ff., 198ff.; Morton Borden, *The Federalism of James A. Bayard*, pp. 73ff.
[13] Burr to Samuel Smith (Jefferson's lieutenant in the House of Representatives), 16 December 1800, printed in Matthew L. Davis's *Memoirs of Aaron Burr, 1756–1856*, 2:75. This letter was widely circulated in the newspapers of the day.
[14] Beveridge, *Life of John Marshall*, 2-541ff.; Paul A. W. Wallace, *The Muhlenbergs of Pennsylvania*, pp. 294ff.; John Bach McMaster, *A History of the People of the U.S. from the Revolution to the Civil War*, 5:517; John Spencer Bassett, *The Federalist System, 1797–1801*, p. 292; Schachner, *Burr*, p. 201.

Bands of enthusiastic Republicans picketed Stella's Hotel in Washington, where most of the Federalist congressmen lived, "howling in tones more discordant than the brays of an ass, 'Jefferson or no constitution.'" Others waylaid carriages in the streets and compelled their occupants to get out in a torrential rain to "huzza for Jefferson."[15]

During the first week of February Samuel Chase went to Washington to resume his seat on the Supreme Court. With him went Luther Martin and the rest of that brilliant phalanx referred to as "the Maryland lawyers"[16] to argue cases there pending for clients along the whole length of the Atlantic seaboard.[17] The Republican newspapers complained that between sessions of the Court Martin and other Federalists were importuning members of Congress and haranguing crowds on the streets and in the taverns in support of their plan to maintain the deadlock until 4 March.[18] The way would then be clear for Congress to elect Jay, Marshall, or some other Federalist as interim president. However, on 17 February, at the urging of Hamilton, James Bayard, the lone representative from Delaware, broke the deadlock: he cast a blank ballot, as did the Federalists from Maryland and Vermont. With these votes lost to Burr, Jefferson carried those three states, for a total of ten and the Presidency.[19]

It was at about this time that the public began to take note of Martin's alcoholism. Sometimes the reference was highly critical,[20] sometimes merely jocular: during the balloting for president in the House of Representatives, the correspondent for the *Baltimore American* noted that "the times must be momentuous [*sic*] indeed: for on pretty good authority I have it that for the whole week Luther Martin has resided at Washington, he has not once been seen intoxicated in the public streets! Such is the fact told to me; if, however, my information is not founded, I throw myself on the mercy of Mr. M. to forgive an assertion so derogatory to his general character."[21] It is impossible to be sure of the reason for this affliction. Martin's wife had been dead for about five years, one daughter was married and the other two were away at school, and he was undoubtedly lonely. He may have used

[15] Luther Martin to Alexander Martin, *American*, 11 April 1801, reprinted in the *Federal Gazette*, 18 April 1801.

[16] This group included Martin, John Thompson Mason, Philip Barton Key, and Robert Goodloe Harper (see Warren, *A History of the American Bar*, pp. 258ff.).

[17] Warren, *The Supreme Court*, 1:184–85; letter of 16 February 1801, James A. Bayard Papers.

[18] *Philadelphia Aurora*, 16 February 1800; *American*, 16 February 1801. See also *Philadelphia Aurora* for 10 and 15 January 1801. The Court had been unable to muster a quorum during the latter half of 1800: Chief Justice Ellsworth was in Europe as envoy to France, Cushing was ill, and Samuel Chase was busy electioneering for Adams in Maryland.

[19] Borden, *James A. Bayard*, chap. 7 *passim*; McMaster, *History of the People of the U.S.*, pp. 525–26. With characteristic recklessness and poor judgment in political matters, Martin lost two hundred guineas (over nine hundred dollars) to Tench Ringgold on his bet that Adams would win the election (Tench Ringgold to Martin, 13 March 1801, Chicago Historical Society).

[20] *American*, 24 July 1800; *Federal Gazette*, 6 April 1801.

[21] 16 February 1801.

alcohol as a stimulant to enable him to handle his ever-increasing private practice, his duties as attorney general, and his burgeoning practice in the federal courts. He frequently traveled to Philadelphia, to New York, and even to Boston for consultations and trials, and he was the most widely retained appellate lawyer in Maryland. The reports of appealed cases argued for this period show that he was counsel on one side or the other in over 80 (or 53 per cent of some 150 appeals reported.[22] There were, of course, many other unreported cases in which he also appeared.[23] Today's lawyer's five-day week, with five to six hours a day in court, was far in the future: Martin was in court from nine in the morning until six or eight in the evening, six days a week. His account of one ten-month period in 1801-1802 indicates his schedule. From 12 to 26 April 1801 he attended the Eastern Shore General Court at Easton; from 10 May to 15 June he argued cases before the Western Shore General Court at Annapolis; from 2 to 29 July he was in New York and Boston on professional engagements; from 3 to 24 September he was at Easton attending sessions of the Eastern Shore General Court; from 17 to 31 October he was at Annapolis trying cases before the Western Shore General Court; on 2 and 3 November he appeared before the Court of Appeals at Annapolis; on 5 and 6 November he argued cases before the United States Circuit Court in Baltimore; from 7 to 17 November he argued cases before the Court of Appeals at Annapolis; from 18 November to 5 December[24] he tried cases daily before the Criminal Court of Baltimore County; from 7 to 23 December he was in Washington arguing cases before the United States Supreme Court; from 1 January to 5 February 1802 he argued cases daily before the General Court, the Court of Appeals, and the Chancery Court in Annapolis.[25]

[22] See 4 Harris and McHenry, and 1 Harris and Johnson, *passim*, briefing the arguments and giving the opinions of the General Court and the Court of Appeals in a selected body of cases during the approximate period 1799–1805. Martin's professional activity in court for the ten-year period 1795–1805 can be derived from these sources. Harris and McHenry report a total of 94 cases, of which Martin took part in 43, or 46 per cent, all in the General Court; he won 28, or 65 per cent. In the Court of Appeals he participated in 16 cases; of these he won 10, or 63 per cent. Harris and Johnson report a total of 153 cases, of which Martin took part in 82, or 54 per cent. Of his 80 cases in the general court, he won 44, or 55 per cent; of his 31 cases in the Court of Appeals, he won 16, or 52 per cent. As of final appeal, Harris and McHenry's tally of all Martin's cases (not including those settled, abated, etc.) was 28 of the total of 42 won, or 67 per cent. Harris and Johnson report a total of 82 cases, of which he won 44, or 52 per cent.

[23] E.g., Dixon v. Slade (Maryland General Court, 1803), Hall's *American Law Journal*, 1 (July, 1808):334.

[24] In the middle of this docket, on 28 November 1800, Martin went to Annapolis to argue the validity of state insolvency laws before the House of Delegates. The *Baltimore American* for 1 December 1800 reported that Martin "contended with great ability the constitutional powers of the State to make and exercise insolvent laws to their fullest extent. . . . [A] speech of more than two hours length received the most marked and undivided attention."

[25] Compiled from data incidentally mentioned in his account of his and his daughters' activities during this period in *Modern Gratitude*.

In this same period he was also riding circuit trying his own and the state's cases before county nisi prius judges and juries. He would board the mail coach for Philadelphia in the morning, travel all day and all night, and arrive at his destination the following morning. He often took the night stage at Baltimore, rode all night, and arrived at Annapolis for breakfast, just in time to meet the morning's docket. His research was done and his arguments, particularly for his many cases on appeal before the general courts and the Court of Appeals, were blocked out during the evenings in the poorly lit, poorly heated law libraries of the period. (Many a lawyer today would feel in need of a drink merely from contemplating such a schedule.)

At this time Martin met Mrs. Mary Magdalena Hager, the handsome, thirty-three-year-old widow of Jonathan Hager, Jr., son of the founder of Hagerstown,[26] and began to pay court to her. He made Mrs. Hager the following proposal, probably while he was in Washington County in the spring of 1800 trying cases:

Dear madam—I twice called at Mrs. Wyant's yesterday to see you, and you were not at home; being obliged to leave town this morning, I take the liberty of expressing to you in writing those sentiments which I should have been happy to have done in person. You have a charming little daughter who wants a *father*. I have two who stand in need of a *mother*. By doing me the honor to accept my hand, our dear children may have the one and the other, and I promise you most sacredly that in me you shall ever find a tender, indulgent and affectionate husband; and your sweet little daughter shall find in me every thing she could wish for in a father.

My fortune, my dear madam, is not inconsiderable; I have a large landed estate in Maryland[27] and Virginia and my practice brings me more than $12,000 a year. Our estates, united, will enable us to live in a stile [sic] of happiness and elegance equal to our wishes. And so far am I, my dear madam, from wishing my little girls to be benefitted [sic] by your estate, that if we should not increase our family, your fortune, whatever it may be, shall be your own, if you survive me or if you should not survive me, your daughter's. Forgive, my dear madam, the liberty I have taken in thus laying before you my wishes and my hopes, and do me the honor to write to me and treat me with the same candor. Should your answer be favorable, I will fly to you the first moment in my power, and express my gratitude at the feet of her on whom, from that time, I shall depend for my happiness. With most perfect esteem and affection, I am, my dear madam, your sincere

friend and lover,
Luther Martin[28]

---

[26] She was the daughter of Christian Orendorff, who was in all probability the Captain Orendorff referred to in Chapter 6 above, in connection with the Fredericktown Tory conspiracy.

[27] Among other properties, Martin owned an 1,100-acre tract known as "Oakland Manor," just off the Columbia Turnpike near Ellicott City, in Howard County.

[28] *Report of the Fourth Annual Meeting of the Maryland State Bar Association*, p. 70ff.

Mrs. Hager was evasive, and Martin pursued his courtship for over a year. On one occasion, he called on her when he was quite drunk, and a week later made her a written apology:

My very Dear, Amiable Mrs. Hager:

I have been told since you left town, that on last Sunday week, in the evening, I was at your lodgings; of this I had no possible recollection. I doubt not I made a very foolish figure, but think it impossible that I should have behaved with rudeness or impropriety; but be assured you shall never see me again in a situation that I know not what I do, unless it shall proceed from the intoxication of love! In the heat of summer my health requires that I should drink in abundance, to supply the amazing waste from perspiration, but having found that I was so unexpectedly affected as I was by cool water and brandy, I have determined to mix my water with less dangerous liquors; nay, I am not only confining myself to mead, cyder, beer, hock mixed with soda water, but I am accustoming myself to drink water alone. Thus if we live to see each other again, you will find me most completely reformed and one of the soberest of the sober.[29]

In the summer of 1801 Martin finally tired of dancing attendance on Mrs. Hager:

My dearest Madam:

To a long letter of mine, you have sent me a very short one. To my inquiries you say you "are repairing your house," where you "mean to live the *Summers, and in the Winters* you intend to live in Baltimore, *where you shall have the pleasure of my company.*" Tell me, my dear Madam, do you mean by these expressions that *I shall have the pleasure of your company*, or, in other words, that my dear Mrs. Hager will then reward me for my affection for her, and bestow herself upon me? If not, let me know, for I am determined not to be cheated of happiness by her for another year; but will, against the approach of Winter look out for some other companion, unless she will promise me to be herself that companion. You see, my dearest Madam, I give you fair notice, and therefore, whatever may be the event, you cannot charge anything to your friend, your lover,

Your Martin.[30]

Whatever Mrs. Hager's answer, this courtship came to naught, and she married Captain Henry M. Lewis instead.

At this time, there was a protracted and unhappy crisis in Martin's own family. Early in 1799 a handsome young man by the name of Richard Reynal Keene came to Baltimore. He knew that Martin frequently took on one or more law clerks to study and work in his office and applied for such a position. Martin agreed and, as he was maintaining bachelor quarters (his two unmarried daughters were at

---

[29] *Ibid.*
[30] See Mary V. Mish, *Jonathan Hager, Founder*, p. 42ff. Ironically, Captain Lewis, whom Mrs. Hager chose instead of the alcoholic Martin, died an alcoholic.

school in New Jersey), he suggested, with characteristic generosity, that Keene might take his meals at his home if he liked.[31]

Two years later, in January 1801, Martin's two unmarried daughters returned home. The younger, Eleonora, was then just fourteen. Keene, who was at least ten years older, wooed her ardently and surreptitiously for some months before he finally told Martin of his affection.

Taken by surprise, Martin told Keene quite frankly that "he was not the man whom I had ever contemplated as the husband of either of my children" and that he "had different views for them." They had been brought up "under the most unbounded indulgence" and "knew but little the value of money." He had sent them to the best girls' schools; they belonged to the same social set as the daughters of Mr. Justice Samuel Chase and Robert Patterson, the banker and shipping tycoon, and might expect to marry a husband of some means. Above all, Martin was concerned about his daughter's youth and the disparity between her age and Keene's. He reminded Keene that many girls who married too young died early. As he later reported the conversation, he promised Keene that if in a few years, when Eleonora reached maturity, he had attained some standing in his profession and could support a family, "I should then have considered him as having a right in an honourable manner to avow himself a competitor for the affections of my child against any other person . . . , and should have thought it no arrogance in him, nor degradation to her."[32] Keene continued to press his attentions, however, and less than a year later the couple eloped to New York City, where they were married on 27 January, 1802, two months after Eleonora's fifteenth birthday.[33]

In accordance with the custom of the time where matters of family or of honor were involved, Martin and Keene aired the whole affair in a series of bitter, recriminatory letters in the newspapers.[34] They make tiresome reading but provide many details of Martin's family, youth, and later life, of which there would otherwise have been no record. His fears were justified: a few years later, on 17 November 1807, after giving birth to a son, Eleonora died at Greenwich, New York.[35]

[31] *Modern Gratitude*, p. 3ff. *et passim.* At this time Martin's office was on Calvert Street and his home was about a mile away in the old Fell mansion, a "country seat" on Hampstead Hill, now the site of The Johns Hopkins Hospital (see John Mullin, *The Baltimore Directory for 1799*, p. 44; Sioussat, *Old Baltimore*, pp. 73, 169).

[32] *Modern Gratitude*, p. 25.

[33] *New York Evening Post*, 6 February 1802.

[34] Martin wrote five letters, which were published in the *Federal Gazette* (Baltimore) in 1801. In 1802 he reprinted them in his pamphlet *Modern Gratitude*. Keene immediately responded in kind, in *A Letter from Richard Reynal Keene to Luther Martin, Esq. . . . upon the Subject of His "Modern Gratitude."*

[35] *New York Evening Post*, 18 November 1807. The boy, named for his grandfather, Luther Martin Keene, is supposed to have died before maturity (see Cresap and Cresap, *The History of the Cresaps*, p. 317). There is extant, however, a letter from Martin to Aaron Burr dated 19 October 1821, asking Burr to help young Keene, then about eighteen, who was "destitute of the means of getting home" from New York (see *The Collector*, March 1960).

While Martin was harassed by these personal and family troubles, the dockets of the courts continued to produce their tide of cases to be tried and appeals to be argued. His litigation in the lower and appellate courts of Maryland included the usual large number of actions of ejectment and to try title to "Jarrett's Disappointment," "Land of Promise," "Hills of Poverty," "The Silent Cyphers of Africa," "Resurvey on Cold Friday," and a hundred other quaintly named tracts. Such litigation, while routine to the practicing lawyer of his day, involved principles and distinctions more abstruse and complicated than are found in any area of legal practice today.

Among his cases, for the most part dull if lucrative, there were a number of more than ordinary interest. In *Russell's Lessee* v. *Baker*[36] it was held that even though the Lord Proprietary of Maryland could acquire real estate by escheat from a convicted murderer, just as the king of England might, he did not enjoy all the royal rights of the king, but could lose his title to the land by the adverse possession of another. The issue in the case required Martin to outline to the court at length "what royal rights were ever granted to the *Bishop* of *Durham*, in order to find out what have been granted to the Lord *Proprietary* of Maryland" by the terms of the latter's charter. *Whittington* v. *Polk*[37] although little known, has an important place in the history of the uniquely American principle of judicial supremacy. Martin's client, Whittington, complained that the General Assembly had enacted a "ripper bill" abolishing the county courts, redistricting the state, and authorizing the governor to appoint a new set of judges to a new set of courts.[38] The defendant, Polk, now occupied the office of chief justice of the Eastern Shore fourth circuit, a position which had been Whittington's.

Martin's first problem was to find a type of action by which he could contest in court Polk's right to hold Whittington's position. None of the usual writs available at that time fitted the circumstances or were adapted to grant the relief sought. Thereupon, Martin resorted to the almost legendary black-letter learning, in which he was without a peer. He sued out a writ, long forgotten and unused, and called an assize of novel disseisin, by which a property owner wrongfully ousted could file suit to be put back in possession by the court. "And if," says Blackstone, "upon trial, the demandant can prove, first, a title; next, his actual seisin in consequence thereof; and lastly, his disseisin by the present tenant; he shall have judgment to recover his seisin, and damages for the injuries sustained."[39]

The argument was heard at Easton early in 1802 before the General Court for the Eastern Shore, with Chief Judge Jeremiah Townley

---

[36] General Court (E.S.) 1 Harris and Johnson 71 (1800).
[37] 1 Harris and Johnson 236 (1802).
[38] Act of 1801, ch. 74.
[39] *Commentaries*, 3:187.

Chase[40] and Judges Duvall and Done sitting. Martin, with Robert Goodloe Harper, made four points: that an act of the General Assembly repugnant to the state constitution was void; that the court had a right to determine such an act void by reason of its unconstitutionality; that the act in question, so far as it respected the plaintiff, was unconstitutional and void; and that the assise of novel disseisin was the proper action by which to recover his judicial office for the plaintiff. The first two points had been the subject of discussion and debate for many years: indeed, there had been numerous decisions from various state courts, both before and after the Constitutional Convention of 1787, asserting this inherent judicial power to determine the invalidity of a state law under a state constitution.[41] It was inevitable in a government, state or national, founded upon a written constitution with a separation of executive, legislative, and judicial powers that the question of the validity of a statute enacted in violation of the basic law should occur and recur. Even Jefferson and his followers vehemently denounced the federal Alien and Sedition Acts as unconstitutional and invalid.[42] However, Jefferson's solution was to allow each department of the government—indeed, in the case of a federal statute, each state—to determine for itself the constitutionality, validity, and binding effect of such law. In principle, Martin's position was the same here as it had been fifteen years before at Philadelphia: "And as to the constitutionality of laws, that point will come before the judges in their proper official character. In this character they have a negative on the laws."[43]

The Court did not deliver its opinion until that June. The decision, written by the chief judge, noted that the first two points set out "were conceded by counsel for the defendant; indeed they have not been controverted in any of the cases which have been brought before this

[40] Beveridge (*Life of John Marshall*, 3:612) and Charles Grove Haines (*The American Doctrine of Judicial Supremacy*, p. 162) both state erroneously that the presiding judge was Samuel Chase. Haines also errs in stating that "Chase was later appointed a Justice of the Supreme Court of the United States" (Samuel Chase was appointed to the Court more than six years earlier, in January 1796; Jeremiah Townley Chase, of course, was never appointed to the Supreme Court).

[41] See the cases collected in Haines, *Judicial Supremacy*, p. 148ff.; Andrew C. McLaughlin, *A Constitutional History of the United States*, pp. 312–13. The necessity for the Supreme Court to determine the validity of state laws under the federal Constitution has always been acknowledged. Every judiciary act, from the first one of 1789 to the present (including the Act of 1802 enacted by Jefferson and his Republican Congress) has granted the Court jurisdiction to review state action or statutes. This places the opponents of judicial supremacy upon the horns of a nice dilemma: either the Court must accept and exercise such jurisdiction in obedience to the act of Congress, or it may refuse to carry out this legislative mandate, but only by declaring such an act of Congress unconstitutional.

[42] See the Kentucky and Virginia Resolutions of 1798. Note also Jefferson's recommendation of federal judicial review of the constitutionality of state legislation (see Chapter 13, p. 117, above). See also Jefferson's own statement asserting the right of each department of the federal government and of each state to determine for itself the constitutionality and validity of an act of Congress (Beveridge, *Life of John Marshall*, 3:605–6).

[43] See Chapter 13 above.

court." Nonetheless, since the Court was deciding these important principles for the first time in Maryland, it deemed it necessary "to communicate the reasons and grounds of their opinion," which was as follows:

The Legislature, being the creation of the Constitution, and acting within a circumscribed sphere, is not omnipotent, and cannot rightfully exercise any power, but that which is derived from the instrument.

The Constitution having set certain limits or land-marks to the power of the Legislature, whenever they exceed them they act without authority, and such acts are mere nullities, not being done in pursuance of power delegated them: Hence the necessity of some power under the Constitution to restrict the Acts of the Legislature within the limits defined by the Constitution.

The power of determining finally on the validity of the acts of the Legislature cannot reside with the Legislature, because such power would defeat and render nugatory, all the limitations and restrictions on the authority of the Legislature, contained in the Bill of Rights and form of government, and they would become judges of the validity of their own acts, which would establish a despotism, and circumvent that great principle of the Constitution, which declares that the powers of making, judging, and executing the law, shall be separate and distinct from each other. . . .

It is the office and province of the Court to decide all questions of law which are judicially brought before them, . . . and to determine whether an Act of the Legislature, which assumes the appearance of a law, and is clothed with the garb of authority, is made pursuant to the power vested by the Constitution in the Legislature; for if it is not the result or emanation of authority derived from the Constitution, it is not law, and cannot influence the judgment of the Court in the decision of the question before them.[44]

The decision acknowledged that the ripper bill, in depriving the plaintiff of his position, was "an infraction of his right, and incompatible with the principles of justice, and does not accord with sound legislation." Nonetheless, since the office was created by the legislature, as distinguished from the state constitution, it was not a vested property right and was subject to abolition by the General Assembly at its pleasure. On this point, accordingly, Martin lost the case.

The importance of this decision lies in the fact that Martin's argument persuaded the Court to write an opinion which was followed in detail a year later in *Marbury* v. *Madison*.[45] There John Marshall announced the principle that the United States Supreme Court has the necessary, inherent judicial power to review acts of Congress when they are challenged as being in violation of the federal Constitution. A comparison of Marshall's historic and far-reaching opinion with that of Chief Judge Chase demonstrates without any question that while much longer and more philosophical in its terminology, it followed step

[44] 1 Harris and Johnson 236, 243.
[45] 1 Cranch 137 (1803).

by step the reasoning and logic of Chase's exposition of Martin's and Harper's argument.

An interesting colloquy between Martin and Chief Judge Jeremiah Townley Chase took place during the course of the argument in *Harper v. Hampton*.[46] This was an action on a contract, and the question was whether there was sufficient evidence in the case to support a finding by the jury that the principals had had notice of their agents' contract within ten days of its execution. The Court assumed that all parties concerned were in Philadelphia, while those who were entitled to have notice were actually located in South Carolina (in those days nearly three weeks' traveling time away). When Chief Judge Chase ruled that there was "competent and sufficient evidence for the jury to presume and find that the plaintiff in this cause had notice, within ten days from the execution of that contract, of the covenant specified therein," Martin expostulated that "none but an angel on the wings of the wind could give notice in ten days at such a distance," at which the other lawyers and clients in the courtroom burst into sympathetic laughter. Still under a misapprehension as to the location of the parties, the chief judge sharply reprimanded Martin, stating that "he had a right to take an exception to the opinion of the Court, but that he had no right to make any observations which tended to reflect on the Court, or to induce bystanders to believe the Court had been guilty of an absurdity. That Mr. Attorney had been too much in the habit of such conduct, and he was, so far as related to himself, determined to submit to it no longer; that as long as he held a seat on the Bench (and he did not know how long that might be), he was resolved to have a proper respect paid to the Court. He could not conceive what the distance of South Carolina from Philadelphia had to do with the opinion of the Court."

At this point, Robert Goodloe Harper, arguing the case with Martin, interceded and clarified the circumstances. The Chief Judge then "confessed that he had been under a mistake. . . . This will give a different complexion to the case—and the Court withdraw the opinion just given."

Two cases argued together in the Court of Appeals at its June term in 1805, *Luther Martin v. State* and *Claypole v. Martin*.[47] illustrate the leisurely manner in which appeals were sometimes heard. In 1778, only a few months after Martin first became attorney general, he issued an attachment of contempt against a juror for non-attendance at the September term of court. The question in *Luther Martin v. State* was whether, under an act of 1715, this constituted an "action" entitling Martin to a fee. The second case raised a similar question with regard to the fee that Martin was authorized to collect in a case where an accused had been presented by the grand jury in 101 cases for assaults

[46] 1 Harris and Johnson 622 (1805), 715ff.
[47] 1 Harris and Johnson 721.

and batteries, had appeared and confessed the charges, and had submitted to the court, which then imposed a fine in each case.[48] The first case involved only £5, but in the second suit fees of something over £150 were at stake.[49]

Martin argued both cases as though his personal honesty were being impugned. In the unabridged report of *Claypole* v. *Martin*, the abstract of his argument fills nearly eighteen closely printed pages.[50] He reviewed the practice from the earliest provincial courts to that date, cited black-letter authorities from Bracton to Coke on Littleton, and even quoted Samuel Johnson's *Dictionary*. He insisted that he was arguing a matter of principle only, since the £150 in fees in the Claypole case had been paid not to him but to the deputy attorney general, from whom he took no payment. In reply, William Pinkney announced that he would not long trespass on the court's patience, "which had been already so severely taxed by the long, though learned, argument of the Attorney-General—whose speech, however, was distinguished by these two qualities: that of being remarkably *redundant* and remarkably *deficient*. He had resorted to authorities without number to support principally what nobody denied, and abandoned the field of fair argument." Pinkney absolved Martin of "all criminal motives," saying that no man was better acquainted than he with Martin's "generosity and utter negligence in pecuniary concerns. No doubt he received the fee under an entire conviction that he had a right to it. The honor of the Attorney-General is not in question. He must stand upon a legal bottom. Upon the last only we are at issue."[51] The Court of Appeals affirmed the General Court's rulings that the attorney general was not entitled to the fees collected in either case.

It was inevitable that a lawyer of such eminence and success in the state courts would be in demand to argue cases in the federal courts, especially before the United States Supreme Court. Martin's first argument before the latter tribunal was in the famous case of *Little* v. *Barreme*.[52] *Murray* v. *The Schooner Charming Betsy*,[53] argued two years

[48] The defendant in this case was one Peter Martin. Inasmuch as only the matters of fees and costs were at issue on this appeal, no facts are given to account for the unusual number of indictments against a single individual, and one can only speculate at the energy of this Peter Martin.

[49] The attorney general's statutory fee (as claimed) was "200 lbs. of tobacco, or 25 shillings" on each indictment.

[50] Brantley's edition of 1883 condenses Martin's argument to half a page.

[51] 1 Harris and Johnson 721, p. 741.

[52] Reported in 2 Cranch 170. The case was argued at the December 1801 term but was not decided until 27 February 1804. This was due in part to the fact that Congress suspended the sessions of the Supreme Court from December 1801 until February 1803 (Warren, *The Supreme Court*, 1:222–24). The first Supreme Court case of Martin's reported by Cranch was Pennington v. Coxe, 2 Cranch 33, which was not argued until 1803, though the Court's opinion was handed down on 22 February 1804. This case was the equivalent of today's action for declaratory judgment, accomplished then by a "feigned issue," viz., a declaration upon an alleged wager. Martin, with Jared Ingersoll and Robert Goodloe Harper, opposed by United States Attorney General Levi Lincoln and Alexander Dallas, was successful in his construction of an excise tax statute.

[53] 2 Cranch 64 (1804).

later but decided at the same term, raised a similar question. Both cases arose out of the undeclared war with France and involved the seizure of merchant ships by vessels of the young United States Navy. They were decided shortly after the Supreme Court's ruling in *Marbury* v. *Madison*, which Jefferson had seen as a gratuitous usurpation of legislative power by Marshall. These admiralty cases—both won by Martin —show, however, that Marshall played no favorites: the decision held executive actions by the Federalist president John Adams, purportedly under an act of Congress, to be equally unlawful when they exceeded statutory authorization.

Ogden v. *Blackledge*[54] was the first case argued in the Supreme Court under the "obligation of contracts" clause of the Constitution, which Martin had vigorously opposed at the convention. It arose from the circuit court of North Carolina and concerned the collectability of a British debt. At issue was the validity of a 1799 act of the North Carolina state legislature reinstating retroactively the provisions of a 1715 statute of limitations which had been repealed in 1789. Martin and Robert Goodloe Harper argued that the 1799 law could not affect the case because "to declare what the law is, or has been is a judicial power; to declare what the law shall be, is legislative. One of the fundamental principles of all our governments is, that the legislative power shall be separated from the judicial." At that point, the court interrupted observing that it was unnecessary to argue that proposition further, and another strut in the structure of judicial supremacy was secured.

In *Head and Amory* v. *Providence Insurance Co.* and *Graves and Barnewall* v. *Boston Marine Insurance Co.*,[55] Martin appeared as counsel in the only cases involving questions of corporation law that had come before the Supreme Court since 1790. It was after hearing the argument in these two cases that John Quincy Adams wrote in his diary, "On the whole, I have never witnessed a collection of such powerful legal orators as at this session of the Supreme Court."[56]

With Richard Stockton, of New Jersey, Martin argued the case of *Church* v. *Hubbart*[57] against John Quincy Adams and Jeremiah Mason. Adams had written his client that he had resolved to retain associate counsel to argue the case with him and had decided on Luther Martin, "a gentleman whose general professional eminence, as well as his particular familiarity with causes of a commercial nature are universally recognized by those who have had the means of knowing him."[58] He offered Martin one hundred dollars as a retainer, but, as he soon discovered, Martin had already been engaged by the other side. Martin and Stockton were successful in reversing the lower court on the

---

[54] 2 Cranch 272 (1804).
[55] 2 Cranch 127 (1804); 2 Cranch 419 (1805).
[56] *Memoirs*, 1:295.
[57] 2 Cranch 187 (1804).
[58] Adams to Peter Chardon Brooks, 21 January 1804, *Writings*, 3:31. See also his *Memoirs*, 1:295.

technicality that certain Portuguese papers in the case had not been properly authenticated. Indeed, he was successful in six of the eight cases he argued before the Supreme Court at its 1804 term.

Despite his frequent drunkenness, his loud good-fellowship, his un-yielding Federalism, his outspoken dislike of Jefferson, his prolix and persistent letters to editors, Luther Martin was both respected and liked. His practice, official and private, had made him the best-known man in Maryland. He was a familiar figure in his unpressed, unbrushed clothes, old-fashioned ruffles edged with lace, rich but badly soiled, at his wrists, plodding the streets from office or tavern to court and back, his nearsighted face habitually buried in a book.[59] Baltimoreans told the story of the time that he bumped into a cow on Baltimore Street, respectfully bowed and apologized to her, and absentmindedly went on his way. More than a character, more than a great lawyer, he was already a Maryland institution.

The following illustrates the mingled affection and esteem in which Martin was held. It will be recalled that he accepted the post of attorney general after it had been offered to and declined by Benjamin Galloway.[60] This decision haunted Galloway all his life. Someone was forever accusing him either of Toryism or of cowardice, and, being of a naturally contentious disposition he denied such charges vigorously and sometimes pugnaciously, insisting that he had declined the office in deference to the apprehensions of his father, who feared that the Revolution might not succeed. Martin's wealth and achievements as attorney general were a constant source of resentment to Galloway.[61]

In June 1803 he and Martin opposed each other in a case tried at Annapolis, and Galloway reported to President Jefferson, at length and in detail, that "with intention of gratifying a malevolent disposition, he [Martin] introduced your name in his address to the jury; and you will not be surprised to learn that his representation of your conduct was not calculated to impress on the public mind a *very favorable* opinion." Galloway complained that in the course of his speech to the jury, Martin had declared him to be "a most *outrageous* character, and as proof . . . , had the Effrontry to tell the Jury that after I came from England . . . , I resided twenty years in Anne Arundel County; that scarce a court met that an action of Ass't and Batt'y or Slander was not brought agst. me; that I had lived eight yrs. in Washington Cy. and the Docquets [*sic*] of the County would prove on search that my Con-duct had been equally *exceptionable* and *outrageous there also.*" Upon the

[59] The best contemporary description of Martin as of about 1800 is provided by Chief Justice Roger B. Taney (see Appendix C to this volume).

[60] See Chapter 6 above. For a brief biographical sketch of Galloway, see T. J. C. Williams, *History of Washington County*, 1:198-99.

[61] On coming to Maryland in the early 1770s he first settled in Anne Arundel County, and it seems probable that Martin, both as attorney general and as a practicing attorney, prosecuted him from time to time, both criminally and civilly, for assaults and batteries resulting from his quarrelsome disposition (see Galloway to Thomas Jefferson, 11 October 1803, Jefferson Papers, 135:23384).

conclusion of the case, Martin approached him outside the courtroom, Galloway reported, and offered "a personal apology . . . for (as he said) *one* expression which he had used in his *Philippic* against me." Upon Martin's affirmative reply to Galloway's question as to whether the apology was confined to one statement only, Galloway declined speaking further with him, whereupon, according to Galloway, Martin "*speedily* took his departure; and being more than *half Seas over, reeled* into the General Court."[62]

By coincidence, Galloway at the time was under a bond to keep the peace because of another altercation. He asserted that Martin was aware of this and intended to provoke him into a breach of the peace, which would bring about the forfeiture of a substantial bond of five hundred pounds. He wrote Jefferson that he was about to go to Annapolis the following Saturday to argue a motion for a new trial in that case and expected that Martin would use the same "black-guard" tactics as he had in June. "I have the best ground to *believe*," Galloway continued, "that if he should misbehave on Saturday next, as he *did in June*, Mr. Attorney General will be put in *durance vile*."

Disappointed in the latter prediction, the following month Galloway presented a petition to the General Assembly of Maryland asking Martin's impeachment as attorney general.[63] He alleged that Martin had indulged in "the almost daily practice of appearing in the Courts of Justice . . . intoxicated with spirituous Liquor, and that the Dignity of the State of Maryland is severely wounded by reason of the appearance of the Attorney General in its Courts of Justice, in said condition." He asked the General Assembly to consider the matter seriously "with a view to removing said Luther Martin from office, and to administer such Relief to their County and Fellow Citizens as the United Wisdom of the Legislature and the Dignity of the State call for in a Trumpet-like voice." As witnesses to his allegation that Martin had repeatedly appeared in court drunk, Galloway appended a page-long list of judges and lawyers in the state. The House of Delegates considered both the source and the object of the petition, and took action. According to the terse report in its *Journal* for 2 January 1804, "On motion, the question was put, That the said letter be ordered to lie on the table? Determined in the negative. ORDERED, that the said letter be thrown under the table."[64]

[62] Galloway's petition for impeachment of Martin (copy enclosed by Galloway in his letter to Jefferson [Jefferson Papers, 128:22167]).

[63] Galloway sent a copy of this petition to Jefferson on 5 January 1804 (Jefferson Papers, 128:22167).

[64] *Votes and Proceedings*, Nov. Sess. 1803, p. 85 (January 2, 1804).

21

The Chase Impeachment, January–March 1805

> We [the Senate] have authority to remove a judge if he is disagreeable in his office or wrongheaded, and opposed to the administration, though not corrupt in conduct.—Senator Giles to Senator Plumer, November 1804

> I assuredly believe that the independence of the Judiciary, which is the boast of the Constitution, hangs on this pivot.—Simeon Baldwin, 5 January 1805

> If any student of American history, curious to test the relative value of reputations, will read Randolph's opening address, and then pass on to the argument of Luther Martin, he will feel the distance between show and strength, between intellectual brightness and intellectual power.—Henry Adams, *John Randolph*

Early in 1805 Luther Martin volunteered his talents in the defense of his close friend of thirty years' standing, Samuel Chase, Associate Justice of the United States Supreme Court. This was one of the two greatest state trials in American history and of tremendous importance to our constitutional system: it established for more than a century to come the independence of the federal judiciary from the executive and legislative branches of the government. It also provided the occasion for one of the greatest forensic arguments in the history of the bar.[1]

The Chase trial was the climax of Jefferson's war on the federal courts. In the first three terms of the presidency, Washington and John Adams had filled the federal judiciary, from district to Supreme Court, with Federalists. Most of these men were able lawyers and sound judges whose actions were not governed by party politics. Some, however, were so convinced of the wrongheadedness, if not downright wickedness, of those whose beliefs were more democratic and liberal than their own

[1] This appraisal of Martin's defense is the conclusion of such historians as Henry Adams (*History of the United States of America during the Administrations of Jefferson and Madison*, 2:232; *John Randolph*, pp. 146–47); Albert G. Beveridge (*Life of John Marshall*, 3:201–6); William Draper Lewis (*Great American Lawyers*, 2:23–24); Horace H. Hagan (*Eight Great American Lawyers*, pp. 11–13); and Andrew C. McLaughlin (*Constitutional History*, p. 322).

that they assumed the propriety, indeed, the necessity, of using their offices to suppress contrary doctrines and to maintain the Federalist Party in power.

In 1798 the Federalists passed the Sedition Act, sec. 2 of which made it a crime, punishable by a fine of as much as two thousand dollars and imprisonment of up to two years, to "write, print, utter or publish . . . any false, scandalous and malicious writing . . . against the government . . . , or either house of Congress . . . , or the President of the United States, with intent to defame . . . or to bring them, or either of them, into contempt or disrepute."[2] The unconstitutionality of such a law under the First Amendment[3] is today so obvious that it could not be passed, much less enforced. James Thompson Callender, for example, was indicted and tried for libel under the Sedition Act for writing and publishing a scurrilous Antifederalist pamphlet entitled *The Prospect before Us.* Justice Chase presided at Callender's trial, which resulted in a conviction. He was sentenced to nine months' imprisonment and a fine of two hundred dollars.

In presiding over prosecutions of Republican officeholders, politicians, and editors and in stirring up indictments for alleged violations of this law, some Federalist judges acted more like avenging angels than impartial administrators of justice, and thus aroused widespread popular hatred.[4] In the same spirit, those who forcibly resisted the federal direct tax on property were tried for treason and, if convicted, were sentenced to death.[5]

The first item on Jefferson's agenda, upon becoming president, was the reformation of the federal judiciary. The Federalists, while still in power, had done what they could to set up a check upon the incoming Republican administration. By the Judiciary Act of 13 February 1801 (enacted by the lame-duck Congress defeated at the polls the previous November), the Federalists had reduced the number of associate justices on the Supreme Court to four, hoping thereby to preclude any new appointments by Jefferson. They had increased by five the number of district judges and created six new circuit courts, requiring some sixteen more judges. These sixteen, all Federalists, were the famous "Midnight Judges" appointed by Adams in the last days of his administration.[6] Most important of all, when Chief Justice Ellsworth resigned because of illness in September of 1800, Adams appointed John Marshall in his place. This not only prevented Jefferson from giving the

[2] *Statutes at Large,* 1:596–97.
[3] "Congress shall make no law . . . abridging the freedom of speech, or of the press." See Zechariah Chafee, Jr., *Free Speech in the United States,* pp. 27–28, 174.
[4] See, for example, trials of Matthew Lyon, Thomas Cooper, Anthony Haswell, and James Thompson Callender, in Wharton's *State Trials,* pp. 333ff., 659ff., 684ff., 688ff.; *American State Trials,* 10:774ff., 813ff.; Smith, *Freedom's Fetters, passim.*
[5] See the trials of John Fries, in Wharton's *State Trials,* pp. 482ff., 610ff.; *American State Trials,* 11:1ff., 146ff. President John Adams pardoned Fries, Hainy, and Getman (McMaster, *History of the People of the U.S.,* 2:435–39; Beveridge, *Life of John Marshall,* 2:429).
[6] See Kathryn Turner, "The Midnight Judges," p. 494.

position to his friend, cousin, and fellow Republican states'-righter Spencer Roane of Virginia, but it established in that office, for life, a man whose entire philosophy—political, economic, and constitutional—was diametrically opposed to Jefferson's.

Jefferson felt that through these appointments the Federalists had given the judiciary the power to thwart the will of the people as expressed in his election and that of other Republicans. Accordingly, he set about to reverse, insofar as he could, the Federalist "seizure" of the judiciary and to bring that department of the government into line with Republican principles. His Congress thereupon repealed the Judiciary Act of 1801, postponed the next term of the Supreme Court until February 1802 (in part to prevent the Court from declaring the repeal unconstitutional), and restored the Supreme Court to its original size of six members, thus giving Jefferson the power to make appointments of his own men.

As though to substantiate the Republicans' worst fears, Marshall and his court in *Marbury* v. *Madison*[7] declared the power of the Supreme Court to hold an act of Congress invalid and inoperative if it was in violation of the Constitution. Marshall had managed the decision with consummate adroitness. The universal assumption of the Republicans was that he would order Madison to give Marbury his commission, and the decision that Madison was not required to do so was a victory for the Republicans. Moreover, the Court showed restraint in refusing to accept jurisdiction from Congress beyond that given it by the Constitution. At the same time, the opinion branded Madison (and, through him, Jefferson) as one who unlawfully, and even immorally, refused to accord to another the rights and privileges to which he was clearly entitled. Even if the part of the opinion adopting the doctrine of judicial review be considered as incidental, Marshall announced it so forthrightly and so clearly that the tail of the dictum wagged the dog of the decision.

This event gave the final impetus, if any had been necessary, to the Republicans' plan to clear the national judiciary of its Federalist judges through the constitutional machinery of impeachment and to replace them with Republicans. There was no secret about this scheme: Jefferson and his leaders in Congress openly announced this as their purpose, ignoring the only basis for impeachment specified by the Constitution, namely, "Conviction of Treason, Bribery, or other high Crimes and Misdemeanors."[8] They resolved to try to convict Federalist judges upon any ground which would serve the purpose, such as failure to observe "good behavior" or legal judgments contrary to the opinion of a majority of Congress. Senator William Branch Giles, of Virginia,

---

[7] 1 Cranch 153 (1803). The earliest case in which the Court passed upon the constitutionality of an act of Congress, sustaining its validity, was Hylton v. United States, 3 Dall. 171 (1796). See Warren, *The Supreme Court*, 1:146ff.

[8] Art. II, sec. 4.

speaking for the Administration, bluntly declared, "*We want your offices, for the purpose of giving them to men who will fill them better.*"[9] As John Quincy Adams concluded, "the impeachment system is to be pursued, and the whole bench of the Supreme Court to be swept away because *their offices are wanted.*"[10]

The first impeachment in a series which was planned to culminate with the removal of John Marshall and all the other judges of the Supreme Court except the last one appointed,[11] was initiated by Jefferson himself. On 3 February 1803 he sent a message to the House of Representatives enclosing affidavits regarding the judicial conduct of United States District Judge John Pickering of New Hampshire and suggesting to that body that "the Constitution has confided a power of instituting proceedings of redress if they shall be of opinion that the case calls for them."[12] As the testimony in that case later revealed, Judge Pickering was hopelessly insane, and his often violent irrationality was compounded by pathological alcoholism. The fact that a man so afflicted could not normally be convicted of "high crimes and misdemeanors" was seized upon by the Republicans as a case made to order for establishing their theory that impeachment did not require criminal conduct but only general incapacitation.[13] Within six weeks, on 12 March 1803, the Senate had tried and convicted Pickering *in absentia*; it deliberately avoided the delicate constitutional question presented by voting Pickering guilty "as charged" rather than of "high Crimes and Misdemeanors."[14] The machinery was thus set in motion for ridding the federal judiciary in general, and the Supreme Court in particular, of the obnoxious Federalists who manned it, the chief and ultimate objective, of course, being John Marshall.

The second step to this end was the impeachment of the most widely disliked of all the federal judges, Samuel Chase of the Supreme Court. Chase was somewhat older than Luther Martin, having been born in

[9] Giles to Israel Smith, Republican Senator from Vermont, quoted in Adams, *Memoirs*, 1:322–23, 21 December 1804. Cf. Giles's argument on the floor of the Senate on 20 December 1804, reported in the *Federal Gazette* (Baltimore) for 3 January 1805, that the Senate was required by the Constitution to remove from office a judge convicted of "Treason, Bribery, or other high Crimes and Misdemeanors" but was allowed to try a judge for other and lesser offenses and, if he were convicted, to suspend or remove him from office or not, at the discretion of the Senate. This remarkable argument had never been heard before and has not been heard since. See also Adams, *Memoirs*, 1:321.

[10] *Memoirs*, 1:321.

[11] Giles to Smith, in *ibid*. The most recently appointed judge was William Johnson, a Republican named to the Supreme Court by Jefferson on 26 March 1804 and, accordingly, not included in the Republicans' impeachment plan.

[12] *Annals of Congress*, 7th Cong., 2d sess., 1803, p. 460.

[13] The Federalist Judiciary Act of 1801, repealed by the Republican Judiciary Act of 1802, provided for replacement of an incapacitated judge by the circuit court.

[14] Henry Adams, *History of the United States*, 2:157; Beveridge, *Life of John Marshall*, 3:167; John Quincy Adams, *Memoirs*, 1:307–8. Jefferson rewarded the principal witnesses against Pickering with lucrative federal appointments, one of them to Pickering's own seat on the bench (William Plumer, Jr., *Life of William Plumer*, p. 274; Beveridge, *Life of John Marshall*, 3:181).

Somerset County, on the Eastern Shore of Maryland, in 1741. At the age of eighteen he went to Annapolis to study law, and he was admitted to practice there in 1761. An organizer of the Sons of Liberty and a delegate from Maryland to the first Continental Congress in 1774, he was an early, fiery, and active participant in the Revolutionary movement. He became a member of the Maryland Council of Safety in 1775 and later that year attended the state convention at Annapolis, where it is probable that he and Martin, also a delegate, first met.[15]

As already recounted, it was Chase's unflagging efforts, more than those of any other single person, that induced the Maryland legislature to instruct its delegation to Congress to vote for complete independence from England in July 1776.[16] Chase returned to Philadelphia and signed the Declaration of Independence in August. A prodigious worker, he served on twenty-one congressional committees in 1777 and thirty in 1778. He joined Martin in opposing Maryland's adoption of the Federal Constitution in the spring of 1788.[17] After a brilliant and highly successful career at the bar, Chase was appointed chief judge of the Baltimore Criminal Court in 1788 and, three years later, became chief judge of the Maryland General Court. As an attorney and judge, he had acquired experience in every field of the law and with every type of lawyer and legal maneuver. Like Martin, he was orginally an Antifederalist, but for reasons not known he changed to Federalism in the early 1790s. In 1796, Washington appointed him to the United States Supreme Court. From then until the appointment of Marshall in 1801 Chase was the outstanding member of that Court. His opinions were impartial,[18] learned, colorful, and dogmatic.

Chase was over six feet tall and broad in proportion. In the words of one of his counsel, "of an ardent mind and sanguine habit, he . . . evidenced more warmth than weaker heads and colder constitutions."[19] He was hearty, gruff, witty, and popular with young people.[20] His complexion was brownish red in color, resulting in the nickname "Old Bacon Face." Joseph Story called him the "living image" of Samuel Johnson, "in person, in manners, in unwieldy strength, in severity of reproof, in real tenderness of heart; and above all in intellect."[21]

[15] It is possible that Martin, who was practicing law in Somerset County at that time, first met Chase there.
[16] See Chapter 5 above.
[17] See Chapter 16 above.
[18] Since he was counsel for Maryland debtors in the British debt litigation (see Chapter 17 above), he begged to be excused from participating in Ware v. Hylton (3 Dall. 199 [1796]). Upon the insistence of the rest of the Court, he reluctantly sat and wrote the opinion sustaining the British claims (see Warren, *The Supreme Court*, 1:144).
[19] Philip Barton Key's description, quoted in Charles Evans' shorthand report (*Trial of Chase*, p. 161). This passage does not appear in the *Annals of Congress*.
[20] Henry Marie Brackenridge, *Recollections of Persons and Places in the West*, p. 129.
[21] Letter of 25 February 1808 in William Wetmore Story, ed., *Life and Letters of Joseph Story, Associate Justice of the Supreme Court of the United States*, 1:166, reprinted in Warren, *The Supreme Court*, 1:465. See also Brackenridge, *Recollections*, pp. 154–55.

Because of his reputed heavyhanded procedure while presiding over the trials of John Fries, James Thompson Callender, and others, Chase had also acquired the epithet, "the American Jeffreys." On 2 May 1803 he delivered the Court's customary address to the federal grand jury in Baltimore, larding it with highly critical comments regarding the political attacks on both the federal and Maryland judiciaries, the adoption of universal suffrage in Maryland, and the newfangled theories as to the "equality of liberty and rights" in a democratic society. "Our republican constitution will sink into a mobocracy," he lamented, "the worst of all possible governments," and predicted that "peace and order, freedom and property, [will] be destroyed."[22]

Jefferson seems never to have lacked for informers, and a young Republican reporter, James Montgomery, sent the President a copy of the *Baltimore American* for 13 June 1803, containing his highly excited and inaccurate account of Chase's address, which attributed to Chase observations on the Jefferson administration which, although he may have had them in mind, he certainly did not express to the grand jury.[23] Jefferson forwarded the newspaper to Joseph Nicholson, a Representative from Maryland, asking whether "this seditious and official attack on the principles of our Constitution, and on the proceedings of a State [should] go unpunished? And, to whom so pointedly as yourself will the public look for the necessary measures?" Then, lest he show his hand too plainly, he added, "For myself, it is better that I should not interfere."[24]

Nicholson felt that it would be indelicate for him to sponsor such action, as he was reported to have been promised Chase's seat after the impeachment.[25] The leadership in the project was therefore assumed by John Randolph of Roanoke. On 5 January 1804 he rose in the House of Representatives to ask that a committee be appointed "to inquire into the official conduct of Samuel Chase . . . , and to report their opinion, whether the said Samuel Chase hath so acted in his judicial capacity, as to require the interposition of the constitutional power of this House."[26] The resolution was amended to include an inquiry into the conduct of Richard Peters, United States District Judge for Pennsylvania, but the committee report recommended that only Chase be impeached. On 12 March, the day on which Judge Pickering's impeachment was voted by the Senate, the House agreed to the committee

[22] Evans, *Trial of Chase*, p. 61.
[23] "Upon the liability to *Impeachment* of *Judge Chase* for alleged misbehavior in office," reprinted in Evans, *Trial of Chase*, p. 101ff.; *Annals of Congress*, 8th Cong., 2d sess., 1804 (cited hereafter in this chapter as *Annals*), p. 247ff.
[24] Letter of 13 May 1803, in H. A. Washington, ed., *The Writings of Thomas Jefferson*, 4:484. See McMaster, *History of the People of the U.S.*, 3:162–69.
[25] See William E. Dodd, *Life of Nathaniel Macon*, p. 188; McMaster, *History of the People of the U.S.*, 3:170.
[26] *Annals of Congress*, 8th Cong., 1st sess., 1804, p. 806; Evans, *Trial of Chase*, p. [1].

report, which recommended the impeachment of Chase, by a vote of seventy-three to thirty-two.[27]

Two weeks later Randolph submitted a further report consisting of a draft of seven articles of impeachment against Chase, which was ordered to lie on the table.[28] (It was not, in fact, acted upon until the next session of Congress, over six months later.) Chase at once expostulated that the result, if not, indeed, the intention of this maneuver, was to make available to the public, through the newspapers, charges highly prejudicial to him which he could not refute because they had not been adopted by the House.[29] This, of course, was all part of the Republican strategy. Jefferson was one of the first American politicians to appreciate and exploit the power of the press for his own political purposes.[30] Most of the accusations against Chase were based on events already three or four years old, but formal action against him was purposely delayed so that the public could be conditioned by speeches, newspaper articles, and other pronouncements to accept Chase's guilt as proved.[31]

Congress reconvened on 5 November, and on 30 November Randolph reported out a new set of articles of impeachment. The fifth and sixth articles were entirely new and concerned alleged misapplication of Virginia law by Chase in the course of Callender's trial. These articles presented issues which had not even been raised there, much less argued; they were brought forth now in support of the Republican theory that a mere legal mistake made by a federal judge was sufficient ground for his impeachment and removal from office. On this theory, every federal judge, from the Supreme Court down, could be removed for any decision with which the party in power disagreed. In addition, a new article was appended charging Chase with improper conduct in his address to the Baltimore federal grand jury. As so amended and enlarged, the articles were adopted by the House on 3 and 4 December 1804, and presented at the bar of the Senate on 7 December.[32]

To prosecute the impeachment the House appointed a miscellaneous and, for the most part, undistinguished group headed by John Ran-

[27] Evans, *Trial of Chase*, p. 5; *Annals of Congress*, 8th Cong., 1st sess., 1804, p. 85.

[28] 26 March 1804 (*Annals of Congress*, 8th Cong., 1st sess., 1804, p. 1237ff.).

[29] *Federal Gazette* (Baltimore), 30 March 1805, reprinted in Evans, *Trial of Chase*, p. 5ff.

[30] While he was in Washington's cabinet, Jefferson persuaded Philip Freneau to set up an opposition newspaper, the *National Gazette*, and subsidized it with State Department funds. When President Washington questioned him about the matter, he was, to put it kindly, something less than candid (see Frank Luther Mott, *Jefferson and the Press*, p. 16ff.).

[31] The Republicans had gathered "a volume of ex parte evidence" against Chase and had published it in pamphlet form, which pamphlets they distributed widely, and also published in the "Court Gazette" (the Washington *National Intelligencer*), from which it was reprinted by newspapers all over the country (Plumer to Smith, 11 March 1804, Plumer Papers, Library of Congress, Washington, D.C.; Beveridge, *Life of John Marshall*, 3:171).

[32] *Annals*, pp. 87–88.

dolph. Randolph was poorly equipped for this assignment: he was in poor health and, not being a lawyer, could not handle the difficult constitutional and legal questions it presented. In addition to that brilliant but erratic genius, the House appointed George Washington Campbell, Joseph Hopper Nicholson, Peter Early, John Boyle, Christian Clarke, and Caesar Rodney. The counsel for the defense provided a sharp contrast. In addition to Chase himself, there were five lawyers of ability and national reputation: Joseph Hopkinson, Charles Lee, Philip Barton Key, Robert Goodloe Harper, and the man who framed and directed the defense strategy, described by Henry Adams as the "most formidable of American advocates . . . the rollicking, witty, audacious Attorney-General of Maryland; boon companion of Chase and the whole bar; drunken, generous, slovenly, grand; bull-dog of federalism, as Mr. Jefferson called him; shouting with a school-boy's fun at the idea of tearing Randolph's indictment to pieces and teaching the Virginia democrats some law,—the notorious reprobate genius, Luther Martin."[33]

Under the direction of Vice-President Aaron Burr, the Senate chamber was decorated for the impending proceedings. On the model of the House of Lords chamber during the impeachment of Lord Hastings, benches covered with crimson cloth were placed to left and right in a line with the president's chair and were assigned to the members of the Senate. Chairs covered with blue were set on the right and the left of the president for the managers of the House and for Chase's counsel. In the center of the room seats were reserved for members of the House of Representatives, covered in green. A special temporary gallery was erected below the permanent gallery, with boxes at each end, "fitted up with peculiar elegance, intended primarily for the accommodation of ladies. But this feature of the arrangements . . . was at an early period of the trial abandoned, it having been found impracticable to separate the sexes."[34] Only Chase had been forgotten. When he first appeared before the Senate on 2 January 1805 no chair had been provided for him and he had to ask for one. Thereafter, he sat with his lawyers until his gout compelled him, with the consent of the Senate, to retire halfway through the case. His address to the Senate asking for time to prepare a formal and detailed answer was interrupted by Burr several times in a peremptory manner.[35] On 3 January Chase therefore filed with the Senate an affidavit stating that he required at least two months to investigate the factual basis of the charges against him, to contact witnesses, procure evidence, and consult with his counsel. After debating the matter, the Senate granted him half the time requested and set a date of Monday, 4 February.

[33] *John Randolph*, p. 141.
[34] *Annals*, p. 100.
[35] *Ibid.*, p. 91ff.; *Federal Gazette* (Baltimore), 5 January 1805; Plumer to James Sheafe, 9 January 1805, Plumer Papers.

On that date Chase appeared with his counsel, who read his formal answer.[36] This long paper, in which the hand of Martin is clearly discernible in almost every paragraph, discussed, article by article and point by point, the facts and the law upon which Chase's defense was based. Its clarity and detail made a deep impression on the public in general and on the Senate in particular. Randolph was then granted permission to file a replication on behalf of the House, and the trial began on 9 February.[37] Randolph opened the proceedings with a statement setting forth, in rambling and disconnected fashion, the evidence which the House expected to adduce in support of its charges.[38]

At the sessions of the impeachment proceedings the room was packed. Every seat and standing place was occupied, and more than a thousand spectators were reported in attendance.[39] Previous commentators on the Chase impeachment have failed to mention that the Senate was to base its verdict on the evidence produced before it, under oath, and subject to cross-examination, at the trial. Accounts of Chase's conduct of the Fries and Callender trials,[40] whether from newspapers, self-appointed court reporters, casual bystanders, or other sources, were therefore quite irrelevant. Such evidence was hearsay at best, was not given under oath, and to this day has not been subjected to cross-examination or refutation by independent witnesses. When he came to vote, each member of the Senate presumably made up his mind on the basis of the testimony at that hearing. Accordingly, it is important to examine the evidence there produced: as in the case of all judicial proceedings, the allegations set forth in the articles, Chase's defense, and the speeches of counsel were not (and are not) evidence for or against Chase except insofar as they were supported by credible testimony.

In view of the number and gravity of the charges against Chase, the bitter determination with which they were publicized over a period of years by the Republican press and politicians, and the vehemence with which they were prosecuted by the House managers, an examination of the articles of impeachment[41] and the evidence introduced is rather startling.[42] Article I accused Chase, the presiding judge in the trial of John Fries, of having conducted himself "in a manner highly arbitrary,

[36] Evans, *Trial of Chase*, p. 7ff.; *Annals*, pp. 102–50.
[37] Evans, *Trial of Chase*, p. 40.
[38] *Ibid.*, p. 13ff. Plumer (*William Plumer's Memorandum of Proceedings in the United States Senate, 1803–1807*, p. 260) called it "the most feeble—the most incorrect that I ever heard him make."
[39] *Federal Gazette* (Baltimore), 23 February 1805.
[40] See nn. 4–5 above. In addition, contemporary newspapers were full of accounts, solicited and otherwise, by partial observers on each side.
[41] Especially arts. I–IV.
[42] The proceedings are published in Evans, *Trial of Chase*; in another shorthand report taken by Samuel H. Smith and Thomas Lloyd, *Trial of Samuel Chase*; and in *Annals of Congress*, 8th Cong., 2d sess., 1804, pp. 80–675. Smith and Lloyd are apparently identical with the *Annals*, but in many places, particularly the evidence of witnesses, these two differ greatly from Evans in wording. The speeches of counsel are also reported in *Columbian Eloquence, Being the Speeches of the Most Celebrated American Orators, as Delivered in the Late Interesting Trial of the Hon. Samuel Chase.*

oppressive, and unjust," in the following particulars: he delivered a written opinion upon a question vital to Fries's defense, tending to prejudice the jury against the accused before his counsel had been heard in his defense; he prevented Fries's counsel from relying upon certain English cases for the defense; and he ruled that Fries's counsel might not argue to the jury certain questions of law, which he held to be for the Court to determine.

Fries's counsel, William Lewis and Alexander Dallas, called as witnesses by the House, immediately cast some doubt on their evidence by admitting that their recollections of these events of almost five years earlier were somewhat hazy. They went on to testify that before the trial started Chase had given counsel a written opinion as to the law of the case, based upon previous rulings both in Fries's first trial[43] and in other similar cases in the same circuit. This action, while not usual, was certainly not irregular under the circumstances and merely served to advise counsel as to the ruling of the court on those matters of evidence and law which had been decided at the earlier trial. Counsel for Fries did not attack Chase's rulings on the basis that they were contrary to law but on the basis that they were announced in advance.

This opinion offered an opportunity to make Fries's conviction, which Lewis and Dallas believed to be inevitable, appear the result of the judge's misconduct rather than of guilt, and they therefore withdrew from the case in apparent high dudgeon. They not only abandoned their client but advised him not to accept another lawyer, even if the court should offer to appoint one for him—highly irresponsible advice for a lawyer to give a client in a capital case. The testimony of Lewis and Dallas[44] raises two questions: why Judge Griffin, who sat with Chase and concurred with him in every decision, was not impeached as well; and why, if Chase's conduct was clearly prejudicial and his rulings flagrantly in error, they did not persevere in making a record that would ensure a reversal of the judgment on appeal.

Edward Tilghman and William Rawle now added their testimony. Rawle, who had been United States district attorney for Pennsylvania, disclosed that, on the day after the dispute with Fries's counsel, Chase and Griffin had withdrawn their opinion and had given the two lawyers permission to proceed with their argument of the law. After Fries's lawyers had withdrawn, Chase announced, according to Rawle, that "by the blessing of God, the court will be your counsel, and will do you as much justice as those who were your counsel." He thereupon "took particular pains to inform Fries of his right to challenge" and enabled Fries to use thirty-four of the thirty-five peremptory challenges allowed him. He also reminded Fries of his right to cross-examine the government's witnesses, at the same time warning him not to ask

---

[43] Fries was convicted of treason before Judges Iredell and Peters in 1799 but was granted a new trial because of alleged prejudice of a juror.

[44] Reported in full in Evans, *Trial of Chase*, p. 18ff.; *Annals*, pp. 166ff., 174ff.

any questions that might tend to incriminate him.[45] The defense testimony on this article[46] merely reinforced the prosecution's own witnesses.

One can show, article by article, how the prosecution's testimony failed to substantiate the offenses charged to any material degree. Articles II, III, and IV alleged not only incorrect legal rulings by Chase during the trial of Callender at Richmond in May of 1800 for violation of the Sedition Act, but also "manifest injustice, partiality, and intemperance." It is apparent that Chase was frequently brusque with Callender's counsel and that he was upon occasion sarcastic, even undignified, if humorous. But it is also evident, from the House's own witnesses, that the defense was using the Callender trial primarily as a political arena. To this end, they baited Judge Chase endlessly, asking for postponement after postponement, offering again and again evidence and arguments that the Judge had already excluded or overruled. George Hay openly admitted that his "chief object" in representing Callender was not to defend his client, but to "address the public on the constitutionality" of the Sedition Act.[47] Furthermore, Chase repeatedly reminded counsel that, as he was human, he might be in error and thus subject to reversal on appeal. He offered every aid to counsel to prepare the record and to expedite an appeal to the Supreme Court.[48]

[45] Evans, *Trial of Chase*, pp. 26, 29–31, 63; *Annals*, pp. 178, 180, 187, 246. The reports do not show which side called Rawle or which counsel examined him. Hopkinson stated, however, that he was a witness for the House managers (Evans, *Trial of Chase*, p. 128; *Annals*, p. 369).

[46] Testimony of William Meredith (Evans, *Trial of Chase*, pp. 62–63; *Annals*, pp. 245–46).

[47] Evans, *Trial of Chase*, pp. 37–38; *Annals*, p. 206. "It was a political affair, in public estimation, and the retirement of counsel, under the pretext of being driven off by the hectoring temper of the judge politically hostile to the prisoner, was likely to be regarded not as a confession of the guilt of their client, but as an appeal to the jury, and an invitation to them to take him into their protection" (Kennedy, *Life of William Wirt*, p. 81).

[48] Evans, *Trial of Chase*, pp. 46, 67; *Annals*, pp. 222, 256, 414. It has been suggested, in support of the conduct of Fries's and Callender's counsel, that perhaps no appeal lay in criminal cases under the Judiciary Act of 1789, in force at the time of those trials (spring of 1800). The Act, in fact, was silent on this point, neither specifically granting nor denying such review. There is no doubt, however, that both the court and counsel believed, at the time of these trials, that the accused did have such right to appeal, if convicted.
During the course of the Callender trial, Chase frequently reminded counsel: "I am a fallible man and it is possible that I may be in error and therefore the whole case may be stated in writing, and I will assist the counsel in making out a writ of error, and allow them to take the case up to the supreme court as soon as possible" (Evans, *Trial of Chase*, pp. 46, 67). Counsel for the accused never questioned this assumption. The Supreme Court, in United States v. Simms (decided 3 February 1803, 1 Cranch 252), actually reviewed a criminal conviction on a writ of error, with the right of appeal still not questioned. It was not until More v. United States (3 Cranch 159, decided 2 March 1805, the day after the Chase trial ended), that the Supreme Court dismissed a criminal appeal for lack of jurisdiction when this issue was raised for the first time. Harper suggested in the Chase trial that review by the Supreme Court might have been had upon a "case stated for the consideration of the court" (Evans, *Trial of Chase*, pp. 227–28). Indeed, the Judiciary Act was amended in 1802 (2 Stats. 59) to permit certification of questions to the Supreme Court upon division of opinion in the circuit court. Cf. *Ex parte* Bollman, 4 Cranch 59 (1807) (appeal to Supreme Court from circuit court denial of writ of habeas corpus).

Inexplicably, the defense counsel throughout ignored the right of appeal.

Articles V and VI alleged no more than error on Chase's part in construing local Virginia law of criminal procedure, viz., whether one accused of crime should be brought to court by a summons or by a writ of capias, and whether an accused should be tried at the same term as the one in which he was indicted or at the next term following.

Article VII charged that Chase had held over a Delaware grand jury for one day (making its total service two days) to investigate a possible violation of the Sedition Act by a local printer. The added information that it was haying season and that the jurymen were anxious to return home does not seem today, and did not then seem, sufficient to justify a judge's impeachment.[49] Indeed, so trivial were these three charges (V, VI, and VII), and so slight the evidence adduced to support them, that all three received a total of only fourteen votes for conviction to eighty-eight for acquittal.

Article VIII accused Chase of making "an intemperate and inflammatory" political harangue to the Baltimore grand jury in May 1803, and, in addition to offensive language, of vehemently attacking the Republican administration. The defense called James Montgomery, whose account of this speech to Jefferson had triggered Chase's impeachment.[50] The evidence of other witnesses, however, indicated that Chase's written copy of this address was accurate and that the language reported by Montgomery was the product of his own Republican zeal. The Federalists had attempted to silence Republican critics of their Administration by prosecutions under the Sedition Act; the Republicans now sought to silence Federalist critics by impeachment proceedings.

The testimony of some of the House witnesses was so lacking in initial credibility and so thoroughly refuted by other witnesses that it reflected discredit on the prosecution's entire case.[51] The disparity between the allegations made in the articles and the evidence brought forth to support them was so great that Hopkinson's observation to the Senate was no flight of fancy but a fact apparent to all:

I admit indeed that the honorable managers are . . . under the necessity of making their election between the articles and the evidence as the foundation of their argument; for they are so totally dissimilar that they could not take them both; they meet in so few and such immaterial points, that no man can argue from them both for five sentences. This being the situation of the gentleman, he has thought proper to select the articles and the facts therein set forth

---

[49] Evans, *Trial of Chase*, p. 49; *Annals*, p. 230. (Twenty-four of the thirty-four senators voted not guilty on this article.)

[50] For an account of his testimony, see Evans, *Trial of Chase*, p. 100ff.; *Annals*, p. 291.

[51] See, for example, that of John Heath (Evans, *Trial of Chase*, pp. 43–45; *Annals*, p. 218. Cf. also the testimony of William Marshall (Evans, *Trial of Chase*, pp. 65–66) and David Randolph (*ibid.*, pp. 68–69; *Annals*, p. 258ff.).

as the foundation of his argument in defiance of the testimony. In the observations I shall have the honor to submit, I propose to take the evidence as my text and guide, and leave the articles to shift for themselves, under the care and patronage of our honorable opponents.[52]

Throughout the trial, most of the defense's direct examination of its witnesses was done by Harper.[53] Martin took the stand briefly to state that he had purchased a copy of Callender's *The Prospect Before Us* in New York and later gave it to Chase. More important, however, he frequently took part in cross-examination and argued points of law regarding the admissibility of evidence with his customary clarity and force.[54]

The factual basis for the prosecution was, then, at best tenuous and insubstantial,[55] but the legal foundation was even more doubtful. The Constitution provides that any civil officer (a category that includes judges) may be removed from office "on impeachment for and conviction of treason, bribery or other high crimes and misdemeanors."[56] It was the consistent position of the defense that none of the charges, whether or not they could be proved, amounted to "treason," "bribery" or other "high crimes" or "misdemeanors." They insisted that the Constitution required an indictable violation of law, and it was obvious that, however injudicious or unjudicial Chase's conduct might have been, he had done nothing indictable by being sarcastic or petulant to counsel, by announcing in writing the "law of the case," by making a mistake in construing a local statute, or by delivering a political speech which offended the members of another party. Not only was this proposition argued by the defense with more skill than the prosecution could match, but its legal position was immeasurably the stronger.

The case against Chase appears today to be weak on facts and even weaker in law, but it must be remembered that the "jury" was composed of thirty-four senators, twenty-five of whom were Republicans and personal and political friends of Jefferson. A two-thirds majority was required to convict, and Jefferson thus had, at least nominally, more than the necessary votes. Some senators openly stated, before they had heard a single word of the testimony or a minute of the argument,

[52] Evans, *Trial of Chase*, p. 124; *Annals*, p. 365.
[53] Robert Goodloe Harper was a social lion, something of a dandy, pompous in manner and speech. He grew up in North Carolina and graduated from the College of New Jersey in 1785. He settled in South Carolina, where he taught school and read law. In 1794 he was elected to Congress as a Republican, but after his marriage to the daughter of Charles Carroll of Carrollton he switched his allegiance to the Federalist Party. He moved to Baltimore about 1801 and built up a large and lucrative law practice there. A year before the Chase trial he represented Judge Pickering when the latter was impeached.
[54] See, for example, Evans, *Trial of Chase*, pp. 27, 33, 49, 61; *Annals*, pp. 181, 194, 230, 243.
[55] Plumer reported that Randolph "thanked God that the Impeachment did not depend upon the testimony of witnesses" (*Proceedings*, pp. 300-1). Cf. a similar comment by Adams (*Memoirs*, 1:358).
[56] Art. II, sec. 4.

that they would vote to convict. Senator Giles, though a judge at the trial, saw no impropriety in conferring regularly with Randolph during its course,[57] and the relatives and friends of the presiding judge, Burr, were showered with appointments to the juiciest posts at the disposal of the Administration.[58] The defense knew that the nine Federalist senators would have to be held and that, in addition, a minimum of three Republicans would have to be won over. The fact that at least fifteen votes were cast for acquittal on every article and that the vote was unanimous for acquittal on one was clearly the result of the skill and persuasiveness of Chase's counsel, as well as of the weakness and inconsistencies of the prosecution.

Representative Peter Early opened the argument for the prosecution on Wednesday morning, 20 February.[59] In a short speech, which John Quincy Adams characterized as "chiefly declamatory, though in some parts argumentative," he "travelled over the whole ground of the articles."[60] He was followed by Representative Campbell, who, after apologizing for his inadequacies, entered upon a pedestrian discussion of the law and the evidence in support of the first article (one observer wrote that his "long, dry, tedious sermon . . . drove away almost the whole of his audience."[61]) Declaring himself to be "feeling much indisposed,"[62] he then announced that he could not proceed until the next day. On Tuesday he resumed his argument, discussed briefly the second, third, and fourth articles, which dealt with Callender's trial, and closed after devoting a total of less than two minutes to the seventh and eighth articles.[63] Next Representative Clarke, "in order that the case may be fully opened," as he said, made a cursory, eight-minute examination of the law of Virginia pertinent to the fifth and sixth articles and then announced (with unconscious irony) that "the opening of the prosecution," however scantily disclosed, was then "fully closed."[64] The presentation thus far had been uninspired, perfunctory, desultory, and filled with misstatements of law and of evidence. Both representatives and visitors for the first time fled the hearing in droves.[65]

Happily, Chase's defense decided to have its argument opened by Joseph Hopkinson.[66] A handsome man, not yet thirty-five, he was graduated from the University of Pennsylvania in 1786 and was admitted to the bar five years later. His practice in Philadelphia was an

[57] Beveridge, *Life of John Marshall*, 3:197; Adams, *Memoirs*, 1:353.
[58] Beveridge, *Life of John Marshall*, 3:181–82; McMaster, *History of the People of the U.S.*, 3:175–76; Schachner, *Burr*, pp. 262–63.
[59] Early, a congressman from Georgia, had studied law, but his legal career had been undistinguished, and he was best known as a Jeffersonian Republican.
[60] *Memoirs*, 1:355.
[61] *Federal Gazette* (Baltimore), 23 February 1805.
[62] Senator Plumer commented that he did not "wonder at his illness for he drank nine tumblers of water during his speech" (*Proceedings*, p. 296).
[63] For his argument, see Evans, *Trial of Chase*, p. 101ff.; *Annals*, p. 312ff.
[64] Evans, *Trial of Chase*, p. 115; *Annals*, p. 352.
[65] Plumer, *Proceedings*, pp. 295–96.
[66] Evans, *Trial of Chase*, p. 116; *Annals*, p. 353.

immediate success. With great solemnity, he began by invoking another "dread tribunal": "then comes a just and impartial posterity, who without regard to persons or to dignities, will decide upon your decision—then, I trust, the high honor and integrity of this court, will stand recorded in the pure language of deserved praise, and this day will be remembered in the annals of our land, as honorable to the respondent, to his judges, and to the justice of our country." He argued that a man may not be impeached for supposed wrongs as decided from time to time by the House of Representatives, but only for "treason, bribery, and other high crimes and misdemeanors," and that such offenses must be indictable violations of the law, not legal errors in the trial of a case, or instances of judicial impropriety, or discourtesy to counsel. Were this not true, he said, the House of Representatives could "create offenses at their will and pleasure, and declare that to be a crime in 1804, which was only an indiscretion or pardonable error, or perhaps, an approved proceeding[,] in 1800." The House managers' theory would place not only the judiciary but also the executive officers of the country at the mercy of an "omnipotent house of representatives—and may God preserve us."[67]

The next day, Friday, 22 February,[68] Philip Barton Key continued the argument.[69] He discussed the second, third, and fourth articles, all concerned with Chase's conduct at Callender's trial, in the light of the testimony and of settled legal principles and showed that the charges set forth in the articles were without basis in fact and unsupportable in law. His argument was closely reasoned and vigorously expressed, despite an illness which had left him nearly voiceless.[70]

Charles Lee then proceeded to an examination of the fifth and sixth articles.[71] These were the last-minute interpolations of John Randolph, based upon supposed misconstructions by Chase of the local Virginia law of criminal procedure, and were brought forward now on Randolph's theory that impeachment was an "inquest of office." To Lee, a

---

[67] That night the Reverend Manasseh Cutler, a member of the House from Massachusetts, noted in his diary that, though Hopkinson's delivery "had nothing to recommend it," his speech itself had been "lucid, pointed, and convincing" (Julia Perkins Cutler, *Life, Journals and Correspondence of Rev. Manasseh Cutler, LL.D.*, 2:184).

[68] Evans (*Trial of Chase*, p. 116) dates Hopkinson's speech 22 February. The *Annals* (pp. 343, 354) and John Quincy Adams (*Memoirs*, 1:356) both place it the day before.

[69] Key, an uncle of Francis Scott Key (not a brother, as stated by Beveridge [*The Life of John Marshall*, 3:185, 201]), was captain of a regiment of Maryland Loyalists during the Revolution. He was graduated from the Middle Temple in London in 1784 and developed a lucrative practice in southern Maryland and Annapolis. Adams appointed him chief judge of the Fourth United States Circuit Court in 1800, but when this office was abolished in 1802, he resumed his legal practice in Montgomery County.

[70] Adams, *Memoirs*, 1:356; Evans, *Trial of Chase*, pp. 149, 162; *Annals*, p. 394.

[71] Evans, *Trial of Chase*, p. 162ff.; *Annals*, p. 413ff. A brother of Light-Horse Harry Lee, he graduated from the College of New Jersey in 1775. He was appointed attorney general of the United States by President Washington in 1795 and held that position until Jefferson's election in 1801. He was one of John Adams' "Midnight Judges."

220

Virginia lawyer, was given the thorny task of expounding fine legal points upon which hardly any two Virginia lawyers, whatever their politics, could agree. However, he was able to demonstrate that Chase had acted strictly in accordance with the law.

On Saturday morning, 23 February, the galleries were overflowing with people who had come to hear Luther Martin make the principal argument for the defense. There was a sense that his speech would be the high point in the defendant's case and would decide the fate of the impeachment proceedings. In 1805 Martin had no peer in ability, fame, and success as a lawyer. Of only medium height, with thinning hair and features distinguished only by the ravages of alcohol, a voice far from melodious and a sputtering, saliva-spraying delivery, he was a far less impressive figure than the scintillating Hopkinson and Pinkney or the suave Harper and Wirt. As Senator Plumer noted in his diary the night of Martin's address on behalf of Chase, "Mr. Martin really possesses much legal information & a great fund of good humor—keen satire & poignant wit. He is far from being a graceful speaker. His language is often incorrect—inaccurate, & sometimes is too low. But he certainly has *talents*."[72] He could be coarse, ungrammatical, and unnecessarily prolix, but he had a phenomenal memory for precedents, a firm grasp of almost every field of the law, and an ability to show the reasons for, and the reasonableness of, the law as he expounded it. Added to these attributes was, as Plumer noted, his broad and disarming sense of humor—a trait uncommon among lawyers—and a gift for perfectly timing his most devastating arguments.

"Did I *only* appear in defense of a friend, with whom I have been in habits of intimacy for nearly thirty years," he began, "I should feel less anxiety on the present occasion, though that circumstance would be a sufficient inducement; but I am, at this time, actuated by superior motives. I consider this cause not only of importance to the respondent and his accusers, but to my fellow citizens in general (whose eyes are now fixed upon us), and to their posterity, for the decision at this time will establish a most important precedent as to future cases of impeachment." He warned that his argument would not be brief: "In the discussion of this cause, I fear I shall occupy a greater portion of your time, than I could wish, but, as the charges are brought forward by such high authority as the House of Representatives of the United States, it becomes necessary to bestow upon them more attention than they would deserve, were they from a less respectable source."

He then asked rhetorically why the Senate had been given power of trying impeachments and, after disposing of the reasons given by Representative Campbell as utterly "fallacious," offered the following explanation: "I see two honourable members of this court,[73] who were

---

[72] *Proceedings*, p. 300.
[73] Abraham Baldwin of Georgia and Jonathan Dayton of New Jersey. Baldwin voted Chase guilty on the first, third, and eighth articles and not guilty on the others. Dayton voted for acquittal throughout.

with me in the convention, in 1787, who as well as myself, perfectly know why this power was invested in the senate. It was, because, among all our speculative systems, it was thought this power could no where be more properly placed, or where it would be less likely to be abused. A sentiment, Sir, in which I perfectly concurred; and I have no doubt, but the event of this trial will show that we could not have better disposed of that power."[74]

At this point, Martin reviewed the Constitution on the subject of impeachments, and reaffirmed the position stated by Hopkinson and Key: impeachment under the Constitution of the United States lies only for indictable crimes and misdemeanors: "Admit that the House of Representatives have a right to impeach, for acts which are not contrary to law and that thereon the senate may convict, and the officer be removed," he warned, and "you leave your judges, and all your other officers at the mercy of the prevailing party. . . . They must be the tools or the victims of the victorious party."[75] He supported this stand with such logic and upon such principles that no other theory of impeachable offenses has since displaced his argument.

Proceeding now to the specific, Martin took up the conduct of the court and counsel in the Fries case. He began by establishing his credentials to speak of the rights, duties, and responsibilities of judges, juries, counsel, and clients: "I believe I speak moderately, when I say that I have attended on behalf of the State, at least five thousand criminal trials in that [Baltimore County] court."[76] As for the conduct of Lewis and Dallas in their defense of Fries, "The duty of a lawyer is most certainly, in every case, to exert himself in procuring justice to be done to his client, but not to support him in injustice."[77] It appeared from Lewis' own testimony, said Martin, that when Judge Chase

delivered at the clerk's table, the copy of the opinion designed for the defendant's counsel, having taken it in his hand—without opening it—without reading one word—Mr. Lewis contemptuously threw it from him, publicly declaring, that "he would never contaminate *his hand* by receiving into it a *prejudicated opinion*, in any cause where he was concerned, from any judge whatever." What insolence! Would to God, no lawyer may ever *contaminate his hand* in a more *disgraceful* manner, than by receiving therein a sensible, correct, legal opinion, in a cause about to be tried, at whatever time it may be delivered to him!

. . . I have long been at a loss, Sir, for the enmity the State of Pennsylvania has shewn for its bar, and the desire of its citizens to get rid of their lawyers; but if such is the manner, in which lawyers conduct themselves to their courts—if they . . . claim the constitutional right, uncontrolled by the court, instead of furthering justice, to pervert it; I wonder no longer why the citizens of that state wish to be freed from them. And will readily join in the sentiment, "the sooner the better."

---

[74] Evans, *Trial of Chase*, pp. 173–74; *Annals*, pp. 429–31.
[75] Evans, *Trial of Chase*, p. 177; *Annals*, p. 433.
[76] Evans, *Trial of Chase*, p. 187; *Annals*, p. 442.
[77] Evans, *Trial of Chase*, p. 192; *Annals*, p. 450.

Martin then dismissed Lewis' characterization of Chase's opinion as "prejudicated" as a mere pretext:

To *prejudge* any case, I consider as meaning, that a person without competent knowledge of facts, hath formed an opinion injurious to the merits of the case. If the term, prejudication, is used in this sense, there is no pretence that my honorable client gave a *prejudicated* opinion in the case of Fries; for it is not alledged [*sic*] that the opinion given, was not strictly legal and correct. Neither Mr. Lewis nor Mr. Dallas have ever attempted to hazard their characters by suggesting the contrary, nor have the honorable managers taken that ground; they do not contest its propriety. Should they in their reply, I shall cheerfully rest that question upon the well known legal abilities of Judges Iredell, Paterson, my honorable client, the associate judges, who concurred with them, and the legal knowledge of this honorable court.

But if by a prejudicated opinion, is meant, that a judge, from his great legal knowledge, and familiar acquaintance with the law, as relative to the doctrine of treason, particularly levying war against the United States, had formed a clear decided opinion that the facts stated in the indictment against Fries, if proved, as laid, amounted to treason, I will readily allow that I have no doubt my honorable client had *thus* prejudicated the law, not only before Fries was brought to trial, but before he had committed the treason for which he was tried. But if this manner of prejudicating the law, is thought improper, nay, criminal, in a judge, a prejudication which is nothing more than an eminent and correct knowledge of the law, why I pray are gentlemen of great talents, and high legal attainments sought for in your appointments of judges? . . .

If, Sir, judges are to be censured for possessing legal talents, for being correctly acquainted with the law in criminal cases, and for not suffering themselves to be insulted, and the public time wasted by being obliged to hear arguments of counsel upon questions which have been repeatedly decided, and on which they have no doubt; I pray you let not our courts of justice be disgraced, nor gentlemen of legal talents and abilities be degraded by placing them on the bench under such humiliating circumstances! But let us go to the cornfields, to the tobacco plantations, and there take our judges from the plough, and the hoe. We shall there find men enough possessed of what seems to be thought, the first requisite of a judge, a total ignorance of the law! That degradation, which *no gentleman* of merit and abilities *could endure, they will not feel.*[78]

Martin spoke from eleven o'clock in the morning to three in the afternoon without a break. At three he asked whether he should proceed to discuss the fourth article. A recess was called, and after half an hour he resumed, apparently as fresh as ever. In discussing Chase's supposed "rudeness" to counsel, Martin goodhumoredly observed:

As to this part of the charge, there is but little of a legal nature contained in it, I shall therefore hastily pass over it. If true, it seems to be rather a violation of the principles of politeness, than of the principles of law; rather the want of decorum, than the commission of a *high crime and misdemeanor*. I will readily agree that my honorable client has more of the "fortiter in re" than the "suaviter in modo," and that his character may in some respects be considered to bear a

---

[78] Evans, *Trial of Chase*, pp. 193–94; *Annals*, pp. 451–52.

stronger resemblance to that of lord Thurlow than to that of lord Chesterfield; yet lord Thurlow, has ever been esteemed a great legal character, and an enlightened judge."

As for Callender's counsel, Philip Norborne Nicholas, George Hay, and William Wirt, Martin took the offensive:

What was the conduct of Callender's counsel? Was it not such as immediately tended to inflame the minds of the by-standers, and to excite their indignation against the court,—and highly insulting to the judges? . . . Was this even to serve Callender? No, they avow they did not appear to serve him, but to serve *the cause.*

In the next place, when the jury were about to be sworn, they challenged the array in order to set aside the whole panel. . . . The reason assigned was, that one of the jurors who was returned had expressed sentiments inimical to Callender. This, if true, might be a good cause to challenge the individual juror for favor, but no boy, who had read in an office six months, would have supposed this a sufficient cause to have challenged the array. . . . Is it possible to believe that legal characters of so great estimation, that one of them was then the attorney general of the state of Virginia, another almost immediately after appointed attorney general of the United States for the district of Virginia, and the third, appointed one of the chancellors of that state, should have been so utterly ignorant of the law. . . as to have made the motion they did? If not, it must be presumed their conduct was influenced by a wish to embarrass the court; to hold up the prosecution as oppressive; to excite public indignation against the court and the government, who endeavored to enforce it, by attempting to impress a belief on the public mind, that even their marshal had in the very beginning, violated his duty to gratify the wishes of an oppressive government, and that for that purpose he had unfairly packed a jury![79]

Martin further suggested that the reason for Chase's jocular behavior on the bench at the trial was his fear that the irate spectators might forcibly set Callender free and that, accordingly, he had attempted "to keep the by-standers in good humor, and to amuse them at the expense of the very persons who were endeavoring to excite the irascibility of the audience against him. Hence the mirth, the humor, the facetiousness, by which his conduct was marked during the trial."

In ringing terms, Martin reasserted Chase's duty to enforce all laws, regardless of their popularity:

would you really wish your judges, instead of acting from principle, to court only the applause of their auditors? Would you wish them to be . . . the most contemptible of all characters, popular judges: Judges who look forward in all their decisions, not for the applause of the wise and good; of their own consciences; of their God; but of the rabble, or any prevailing party? I flatter myself that this honorable senate will never, by their decision, sanction such principles! Our government is not, as we say, tyrannical, nor acting on whim or caprice. We boast of it as being a government of *laws.* But how can it be such, unless the laws, while they exist, are *sacredly* and *impartially*, without regard to

---

[79] Evans, *Trial of Chase,* p. 212; *Annals,* p. 475.

popularity, carried into execution? What sir, shall judges discriminate? Shall they be permitted to say, "this law I will execute, and that I will not; because in the one case I may be benefited, in the other I might make myself enemies?" And would you really wish to live under a government where your laws were thus administered? Would you really wish for such unprincipled, such time serving judges? No, sir, you would not. You will with me say, "Give me the judge who will firmly, boldly, nay, even *sternly*, perform his duty, equally uninfluenced, equally unintimidated. . . . —Such are the judges we *ought* to have; such I hope *we have and shall have*. Our *property*, our *liberty*, our *lives*, can only be protected and secured by *such judges*. With this honorable court it remains, whether we *shall have such judges*!

The article had disparagingly compared Chase's action with that of a "public Prosecutor," and Martin felt obliged to object to the derogation of that officer, who is, he said,

as much the protector of innocence, as the avenger of guilt; his duties are as clearly marked as those of a judge. They have both one common object in view, though acting in different characters. The prosecutor and the judge are *equally* bound to shield the innocent, and to punish the guilty. The prosecutor does the same benefit to his country by saving the innocent from punishment, as by preventing the guilty from impunity. . . . Such, sir, are my ideas. Such, sir, I have ever understood the duties of an *office*, which I have held in the state of Maryland, for twenty-seven years or more; and if my conduct had not been during that period, consonant to these sentiments, I should indeed feel myself degraded and dishonored.[80]

It was now five o'clock, and Martin had been speaking for more than five hours. He apologized for the length of his address but reminded his audience of the seriousness of the occasion and the impossibility of knowing which charges the managers, in closing the case, would most rely upon. He then asked that he be allowed to conclude on Monday. On that day he began with the testimony of James Triplett that Chase had told him that because the marshal had not arrested Callender, "I am afraid that we shall not be able to get the damned rascal this court."[81] In order to show that this statement did not indicate, as was charged, Chase's "predetermination to oppress, to do injustice to Callender," Martin decided upon a bantering tone:

I have, sir, heard, I believe more than one hundred of the most respectable gentlemen of all political parties use similar expressions, not only when speaking of Callender, but also of some other printers. . . .

As to the word "damned," which has been introduced in the conversation, however it may sound elsewhere in the United States, I cannot apprehend it will be considered *very* offensive, *even* from the mouth of a judge, on this side of the Susquehanna; — to the southward of that river it is in familiar use, generally introduced as a word of comparison,—supplying frequently the place of the word "very," not confined to cases where we mean to convey censure, but

---

[80] Evans, *Trial of Chase*, p. 219; *Annals*, p. 483.
[81] Evans, *Trial of Chase*, p. 44; *Annals*, p. 218.

225

frequently connected with subjects the most pleasing;—thus we say indiscriminately a very good or a damn'd good bottle of wine,—a damn'd good dinner, or a damn'd clever fellow.[82]

As far as the fifth and sixth articles were concerned, Martin's analysis of the law of Virginia pertaining to arrests and trials was convincing: Section 34 of the Judiciary Act of 1789 did not require Chase to follow Virginia practice on service of process, as distinguished from questions of substantive law; and, in any event, Chase had correctly construed and followed the applicable law of Virginia.

Martin closed his argument with a brief reference to art. III, sec. 2, of the Constitution, which gives the Supreme Court appellate jurisdiction in matters of fact as well as of law. This provision intended that the Supreme Court was to have the last appellate word on both the law and the evidence, he said, and it was inconceivable that "the framers of the Constitution ever contemplated giving power of counsel to argue to jurors *against the opinions of their judges—or to juries to decide against such opinions.*" With thanks to the Senate for its attention and to Burr for "the high sense I have of the impartiality, politeness and dignity with which you have presided during this trial,"[83] Martin returned to his seat.

The rest was anticlimax. The House managers were unable to meet Martin's argument. Henry Adams' conclusion is as sound as it is well said: "Nothing can be finer in its way than Martin's famous speech. Its rugged and sustained force; its strong humor, audacity, and dexterity; its even flow and simple choice of language, free from rhetoric and affectations; its close and compulsive grip of the law; its good-natured contempt for the obstacles put in its way,—all these signs of elemental vigor were like the forces of nature, simple, direct, fresh as winds and ocean, but they were opposite qualities to those which Randolph displayed."[84]

To Robert Goodloe Harper, who followed Martin, the seventh and eighth articles were assigned. Harper started out well enough, arguing that the actions of the Senate in this very case, by its rulings on evidence in accordance with "the well settled and well known principles of law," had demonstrated that this was not a mere "inquest of office" but the "trial of a criminal case, on legal principles."[85] Then, however, he almost admitted the defense out of court, quite unnecessarily, by suggesting a hypothetical situation in which a judge consistently refused to hold court, so that business could not be dispatched. Harper had "no hesitation in saying, that the judge in such case ought to be impeached," even though such conduct might not be indictable.[86] Fortunately for him, the House managers did not take advantage of this slip. He then

[82] Evans, *Trial of Chase*, p. *223; *Annals*, p. 489.
[83] Evans, *Trial of Chase*, p. 234; *Annals*, p. 501.
[84] *John Randolph*, p. 147.
[85] Evans, *Trial of Chase*, p. 205; *Annals*, p. 502.
[86] Evans, *Trial of Chase*, p. 208; *Annals*, p. 507.

reviewed the evidence and law applicable to the first six articles and went on to the seventh and eighth, which turned, respectively, upon Chase's instructions to a Delaware grand jury about a local printer, and his remarks on the Republican Administration to the Baltimore grand jury. The eighth article was the one on which the Administration rested its highest hopes for a conviction, and Harper's summation of the evidence was masterful.

In closing, Harper reverted to the idea first mentioned by Hopkinson and insisted upon by each succeeding counsel for the defense: "This honorable court, adhering to the principles of the constitution, the positive rules of law, and the plain dictates of justice and common sense, will require, before it convicts, the clear proof of a criminal intent, manifested and carried into effect, by some act done in violation of the laws. Under the shield of this great principle, our honorable client stands secure."[87] It was now seven o'clock in the evening, and the Senate adjourned until the next morning.

The House managers had saved their biggest guns, Joseph Hopper Nicholson, Caesar Rodney, and John Randolph, for the concluding arguments.[88] Nicholson made a meticulous, hair-splitting examination of the evidence in support of the first article.[89] Shortly after noon he gave way to Rodney, who talked until almost seven, at which point he declared that "his knees had failed him"[90] and subsided. He concluded the following morning. His address was the most lawyer-like of all the managers. Like Nicholson before him, however, he confined himself for the most part to a discussion of the evidence and did not attempt to refute the defense analysis of the law of the case or to justify the prosecution itself.

After Rodney had finished, John Randolph, who had been absent the day before, arrived and, after only a few minutes' preparation, announced his readiness to proceed. His summation (Plumer commented that the word "argument" was "inapplicable to his performance"[91]) took about two hours and a half. John Quincy Adams described it as "without order, connection, or argument; consisting altogether of the most hackneyed commonplaces of popular declamation, mingled up with panegyrics and invectives upon persons, with a few well-expressed ideas, a few striking figures, much distortion of face and contortion of body, tears, groans, and sobs, with occasional pauses for recollection, and continual complaints of having lost his notes."[92]

[87] Evans, *Trial of Chase*, p. 244; *Annals*, p. 559.

[88] Nicholson, from Chestertown on the Eastern Shore of Maryland, was a staunch supporter of the President (he had himself carried into the House upon his sickbed every day for seventeen successive days to vote for Jefferson during the Electoral College deadlock in February 1800). Rodney was the best lawyer of the prosecuting group. He had been a member of the Delaware bar for more than a decade, was a signer of the Declaration of Independence, and was to become Jefferson's attorney general and to prosecute Aaron Burr at his trial for treason.

[89] Evans, *Trial of Chase*, p. 237ff.; *Annals*, p. 559ff.

[90] Evans, *Trial of Chase*, p. 243ff.; *Annals*, p. 583ff.; Plumer, *Proceedings*, p. 301.

[91] *Proceedings*, p. 302.

[92] *Memoirs*, 1:359.

Another spectator, somewhat less restrained, described it as "an out-rageous, infuriated declamation, which might have done honor to Marat, or Robespierre."[93] When Randolph sat down "he threw his feet upon the table—distorted his features & assumed an appearance as disgusting as his harangue."[94] Harper then corrected some of his mis-citations and constructions of English cases and texts. Randolph's closing statement, in response to Harper, was quite anticlimactic, and its petulance contrasted sharply with the preceding argument. "If judge Chase is innocent," he cried, "let him not be merely acquitted. Let it be an unanimous vote. Let hosannas be sung to his name, and let it be said, 'thus shall it be done to the man, whom the highest judicial tribunal in the nation delighteth to honor.' "[95]

Two days later the Senate convened to pronounce judgment. The room was packed to suffocation, and Vice-President Burr ordered the ushers to arrest any person who made the slightest disturbance. He then addressed each senator in roll-call order: "Mr. ——, how say you; is the respondent, Samuel Chase, guilty or not guilty of a high crime or misdemeanor, as charged in the first article of impeachment?"[96] The ballot on this article was prophetic: of the twenty-three votes necessary to convict, there were only sixteen for guilty. Ten senators voted guilty on the second article, eighteen on the third and fourth articles, the vote on the fifth article was unanimous for acquittal, four voted guilty on the sixth, and ten on the seventh. The eighth article secured the largest number of votes to convict, nineteen. Burr thereupon announced, "There not being a constitutional majority on any one article, it be-comes my duty to pronounce that Samuel Chase, esq., is acquitted on the articles of impeachment exhibited against him by the house of representatives."[97]

The results of this state trial were three-fold. It represented the last attempt on the part of the federal executive and legislature to control the third branch of government through the device of impeachment and discouraged the executive and legislature from "packing" the Court for many years;[98] it upheld against challenge the power of the courts, state and federal, to determine the constitutionality of legisla-tion; and it established an unwritten law, obeyed with only occasional and individual exceptions, that judges were to confine their public activity to their judicial offices, foregoing participation in partisan politics.

[93] The Rev. Manasseh Cutler, in his *Journals and Correspondence*, 2:184–85.
[94] Plumer, *Proceedings*, p. 302.
[95] Evans, *Trial of Chase*, p. 266; cf. p. 268. The report of Randolph's speech in the *Annals* varies greatly from this one and does not contain this passage.
[96] Adams, *Memoirs*, 1:362; Evans, *Trial of Chase*, p. 268, Appendix p. 62; *Annals*, p. 664ff.
[97] Evans, *Trial of Chase*, p. 268; *Annals*, p. 669.
[98] For other efforts, more or less serious, see Warren, *The Supreme Court*, 2:466ff. (to avoid invalidation of the Reconstruction laws); 517–19 (the unfounded charge that President Grant packed the Court to affect its decision in the Legal Tender case [Hepburn v. Griswold], 8 Wall. 603 [1870]). The most famous such attempt in recent times was President Franklin D. Roosevelt's proposal to enlarge the Court.

22

The Aaron Burr Treason Trial:
1. Prelude to Richmond

> Jefferson . . . pursued Burr with a venomous persecution
> unparalleled in the Presidential annals of the United
> States.—Nathan Schachner, *Aaron Burr, a Biography*

> It was an enterprize against the Mexican provinces, with
> a view to *revolutionize them*—to form an independent em-
> pire, at the head of which Americans would preside.—
> Martin, in *United States* v. *Bollman & Swartwout*

After the acquittal of Justice Chase, Martin returned to Baltimore and
the litigation which had piled up during his absence. In 1805, wide
dissatisfaction with the state judicial system finally brought about the
abolition of the General Court. This Court was a great favorite with
the bar, not only because of its able members but also because they
could argue before it all their own and other lawyers' cases at the same
term and in the same place. For this very reason the Court was generally unpopular with litigants, who, with their witnesses, had to travel
from all over the state and spend many days in the expensive town of
Annapolis while awaiting trial of their cases.[1]

The Act of 1805, ch. 65 (signed 25 January 1806), organized a new
judicial system, with all appeals from the county courts heard by the
newly established Court of Appeals. Martin opposed the change with
all his energy, but to no avail. He realized that it would be impossible
for him to try the cases that came to him from clients all over the state
in the local county courts while continuing to prosecute hundreds of
cases every year on the Baltimore County criminal docket. Accordingly,
with great reluctance, on 2 December 1805 he wrote to the governor
and council resigning his commission as attorney general.[2] Thus ended
the longest incumbency as a state attorney general in American history
—a period of almost twenty-eight consecutive years.[3] During Martin's
tenure the office had been raised from an insignificant political
sinecure to a post of dignity, influence, and importance. He had made
it, and himself, an institution.

[1] See p. 154 above for Roger Brooke Taney's observation on this system.
[2] Executive Papers, 1805, Archives, Hall of Records, Annapolis, Md.
[3] Martin was reappointed attorney general on 11 February 1818 and held the
office until 18 February 1822 (see Chapter 26 below).

His practice continued to be busy[4] and his cases varied. Most involved aspects of the law of real estate. Typical was *Howard* v. *Moale*[5] involving the title to "David's Fancy." At issue were intricate questions of escheat of lands conveyed in fee tail, the docking of entails, the proper construction of courses and calls in ancient deeds, and the effect of the treaty with Great Britain upon a mortgage owed to a British subject. In addition to his state litigation, Martin was in ever-increasing demand to argue cases in the federal courts, particularly before the United States Supreme Court in Washington. He appeared in four cases[6] in the February 1806 Court term and won all four. Although some lawyers attain pre-eminence in one particular area of the law, Martin was apparently equally at home in all fields.

In 1807 one of the greatest trials in this country's legal history took place. After Aaron Burr killed Alexander Hamilton, the head of the Federalist Party, in a duel, he lost much of his following in his own Republican Party. He was defeated for the governorship of New York and was bankrupt financially as well as politically. But Burr was not one to collapse in adversity, and he turned his face to the West to recoup his fortunes and realize his ambitions. Eventually, on the basis of his activities west of the Alleghenies, he was arrested and tried for treason.

Much that historians have uncovered with regard to the principals and their parts in the drama was either unknown or at most only suspected in 1807.[7] The great weight of the evidence, however, both direct and circumstantial, now points to the conclusion that Burr's ultimate plan (whatever his original dream or scheme) was an invasion of Mexico, not a division of the Union.[8] A detailed analysis of the

[4] Martin's participation in the cases of this period, as reported in vol. 2 of Harris and Johnson's Reports, was as follows. Of a total of 96 cases reported, Martin argued 42, or 44 per cent. Of his 30 cases argued in the lower court, he won 18, or 60 per cent. Of his 38 cases argued in the Court of Appeals, he won 24, or 63 per cent. The tally, as of final appeal, of all the cases he participated in was 24, or 57 per cent.

[5] 2 Harris and Johnson 249 (1806). With Martin were Francis Scott Key, John Thompson Mason, and John Johnson, the father of Reverdy Johnson and the third attorney general to be appointed in less than a year of Martin's resignation (William Pinkney was appointed on 21 December 1805 but resigned the next summer to go to England as one of Jefferson's commissioners; he was succeeded by Mason, who resigned three months later). On the other side were Harper and Shaaf, able and clever veterans, and with them, arguing his first case before the Court of Appeals, a young man with a great future, Roger Brooke Taney.

[6] Silsby v. Young & Silsby, 3 Cranch 249 (construction of a will); United States v. Grundy & Thornburgh, 3 Cranch 337 (libel in admiralty); Maley v. Shattuck, 3 Cranch 458 (prize law); Manella Pujals & Co. v. J. Barry, 3 Cranch 415 (agency).

[7] E.g., Burr's conversations with Anthony Merry, the English minister to the United States; Wilkinson's selling out to the Spaniards; and Jefferson's own realization that Burr was not guilty of the crime for which he was to be prosecuted (for this last, see Jefferson to James Bowdoin, 2 April 1807, in *Writings*, 10:381–82).

[8] This was also Jefferson's conclusion: he believed that Burr originally planned to separate the western states but, finding that their allegiance to the Union was firm, diverted his "conspiracy" to an attack on Mexico (see Jefferson's message to Congress, 22 January 1807, in James Daniel Richardson, *A Compilation of the Messages and Papers of the Presidents 1789–1897*, 1:412, 414).

objectives of the so-called conspiracy and the exact nature of Burr's involvement in it is beyond the scope of this biography:[9] our purpose here is to consider Burr's trial from the point of view of the actors in it, the testimony heard, and the mood of the times, and in this light to examine the difficulties surmounted by the defense counsel, particularly Burr's ablest associate, Luther Martin.

From whatever vantage point one views the "Burr Conspiracy," one sees the bulky and sinister figure of Gen. James Wilkinson.[10] This worthy was born in Calvert County, Maryland, in 1757, rose to the rank of brigadier-general in the American Revolution, became involved in the Conway Cabal to oust George Washington from his post as commander-in-chief of the Continental army, and resigned. He had the knack of landing on his feet, however, and soon acquired the position of clothier-general to the army. After the war, with the money he had made in that office he went to Kentucky, where, in 1787, he took a secret oath of allegiance to Spain and became Agent 13 on the Spanish payroll. His allegiance was expensive, and during the years that followed, his Spanish employers paid him thousands of dollars (usually in silver, delivered in canvas sacks) by way of annual "pensions," occasional "loans," and substantial bonuses for particular services rendered. Though many of his contemporaries suspected Wilkinson's duplicity,[11] it was not until the twentieth century, when the Spanish archives were opened to historians, that the full story of Wilkinson's career as a spy became known.[12]

Wilkinson procured an appointment as governor of the Upper Louisiana Territory in 1799. Burr had known him since their days in the Revolutionary army and had kept up a desultory friendship with him thereafter. At the time of the Chase trial in 1805, Jefferson (despite his professions of belief in the separation of military and civil power) appointed this friend of Burr governor of the Territory.[13]

In appearance Wilkinson was a Falstaffian figure, porcine and corpulent, with a flabby face and watery eye. Fond of pomp and display, he exercised the prerogatives of his rank to design his own uniform, and

[9] For such investigations, see Walter F. McCaleb, *The Aaron Burr Conspiracy*; Adams, *History of the United States*, vols. 3 and 4 *passim*; Abernethy, *The Burr Conspiracy*; Schachner, *Burr*; Schachner, *Jefferson*; James Ripley Jacobs, *Tarnished Warrior: Major-General James Wilkinson*; Beveridge, *Life of John Marshall*, vol. 3 *passim*.

[10] See, generally, Schachner, *Burr*, p. 291ff.; Jacobs, *Tarnished Warrior*; Royal Shreve, *The Finished Scoundrel*; Thomas R. Hay and M. R. Werner, *The Admirable Trumpeter*.

[11] See, for example, Daniel Clark, *Proofs of the Corruption of General James Wilkinson*, p. 33ff., published in 1809. Jefferson observed in his notes on his cabinet meeting of 22 October 1806 that "suspicions of infidelity in Wilkinson [have] now become very general" (Franklin B. Sawvel, ed., *The Complete Anas of Thomas Jefferson*, p. 247).

[12] See William R. Shepherd, "Wilkinson and the Beginning of the Spanish Conspiracy," p. 490; J. M. Robertson, *Louisiana under the Rule of Spain, 1789–1807*, 2:325ff.; I. J. Cox, "General Wilkinson and His Later Intrigues with the Spaniards," p. 794; and, generally, Adams, *History of the United States*, and McCaleb, *The Burr Conspiracy*.

[13] Cf. Jefferson to General Smith, 4 May 1806, *Writings of Jefferson*, 5:13.

even his equipment—golden stirrups and spurs and a leopard-skin saddlecloth with claws of solid gold dangling from it.[14] His speech, even on the simplest matters, was pompous, glib, and bombastic— John Quincy Adams aptly called him "Don Adriano de Armado the second."[15]

On 23 May 1804 Wilkinson, always secretive, sent a note to Burr at his New York Home: "To save time of which I need much and have but little, I propose to take a Bed with you this night, if it may be done without observation or intrusion—Answer me and if in the affirmative, I will be with [you] at 30' after the 8th Hour."[16] From this time on, Burr, Wilkinson, and others are known to have visited and corresponded regarding some project of deep secrecy, grand adventure, and high stakes in the West.[17] Many of their letters were in a cipher which referred to the page and line of identical pocket dictionaries each carried. Some facts are clear: early in the spring of 1805, Burr made his first trip west of the Alleghenies. From Pittsburgh, he went by boat down the Ohio, stopping at Blennerhassett's Island, a 250-acre Eden about two miles below Parkersburg. Burr so charmed the owners of that idyllic spot, Harman Blennerhassett, an eccentric Irishman, and his beautiful and accomplished wife, that they asked to join him and to help finance his project. As he continued on down the Ohio and the Mississippi he made many visits and acquired a number of supporters of his plans (whatever they then were): Senators John Smith of Ohio, Jonathan Dayton of New Jersey,[18] and John Adair and John Brown of Kentucky; Andrew Jackson; Henry Clay; Daniel Clark; and a group of prominent New Orleans citizens who were members of a "Mexican Association," actively working to free Mexico from Spain.[19]

This tour had results both favorable and detrimental to Burr: he was met everywhere so hospitably and generously, and with such great acclaim, that he was much encouraged to proceed with his plans; however, it caused a flood of rumors attributing all sorts of plots to him, from the setting up of a family dynasty west of the mountains to an invasion of Mexico by land and sea. These sensational stories were widely copied by newspapers in the east.[20] The basis for these speculations was

[14] John T. Watson to E. B. O'Callahan, 12 September 1806, vol. 18, O'Callahan Papers, Library of Congress, Washington, D.C.
[15] To Louisa Catherine Adams, 8 December 1806, *Writings of Jefferson*, 3:157n. Shakespeare describes the Don thus: "His humour is lofty, his discourse peremptory, his tongue filed, his eye ambitious, his gait majestical, and his general behavior vain, ridiculous and thrasonical. . . . He draweth out the thread of his verbosity finer than the staple of his argument" (*Love's Labour's Lost*, act 5, sc. 1, line 11).
[16] Worthington Chauncey Ford, ed., *Some Papers of Aaron Burr*, pp. 82–83.
[17] See, for example, R. Easton to Jefferson's friend H. Dearborn, 17 October 1807, in *Calendar of the Correspondence of Thomas Jefferson*, pt. 2, ser. 3, vol. 11, no 55.
[18] An old friend of Luther Martin, Dayton was also a graduate of Princeton and was a delegate to the Philadelphia constitutional convention in 1787.
[19] See McCaleb, *The Burr Conspiracy*, pp. 32–33.
[20] See *ibid.*, p. 37ff.; Beveridge, *Life of John Marshall*, 3:296ff.; Wilkinson's *Memoirs of My Own Times*, 2:xxxiii. The *Federal Gazette* (Baltimore) published many lurid rumors concerning Burr's western activities under such headlines as "The Ex-Vice President Turned Traitor," "Col. Burr's Treason," etc.

inherent in the situation: the desire on the part of both Mexicans and Americans to throw out the Spaniards and occupy their lands, and the imminence of war with Spain. Because of his known character, abilities, and ambition, Burr was a marked man from then on.

Upon his return to Washington, Burr began to search for the money to finance his schemes. He had numerous conferences during the winter of 1805–1806 with men who were known, for one reason or another, to have grudges against the Jefferson administration, telling each whatever story was best calculated to obtain his support. Among the disgruntled were "General" William Eaton and Commodores Truxton and Stephen Decatur.

In the late spring Burr received a code letter from Wilkinson dated 13 May 1806; on 29 July Burr sent his answer to New Orleans by two messengers, Dr. Justus Erich Bollman[21] by sea and Samuel Swartwout by land. The actual text of this missive is necessarily in dispute, as Wilkinson admitted having "edited" it before he sent it on to Jefferson some three months later.[22]

War with Spain may have been imminent on the Mexican border, but its actual occurrence depended upon Wilkinson, who had the means to precipitate or prevent it. So far as the "conspiracy" involved an invasion of the Spaniards' western possessions, everything depended upon his course. After dispatching his answer, Burr, accompanied by his daughter Theodosia, set out once more to Pittsburgh. He stopped at the home of Col. George Morgan and his sons, continued down the Ohio, where he contracted for the building and provisioning of some fifteen riverboats in the neighborhood of Marietta, and then moved south.

He visited Andrew Jackson at Nashville, and at Lexington, Kentucky, he purchased several hundred thousand acres of land on the Washita River from Col. Charles Lynch. At this point Joseph Hamilton Daviess, United States Attorney for the District of Kentucky, published a series of articles in *Western World* accusing Burr of plotting not only to attack Mexico but also to separate the western from the eastern states. These charges were picked up by the eastern newspapers and widely publicized. In November Daviess demanded Burr's arrest but on the day appointed for hearing failed to appear in court with his witnesses. Burr appeared with Henry Clay as his counsel and was, of course, discharged. Two weeks later Burr was once more haled into court by Daviess and again dismissed because of the total lack of evidence of any wrongdoing.

[21] Dr. Bollman was not only a practicing doctor of medicine but was famous for his intrigues and adventures, the most notable of which was bringing about Lafayette's escape from prison at Olmütz, Austria.

[22] Reprinted in Appendix D below. See Beveridge, *Life of John Marshall*, 3:307ff., 614–15; Adams, *History of the United States*, 3:253. A photostat of Burr's original letter, beginning "Your letter, post-marked 13th May, is received," is reproduced in Schachner, *Burr*, p. 324. See also Thomas Carpenter, *The Trial of Col. Aaron Burr on an Indictment for Treason*, 3:243ff., 252.

Meanwhile, Swartwout had given Wilkinson Burr's cipher dispatch. After carefully considering how his interest might best be served, the General wrote to Jefferson the first of a series of cleverly-thought-out letters: "A Numerous and powerful Association, extending from New York through the Western States . . . has been formed, with the design to levy & rendezvous eight or Ten Thousand Men in New Orleans, at a very near period; & from thence, with the co-operation of a naval armament, to carry an Expedition against Vera Crux."

Wilkinson claimed that it was not known "under what authority this enterprise has been projected, from whence the means of its support are derived, or what may be the intention of its leaders."[23]

He followed this, the next day with another and even more alarming dispatch to the President:

Although my information appears too direct and circumstantial to be fictitious, yet the magnitude of the Enterprise, the desperation of the Plan, and the stupendous consequences with which it seems pregnant, stagger my belief & excite doubts of the reality, against the conviction of my senses; and it is for this reason I should forbear to commit Names, because it is my desire to avert a great public Calamity, & not to mar a salutary design, or to injure anyone undeservedly. . . . I am not only uninformed of the prime mover & ultimate Objects of this daring Enterprize, but am ignorant of the foundations on which it rests, of the means by which it is to be supported, and whether any immediate or Colateral [sic] protection, internal or external, is expected.[24]

Most important in these letters was Wilkinson's acknowledgment that the "main design" of the project was "attacking Mexico."

Two weeks later, Wilkinson concluded with General Cordero the Neutral Ground Treaty, whereby the Spaniards agreed to remain west of the Sabine and the Americans east of the Arroyo Hondo. On 8 November Jefferson, in complete ignorance of Wilkinson's act, told him to make such terms with the Spaniards as he could.[25] Jefferson's about-face with regard to the Spaniards is usually attributed to his lifelong dread of physical combat. In this instance, however, it seems at least as likely that his desire to thwart Burr's plans for rehabilitating his personal and political fortunes was the motivating factor. Burr had become a popular idol to the people west of the Appalachians, and had a war against Spain been undertaken, Jefferson was well aware

[23] Letter of 20 October 1806, Letters in Relation to the Burr Conspiracy, Library of Congress, Washington, D.C.
[24] Letter of 21 October 1806, Letters in Relation to the Burr Conspiracy.
[25] Wilkinson sent his aide-de-camp, Walter Burling, to Mexico City to solicit Viceroy Iturrigaray for some $120,000 as a reward for standing like "Leonidas in the pass at Thermopylae" and thwarting Burr's threatened "expedition" against Mexico (not a word, of course, about any plot to dismember the American Union). When the Spaniards refused to pay, Wilkinson sent a bill to Jefferson for $1,500 that he alleged he had advanced to Burling for the latter's trip to spy out the land in case of war. Jefferson paid the bill promptly (see the pertinent correspondence in McCaleb, *The Burr Conspiracy*, pp. 144–45; statements of Sra. Maria Iturrigaray and Dr. Patrick Mangan in Davis, *Memoirs of Aaron Burr*, 2:401).

that Burr's success at the head of an army of frontiersmen was highly probable.[26] He therefore decided to nip in the bud any project which would create a popular and dangerous political rival, especially an enterprise which would make a national hero of a man he hated and feared.

Despite the imminent peril of which he had warned Jefferson, Wilkinson proceeded in a leisurely manner to New Orleans, arriving there on 25 November. He at once declared the city in a state of siege and sought to have Governor Claiborne proclaim martial law. When Claiborne refused, Wilkinson took matters into his own hands. On 14 December he arrested Burr's messengers, Swartwout and Bollman, and also Swartwout's companion, Peter Ogden, put the first two on board the ship *Nimrod*, and sent them in irons directly to Jefferson in Washington. Ogden was released upon a writ of habeas corpus. When similar writs were sworn out for Bollman and Swartwout, the General ignored them and took "on himself all the responsibility"[27] therefor. Ogden was arrested again the next day, this time with his lawyer, James Alexander, and Senator Adair, and they too were shipped off to Washington by way of Baltimore.[28]

As the result of Jefferson's official proclamations and statements, the articles in the press, the actions of the governments of the western states, and the propaganda of Wilkinson, Daviess, and others, Burr's

[26] "So popular is an enterprize on that country [Mexico] in this, that we had only to be still, & he [Burr] could have had followers enough to have been in the city of Mexico in 6 weeks" (Jefferson to James Bowdoin, 2 April 1807, Jefferson Papers, Library of Congress, Washington, D.C.; cf. Kennedy, *Life of William Wirt*, 1:161–62).

[27] The General's speech in open court refusing to honor the writ of habeas corpus for Dr. Bollman (*Federal Gazette* [Baltimore], 21 January 1807) is a good sample of his rhetoric:

> Called to account for an act in which I glory, and for which I trust my country will thank me, I shall meet the consequences with the applause of my own breast, which I prize more than the hosannas of the thousands or the popularity of the world: But when I cast my eyes on the movers of this prosecution, my bosom is rent by a conflict of emotions. Sorrow for their depravity; charity for their sympathies; surprize at their indiscretion; and astonishment at their audacity. I would to God that I could here close the proceedings of this day: but my honor, my duty, and the safety of the state forbid me. . . . Treachery is in the midst of us. Treason stalks abroad, and the friends of Burr and rebellion, whilst they ridicule our apprehension, and scoff at our preparations, with trembling solicitude implore his speedy arrival to reward them for their apostacy, and to rescue them from the goadings of guilt and the terror of impending punishment.

[28] See McCaleb, *The Burr Conspiracy*, p. 183. Characteristically, Wilkinson wrote Jefferson that he would expect the government to reimburse him for any damages incurred by these actions. Years later, Adair sued Wilkinson for false arrest and imprisonment, and ultimately recovered $2,500 in damages (the jury stated that much more would have been awarded but for Wilkinson's insolvency). Congress then reimbursed Wilkinson for this amount. All three men were released by writs of habeas corpus upon their arrival in Baltimore. When Judge Joseph Hopper Nicholson wrote Jefferson on 18 February 1807 apologizing for freeing them and asking the President to submit evidence upon which he might have them rearrested, Jefferson responded that he was, as yet, without any such evidence (165:29020–21, 29027, Jefferson Papers).

modest following melted away. In the place of an army of ten, eight, or even two thousand men moving against New Orleans, as Wilkinson charged, Burr's entire force consisted of nine riverboats and less than sixty men. Their arms were a few shotguns and hunting rifles, their cargo seed grain and rations insufficient for more than a short distance. With this "army," the public was led to believe, Burr was setting out to separate the Union, to capture New Orleans, and to liberate all Mexico from the Spanish.

Burr got as far south as Bayou Pierre, in Mississippi Territory, where he was held under bond despite the fact that he had been cleared by the territorial grand jury. Wilkinson had offered a reward of five thousand dollars for his capture[29] and had dispatched naval and army officers (in disguise) to bring him to New Orleans, where he could expect a drumhead court-martial, followed by a firing squad. Accordingly, upon the advice of his friends and his bondsmen, Burr turned his meager equipment and his Washita lands over to his followers, bade them a solemn farewell, and fled east into the wilderness. A month later he was recognized near Fort Stoddert, in Alabama, apprehended, and taken back to Richmond in chains for trial.

Meanwhile, in Washington Jefferson had been receiving a series of ambiguous and conflicting reports about Burr's activities in the West. Some accounts, like those of Davies, were highly sensational, accusing Burr of plotting a western empire of states and territories separated from the Union.[30] Others, including those of his own personal emissaries and advisers in the West,[31] contained no indication of unlawful, much less treasonous, activities on Burr's part. On the basis of Wilkinson's letters and other advice, Jefferson issued a proclamation on 27 November announcing that a conspiracy had been discovered, calling upon all participants to abandon the same, and directing the seizure of all equipment and stores which could be used in furtherance of it.[32] The proclamation was vague both as to the persons and the objectives involved. It was not immediately understood, especially by those citizens west of the mountains, that Jefferson was abandoning all expectations of war with the Spaniards. As for the conspirators, no one but Burr and his lieutenants was known to be engaged in building

[29] Rewards offered by Judge Toulmin and Governor Williams raised the total to eleven thousand dollars (Claiborne to Madison, Letters in Relation to the Burr Conspiracy).

[30] See Schachner, *Jefferson*, 2:827–28; Beveridge, *Life of John Marshall*, 3:315ff. See also the letter of Neville and Roberts of 7 October 1806 to Jefferson regarding Burr's ambiguous language in conversations with their friends the Morgans, near Pittsburgh (Letters in Relation to the Burr Conspiracy). Jefferson had not always been opposed to such a separation: in 1803 he had stated that it was a matter to be decided locally (letter to John Breckenridge, 12 August 1803, *Writings of Jefferson*, 10:409; Beveridge, *Life of John Marshall*, 2:283).

[31] See *Complete Anas*, p. 248; John Graham to Madison, 8 February 1807, Letters in Relation to the Burr Conspiracy.

[32] Richardson, *Messages and Papers of the Presidents*, 1:404; *Annals of Congress*, 9th Cong., 2d sess., 1806, p. 686.

boats and assembling supplies, and when Jefferson referred to "criminal enterprises" and "unlawful designs," it was generally (and naturally) assumed that Burr was engaged in some nefarious plot against the country.

On 2 December 1806 Jefferson delivered his annual message to Congress.[33] He did not name Burr, nor did he suggest any subversive plot against the United States. He mentioned only that filibusters were being organized in the West to attack the Spanish territories, and that the government was taking specific steps to suppress this unlawful activity. Since the newspapers were full of vague but inflammatory accounts of a conspiracy, the message satisfied no one's curiosity.

Accordingly, in mid-January John Randolph rose in the House of Representatives to demand that the President submit to the Congress his information with regard to this conspiracy.[34] A week later Jefferson responded with a special message.[35] Although conceding that there was "little to constitute legal evidence" in the "voluminous mass" of data he had received, he declared that his information had disclosed Burr's "general designs": the separation of the western states from the Union, an attack on Mexico, and the settlement of his Washita lands. The last object, Jefferson declared, was merely a cover for the others. As to Burr's treason, the President proclaimed dogmatically that his "guilt is placed beyond question." General Wilkinson, "with the honor of a soldier and fidelity of a good citizen," had provided the necessary evidence, he said, and appended to the message were letters and an affidavit from Wilkinson, along with his edited version of Burr's cipher letter of 29 July. For obvious reasons Jefferson withheld Wilkinson's letter to him of 21 October 1806.[36]

On 22 January 1807, the day on which Jefferson delivered his message to Congress disclosing his conception of the "conspiracy," Bollman and Swartwout, in chains in the hold of the schooner *Nimrod*, were landed at Annapolis. They were taken at once to Washington under military escort, put into the Marine barracks prison, and guarded night and day by a fifteen-man detachment of marines.[37] They were

[33] *Annals of Congress*, 9th Cong., 2d sess., 1806, p. 11; Richardson, *Messages and Papers of the Presidents*, 1:405.

[34] *Annals of Congress*, 9th Cong., 2d sess., 1806, pp. 336, 357–58.

[35] Richardson, *Messages and Papers of the Presidents*, 1:412; *Annals of Congress*, 9th Cong., 2d sess., 1806, p. 39. Jefferson also drew up legislation authorizing the use of the armed forces for suppressing insurrection and the arrest of any person on suspicion of planning to commit a misdemeanor against the country. He sent the drafts to Congressman John Dawson, asking him to copy and introduce the measures and to burn the drafts, as he was "very unwilling to meddle personally with the details of the proceedings of the legislature."

[36] See p. 234 above. This is the document which Burr and his counsel later sought to have produced at his trial by means of a *subpoena duces tecum* directed to Jefferson himself.

[37] William Plumer, Diary, 30 January 1807, Plumer Papers, Library of Congress, Washington, D.C.; *Federal Gazette* (Baltimore), 23 January 1807.

confined in separate cells eight feet square and denied writing materials and access to friends and counsel. The prisoners had hardly arrived at the capital when Bollman got word to the President of his desire for an interview. Jefferson, supposing that he was ready to confess all and to provide the evidence with which to convict Burr, granted his request immediately. Bollman, however, had two things in mind: first, "to remove from [the President's] mind the false impressions he had received with regard to treason. 2nd, To endeavor to convince him that the interests of the United States would be best consulted by going to war with Spain, and giving countenance to the expedition which Colonel Burr had planned" toward that end. Jefferson called in Madison for a witness and, after assuring Bollman that "nothing which he might say or acknowledge should be made use of against himself," questioned him at length, taking copious notes. They got nothing of value to convict Burr of treason; they also learned (if they did not already know) that Wilkinson had, until a few months before, been an ally of Burr in the proposed invasion of Mexico.[38] The next day Bollman received a note in Jefferson's own hand asking him to put his statements in writing, "Thomas Jefferson giving him his word of honor that they shall never be used against himself, and that the paper shall never go out of his hand."[39] How well Jefferson kept his word will be seen shortly.

Desperate for evidence to keep Burr's messengers in prison and to convict them of treason along with Burr, Jefferson procured from Eaton a lurid affidavit in which he charged Burr with having threatened to "turn Congress neck and heels out of doors, assassinate the President, seize the treasury and Navy; and declare himself the protector of an energetic government."[40] Aside from the fact that even if Burr had had such extravagant insurrectionary plans, he would not have been likely to confide them to a man of Eaton's reputation, there are other circumstances which cast doubt on the affidavit—for example, the fact that upon hearing these murderous revolutionary suggestions, Eaton hurried to the President but, instead of telling Jefferson about them, urged him, for the good of the country, to appoint Burr minister to some European nation.[41] Of greater significance, however, are the circumstances surrounding Eaton's statement. He had been trying un-

[38] Bollman's account is set out at length in Davis, *Memoirs of Aaron Burr*, 2:387ff. Though more succinct, it agrees with Madison's notes of the meeting (Madison, *Letters and Other Writings*, 2:393-401; Brant, *James Madison*, 3:350-51).

[39] Davis, *Memoirs of Aaron Burr*, 2:388. This sequel to the meeting is mentioned neither by Brant nor by most of Jefferson's biographers.

[40] As the "hero of Derna," Eaton attained a nationwide acclaim but soon dissipated his popularity by drunkenness, swagger, and extravagant eccentricities (see Plumer, *Proceedings*, pp. 332-33, 339, 480-81, 496, 542, 550, 583, 613; Francis Rennell Rodd, *General William Eaton, the Failure of an Idea*, pp. 387-88; Charles Prentiss, *Life of the Late General William Eaton*, p. 408. The affidavits of Wilkinson and Eaton (4 Cranch [U.S.] 455ff. [1807]) are reprinted in Appendix 4 to that volume.

[41] Martin later made good use of this paradox to demolish Eaton's credibility; see p. 242 below.

successfully since 1804 to collect from Congress the sum of $7,082.52, which he claimed to have advanced in 1804 out of his own funds to overthrow the Pasha of Tripoli.[42] Suddenly the wheels began to turn: on the day of Bollman's interview with Jefferson Eaton's claim was referred to the Claims Committee of the House of Representatives;[43] three days later he obliged the Administration with his affidavit; within a month, without debate, Congress authorized the settlement of Eaton's claim, and a few days later the government paid him $10,000 (the fact that he was overpaid almost $3,000 has never been explained).

On 23 January, Jefferson's floor leader in the Senate, Giles of Virginia, offered a bill to disallow the writ of habeas corpus and asked for its immediate passage by suspension of the rules. After surprisingly little opposition, it passed the Senate and was taken to the House, where immediate concurrence was asked. However, the House refused the Senate request that the matter be discussed in secret by a vote of 123 to 3, and after a short, acrimonious debate, defeated the measure by a vote of 113 to 19.[44]

Counsel for Bollman and Swartwout were Charles Lee, Francis Scott Key, and Robert Goodloe Harper. They applied promptly on 24 January for a writ of habeas corpus for the release of the prisoners. The United States Attorney, Walter Jones, countered by asking (rather belatedly, as they had been imprisoned since 14 December) for the arrest of the accused. This he did, he stated, "in obedience to instructions received from the President of the United States, whose wish was that they should be surrendered to the civil authorities."[45] After the formal arrest that followed, their counsel moved for their discharge.

Argument on the question of the sufficiency of the evidence to hold them in custody was now heard before the full bench of the federal Circuit Court, Judges Allen Bowie Duckett, Nicholas Fitzhugh, and William Cranch. The courtroom overflowed with members of Congress, the bar, and the curious public—indeed, the Senate was "scarcely able here to form a quorum to do business and the House . . . actually adjourned."[46] The argument lasted almost a week, and the only evidence presented to the court was the affidavits of Eaton and Wilkinson. Jones and Attorney General Caesar Rodney vehemently maintained, for want of anything more tangible, the astounding proposition that Jefferson's message to Congress of 22 January, being an official act of a president sworn to the faithful execution of his office, was "conclusive evidence of the existence of treason." Treason being thus "proved," and the prisoners' participation in it manifested in the Wilkinson affidavit, further argument "would only tend to inflame the public

[42] Rodd, *General William Eaton*, p. 265.
[43] *Annals of Congress*, 9th Cong., 2d sess., 1806, p. 383.
[44] *Ibid.*, pp. 44, 424.
[45] United States v. Bollman & Swartwout (1807), 1 Cranch Circuit Court Reports 373 (1807).
[46] John Quincy Adams to John Adams, 30 January 1807, *Writings*, 3:159.

animosity against the prisoners, and preclude the possibility of a fair trial."[47] Such solicitude would have been amusing had not the very lives of the two been at stake.

The court split along strict party lines: Duckett and Fitzhugh, Republicans appointed by Jefferson, held that the accused should be imprisoned without bail; Cranch, who was originally appointed by Adams but was reappointed by Jefferson, dissented on the sound ground that the evidence against the prisoners on the charge of treason was neither admissible, credible, nor constitutional. A few days later he wrote his father:

I have dared to set the law and the Constitution in opposition to the arm of Executive power, supported by popular clamor. I have dared to attempt to maintain principle at the expense of popularity. . . . I had no doubt whatever, that the Constitution did not justify a commitment upon such evidence. . . .

Never before has this country since the Revolution witnessed so gross a violation of personal liberty, as to seize a man without any warrant or lawful authority whatever, and send him two thousand miles by water for his trial, out of the district or State in which the crime was committed;—and then for the first time to apply for a warrant to arrest him, grounded on written affidavits.[48]

The stage was now set for taking the case to the Supreme Court. On 10 February Harper advised that body that he and Luther Martin had been retained for Bollman, and that on the following day they would address the Court on the difficult points of law presented.[49] Instead of noting a simple appeal from the Circuit Court, the prisoners had applied to the Supreme Court for writs of habeas corpus. This raised a quaint anomaly: it was Mr. Justice Johnson's opinion that Congress could no more invest the Supreme Court with original jurisdiction to issue a writ of habeas corpus than a writ of mandamus, as was held in *Marbury* v. *Madison*.[50] It would have been ironical if Jefferson had been successful in retaining Burr's emissaries in custody on the strength of that earlier decision, which he so execrated and despised. No doubt it was the embarrassment engendered by this dilemma that caused Attorney General Rodney to decline to argue the jurisdictional point at all.

When Harper finished his very able argument upon the question of the Court's jurisdiction in the premises, Martin was to conclude for the prisoners. He took into consideration the comprehensiveness of Harper's address and its apparent effect upon the Court, and with remarkable

[47] See *The Speeches of Messrs. Harper and Martin, on the Trial of Bollman and Swartwout, upon the Habeas Corpus, Before the Supreme Court of the United States,* 1 Cranch Circuit Court Reports 373.

[48] Quoted in Allen C. Clark, *Greenleaf and Law in the Federal City,* p. 53; Warren, *The Supreme Court,* 1:803–4.

[49] *Federal Gazette* (Baltimore), 12 February 1807.

[50] 1 Cranch 137 (1803).

self-restraint, he simply told the Court that his brother had discussed the issues so fully and forcefully that he had nothing further to add. The majority of the Court, after deliberation and an opinion by Chief Justice Marshall, accepted counsel's alternative argument that the jurisdiction which "the court is now asked to exercise is clearly appellate." Mr. Justice Johnson wrote a dissenting opinion (concurred in by Chase) in which he "submitted in silent deference to the decision of my brethren."[51]

Argument on the merits began on 16 February with the leisurely expansiveness customary at the time. Swartwout's counsel, Charles Lee, opened with an address of some three and a half hours, followed by Key with another hour's argument. The next day Rodney and Jones each argued for two hours with Rodney conceding "that none of the evidence now offered would be competent on the trial; nor even if it appeared in proper shape, would it be sufficient to convict the prisoners." Realizing the insubstantiality of an argument based on Jefferson's message, the prosecution now advanced an even more tenuous distinction: the President's speech had not been introduced as "direct evidence" of a war waged by Burr, but only as evidence of the "public notoriety" of the "assemblage of a military force by Col. Burr."[52]

On the following afternoon Harper ended with one and a half hours of analysis of the evidence against the prisoners as contained in Wilkinson's and Eaton's affidavits.[53] On Wednesday, 18 February, Martin closed on behalf of the prisoners. "I feel it my duty," he began,

to make some additional observations in favor of my clients, now before the court. Though considerations of personal regard for one of them, and respect for the family and connections of the other, could not fail to interest me, yet personal considerations were not necessary to induce me to appear before your Honors on this occasion. Were the prisoners, now before you, of the poorest, and lowest condition in society, in the most friendless and forlorn situation, seeing all those rights, which were meant by our change of Government to be sacredly secured to them, trampled under the feet of Military Despotism, viewing them as the victims of a violated Constitution, I should consider myself bound not only as the friend of Humanity, but as the friend of my Country, to assert those little abilities which it has pleased heaven to bestow upon me, for the purpose of procuring them redress.

He pointed out that the evidence showed nothing whatever of a treasonable nature, and that "the utmost which could be suspected from it was a design of revolutionizing the Spanish colonies, and that

[51] *Federal Gazette* (Baltimore), 16 February 1807.

[52] *Ex parte* Bollman and Swartwout, as reported in 4 Cranch (U.S.) 115, 118.

[53] Harper properly cast aside the depositions of Wilkinson's subordinate officers Donaldson, Wilson, and Meade as obvious hearsay and valueless, and neither the Court then nor commentators since have given them any consideration.

predicated upon a Spanish War." Adverting first to Eaton's deposition, Martin observed:

> I have never heard Col. Burr's enemies charge him with want of sense and understanding, nay, they have uniformly allowed him uncommon talents and abilities . . . ; and yet in Mr. Eaton's deposition he figures in the character of a visionary fool and quixotic madman. Nor is Mr. Eaton's account of his own conduct less likely to excite our astonishment; after he had become a depository of all Col. Burr's treasonable designs, as he represents them, he recommends to the President to send Col. Burr to the Court of St. James or to that of Spain.

As for Eaton's statement that Burr had spoken to him of "revolutionizing the western country," Martin sensibly observed:

> And here upon the subject of a separation of the Union, tho' I deprecate the idea, it is a subject upon which every person has a right to hold a different opinion, and in a peaceable manner to propagate the same. There is, I believe, in the United States, a diversity of sentiment on this subject. Should any person, by force of arms, endeavor to compel a separation, it certainly would be a treasonable act; but should a person write from the beginning of the year to the end of it, in order to convince the inhabitants of the western states, that it would be for their interest to separate themselves from the Union, and form themselves into an Independent Empire, I know not that it would be a crime of any nature, but sure I am it would not be *Treason*.

Martin emphasized that the Constitution defined treason as consisting only in levying war against the United States. Where was this war waged, he asked rhetorically, and where had Burr, or the accused, committed a single act of war? The wildest of threats Eaton attributed to Burr, even if one were to believe in them entirely, could not possibly amount to an act of war or an act of treason.

Then addressing himself to Wilkinson's affidavit, Martin dryly noted that it had been sent by the General "under the two-fold sanction of being attested on the honor of a soldier, and on the Holy Evangelists of Almighty God; and which therefore, I suppose, must be considered as entitled to two-fold respect." He then took up the letter which Wilkinson said was "a communication in cipher from Colonel Aaron Burr," the document which so impressed Jefferson and many others since, and examined it point by point, item by item.

First, he said, there was no evidence whatever that the letter was written or sent by Burr. Wilkinson did not claim that it was in Burr's handwriting; it was not signed by Burr; it referred to Burr only in the third person and thus could have been written by anyone. Second, Wilkinson did not claim that his deciphering of it was correct, only that it was "substantially as fair an interpretation as I have heretofore been able to make," whatever that meant. Third, the document was a copy, and Wilkinson was required to send either the original or an exact, certified transcription of it so that counsel or the Court could have an opportunity to decipher it. This last was an important point: either Wilkinson had the key to the cipher or he did not. If he did, he was obviously in league with Burr; if he did not, no one could say what the letter actually meant. As for Bollman and Swartwout, Martin went on, there was no evidence to show that they knew of the existence of the letter or that they assented to its contents. The letter, in fact, contained so many demonstrably false statements that its genuineness was put in serious question. However, assuming it to be genuine, whatever game was afoot, it was clear from the wording that it was to be played with Wilkinson's aid and against some country other than the United States. Did it not promise that "the people of the country, to which we are going" would be friendly if "protected in their religion"? Obviously, the objective was the Spanish possessions. Martin ended with the conclusion reached by most modern historians and investigators of this episode: "From the whole of these depositions, Eaton's, Wilkinson's, and Donaldson's, taken together, there is not the faintest trace of Col. Burr being engaged in any treasonable attempts against the United States, but they clearly and unequivocally prove the contrary, and shew that, if he had any object of a public nature in view, it was an expedition against the Mexican provinces."[54]

Each morning the marshal of the Court produced the prisoners, and each evening, after the day's argument, "the Court, not being sufficiently advised in the premises, and taking further time to consider," remanded them to the marshal for safekeeping until the next day. On Friday, however, the Court released the prisoners under bond, Martin going surety for both of them.[55] The following day, Marshall gave the opinion of the Court.[56] The justices had divided evenly upon the issue of the admissibility of the affidavits against the accused (in all probability, Marshall and Washington were for excluding and Chase and Johnson for admitting them). Even if Eaton's and Wilkinson's statements were admitted as evidence, however, a majority of the Court concluded that there was not sufficient evidence that Swartwout had "levied war" against the United States "to justify his commitment on a charge of treason." There was still less evidence against Bollman. As for the misdemeanor of fomenting war "against the dominions of a power at peace with the United States," it was apparent that no part of it was committed in the District of Columbia. The Court was unanimous, therefore, that the prisoners could not be tried there.

Adverting to the constitutional definition of treason, viz., that it shall consist "only in levying war against the United States," and there being no evidence proffered as to the existence of any such war, the

---

[54] *The Speeches of Messrs. Harper and Martin*, pp. 16ff.

[55] Minutes of the Supreme Court of the United States, M-215, Roll 1, National Archives, Washington, D.C. The original papers in this case are missing.

[56] 4 Cranch (U.S.) 125. Justice Livingston sat (with Marshall, Chase, Bushrod Washington, and Johnson) only on the first day of argument and took no part in the decision of the case.

Court necessarily found that "the crime with which the prisoners stand charged has not been committed, [and] the court can only direct them to be discharged."

Marshall's opinion closed with a reference to what was then and remained, the central flaw in the Administration's case against Burr and his associates: "if those whose duty it is to protect the nation, by prosecuting offenders against the laws, shall suppose those who have been charged with treason to be proper objects for punishment, they will, when possessed of less exceptionable testimony, and when able to say at what place the offense has been committed, institute fresh proceedings against them."[57]

[57] 4 Cranch 136.

23

The Aaron Burr Treason Trial:
2. Richmond,
26 March-17 August 1807

W. [Wilkinson] is the only man I ever saw who was
from the bark to the very core a villain.—John Randolph
to Joseph H. Nicholson, 25 June 1807

My principles and the motives which prompted my
conduct are the good of the country in which I live and
the interest and aggrandizement of the Spanish Monarchy: in faith of which I sign herewith.—Gen. James
Wilkinson, Expatriation Declaration, 22 August 1787

Shall we move to commit L[uther] M[artin]. . . . this
unprincipled & impudent federal bull-dog?—Thomas
Jefferson to George Hay, 19 June 1807

On the evening of 26 March 1807, Aaron Burr was brought in chains
into Richmond, and lodged temporarily, under guard, at the Eagle
Tavern on Main Street. Four days later, Chief Justice John Marshall,
in his capacity of circuit judge, appeared in a "retired room" of the
tavern to hold a hearing on the matter of Burr's formal commitment
by the civil authorities upon charges of treason and high misdemeanor.[1]
It was the strategy of the Republican Administration to conduct the
trial as a spectacle before as large a public as possible. Accordingly, on
the motion of George Hay, Attorney for the United States, the hearing
was adjourned to the courtroom in the capitol the following day. At
that time there was such a large crowd milling around the entrance
that, without objection, Marshall ordered the hearing moved to the
spacious, if dingy, assembly hall of the House of Delegates.[2]

Gathered for the trial was an unusually numerous, able, and picturesque array of counsel. For the government, the young attorney general,
Caesar Rodney, was present for the opening proceedings but was
required by a family illness to return to Washington shortly thereafter.

[1] David Robertson, *Trials of Aaron Burr*, 1:1ff. Francis F. Beirne's *Shout Treason:
The Trial of Aaron Burr* contains much colorful local detail as to Richmond personalities, society, and events of this period.
[2] Robertson, *Trials of Aaron Burr*, 1:8.

The workhorse of the prosecution was the United States Attorney for the District of Virginia, George Hay, the plodding and conscientious but not overly brilliant son-in-law of James Monroe. He was politically and personally devoted to Jefferson, to whom he owed his appointment. Realizing that Hay was out of his depth in a case of such importance and opposed by counsel of such great skill and experience, Jefferson authorized the expenditure of over eleven thousand dollars (not a cent of which was authorized by Congress) to retain counsel to assist him. The ablest of these assistants was William Wirt: handsome, debonair, learned, eloquent, and clever, he was at the threshold of a long and brilliant career. Aiding Hay and Wirt was Alexander MacRae, a competent and successful Richmond lawyer, noted particularly for his cutting, sarcastic tongue and his ill humor. Although Jefferson was not in Richmond in person, he was in fact chief of the prosecution. He corresponded almost daily with Hay,[3] counseling, exhorting, chiding the judges, demanding minute details, and giving careful, peremptory, and often ill-considered and impossible instructions.

The leader of the defense was Burr himself. He was in his own right an able and astute lawyer and in this case was better acquainted with the facts and the witnesses than anyone else. As local counsel, he retained John Wickham, Edmund Randolph, Benjamin Botts, and Jack Baker. Wickham had come to Virginia from Long Island and, by dint of hard work and talent, had become the leader of the Richmond bar. Randolph, older than the others, was a solid, dignified lawyer who had been Washington's attorney general. Botts, the youngest, was witty, courageous, and dynamic. Baker was apparently retained for his wide acquaintance and popularity with the people who would be called to serve on the jury.

The ablest lawyer on either side, however, was Luther Martin. A good friend of Martin's has given us a vivid verbal portrait of him, "warts and all," at this time:

> Luther Martin was a being *sui generis*. In his appearance there could be nothing more common. . . . His voice was thick and disagreeable, his language and pronunciation rude and uncouth. With all these defects he possessed extraordinary powers. He had the finest capacity for discrimination and analysis, the faculty which, perhaps more than any other, distinguishes the lawyer. He had also wit, philosophy, a prodigious memory, and stores of learning, which were unsuspected until the occasion called for their display. On the different occasions on which I have heard him speak, he seemed to blunder along for an hour or two, as if he were merely meditating his subject. . . . It was in his recapitulation that he appeared to be great. He became warm, his language more happy, his leaden eyes seemed to kindle, and for fifteen minutes or half an hour he spoke with admirable force and power. This would probably have been his speech if he had prepared himself in his closet. But his usual prepara-

---

[3] During the actual trial Hay wrote more than fifty letters to Jefferson and received almost as many from him.

tion was drinking enormous quantities of brandy. For twenty or thirty years he was a perfect sot, and it is wonderful how both his constitution and his intellect could withstand the destructive habit.[4]

By the spring of 1807 Jefferson had realized—and privately admitted—that Burr, whatever his original intentions, had not actually been guilty of treason,[5] but having committed himself, his party, and his public to that theory, Jefferson personally undertook to bring about Burr's conviction on that charge. The grand jury was selected after several of those summoned for that duty had been excused "for favour," i.e., for prejudice against Burr both formed and announced.[6] Of the sixteen jurors chosen, fourteen were Republicans.[7] Marshall appointed John Randolph to be its foreman.

Although there were dozens of prosecution witnesses present in town, the government refused to begin the presentation of evidence to the grand jury until its principal witness, General Wilkinson, made his appearance. The government thereupon sought to fill this hiatus by moving to jail Burr, pending his trial, on a charge of treason. After extended argument, Marshall sustained the prosecution's right to so move, and Hay began taking testimony in support of his motion.[8]

On 28 May 1807, in the midst of testimony from some of Blennerhassett's laborers as to extravagant statements supposedly made by that gentleman and his wife, Martin appeared in court to represent Burr.[9] Shortly after he arrived, Marshall objected that the court should not be asked to pass upon the sufficiency of the grounds for holding Burr on a charge of treason until the grand jury had returned an indictment therefor. He suggested that Burr's continued appearance in court could just as well be secured by additional bail. Thereupon, four of Burr's friends, among them Martin,[10] became sureties for Burr in the amount of ten thousand dollars.

[4] Brackinridge, *Recollections*, p. 138.

[5] Jefferson to James Bowdoin, 2 April 1807, Jefferson Papers, 166:29256: "Altho at first he proposed a separation of the Western country, . . . yet he very early saw that the fidelity of the Western country was not to be shaken, and turned himself wholly towards Mexico. . . ." Cf. Jefferson's letter of 3 January 1807 to General Wilkinson stating that Burr's followers believed either that they were to settle on the Washita lands, or that they were going to fight the Spaniards in Mexico. None of them, apparently, knew of any treasonous enterprise.

[6] Among those excused were Sen. William Branch Giles, Jefferson's floor leader in the Senate, and Col. William Cary Nicholas, Jefferson's choice for floor leader in the House (Robertson, *Trials of Aaron Burr*, 1:38ff.; Beveridge, *Life of John Marshall*, 3:409–12). Jefferson protested the excusing of these two, calling them "as far above all exception as any two persons in the U.S." (letter to George Hay, 26 May 1807, Jefferson Papers, 167:29454).

[7] Beveridge, *Life of John Marshall*, 3:413; Jefferson analyzed the grand jury as containing "2 feds, 4 Quids & 10 republicans," and complained that this did "not seem to be a fair representation of the state of Virginia" (to J. W. Eppes, 28 May 1807, Jefferson Papers, 167:29462).

[8] Until this time Burr had been free on bail on the misdemeanor charge of attacking a "friendly nation" (Robertson, *Trials of Aaron Burr*, 1:50ff., 96ff.).

[9] *Ibid.*, p. 97.

[10] *Ibid.*, p. 106.

Inexplicably, Wilkinson still had not appeared, and Marshall recessed the court for a week (as Washington Irving wrote his friend, Mrs. Hoffman, in New York, so that, during this period of inactivity, "they might go home, see their wives, get their clothes washed, and flog their negroes"[11]).

On 9 June the court was again in session, and Burr rose to submit a "proposition." President Jefferson, in his proclamation to Congress on 27 November 1806, had referred to a letter dated 20 October 1806 received by him from Wilkinson. In addition, he asserted, the government had given orders to the army and navy "to destroy" Burr's "person and property." The defense accordingly demanded that these papers, material and necessary for Burr's defense, be produced in court—if necessary, by the issuance of a *subpoena duces tecum* served upon the President. Of course, if Hay produced these documents at the trial, a subpoena would not be necessary.[12]

Hay was in a quandary. Rather than appear to be hiding evidence necessary to the defense, he said that he would try to get the documents if Marshall ruled them relevant, but he declared that the court had no power to issue such a writ on the chief executive officer of the country. He then wrote to Jefferson at once asking that the papers be forwarded to Richmond so that Burr would not be able to charge political persecution. Martin had had, as yet, little chance to exercise his talents on Burr's behalf, and this issue, Hay feared, would give him an opportunity.[13]

Because Hay refused to agree to the subpoena, Marshall asked to hear counsel on the point. Martin now made his first argument of this great trial. "This is a peculiar case, sir," he observed.

The president has undertaken to prejudge my client by declaring[14] that "of his guilt there can be no doubt." He has assumed . . . the knowledge of the Supreme Being himself, and pretended to search the heart of my highly respected friend. He has proclaimed him a traitor in the face of that country, which has rewarded him. He has let slip the dogs of war, the hell-hounds of persecution, to hunt down my friend. And would this president of the United States, who has raised all this absurd clamour, pretend to keep back the papers which are wanted for this trial, where life itself is at stake? It is a sacred principle, that in all such cases, the accused has a right to all the evidence which is necessary for his defence. And whoever withholds, wilfully, information that would save the life of a person, charged with a capital offence, is substantially a murderer, and so recorded in the register of heaven. . . .

It may be suggested, that this is a private and confidential letter from general Wilkinson to the president. It was so said, indeed, yesterday. . . . What, sir, if general Wilkinson had reposed as much confidence, if he had instilled as much poison into the ear of the president, as Satan himself breathed into the ear of

[11] *Life and Letters of Washington Irving*, ed. Pierre Munroe Irving, 1:192.
[12] Robertson, *Trials of Aaron Burr*, 1:113ff.
[13] Hay to Jefferson, 9 June 1807, Jefferson Papers, 167:29510.
[14] In his message to Congress of 22 January 1807.

Eve, the president would have been still responsible to a court of justice, and bound to disclose his communications.[15]

In response, Wirt conceded the power of the court to subpoena the President to testify, but insisted that he could not be required to produce state papers, such as the orders of the Departments of the Army and Navy for the apprehension of Burr. In any event, Wirt insisted, Burr's resistance to them "was itself an act of treason."[16] Martin's response was as soundly based as it was vehement:

We have a right to inspect the orders issued from the war and navy departments, because, if they were illegal, we have a right to oppose them. If they were unconstitutional and oppressive, it was right to resist them. . . . If every order, however arbitrary and unjust, is to be obeyed, we are slaves as much as the inhabitants of Turkey. If the presidential edicts are to be the supreme law, and the officers of the government have but to register them, as formerly in France . . . , we are as subject to despotism, as the people of Turkey, the subjects of the former "Grand Monarques" in France, or those of the despot Bonaparte at this day. If this were true, where would be our boasted freedom? Where the superior advantages of our government, or the beneficial effects of our revolutionary struggles? . . . Resistance to an act of oppression unauthorized by law, can never be criminal, and this is all we contend for.[17]

The next day, Marshall delivered the court's opinion. He dismissed the prosecution's argument that Burr was not entitled to a subpoena to produce evidence until after he should be actually indicted as highly impractical and prejudicial to the accused, who had to prepare his defense before his trial. Proceeding then to the principal question, Marshall held that in this country a *subpoena duces tecum* may be issued to anyone having material relevant to a trial. In closing, he said:

It is not for the court to anticipate the event of the present prosecution. Should it terminate as is expected on the part of the United States, all those who are concerned in it, should certainly regret, that a paper, which the accused believed essential to his defence . . . had been withheld from him. I will not say, that this circumstance would, in any degree, tarnish the reputation of the government; but I will say that it would justly tarnish the reputation of the court, which had given its sanction to its being withheld.[18]

MacRae, the government counsel, smarting under the ruling, misquoted Marshall. The judge had no right to say that the prosecution "wished"[19] the conviction of Aaron Burr, he complained. Such a thought was "completely abhorrent" to their feelings. In response, Marshall quietly noted that "Gentlemen had so often, and so uniformly asserted, that colonel Burr was guilty, and they had so often repeated it

[15] Robertson, *Trials of Aaron Burr*, 1:127ff.
[16] *Ibid.*, p. 140.
[17] *Ibid.*, p. 167.
[18] *Ibid.*, p. 188.
[19] Marshall had said "expected."

before the testimony was perceived, on which that guilt could alone be substantiated, that it appeared to him probable, that they were not indifferent on the subject."[20]

When Jefferson received word of Marshall's opinion from Hay, his anger overcame his common sense. He wrote to Hay directing the weight of his wrath at Martin, who, he believed, had been responsible for this affront to his office. He had received a letter from a John Gordon of Baltimore (Jefferson never lacked for informants), who claimed that one Philip Graybell, "a very worthy old revolutionary officer & an undoubted friend to your Administration . . . told me that Mr. Luther Martin mentioned to him as early as last summer that Burr was then concerting measures to separate the Union."[21] Jefferson suggested to Hay, on the basis of this fourth-hand account, that Martin be indicted along with Burr, and that Graybell be called upon to "fix upon [Martin] misprision of treason at least,"[22] and thus "put down this unprincipled & impudent federal bull-dog, and add another proof that the most glamorous defenders of Burr are all his accomplices."[23]

On Saturday, 13 June, a group of witnesses, including Burr's ill-fated messenger, Dr. Bollman, were called to be sworn before testifying to the grand jury. After Bollman had been released on a writ of habeas corpus by the Supreme Court, Jefferson had instructed Hay to have him taken into custody immediately and sent to Richmond. Jefferson was so thoroughly committed to a belief in Wilkinson's veracity and Burr's treason that he resolved to take any and every step to get a conviction. Accordingly, despite his pledge,[24] he sent Bollman's statement to Hay as a lever to use in extracting from Bollman evidence incriminating to Burr. Jefferson then adopted a suggestion made to him by Wilkinson some months before: he sent Hay a batch of blank pardons, including one for Bollman, to be used by Hay "at discretion." Whenever a witness who was in a position to give evidence against Burr declined for fear of self-incrimination, he was to be bribed or forced with a pardon. If such a witness could be compelled to accept a presidential pardon, he could then be made to testify under pain of contempt of court.[25]

[20] Robertson, *Trials of Aaron Burr*, 1:189.

[21] Letter of 17 June 1807, Letters in Relation to the Burr Conspiracy. Graybell's affidavit, along with a similar one by John Campbell White, M.D., was sent by Jefferson to Hay, who took no action against Martin. See Martin's letter in the *Virginia Gazette* for 10 October 1807, in which he explained the jocular circumstances of the alleged quotations, which did not imply any treasonous matter in any event. The affidavits were furnished to William Eaton for publication in the *Virginia Gazette* for 7 October 1807.

[22] I.e., concealment of treason by silence—having knowledge of it but committing no overt act in furtherance of it.

[23] Letter of 19 June 1807, Jefferson Papers, 168:29547. Jefferson's letter to Hay of 20 May contains a highly equivocating account of his conversation with Dr. Bollman (see Jefferson Papers, 167:29400; Chapter 6 above).

[24] It will be recalled that Jefferson had promised Bollman that the written record of their interview, which he asked Bollman to send him, would be kept confidential (see Chapter 22, p. 238, above).

[25] McCaleb, *The Burr Conspiracy*, p. 321.

In accordance with this plan, on 13 June Hay rose to announce that Bollman had made a "full communication to the government of the plans, the designs, and views" of Aaron Burr. As this statement might incriminate Bollman, Hay said blandly, the President had sent a pardon for him, which he now tendered. "Will you accept this pardon?" he asked Bollman. Bollman unhesitatingly replied, "No, I will not, sir." Thereupon, Hay duly threatened that Bollman might be forced to go before the grand jury, pardon and all, like it or not.[26]

Thus another issue was joined: Martin maintained that a pardon was a nullity and without effect unless and until it were pleaded in court as a defense to an indictment.[27] "Are you willing," Hay blustered, "to have doctor Bollman indicted? Take care in what an awful condition you are placing this gentleman." Martin was unmoved: "Doctor Bollman, sir, has lived too long to be alarmed by such menaces. He is a man of too much honour to trust his reputation to the course which you prescribe for him. . . . As another reason, sir, why doctor Bollman has refused this pardon, permit me to say, is that it would be considered as an admission of guilt. Doctor Bollman does not admit that he has been guilty. He does not consider a pardon as necessary for an innocent man."[28] The upshot for the time being, subject to later adjudication by the court, was that Dr. Bollman went before the grand jury "without any particular notification" and without his pardon. The grand jury called him and examined him for over two hours, and he answered every question that was asked him without exception. The grand jury found the evidence against him insufficient for indictment.[29]

At this point, panoplied in a magnificent major general's uniform of his own design and accompanied by his military retinue (including his son, now an Army lieutenant, whom Burr had gotten admitted to Princeton) and some eight or ten witnesses for the government, General Wilkinson finally arrived in Richmond.[30] He was "too much fatigued," however, to attend court that day. On Monday, 15 June, he made his long-awaited appearance. Washington Irving wrote to his friend Paulding that Burr, on hearing Wilkinson's name called, "swept his eye over [the General's] whole person from head to foot, as if to scan its dimensions, and then coolly . . . went on conversing with his counsel as tranquilly as ever."[31] Wilkinson's report of this encounter to Jefferson was somewhat more grandiloquent: "I saluted the Bench & in spite of myself my Eyes darted a flash of indignation at the little Traitor. . . . This Lyon hearted Eagle Eyed Hero, sinking under the weight of con-

[26] Robertson, *Trials of Aaron Burr*, 1:191.
[27] Martin's prescience is again demonstrated here. On 27 August 1787, at the Philadelphia constitutional convention, he had moved (unsuccessfully) to give the President power to grant reprieves and pardons only after conviction (see Chapter 15, p. 129, above).
[28] Robertson, *Trials of Aaron Burr*, 1:192.
[29] Davis, *Memoirs of Aaron Burr*, 2:391.
[30] Robertson, *Trials of Aaron Burr*, 1:196.
[31] *Life and Letters*, 1:194–95.

scious guilt, with haggard Eye, made an Effort to meet the indignant salutation of outraged Honor, but it was in vain, his audacity failed him. He averted his face, grew pale & affected passion to conceal his perturbation."[32] A third observer, David Robertson, one of the court reporters, declared the meeting a draw: Wilkinson's "countenance was calm, dignified, and commanding; while that of colonel Burr was marked by a haughty contempt."[33] The reader may take his choice.

Immediately after taking the oath, Wilkinson went before the grand jury, where, as Irving wrote, he had "such a mighty mass of words to deliver himself of" that he required "at least two days more to discharge the wondrous cargo."[34] Usually the grand jury's proceedings are a sealed book, and not a word of the testimony before it is known, but the foreman of this jury was John Randolph, who felt little concern for a grand juryman's oath. Accordingly, he gave his friend Judge Joseph Hopper Nicholson a detailed account of the General's testimony.[35]

When Wilkinson exhibited Burr's cipher letter to that body, the General's editing at once became apparent. The very first sentence, "Yours [Wilkinson's] postmarked 13th of May, is received," was omitted in his transcript, and other changes and substitutions for the sake of concealing his involvement in Burr's schemes were also evident.[36] "The mammoth of iniquity escaped," Randolph told Nicholson, "not that any man pretended to think him innocent. . . . Wilkinson is the only man I ever saw who was from the bark to the very core a villain. . . . Perhaps you never saw human nature in so degraded a situation as in the person of Wilkinson before the grand jury, and yet this man stands on the very summit and pinnacle of executive favor."[37]

Despite the fact that fourteen of the sixteen jurymen were Republicans, seven voted to indict Wilkinson along with Burr. Only the fact that a Republican president's political reputation was at stake and that the prosecution was primarily a political matter prevented the case from collapsing at its outset. On 24 June, however, the grand jury interrupted argument before Judges Marshall and Griffin on a collateral matter[38] and solemnly filed into the courtroom. All other business ceased as John Randolph announced to a hushed audience that the grand jury presented Burr and Harman Blennerhassett for

---

[32] Letter of 17 June 1807, Letters in Relation to the Burr Conspiracy.

[33] Quoted in Robertson, *Trials of Aaron Burr*, 1:197n.

[34] *Life and Letters*, 1:145.

[35] Letter of 28 June 1807, Nicholson Papers, 3:1398-C, Library of Congress, Washington, D.C.

[36] Cf. Wilkinson's admission of his "editing" of the letter at Burr's trial for misdemeanor the following September (Carpenter, *Trial of Burr*, 3:245–46; *Annals of Congress*, 10th Cong., 1st sess. [cited hereafter in this chapter as *Annals*], pp. 520–21).

[37] Letter of 25 June 1807, Nicholson Papers, 3-1398-C.

[38] A motion to cite Wilkinson for obstruction of justice for seizing sealed letters to and from Burr from the United States mails; for high-handed arrest and imprisonment, without preference of charges, of persons supposedly connected with Burr's enterprise; for extracting statements from witnesses by means of torture, etc. (Robertson, *Trials of Aaron Burr*, 1:277; McCaleb, *The Burr Conspiracy*, p. 201).

treason against the United States and for misdemeanor by organizing an armed expedition against the territory of the King of Spain, with whom the United States was at peace.[39]

The indictment of Burr for treason declared, in substance, that Burr,

being . . . under the protection of the laws of the United States, and owing allegiance and fidelity [thereto], not having the fear of God before his eyes, . . . but being moved and seduced by the devil,[40] wickedly devising and intending the peace and tranquillity of the same United States to disturb, and to stir, move and incite insurrection, rebellion and war against the said United States, on the tenth day of December, in the year of Christ one thousand eight hundred and six, at . . . Blennerhassett's Island, in the county of Wood, and district of Virginia . . . with force and arms, unlawfully, falsely, maliciously and traitorously did compass, imagine and intend to raise and levy war, insurrection and rebellion against the United States, and in order to fulfil and bring to effect the said traitorous compassings, imaginings, and intentions . . . he, the said Aaron Burr, afterwards [on the same day] at the said island called Blennerhassett's . . . , with a great multitude of persons whose names at present are unknown to the grand inquest aforesaid, to a great number, to wit: to the number of thirty persons and upwards, armed and arrayed in a warlike manner, that is to say, with guns, swords and dirks, and other warlike weapons, as well offensive as defensive, being then and there unlawfully, maliciously and traitorously assembled and gathered together, did falsely and traitorously assemble and join themselves together against the said United States.[41]

There was a great deal more to the same effect. The indictment, however, was noteworthy in two ways: first, other than the assembling on Blennerhassett's Island of a small group of men with an alleged intention to levy war against the United States, no overt act of war was mentioned; and second, although he was alleged to have been present with this "great multitude of persons," no one in fact believed that Burr (who on 10 December 1806 was three hundred miles away in Kentucky[42]) was there.

No other accommodation having been provided, Burr spent the next two nights in the damp, verminous, and overcrowded public jail of Richmond. On Friday, one of his counsel, Benjamin Botts, protested to the court that Burr's place of confinement was not only unhealthy but was so crowded with drunkards, imprisoned debtors, and others that consultation with counsel was virtually impossible. After some discussion with the court, in which the government counsel did not

---

[39] Robertson, *Trials of Aaron Burr*, 1:305–6; *Annals*, pp. 386–87. The next day the grand jury presented Jonathan Dayton, John Smith, Comfort Tyler, Israel Smith, and Davis Floyd (all minor participants in the Burr group's activities) for treason (Robertson, *Trials of Aaron Burr*, 1:330, 350).

[40] In an indictment for felony this allegation had to be made (fortunately, the prosecution was not required to prove it).

[41] J. J. Coombs, *The Trial of Aaron Burr for High Treason*, pp. 140–43.

[42] This fact was later conceded by the government (Robertson, *Trials of Aaron Burr*, 1:530, 532).

participate, it was suggested that Burr be lodged in the dining room of the house rented by Martin, across the street from the Swan Tavern. Benjamin Latrobe, Jefferson's surveyor of public buildings, who was on hand as a possible witness, was ordered to inspect the security of these quarters, and, in accordance with his recommendations, the court ordered the marshal to have the room prepared "by securing the shutters to the windows of the said room by bars, and the door by a strong bar or padlock"; a seven-man guard was ordered placed around the house to prevent Burr's escape.[43] In this room, day after day and night after night, Martin and Burr together planned the defense: the cross-examination of the government witnesses, the subpoenaing of President Jefferson and the letters and documents he was withholding, and the arguments as to the law of the case.

Upon his arraignment, Burr pleaded not guilty and, in the language of the time, "put himself upon God and the country" for his trial.[44] The alleged offense had taken place in Wood County, Virginia (now West Virginia), in the vicinity of Parkersburg, some three hundred miles west of Richmond. When it was impossible or impractical to try a case in the county in which the offense occurred, the law at the time required that at least twelve of the forty-eight jurors selected be residents of that county. To procure a dozen men from the Ohio River and transport them to Richmond took several weeks. Consequently, the court adjourned on 26 June until Monday, 3 August.[45] To avoid a charge of partiality, Burr was removed during this recess to a spacious apartment on the third floor of the new state penitentiary, some five or six miles out of town.[46]

A good deal of nonsense has been written about Martin's supposed infatuation at this time with Aaron Burr's married daughter, Theodosia, a beautiful, charming, well-educated, and accomplished woman. Martin had known her since she was a young girl but had never met her husband, Joseph Alston. However, he wrote to Alston on the night of the adjournment, suggesting that it would be helpful if he attended the trial:

Sir,—I have the painful task to inform you that my much esteemed friend, Col. Burr, was yesterday committed to Prison in consequence of a Bill for Treason being found by the Grand Jury against him. I arrived here the evening of May twenty-seventh, and have been with Col. Burr ever since. Nor shall I leave him until his Trial is at end. Never, I believe, did any Government thirst more for the Blood of a victim than our enlightend [sic], philosophic, mild, philanthropic Government for the Blood of my friend. . . . That Col. Burr is as innocent of every thing of a treasonable nature as the child unborn I remain fully con-

[43] *Annals*, p. 389; B. Henry Latrobe to the U.S. Marshal, 26 July 1807, in Aaron Burr Treason Case Papers, National Archives, Washington, D.C.
[44] Robertson, *Trials of Aaron Burr*, 1:352–357. The "country" is a synonym for the jury.
[45] *Ibid.*, p. 357.
[46] *Annals*, p. 391.

vinced; that he never had any object in view, but what did honor to himself, and would have been greatly useful to the United States, and to all Europe, except France and Spain, I am fully convinced. That a Bill has been found, has been owing to the Jury not being well informed what facts constitute Treason, and to gross perjury in swearing to facts not true. We feel the utmost confidence that he will be acquitted upon his Trial. . . . That Government ardently desire[s] to destroy Col. Burr, that it would feel no more compunction in taking his life, than that with which a philosopher views a rat expiring, with convulsions, at the bottom [of] an exhausted receiver, I have not a doubt. And I am confident that Government does not believe him to have been guilty of a treasonable act or design.

Under Col. Burr's present situation, you may be assured, it would be most pleasing, most consolatory to him, could you visit Richmond. He has many warm friends here at this time, who are not, and have not been deterred from proving their attachment to him in the hour of adversity. And the popular odium, which had been so artfully and so basely excited against him has greatly decreased, and is still decreasing. While Wilkinson is viewed by many as the basest of villains. Nay, such are the sentiments of the Grand Jury concerning him, that they were, yesterday, equally divided on the question, of finding a Bill against him for Treason.

Present my most respectful Compliments to your amiable Lady—tell her my Daughter, Maria, who came to Richmond with me, and who shares in all my sollicitudes [*sic*] for the fate of Col. Burr, wishes to be remembered by her— tell her, that, for her sake as well as her father's, all the professional powers I possess, are devoted to him, with all the zeal and ardency of friendship—tell her that, if on this occasion I had not come forward and offered my aid,—my serv- ices—every exertion of my mind, to shield him from his Enemies, I should have felt myself most deservedly liable to her eternal reproaches—and finally tell her she has my fervent prayers for her happiness.

You will forgive this intrusion upon you by a person, who has not the honor to be *personally* known to you, but who is with sentiments of respect and esteem for you, Your very obedient Servant,

LUTHER MARTIN[47]
Richmond, 26th June 1807

It must be obvious from this that Martin's regard for Theodosia Burr Alston, however deep, however florid in expression, could not have been called an infatuation. Blennerhasset, a highly uxorious man, ob- served that Martin's "idolatrous admiration of Mrs. Alston is almost as excessive as my own. . . . Nor can he see a speck in the character or conduct of Alston, for the best of all reasons with him, namely, that Alston has such a wife."[48]

Shortly after his arrival at Richmond, Martin began a series of letters to the Richmond *Virginia Gazette*, in which he discussed, with characteristic vigor and supporting detail, the background of the Burr prosecution. Probably because of his participation in the case, he signed them "Investigator." In his first letter of 24 June, quoting from

[47] Ford, *Some Papers of Aaron Burr*, p. 83.
[48] Blennerhassett Papers, p. 469.

Wilkinson's letters and statements to the press, he summarized what was known of that worthy's equivocal dealings with the Spaniards. In his next he discussed the advantages to this country, in the event of a war with Spain, of an expedition against the Spaniards led by Burr (this expedition was Jefferson's first charge against Burr, made, without any suggestion of treason, in his proclamation of 27 November 1806). Martin went on to quote Administration newspapers early in November 1806, which suggested, without the least supporting evidence, that the President was about to order Burr's arrest for treason, charges that were widely reprinted and embroidered upon by other newspapers around the country under such sensational headings as "Ex-Vice President Turned Traitor." He pointed out the inconsistencies in General Eaton's affidavits and testimony, and showed that Burr's conduct was consistent in every detail with a plan to lead a force against the Spaniards in case the war which was imminent became actual. He further traced to Jefferson's Administration, if not to the President himself, the origin of the articles in the Alexandria *Expositor* and the Washington *National Intelligencer* ("the presidential paper") suggesting that Burr was to be arrested for treasonously seeking to separate the Union.[49]

The court reconvened on 3 August, but it was not until a week later that Hay had enough prospective jurymen on hand to proceed with the case. More than 130 witnesses had been summoned by the government,[50] along with some four dozen persons from whom the jury would be selected. Every person tried for a crime is, of course, entitled to have an unbiased and impartial jury. The accused may examine each prospective juryman and may have him excused if he has already formed and expressed a conviction of the prisoner's guilt. The first name called was that of Hezekiah Bucky of Wood County. Burr addressed him and all the assembled talesmen, saying that it was possible that they had formed or expressed opinions against him, but that he expected them to "discharge the duties of conscientious men, and candidly answer the questions put to them, and state all their objections against him." Benjamin Botts thereupon asked Bucky, "Have you ever formed and expressed an opinion about the guilt of Colonel Burr?" Hay immediately objected that the question was too broad. If this question were submitted to each man on the panel, he said, he "would venture to predict, that there could not be a jury selected in the state of Virginia; because he did not believe that there was a single man in the state, qualified to become a juryman, who had not, in some form or

---

[49] The issue of 24 June also printed a brief, good-humored letter from Martin, over his own signature, suggesting that the *Gazette* publish (which it did) an uncomplimentary letter which had recently appeared in the Richmond *Enquirer* describing Martin's appearance, manners, and speech. Martin's letters appeared in the issues of 8 and 15 August, 19 and 30 September, and 7 October 1807.

[50] Including the ubiquitous Richard Reynal Keene, Martin's troublesome son-in-law.

other, made up, and declared an opinion, on the conduct of the prisoner." Martin countered that it was "a libel upon Virginia, a blot upon the whole state, that twelve men could not be found to decide such a case, with no other knowledge than what they had picked up from newspapers." Upon further examination, Bucky denied having said that Burr was guilty of treason, only that a "man who had acted as colonel Burr was said to have done, deserved to be hung."[51] Despite the efforts of the prosecution to uncover some evidence of Bucky's impartiality, he was rejected.

This examination was typical of the rest. Almost to a man, each venireman admitted having expressed an opinion, based upon what he had heard or upon the newspaper accounts, that Burr was guilty of high treason. At least half of the panel members attempted to modify their obvious bias by protesting that although they were convinced of Burr's treasonous intentions, they would be openminded on the question of whether he had committed an overt act of treason. By the following morning, out of the forty-eight talesmen, only four had been accepted as jurymen, while some eight or ten others had been tentatively selected, subject to a ruling by the court after argument as to the degree of impartiality required of them.

Counsel for both sides then argued at length on the rule of law to be applied in the selection of a jury in a criminal case. Martin opened for the defense, invoking the Bill of Rights:

The constitution has secured to us a privilege so sacred, that no law, nor this court of justice can take it from us. Sir, so jealous were the citizens of the United States of their rights, that they were dissatisfied with the constitution in its original form, because it did not expressly provide, that there should be a trial of every offense *"by an impartial jury."* They therefore chose to have it secured by the constitution, so that there should be no possibility of being deprived of an *"impartial jury-trial."* The eighth amendment of the constitution provides, that "in all criminal prosecutions the accused shall enjoy the right to a speedy and public trial by an impartial jury of the state and district wherein the crime shall have been committed."

This provision in the constitution, which secures this sacred right, is binding on every judge sitting on the trial of every criminal. It forbids him to force upon him any juror that is not perfectly indifferent. Gentlemen may say, that we must take such men or have no trial at all. Gentlemen do not understand the subject correctly. They take it for granted, that colonel Burr must be tried at all events, and hung, if an impartial jury cannot be had! But I contend that if an impartial jury cannot be found to try him, he cannot be tried at all: because the constitution says, that he "shall be tried by an impartial jury."[52]

Referring to the government's insistence upon qualifying as jurors veniremen who confessed a belief in Burr's treasonable intentions but

[51] Robertson, *Trials of Aaron Burr*, 1:367–69.
[52] *Ibid.*, p. 388.

who claimed an open mind on Burr's commission of an "overt act," Martin, as was his custom, reduced his argument to the simplest terms:

Let me familiarize this case with the common case of burglary, which is the crime of breaking and entering a house in the night time with an intention to steal.[53] Suppose a person is charged with the crime of burglary and a juryman called to act on his trial says, that he has his mind perfectly made up that the person indicted intended to steal; but, that he is not sure that he did enter the house, and the only question is, with what *intent* did he enter the house? (because he may have gone in with a mind perfectly innocent, without intending to take anything.) Could such a juryman be truly said to be impartial? Most certainly he could not. When a man is indicted for burglary, the juror to try him must be as free from the belief that he intended to commit burglary, as that he went into the house. He must be free from every impression when he comes to be sworn. These observations I have made to show, that on principles of common law and justice, every juryman in every case, especially in criminal cases, ought to be without any prejudice.[54]

In closing, Martin adverted to the widespread popular belief in Burr's guilt which had been inspired by the Administration and the press:[55]

How came these impressions to be on the public mind? Did we busy ourselves to mislead or influence it? Was not the Alexandria Expositor and other papers, under the influence of our rulers at Washington, constantly occupied in throwing out dark hints on this subject, long before the proclamation of the president appeared? Have not great pains been taken by inflammatory publications to impress the minds of the people with a belief of his guilt? Those who have done it have to answer for it; and if they have created such a prejudice, that colonel Burr cannot be rightly tried, they alone are to blame.[56]

After some further argument by most of the counsel present, Marshall wrote his opinion with his usual care, attention to the arguments of both sides, and sober, if repetitious, clarity. In resolving the question he was influenced by Martin's analysis of the issues and by the reasoning and analogies which he had employed:

The question now to be decided, is, whether an opinion formed and delivered, not upon the full case, but upon an essential part of it, . . . [shall] disqualify a

---

[53] A rare slip or, more probably, an oversimplification by Martin. The specific intent required for the common-law crime of burglary was (and generally still is) intent to commit *any* felony, whether grand larceny, rape, arson, or whatever.

[54] Robertson, *Trials of Aaron Burr*, 1:389.

[55] Despite his official declaration that Burr's guilt was beyond question and his fomentation of the outcry against him in the press, Jefferson wrote to William Giles on 20 April 1807: "as to the overt acts, were not the bundle of letters in Mr. Rodney's hands, the letters and facts published in the local newspapers, Burr's flight, and the universal belief or rumor of his guilt, probable ground for presuming the facts of enlistment, military guard, rendezvous, threat of civil war, or capitulation, so as to put him on trial?" And he concluded, "Against Burr I never had one hostile sentiment" (*The Writings of Thomas Jefferson*, ed. Andrew A. Lipscomb, 11:187, 191).

[56] Robertson, *Trials of Aaron Burr*, 1:353.

man in the sense of the law and of the constitution from being an impartial juror? . . .

The cases put by way of illustration, appear to the court, to be strongly applicable to that under consideration. They are those of burglary, of homicide, and of passing counterfeit money, . . . cases in which the intention and the fact combine to constitute the crime. . . .

In reflecting on this subject, which I have done very seriously since the adjournment of yesterday, my mind has been forcibly impressed by contemplating the question precisely in its reverse. If, instead of a panel composed of gentlemen who had almost unanimously formed and publicly delivered an opinion, that the prisoner was guilty, the marshal had returned one composed of persons, who had openly and publicly maintained his innocence; who had insisted, that notwithstanding all the testimony in possession of the public, they had no doubt that his designs were perfectly innocent; who had been engaged in repeated, open, and animated altercation to prove him innocent, and that his objects were entirely opposite to those with which he was charged; would such men be proper and impartial jurors? I cannot believe they would be thought so. I am confident I should not think them so. I cannot declare a juror to be impartial, who has advanced opinions against the prisoner, which would be cause of challenge, if advanced in his favour.

The opinion of the court is, that to have made up and delivered the opinion that the prisoner entertained the treasonable designs with which he is charged and that he retained those designs, and was prosecuting them when the act charged in the indictment is alleged to have been committed, is good cause of challenge.[57]

Accordingly, the ten suspended jurymen were called and dismissed for lack of impartiality. Upon instructions from the court, the marshal then undertook to gather another panel of forty-eight veniremen. It was several days before such a group could be assembled and a list of their names given to the defense. When the court convened, Burr arose and offered a proposition to reduce the time and effort required to strike a jury. He suggested that the defense would be willing to select eight men from the new panel, place them in the box with the four tentatively chosen the previous day, and go to trial. Burr, after consultation with his counsel, had apparently selected the eight because their character and reputation was such that it could be hoped that they would render a verdict upon the evidence and the law, regardless of their previous opinions.

The government assented, subject to examination of the men. When Christopher Anthony was "called to the book," he stated that "his general opinions had been precisely the same that had disqualified (as he understood) several other gentlemen."[58] His objections, however, were overruled. Similarly, John Sheppard stated that he believed that

---

[57] *Ibid.*, p. 414ff.

[58] *Ibid.*, p. 423. Anthony further stated that he "had come to town with a hope of being placed on this jury, and if I were, I would hang colonel Burr at once without further inquiry."

Burr's "intentions were hostile to the peace and safety of the United States; in short, that he had intended to subvert the government of the United States." Miles Bott announced a fixed bias against Burr. When Martin suggested that perhaps it was based only on the supposition that the facts upon which it was founded were true, Bott announced, "I have gone as far as to declare, that colonel Burr ought to be hanged." In deciding to accept him, Burr stated that he was under the necessity of taking men "in some degree, prejudiced against me" and took Bott "under the belief that he will do me justice." Henry Coleman also stated that he "had conceived and expressed an opinion, that the designs of colonel Burr were . . . inimical to the United States."[59] Only Rueben Blakey, Benjamin Graves, and Richard Curd stated that they had no prejudice against Burr.[60]

The jurymen having been sworn and the indictment read to them, George Hay made his opening address outlining the government's case. He laid special emphasis, of course, on Marshall's definition of treason in Bollman's and Swartwout's habeas corpus case,[61] i.e., that all persons allied with those who have assembled for a treasonable purpose, "however remote from the scene of action . . . are to be considered as traitors." For its first witness, the government called "General" William Eaton. The defense immediately objected, stating that the case revolved around the question of whether Burr had committed the overt act required by the Constitution as a prerequisite to a conviction for treason and that Eaton's testimony, as everyone knew from his widely publicized affidavit, only concerned conversations supposed to have taken place between him and Burr in Washington in February and March 1806. Any statements made by Burr at that time and place, whether the jury believed them or not, could not possibly constitute an overt act of treason on the Ohio River ten months later, as alleged in the indictment.

The defense insisted that if the government had any testimony of Burr's commission of an overt act on Blennerhasset Island on 10 December 1806, it should be produced. If the government had no such testimony, there was the end of the case. A federal prosecution for treason must meet the definition of the crime and the requisites of proof set out in the Constitution. To convict Burr of treason, the defense insisted, the government must show that there had been a "war"—not one in the newspapers, but one in fact. Beyond this, the government was bound to present the testimony of at least two witnesses that Burr had engaged in "levying" that war against the United States specifically, and at the time and place named in the indictment. The government argued that it might present its case and its witnesses in any order it chose, and that

---

[59] *Ibid.*, p. 425ff.
[60] The other jurymen of this group were Edward Carrington, David Lambert, Richard E. Parker, Hugh Mercer, and James Sheppard.
[61] See Chapter 22, p. 240ff., above.

it was entitled to adduce evidence of an intent on the part of Burr to commit treason before providing testimony as to any actual overt act.

This point was argued earnestly and learnedly until the close of the court on Monday. As usual, Marshall wrote his opinion that evening and delivered it the next morning. He ruled that inasmuch as both intention to commit treason and the actual levying of war, which constituted the required act of treason, were relevant, the government could prove these matters in any order it pleased. The court pointed out, however, that testimony about collateral matters not related to the levying of war at the time and place specified would be excluded. With these ground rules, on 17 August, William Eaton was called to the stand to give his evidence.

24

The Aaron Burr Treason Trial:
3. Richmond, 17 August–20 October 1807

No person shall be convicted of treason unless on the
testimony of two Witnesses to the same overt Act, or on
Confession in open Court.—Constitution of the United
States, art. III, sec. 3

Wirt is sick, my strength and flesh are declining, and
everybody almost complains except Luther Martin. His
speech lasted 14 hours and does not appear to have had
the slightest effect even in his voice. I believe that the
judge by cutting off all the trials for treason has saved
my life.—Hay to Jefferson, 1 September 1807

The declaration which I made in court in his [Wil-
kinson's] favour some time ago was precipitate. . . . My
confidence in him is shaken if not destroyed. . . . I am
sorry for it, on his own account, on the public account,
and because you have expressed opinions in his favour;
but you did not know then what you soon will know.—
Hay to Jefferson, 15 October 1807

Regardless of one's preconceptions about Aaron Burr's innocence or
guilt, a review of the actual testimony produced at his trial is bound to
be startling. Particularly striking is the weakness of the government's
case in support of the crime charged, as defined in the Constitution and
specified in the indictment. No one was shown to have engaged in
"levying War" against the United States; the country had no "Enemies" to whom "Aid and Comfort" was given; and no "overt Act" of
war was charged against Burr personally. Indeed, the government was
forced to concede that he was some hundreds of miles away from the
place of the alleged crime.[1]

The government could prosecute Burr only upon a theory of "constructive treason," attributing to him acts of treason (if such they were)

[1] Robertson, *Trials of Aaron Burr*, 1:473–530; Carpenter, *Trial of Burr for Treason*,
2:124–85; Coombs, *Trials of Aaron Burr*, pp. 150–215.

committed by others, supposedly on his behalf and in his absence. Moreover, even on such grounds, the evidence of the levying of war against the United States—supposedly waged by some thirty leaderless men and boys, equipped with a few guns, less than a dozen flatboats, and a small quantity of seed grain—was so slight as to be ludicrous in fact and *de minimis* in law. All the power of Jefferson's government was behind the prosecution of this artificial case: the best counsel that government money could attract were hired, and the country was scoured for whatever evidence pressure or patronage could produce.[2] The result was the most over-tried and under-proved case in the legal history of the United States.

The public, barraged by a constant flow of sensational articles in the press[3] and propaganda of Republican politicians, was convinced of Burr's guilt long before he was indicted. On a typical Fourth of July outing in 1807 in Elkton, Maryland, for example, as was usual, a series of seventeen previously prepared resolutions were adopted in the style of toasts, with the customary liquid accompaniment. These were followed by an indeterminate number of "volunteers" expressing sentiments understandably more impromptu and necessarily less responsible than those of the first group. The proceedings were reported in the Baltimore press and came to Martin's attention while he was there during the court recess.[4] He dismissed the "volunteers" with humor: "After seventeen bumpers had been drank, I can make allowances for any thing that took place; but for toasts deliberately prepared, and agreed to be drank on that day, myself, my fellow citizens, and the world at large, do and will hold you answerable."[5] Martin took particular exception to three of the formal toasts:

The grand jurors lately impanelled at Richmond, to indict the traitors of their country—May their zeal and patriotism in the cause of liberty, secure them a crown of immortal glory, and the fruits of their labour be a death wound to all conspirators.

Luther Martin, the ex-attorney general of Maryland, the mutual and highly respected friend of a convicted traitor—May his exertions to preserve the Catiline [*sic*] of America procure him an honorable coat of tar, and a plumage of feathers that will rival in finery all the mummeries of Egypt.

Aaron Burr, the man who once received the confidence of a free people—May his treachery to his country exalt him to the scaffold and hemp be his escort to the republic of dust and ashes.[6]

---

[2] See the questionnaire sent to all United States attorneys and other federal officers in a desperate attempt to turn up some evidence against Burr (Letters in Relation to the Burr Conspiracy).

[3] See Jonathan Daniels, *They Will Be Heard*, chap. 5, for an account of the lurid articles in the Lexington, Kentucky, *Western World* during the fall of 1806.

[4] The court recessed from 27 June to 3 August, while prospective jurymen were being brought from Wood County on the Ohio to Richmond.

[5] Samuel L. Knapp, *The Life of Aaron Burr*, p. 161 ff.

[6] Quoted in *ibid*.

In view of the fact that Burr's trial had hardly begun, Martin's philippic protest was justified:

Gentlemen, have you any knowledge that Colonel Burr is guilty of treason, or of any other offense? Doth either of you know of one single fact to prove upon him guilt of any kind? Why have you not come forward and informed your government? And why had I not the pleasure of seeing you as witnesses at Richmond?

I know your answer. You must confess that you have no personal knowledge of any thing criminal that has been committed by Colonel Burr, but in the Aurora, the Argus, and many other democratic papers, you have seen him charged with not only misdemeanours but treason; nay, you will probably say, that the president of the United States, in his message to congress, declared his *guilt to be placed beyond doubt*. . . .

And now let me inquire who is this gentleman whose guilt you have pronounced, and for whose blood your *parched* throats so thirst? Was he not, a few years past, adored by you next to your God? . . . He was then in power. He had then influence. You would then have been proud of his notice. . . .

Go, ye holiday, ye sunshine friends—ye time servers—ye criers of hosanna to-day and crucifiers to-morrow—go hide your heads, if possible, from the contempt and detestation of every virtuous, every honourable inhabitant of every clime. . . .

In your toast you have particularly noticed me, as "the mutual and highly respected friend of an indicted traitor."

Remember, gentlemen, a few years only have passed since you boasted of your friendship for Colonel Burr. . . . He was then your political friend; *such he never has been to me*. Our friendship has been *personal*, our politics have ever been *different*.[7]

On 18 August Burr's jury was chosen, and the trial resumed. The first witness was William Eaton, who had been cutting quite a figure in Richmond for weeks, swaggering up and down the streets in his Oriental costume. He had been going from tavern to tavern, drinking, bragging, and laying bets on Burr's conviction, and, in the process, casting considerable doubt on his character and reliability as a witness. At the outset he testified that he had no knowledge of any overt act of treason committed by Burr but that "concerning colonel Burr's expressions of treasonable intentions" he knew much.[8] He reported conversations he had had with Burr during the winter of 1805 in which Burr intimated that he was organizing an expedition against the Spanish for the war that appeared inevitable. After a while, Eaton said, he came to believe that Burr had other projects in mind for which the Spanish war would serve as a screen. Burr sympathized with his failure to obtain reimbursement from the government for his expenditures on behalf of

---

[7] *Ibid.* After Martin's return to Baltimore following the Burr trials, he was given the names of a number of persons present at the Elkton outing who had dissented from the toasts there offered. These names Martin published in a letter to the editor of the *Federal Gazette* for 6 November 1807.

[8] Robertson, *Trials of Aaron Burr*, 1:473.

the United States and suggested that there were other ways by which he could be repaid. He drew Burr out by pretending sympathy with his plans, Eaton testified, and Burr "laid open his project of revolutionizing the territory west of the Allegheny; establishing an independent empire there; New-Orleans to be the capital, and he himself to be the chief; organizing a military force on the waters of the Mississippi, and carrying the conquest to Mexico." In other discussions Burr indicated that General Wilkinson and many other prominent citizens of the western country were allied with him in the project.[9]

On cross-examination, Eaton publicly conceded for the first time that the federal government accounting department had claimed a balance due from him. Despite this, Eaton insisted that instead the government owed him money for his private expenditures on its behalf. He admitted that the government had withdrawn its claims and had paid him "about $10,000"[10] immediately after he made an affidavit containing these charges against Burr. He further admitted that he had recommended Burr to Jefferson for an ambassadorship after Burr's alleged revelation of his plans to bring about a secession of the western states.[11] On redirect, Eaton insisted only that Congress had not awarded him a fixed sum but merely authorized the State Department to settle with him "on equitable principles."

Commodore Truxton, to whom Burr had offered the command of his naval forces, was next called and testified to their lengthy conversations in July of 1806. Burr's plans, as revealed to him, went no further than "an expedition to Mexico, in the event of a war with Spain, which he thought inevitable." On cross-examination, he stated positively that though he and Burr had talked intimately and without reserve, he had never heard Burr "speak of a division of the union."[12]

Peter Taylor, Blennerhassett's gardener, then recounted that in October of 1806 Mrs. Blennerhassett had sent him to warn Burr that people were so agitated and alarmed by rumors that it would not be safe for him to return to Blennerhassett Island. Taylor found Burr in Lexington, Kentucky, where he gave him some letters. Shortly thereafter, Taylor also met Blennerhassett, who was then recruiting "good, orderly, young men" from the Lexington area to settle the large Washita tract of land bought by Burr and his friends. According to Taylor, Blennerhassett was full of great plans: "We are going to take Mexico," he said. Burr was to be King of Mexico and Theodosia Burr Alston its queen. As for the rumors that Burr wanted to divide the Union, Taylor quoted Blennerhassett as protesting that he and Burr could not possibly accomplish this alone. With regard to the assembly on Blennerhassett Island on 10 December, Taylor said that there had

[9] *Ibid.*, p. 474ff.
[10] Some three thousand dollars more than he had claimed (see Chapter 22, pp. 238–39, above).
[11] Robertson, *Trials of Aaron Burr*, 1:480ff.
[12] *Ibid.*, p. 485ff.

been four boats and about thirty men. Some of the men had guns and went hunting; Taylor did not know how many guns the group had or whether they were rifles or muskets. What was most important to the defense was the witness's testimony that Burr was not present on the island at that time, nor even, he understood, "in that part of the country."[13]

Gen. John Morgan then testified that when Burr visited his home at Morganza, near Pittsburgh, in August of 1806, he observed that "the union of the states could not possibly last; and that a separation of the states must ensue as a natural consequence, in four or five years." (Such observations, of course, did not constitute treason and were heard all over the country—Jefferson himself is known to have made a similar statement.[14]) Morgan attributed other extravagant statements to Burr, such as the claim that with two hundred men he could "drive the president and congress into the Potowmac; and with four or five hundred he could take possession of the city of New-York." It was after these conversations, Morgan said, that he advised his father to write President Jefferson that "something was going on."[15] His brother and father confirmed this testimony.

The government then called Jacob Allbright, another of Blennerhassett's employees, in order "to prove directly the overt act," according to Hay. Allbright testified that Mrs. Blennerhassett had told him that her husband and Burr were going to "lay in provisions for an army for a year." He told of about twenty or thirty men with four boats assembling on Blennerhassett Island in the first week in December. They made a supply of bullets and loaded the boats with wooden crates. While this was going on, an officer from Ohio named Tupper abruptly appeared on the island and attempted to arrest Blennerhassett (on Virginia soil) in the name of the commonwealth of Ohio. When seven or eight muskets were leveled at him, he wished Blennerhassett luck and departed as abruptly as he had come. Allbright testified that Burr was not present on the island at the time and had not been there for six weeks.[16] Other witnesses gave evidence to the same general effect, without adding anything to the government's case: twenty to thirty men had met on Blennerhassett's Island on 10 December; Burr was not there; some of the men were armed, some not; one or two of the men went hunting, and made a few bullets; there was no disturbance of any kind.

The prosecution had now adduced all the evidence it had with regard to the events on the date and at the place specified in the indictment. Counsel for Burr proceeded to argue that sufficient evidence

[13] *Ibid.*, p. 491ff.
[14] Letter to John Breckenridge, 12 August 1803, Jefferson Papers, 134:23144ff.
[15] Robertson, *Trials of Aaron Burr*, 1:497ff.
[16] *Ibid.*, p. 506ff.

of an overt act on the part of Burr had not been shown, as required by the Constitution, and moved, accordingly, that no further evidence of collateral acts and words elsewhere be admitted. Wickham argued throughout most of Thursday and part of Friday's session. He was followed by Edmund Randolph,[17] at the close of whose argument the prosecution asked for a postponement until Monday morning, in order to prepare its reply. Unusual as this request was (Saturday was then as full and as long a day in court as any other), Marshall granted it.

On Monday morning, MacRae opened for the government with characteristic fire and sarcasm.[18] He was followed on Tuesday by Wirt, who delivered a lengthy exordium, abstracting, explaining, and distinguishing treason cases from the time of the Year Books to that moment. The one bright spot of the speech, which was reprinted in school readers and used as a declamatory exercise for over a century, was a brilliant passage in which he contrasted the roles and characters of Burr and Blennerhassett.[19] This passage, more than anything else, is responsible for the public conviction of Burr's guilt. Botts answered for the defense, bringing court, counsel, and spectators back to earth with his humorous sallies at Wirt's "tropes and figures" and with a simple summary of the scanty evidence produced by the government in support of its case.[20]

On Wednesday, Hay rose to reply. He began with an ineffectual attempt to withdraw the government's previous admission that Burr was nowhere near Blennerhassett's Island on 10 December. When challenged, Hay admitted "his own *belief* . . . that the accused was not then present." but insisted that this did not affect the prosecution's theory of the case.[21] Though he added nothing to the weight of the government's argument, he suggested, none too subtly, that Marshall might be impeached as Chase had been if he ruled in favor of the defense.[22] The Chief Justice chose to pass this off as argument rather than threat.[23]

It had been known for days that Martin would close for the defense. When Charles Lee finished on the afternoon of 27 August, the court was advised that Martin was "not yet ready."[24] The following morning, before a room crowded with spectators come to see and hear the famous reprobate advocate from Maryland, he appeared for one of the greatest efforts of his career.

[17] *Ibid.*, 2:3ff.
[18] *Ibid.*, p. 27ff.
[19] *Ibid.*, p. 96ff.
[20] *Ibid.*, p. 123ff.
[21] *Ibid.*, pp. 196–97.
[22] *Ibid.*, p. 193.
[23] *Ibid.*, p. 238.
[24] *Ibid.*, p. 260. Without denying Martin's chronic alcoholism, it must be noted that Beveridge's statement (*Life of John Marshall*, 3:501) that Martin "had been drinking even more than usual throughout the proceedings" is not supported by his sources, Blennerhassett's diary for 30 August and 2 and 27 October 1807 (Blennerhassett Papers, pp. 377, 438, 463).

Addressing Chief Justice John Marshall and Judge Cyrus Griffin, he opened his argument:

May it please your Honours.

I shall now endeavour to close the important debate before the court, and to show that our motion ought to be granted. It involves certain great principles, on the correct settlement of which, greatly depend the welfare and happiness of the people of this country. I shall therefore make no apology for any length of time I may occupy in the discussion of the question. When we are defending the life of a human being, and discussing principles of such vast importance to the interests of the community and of posterity, time ought not to be regarded.[25]

After reviewing the proceedings, Martin expounded the common law as to principals and accessories in felonies set out in the classic texts of Hawkins, Blackstone, Hale, Foster, and East. He execrated the British doctrine of constructive treason, "this legal ubiquity by which a man may be said by the instrumentality of his agents, to be present—like the Deity—in any and every part of the United States." A "levying of war," he insisted, "must mean more than the mere enlistment of men, and yet it was evident that in this case "the *violence of actual war* has never been known to take place. If such a war have taken place, it was a mighty strange kind of war, which neither man, woman nor child has ever seen or heard. Though there was a great war . . . from New Hampshire to New Orleans, and a great number of persons were engaged in it, yet in this great war, not a single act of violence can be proved by any human being to have happened."[26] All the English and American cases specified as an overt act some evidence that force had been used: with that element absent, treason could not properly be alleged, much less proved.

The next morning, after recapitulating his previous argument, Martin went on to direct his remarks to Chief Justice Marshall's language in the Bollman-Swartwout case.[27] He demonstrated from the record of that case that Colonel Burr's presence, actual or constructive, on Blennerhassett Island was not there in issue; that even the name of the place was not there mentioned; that, considering the evidence which was put before the court there (the depositions of Eaton, Wilkinson, and others, along with the famous cipher letter), that court had held unanimously that there was no proof of treason on the part of Bollman, Swartwout, Burr, or anyone else. His conclusion was that "there was not the least proof of treason; that if there were any proof, it was no more than of an expedition which, as it depended on a war with Spain (of which there was then the greatest probability), would have been honourable if war took place, and no treason if the war did not take place: a war in which if he [Burr] succeeded, he would have acquired honour and glory: and which in any event would have been but a mis-

[25] Robertson, *Trials of Aaron Burr*, 2:26off.
[26] *Ibid.*, p. 265.
[27] *Ibid.*, p. 332ff. See Chapter 22 above.

demeanor, by which neither his honour nor reputation could have been sullied."[28] The reference in Bollman-Swartwout to other persons, places, and circumstances not then before the court, Martin argued, was necessarily only dictum and without authority: "As a binding judicial opinion, it ought to have no more weight than the ballad or song of Chevy Chase."

The government had proposed to offer testimony concerning Burr's actions further down the Ohio, at the mouth of the Cumberland, as evidence of overt acts of war. Not only was such testimony irrelevant to the charge laid in the indictment, Martin insisted, but the court was bound to so declare it, and to exclude it, even in the face of threats of impeachment if it should "decide against the wishes of the government."[29]

Martin reminded his audience of the cruelty with which the doctrine of constructive treason had been applied in England and pointed out that the language of the Constitution had been carefully drawn to prevent just such political persecution here: "If innocence had never been persecuted, if innocence were never in danger, why were no many checks provided in the constitution for its security?" he asked. "We know the summary and sanguinary proceedings of former times, as recorded in faithful history. In those times of oppression and cruelty, they never troubled courts or juries with their accusations, proofs and legal forms, but declared the intended victim guilty of treason, and proceeded to execution at once. We wish to prevent a repetition of those scenes of injustice and horror."[30]

Martin's peroration was characteristically vigorous and directed to the heart of the matter and to the minds of the court. He exhorted the latter to perform its solemn duty regardless of popular clamor:

We are unfortunately situated. We labour against great prejudices against my client, which tend to prevent him from having a fair trial. I have with pain heard it said that such are the public prejudices against colonel Burr, that a jury, even should they be satisfied of his innocence, must have considerable firmness of mind to pronounce him *not guilty*. God of heaven! have we already under our form of government (which we have so often been told is the best calculated of all governments to secure all our rights) arrived at a period when a trial in a court of justice, where life is at stake, shall be but a solemn mockery, a mere idle form and ceremony to transfer innocence from the gaol to the gibbet, to gratify popular indignation excited by bloodthirsty enemies! But if it require in such a situation firmness in a jury, so does it equally require fortitude in judges to perform their duty. And here permit me again most solemnly and at the same time most respectfully to observe that in the case of life and death, where there remains one single doubt in the minds of the jury as to facts, or of the court as to law, it is their duty to decide in favor of life. If they do not and

[28] *Ibid.*, pp. 333–34.
[29] *Ibid.*, p. 369.
[30] *Ibid.*, p. 375.

the prisoner fall a victim, they are guilty of murder in *foro coeli* whatever their guilt may be in *foro legis*.

When the sun mildly shines upon us, when the gentle zephyrs play around us, we can easily proceed forward in the straight path of our duty; but when bleak clouds enshroud the sky with darkness, when the tempest rages, the winds howl and the waves break over us—when the thunders awfully roar over our heads and the lightnings of heaven blaze around us—it is *then* that all the energies of the human soul are called into action. It is *then* that the truly brave man stands firm at his post. It is *then* that by an unshaken performance of his duty, man approaches the nearest possible to the divinity. Nor is there any object in the creation on which the supreme Being can look down with more delight and approbation than on a human being in such a situation and thus acting. May that God who now looks down upon us, who has in his infinite wisdom called you into existence and placed you in that seat to dispense justice to your fellow citizens, to preserve and protect innocence against persecution—may that God so illuminate your understandings that you may *know* what is right; and may he nerve your souls with firmness and fortitude to *act* according to that knowledge.[31]

The court adjourned until Monday to consider and write its decision. The following evening, Blennerhassett recounted, Martin ("the whole rear-guard of Burr's forensic army") dropped by the prison to visit him. At Blennerhassett's recommendation of his brandy as "superior," Martin poured out a pint and drank it down on the spot. He then summarized for the prisoner the proceedings of the trial, giving lengthy quotations from memory from the speeches of counsel on both sides (including, Blennerhassett noted, long excerpts from his own); recited verbatim, by the half-column, letters he had written to the *Virginia Gazette* over the signature "Investigator"; recapitulated the history of his acquaintance with Burr; and interspersed in all this anecdotes, denunciations of some characters connected with the trial, and praise of others—all in the space of thirty-five minutes![32]

The following morning Marshall read the court's opinion. To a large extent it was based on Martin's analysis and exposition: the defense had maintained that under the Constitution no man might be convicted of treason who was not actually present when the war alleged was levied, and that no testimony charging one man with the overt acts of others might be admitted until those acts as laid in the indictment had been proved to the satisfaction of the court.[33] Marshall discussed the meaning of the phrase "levying war," historically and textually, and concluded that "war could not be levied without the employment and exhibition of force," and that no such force or violence had been used on Blennerhassett Island. Next he held that to prove Burr's guilt the government must produce at least two witnesses to show that he was either present in person at the time and place laid in the indictment or had himself organized a treasonable assemblage there. It was conceded

[31] *Ibid.*, pp. 377–78.
[32] Blennerhassett Papers, p. 377.
[33] Robertson, *Trials of Aaron Burr*, 2:401.

that Burr was some hundreds of miles distant from the island on the date in question, and to establish his role in organizing the meeting the government had produced no witness and had put in evidence only "subsequent transactions at a different place and in a different state." Such testimony was irrelevant and inadmissible.

In this state of the law and the evidence, the jury's ensuing "Scotch verdict" on 1 September, that "Aaron Burr is not proved to be guilty under this indictment by any evidence submitted to us" was as inevitable as it was grudgingly rendered. Marshall's ruling requiring actual rather than "constructive" presence at the commission of overt actions of treason, bitterly as it was condemned by Jefferson, has been accepted in this country from that day to this.[34]

At Jefferson's insistence, however, proceedings on Burr's indictment for the misdemeanor of conspiring against a government at peace with the United States were undertaken.[35] Dozens of witnesses were examined, but nothing more was proved than Burr's intentions to occupy his Washita property, and from there to attack the Spanish in the event of war between Spain and the United States. When General Wilkinson took the witness stand, his testimony about his relations with Burr was evasive and slippery. He had convenient lapses of memory and "corrected" and emended his account from day to day, as "further reflection" dictated.[36] Under the persistent cross-examination of Martin and Wickham, he was forced to admit the discrepancies between the original of the letter of 29 July 1806, supposedly sent to him by Burr, and the translation of it which he sent to the President. He acknowledged the "convention," unauthorized by the United States government, between himself and the Spaniards.[37] He further admitted sending army officers disguised as civilians to capture Burr, and rifling the mails and arresting private citizens in New Orleans in an effort to establish his dictatorship there. He repeatedly declined to answer questions for fear of incriminating himself, while continuing to insist that he was "prompted by that pure patriotism which has always influenced my conduct and my character which I trust will never be tarnished."[38] He left the witness stand completely discredited in the eyes of the defense, the public, and even the government counsel.

On 15 September, the jury, after half an hour of deliberation, brought in a verdict of not guilty,[39] but the end was not yet in sight. At

---

[34] Edward S. Corwin's argument that Marshall's rulings were based more on personal and political antagonism to Jefferson than on sound legal principles (*John Marshall and the Constitution*, pp. 86–120) has been ably refuted by Willard Hurst, "Treason in the United States"; Bradley Chapin, *The American Law of Treason: Revolutionary and Early National Origins*, pp. 98–113; and Robert K. Faulkner, "John Marshall and the Burr Trial," p. 247ff.

[35] Robertson, *Trials of Aaron Burr*, 2:539.

[36] *Ibid.*, p. 512ff.

[37] See Chapter 22 above.

[38] *Annals of Congress*, 10th Cong., 1st sess., 1807, p. 550. One is reminded of Samuel Johnson's definition of patriotism as the last refuge of a scoundrel.

[39] Blennerhassett Papers, p. 404; Robertson, *Trials of Aaron Burr*, 2:539.

Jefferson's insistence, Hay proposed that the court should hear evidence on the question of holding Burr for trial on charges of treason and misdemeanor in Ohio, Kentucky, or the Mississippi Territory. Despite the protests of Burr's counsel that such proceedings constituted double jeopardy and that the evidence, in any event, was too flimsy to justify such a commitment, Marshall deemed it politic to proceed as requested. After three weeks of hearing much the same testimony twice heard before, from much the same witnesses (including another sorry performance by Wilkinson), Marshall held that the evidence was insufficient to commit Burr for treason. However, he did hold both him and Blennerhassett for trial in Ohio on the misdemeanor charge.[40] They were allowed bail, Martin going surety for Burr, who was scheduled to appear at Chillicothe on 4 January 1808,[41] along with a Dr. Commins. (Unfortunately for Martin, Burr departed for Europe after the trial and did not return until 1812, thus forfeiting his bail.) With his customary generosity, Martin insisted that he would go to Ohio to defend Burr and Blennerhassett,[42] but the government never brought the case to trial.

[40] Carpenter, *Trial of Burr for Treason*, 3:160ff.; Blennerhassett Papers, p. 430ff.
[41] Blennerhassett Papers, p. 461.
[42] *Ibid.*, pp. 471, 487, 499, 508.

25

Supreme Court Advocate, 1807-1810

Luther Martin is certainly one of the most benevolent men alive. His heart is overflowing with the milk of philanthropy, which his potations may sometimes coagulate, but will never acidify.—Harman Blennerhassett, 29 October 1807

In the enumeration of the great men of the bar, I have placed Luther Martin first.—Roger Brooke Taney, *Autobiography*

You should hear of Luther Martin's fame from those who have known him long and intimately, but you should not see him.—Justice Joseph Story to Samuel P. Fay, 16 February 1808

Accompanied by Harman Blennerhassett and Dr. Commins, his fellow bondsman, Martin left Richmond for Baltimore by coach at 3:00 A.M. on 24 October. Despite his heavy and constant drinking, his vitality was phenomenal. Blennerhassett recounted that "neither the privation of sleep, nor the fatigue of the journey, have in the least checked his loquacity, or lessened his good humor. He read to me an able pamphlet, on the subject of Jefferson's rejection of the new British treaty, while we were jolting and jarring over as bad a road as any country can lament, with more dispatch than I could peruse it in my chair."[1] The party arrived in Baltimore on 31 October.[2]

Martin promptly got off a letter to the *Federal Gazette* in which he called attention to the fact that the Burr trials at Richmond had saved "seven worthy American citizens from that ignominious death to which the administration had destined them." He and his fellow defense lawyers, he went on, had also "saved from a life of agonizing misery, one of the most amiable and accomplished ladies in America, with

[1] Blennerhassett Papers, p. 463ff.
[2] Martin first appeared in Richmond as Burr's counsel on 28 May 1807, came back to Baltimore for a few weeks in midsummer, and returned to Richmond around 1 August.

whom I have been acquainted from her early youth."[3] His letter continued:

We have proved that in America there are lawyers who cannot be intimidated by fear of presidential vengeance, nor by the frenzy of a deceived, misguided people, from securing even to those destined to be the victims of power, those rights, for the enjoyment of which the constitution is and ought to be their sacred and inviolate pledge. . . .

For the share I have had in, and the sacrifices I have made for obtaining those events, I ask not the *approbation*, much less the *applause* of my fellow citizens; that will be bestowed upon my *memory* by *their children*, and in the meantime be received by me from the good and worthy of every *other* country.[4]

This letter was noticed in an editorial by the local pro-Administration newspaper of the day, the *Baltimore American*, whose editor suggested that Martin's letter might result in public riots and went on to "just hint the good effect that would be produced by putting Luther Martin in a straight waistcoat."[5] There were many people eager to take such a hint. At this time Martin resided at Nine South Charles Street, just south of Market (now Baltimore) Street, where he maintained a combination of home, office, and private law school. One of his students brought word that a mob was forming to attack him, Burr, and Blennerhassett at his home and displayed a copy of a handbill which was being circulated throughout the city. Under the heading "AWFUL!" it announced that "the Public are hereby notified that four 'Choice Spirits' are this afternoon, at three o'clock, to be Marshalled for execution by the Hangman on 'Gallows Hill'." The four to be so "honored" were the Chief Justice, John Marshall; "His Quid Majesty," Burr; Blennerhassett, "the Chemist"; and "Lawyer Brandy Bottle."[6]

While Captains Samuel Hollingsworth and William Barney and the First Baltimore Hussars, together with Martin's students, stood guard around his house and Blennerhassett watched from the attic of Evans' Hotel, a mob of some fifteen hundred persons, with a fife and drum corps playing the "Rogue's March," went howling by, dragging the effigies of the four "Choice Spirits" in a pair of carts. As they passed Martin's house, they broke some of his windows with stones but did little other damage.[7]

One sequel to the Burr trials proved to be a left-handed compliment to Martin. John Smith, a United States senator from Ohio, former Baptist preacher, and early supporter of Burr's Mexican schemes, was one of many implicated (without supporting evidence) by the government in the "conspiracy." With Burr's acquittal Smith's indictment

---

[3] This is a reference, of course, to Theodosia Burr.
[4] Published on 2 November 1807, p. 3.
[5] Wednesday, 4 November 1807, p. 3.
[6] Blennerhasset Papers, p. 477ff.; Beveridge, *Life of John Marshall*, 3:536.
[7] As reported in the *Federal Gazette* (Baltimore), 4 November 1807, p. 2; recalled editorially in the *Federal Republican* (Baltimore), 21 September 1810.

for treason was dropped. When he resumed his seat in the Senate, however, his right to it was challenged. The chairman of the committee appointed to investigate and make a recommendation was John Quincy Adams, who made the assumption that all persons implicated by the government were guilty.[8] After hearing much testimony against Smith, the committee filed a report recommending his expulsion from the Senate. Smith thereupon made a formal motion that he be informed of the specific charges against him, that he be allowed to make a defense to the charges and to call witnesses on his behalf, and that he be represented by counsel. The Senate granted his request but reserved the right to pass upon his choice of counsel. Smith announced that he had retained Luther Martin and Francis Scott Key. The Senate agreed to Key but refused to accept Martin.[9] Accordingly, Martin turned his attention to his private practice.

A great deal of work had accumulated during his absence in Richmond, many of his cases, because of his skill and success in handling them, involving abstruse questions in the law of real property—contingent remainders, the law of waste, estates in fee tail, and other recondite problems no longer litigated today.[10] In one way or another, the institution of slavery continued to impinge upon his practice.[11] In Maryland, as in other states below the Mason and Dixon line, any Negro might be arrested merely upon "suspicion of being an escaped slave," and on him was the burden of proving, by manumission papers or otherwise, his free status. Upon arrest, such a person was confined in a foul slave detention prison and held while his description was advertised so that his owner, if any, could claim him upon payment of the jailer's charges for his keep. If during the statutory period of advertisement, no owner claimed him—if he were free, of course, he had no owner who could claim him—then he would be sold off to slavers, who paid the jail charges and resold him for whatever profit he might bring.

To test the legality of this vicious system, late in the summer of 1810 writs of habeas corpus were sued out in Baltimore for five Negroes so imprisoned. The cases were heard by the Chief Justice of the Baltimore Court of Oyer and Terminer, John Scott.[12] The courtroom was packed

[8] Bennett Champ Clark, *John Quincy Adams, "Old Man Eloquent,"* pp. 94–97.
[9] *Annals of Congress,* 10th Cong., 1st sess., 1807, pp. 66ff. The Senate ultimately voted for Smith's expulsion nineteen to ten; however, a two-thirds vote was required, and Smith thus retained his seat by one vote (Clark, *John Quincy Adams,* pp. 94–97).
[10] Martin's participation in the Maryland appealed cases of this period, as reported in vol. 3 of Harris and Johnson's Reports, was as follows: of 126 cases reported, he argued 53, or 42 per cent. Of his 53 cases argued in the lower court, he won 21, or 40 per cent; of his 52 cases argued in the Court of Appeals, he won 24, or 46 per cent. Cases argued before and decided by the Court of Appeals in 1809 were for some reason not reported. Vol. 2 of Harris and Johnson covers the years 1806–8, vol. 3 the years 1810–15.
[11] See Chapter 18 above for Martin's earlier involvement in the legal aspects of slavery.
[12] See the Baltimore *Scourge* for 15 and 22 September 1810, Baltimore *Whig* for 18 September 1810.

for the occasion with antislavery advocates, as well as many professional slave-catchers, "negro-apprehending constables, Georgia factors, slave agents, purchasers and pimps." The attorneys for the jailer were Theodorick Bland, T. B. Dorsey, and Luther Martin. After argument, to the chagrin of the slavers and the surprise of everyone, Judge Scott released the prisoners.

Writs were thereupon sued out for the release of five more Negroes similarly confined. In this case, Martin argued for six and a half consecutive hours that such a practice was necessary for the public safety. He pointed out that escaped slaves usually gave fictitious names and addresses and thus could not be recognized by their owners from advertisements in distant newspapers unless they had (as they often did) whiplash scars on their backs, or marks from cutting or branding given as a means of identification. He urged that many thefts, murders, and arsons were committed by escaped slaves, and that unless Negroes wandering at large were apprehended and confined, Baltimore would become a haven for desperate escaped slaves from all over the South. In the end, Judge Scott released two prisoners whose slave status could not be proved by the jailer, retained two who confessed that they were escaped slaves, and held sub curia, pending receipt of proofs of manumission, one woman who had lived free and independent for years, supporting herself as a seamstress. (There is no record of any great increase of serious felonies in Baltimore following these decisions, as Martin feared.)

The case of *Burk* v. *State*,[13] on the other hand, affords an example of the zeal which Martin was equally willing to expend in defending a Negro client. Burk was an indigent slave, indicted for the rape of a ten-year-old girl. An indictment was found by the grand jury of Frederick County charging Thomas Burk with rape (a felony), as well as with an assault with intent to commit rape (a misdemeanor) on the body of Catharine Maria Brawner. The public was so aroused against the prisoner that, upon Martin's motion, the court granted a removal to neighboring Washington County. The case was tried on the first count only, before Chief Judge John Buchanan.

After a long and acrimonious trial, the jury returned a verdict of guilty, as expected.[14] Martin then made a motion in arrest of judgment based on defects in the indictment, the manner of the summonsing of additional talesmen after exhaustion of the first panel, and the charge to the jury. After deciding that "upon the whole" sufficient cause for a new trial had not been shown, Judge Buchanan sentenced Burk to be hanged. Martin had argued his motions and objections so tenaciously that when the case was over and he attempted to board the stagecoach in which Judge Buchanan was sitting, the infuriated jurist struck him with his cane.[15]

[13] 2 Harris and Johnson 426 (1809).
[14] *Maryland Herald* (Hagerstown), 31 May 1809.
[15] See Williams, *History of Frederick County*, 1:179.

Martin took the case to the Court of Appeals upon a writ of error and there, aided by Taney and Upton Lawrence,[16] urged the same grounds of error. Of particular interest is his brief before the Court of Appeals in which he cited nearly a hundred cases, ancient and modern, as well as numerous other authorities. The lower court's judgment was affirmed, however, and the death warrant was issued for Burk's execution on 28 July. The prisoner had other plans, however, and on 4 July made his own declaration of independence by breaking out of the Hagerstown jail.[17] Despite a hundred-dollar reward for his apprehension, he was never seen again.

Shortly after the turn of the century, for a variety of reasons, the wages of unskilled laborers began to rise perceptibly; at the same time, there being no corresponding increase in the pay of skilled workmen, the latter began to form organizations for collective action in regulating wages and in imposing a closed shop.[18] The Baltimore journeymen tailors, for example, actually went on strike as early as 1795 and again ten years later. To combat these activities, prosecutions were brought against the workmen involved for the common-law crime of conspiracy. The first of these trials took place in Philadelphia in 1806 and was followed by others in various states along the Atlantic seaboard.

On 17 January 1809 the "Journeymen Cordwainers [i.e., shoemakers] Society of Baltimore" ordered a general strike. A grand jury returned 270 indictments against some three dozen shoemakers for conspiracy to prevent another journeyman, who had been excluded from their society, from being hired by a master cordwainer.[19] The trial of one of the defendants, begun as a test case (*State v. Powley*), started on 8 August, and that redoubtable champion of the underdog, Martin, appeared for the defense.[20] After two weeks of testimony and argument, Chief Justice John Scott, of the Court of Oyer and Terminer, submitted the case to the jury, reserving "under advisement" the questions of law raised by Martin. After deliberating overnight, the jury returned a verdict of guilty. Martin immediately filed a motion for a new trial based upon the reserved questions of law.

There is some indirect evidence that his motion was denied,[21] but in the end the cordwainers were successful, since the docket shows that no sentence was ever imposed. Furthermore, perhaps frightened at the

[16] An able Hagerstown lawyer, Lawrence was married to the daughter of Mary Magdalina Hager, the widow of Jonathan Hager, Jr., whom Martin had courted.
[17] *Federal Gazette* (Baltimore), 11 July 1809; *Maryland Herald* (Hagerstown), 19 July 1809; Scharf, *History of Western Maryland*, 2:1108.
[18] See, generally, McMaster, *History of the People of the U.S.*, 3:510ff.; John R. Commons et al., eds., *A Documentary History of American Industrial Society*, vol. 2 *passim*; James Wallace Bryan, *The Development of the English Law of Conspiracy*, chap. 5.
[19] *Federal Gazette* (Baltimore), 22 August 1809.
[20] *North American* (Baltimore), 22 August 1809.
[21] Commons et al., *History of Industrial Society*, p. 249; T. W. Glocker, "Trade Unionism in Baltimore before the War of 1812," p. 26ff. In the case of the Journeymen Cordwainers of New York, reported in Commons, p. 379, the Baltimore case is apparently referred to as one where, on demurrer to the evidence, there was a judgment for the defendant.

prospect of trying almost forty more cases at two weeks each, the state never brought any other indictment to trial. The Republican press of the day criticized the decision bitterly: "The *lawyers* say it is *lawful* for the masters and employers (*if good federalists*) to associate as they please, to *lower* the wages of their workmen, but that it is a high *crime* and *misdemeanor* for journeymen to have a society intended *to regulate the price of their labor.*"[22] In any event, the judgment in the case anticipated by a third of a century the famous decision of Justice Shaw of the Supreme Judicial Court of Massachusetts,[23] which has become the accepted law of the land.

During the first years of the nineteenth century, this young nation was struggling to maintain its commercial and naval independence and to avoid being caught in the maelstrom of European power politics. As a result of the Napoleonic wars, American shipping was constantly harassed and often seized by French, British, Spanish, or Portuguese privateers or men-of-war for violation of the laws of neutrality. Out of these seizures arose litigation involving the liability of marine insurers for losses of ships and cargoes seized by one or another belligerent. These cases frequently, if slowly, found their way to the docket of the United States Supreme Court.[24]

In 1804, in *Church* v. *Hubbart*,[25] the Court sustained a lower court's ruling that a belligerent has the right to search a neutral vessel upon the high seas for contraband. Martin, representing the ship- and cargo owners, procured a reversal upon the narrow, collateral ground that certain Portuguese edicts had been allowed in evidence without proper authentication. Four years later, a similar question arose in a group of cases reported under the title of *Rose* v. *Himely*.[26] A galaxy of legal talent argued the case before the Court: Robert Goodloe Harper, Charles Lee, Samuel Chase, Jr., Alexander Dallas, William Rawle, Jared Ingersoll, and John Drayton for the various libellants, with Pierre Duponceau, Edward Tilghman, and Luther Martin for the respondents.

After an extensive hearing lasting nine days, the Court, in an opinion by Marshall, diverged from its decision in the Church case and held that a French court had no power to condemn a ship and cargo seized by the French upon the high seas but never taken into French waters. The decision here was against Martin and his clients. However, shortly thereafter, in the two cases entitled *Hudson* v. *Guestier*,[27] Martin got the court to overrule *Rose* v. *Himely* and to hold that the courts of a belligerent did have jurisdiction over ships and cargo seized as contraband, though never physically brought into that country's waters. Indeed, Chief Justice Marshall felt obliged to confess error, in a concurring

---

[22] *Evening Post* (Baltimore), 23 August 1809.
[23] Commonwealth v. Hunt, 4 Met. 45 (1842).
[24] Martin alone argued some fifteen cases of this type before the Supreme Court.
[25] 2 Cranch 187; see Chapter 4 above.
[26] 4 Cranch 241 (1808).
[27] 4 Cranch 293 (1808) and 6 Cranch 281 (1810).

opinion in the second case, stating that in *Rose* v. *Himely* he had assumed that four judges of the court had concurred in the judgment when, in fact, he was mistaken about this.[28]

Writing to a friend in Boston,[29] Joseph Story, who was an interested spectator, gave thumbnail descriptions of most of the counsel in the case: Harper was "diffuse, but methodical and clear"; Dallas was "a book-man, ready, apt, and loquacious, but artificial"; Rawle "argues with a very pleasant voice, and has great neatness, perspicacity, and even elegance" (Story, as we shall see, was susceptible to forensic "elegance"); Ingersoll was "learned, laborious, and minute"; Duponceau was "ingenious . . . in the display of his learning"; and Tilghman's argument was "strong, clear, pointed and logical." But the future justice's longest description was reserved for Luther Martin,

that singular compound of strange qualities. With a professional income of $10,000 a year, he is poor and needy; generous and humane, but negligent and profuse. He labors hard to acquire, and yet cannot preserve. Experience, however severe, never corrects a single habit. I have heard anecdotes of his improvidence and thoughtlessness which astonish me. He is about middle size, a little bald, with a common forehead, pointed nose, inexpressive eye, large mouth, and well-formed chin. His dress is slovenly. . . . All nature pays contribution to his argument, if, indeed, it can be called one. . . . But every one assures me that he is profoundly learned, and that though he shines not now in the lustre of his former days, yet he is at times very great. He never seems satisfied with a single grasp of his subject; but urges himself to successive efforts, until he moulds and fashions it to his purpose. You should hear of Luther Martin's fame from those who have known him long and intimately, but you should not see him.[30]

Martin's alcoholism was no doubt closely connected with overwork. As his clients and their cases grew more and more numerous, the amount of liquor that he drank also increased. Its effects on him physically, socially, and professionally were legendary in his own day. One evening he traveled by stagecoach with Roger Brooke Taney from Frederick to Hagerstown to try a very important and difficult action of ejectment the next morning. Every five miles along the twenty-six-mile route, the coach stopped to change horses. A compulsive drinker, Martin took advantage of each occasion to imbibe as much as possible in the short time available—whiskey, when he could get it, when he could not, ale, and when neither was at hand, even buttermilk. On reaching their hotel in Hagerstown, the two lawyers had a late supper and then went to their rooms for a brief rest before they reviewed the case to-

[28] 4 Cranch 285. See Donald G. Morgan, *Justice William Johnson, the First Dissenter*, pp. 177–78.

[29] Letter to Samuel P. Fay, 16 February 1808, in Story, ed., *Life and Letters of Joseph Story*, 1:162ff. Story was not appointed to the Supreme Court until late in 1811.

[30] Duponceau has provided an interesting description of the Philadelphia bar; see Warren, *A History of the American Bar*, p. 257.

gether. When Taney went to Martin's room a short time later, he found him sprawled across his bed, sound asleep, fully clothed (except for one boot) even to his hat. Unable to wake him, Taney went back to his room and worked on the case alone most of the night. Before leaving the hotel for court in the morning, he went to Martin's room again but found the door locked and all quiet. Fearful that he would have to argue the case himself, Taney went on to court. Just as the clerk called the case, however, Martin walked into the courtroom and, said Taney, "in none of his forensic efforts did he excell his skill in the management of this cause."[31]

On another occasion, Martin undertook to represent a Baltimore Quaker in a tricky real property action. His client exacted a promise from him that he would not "drink a drop of liquor" during the trial. At the beginning of the trial Martin was true to his word, but the strain that his abstinence placed upon his system was so great that he was completely ineffectual. At the noon recess he was faced with a difficult ethical dilemma: should he keep his word and lose the case or break it and give his client the benefit of his best efforts? His solution showed his characteristic sense of humor: he went to a bakery and bought a loaf of bread, thence to a tavern and bought a bottle of brandy, then to an inn, where he placed the bread on a plate, poured the brandy over it, and ate it with a knife and fork. That afternoon, he won his case.[32]

The results of his excessive drinking were not always so lucky. In the summer of 1810 he argued an insurance case involving the ship *Herkimer*[33] in the federal Circuit Court in Baltimore, presided over by his old friend Justice Samuel Chase, sitting as circuit judge. Martin, who was apparently somewhat tighter than usual, was reprimanded by Chase, who said, "I am surprised that you can so prostitute your talents." Martin, drawing himself up as straight as he could, replied to Chase, "Sir, I never prostituted my talents except when I defended you and Colonel Burr," at which, turning to the jury, he added confidentially, "a couple of the greatest rascals in the world." Chase angrily instructed the clerk to draw up a citation of Martin for contempt of court, but when it was presented for his signature, that choleric old man, recollecting their forty-year friendship and all that he owed Martin, put the quill pen back in its holder, saying, "This hand could never sign a citation against Luther Martin."[34]

Martin argued over two dozen cases before the Supreme Court during the February terms of 1808, 1809, 1810, 1812, and 1813.[35] Over

---

[31] Tyler, *Memoir of Roger Brooke Taney, LL.D.*, p. 122.

[32] Sioussat, *Old Baltimore*, pp. 168–69.

[33] Livingston and Gilchrist v. Maryland Insurance Co., 6 Cranch 274 (1810); 7 Cranch (U.S.) 506 (1813).

[34] Aaron Burr was told this anecdote by one of the jurors present at the time and relayed it to his daughter, Theodosia (Burr, *Journal*, 2:68). Burr (who was in France at the time) erroneously reports the incident as taking place in Boston.

[35] Owing to illnesses and deaths among the justices, the Supreme Court could not seat a quorum and hence heard no cases during the February term of 1811.

half these cases involved questions of prize, admiralty, and marine insurance law. The others raised issues in the law of evidence, sales, wills, ejectment, and constitutional law. The most famous and important of the last group was *Fletcher* v. *Peck*,[36] which grew out of the so-called Yazoo land frauds. After the Revolution the state of Georgia asserted a claim under her original charter to the large tract of land lying to the west of her western boundary and running all the way to the Mississippi River. This area roughly comprised the area of the present states of Alabama and Mississippi, nearly a hundred thousand square miles. There were, however, other claimants to this territory: South Carolina asserted title under her original charter; Spain belligerently claimed ownership by right of discovery; the Creek, Choctaw, and Cherokee Indians claimed it by right of immemorial occupancy and by treaty; the white backwoodsmen and traders asserted their claims as explorers and settlers; and, most important, the federal government asserted paramount title under the terms of its treaty of peace with England.[37]

Georgia, one of the poorest of all the states, saw an opportunity of realizing ready cash without taxation by selling off these lands. After a number of abortive efforts to consummate a sale, the Georgia legislature enacted a measure, signed by Gov. George Matthews in January of 1795, selling a tract of thirty-five million acreas for five hundred thousand dollars in specie (about a cent and a half per acre) to four groups of land speculators: the upper Mississippi, Tennessee, Georgia Mississippi, and Georgia companies. About two million acres were reserved for sale to Georgia residents at a nominal price. All but a few members of the Georgia legislature had been "handsomely provided for": gifts of shares of land-company stock redeemable for thousands of acres of land or of slaves were made in return for votes for the bill.[38]

When knowledge of this giveaway of public resources became public, a storm of protest swept the state. A mob assembled and attempted to lynch the guilty legislators. Protest meetings were held in almost every city and town, and resolutions were passed demanding the repeal of the hated law. At the next election of state legislators nearly every "Yazoo man" was defeated by a candidate pledged to rescind the sale.

By an overwhelming vote a new bill was approved declaring that the land-grant act was the result of "atrocious peculation, corruption, and collusion" and was "null and void," that title still remained in the state, and that all claims arising out of this act were declared annulled. The copy of the obnoxious act was removed from the state archives and

---

[36] 6 Cranch (U.S.) 87 (1810).

[37] For the background of this episode, see, generally, Shaw Livermore, *Early American Land Companies*, p. 146ff.; Warren, *The Supreme Court*, 1:392ff.; Beveridge, *Life of John Marshall*, 3:546ff.; C. Peter Magrath, *Yazoo: Law and Politics in the New Republic*, passim.

[38] See the twenty-odd affidavits attesting to bribery of state legislators in *American State Papers, Public Lands*, 1:144ff.

burned by fire drawn from heaven with a sun glass, in the presence of the legislature and a large throng of citizens.

Meanwhile, each of the four land companies had received its share of the tract. James Greenleaf engineered an immediate resale of the entire Georgia Mississippi Company's interest (eleven million acres), together with four million acres of the Georgia Company's allotment, to a Boston syndicate for $1,375,000. This represented a profit over a few months of more than a million dollars on an original investment of about $215,000. Once sold, these lands were feverishly bought at from eleven to fourteen cents an acre by other speculators, sometimes for cash, sometimes for notes, which were promptly negotiated as commercial paper.

When word reached Boston of the repudiation of the sale by the Georgia legislature, there was great excitement, and immediate efforts were made to have the matter settled either by Congress or by the courts. Pamphlets for and against the right of a state legislature to repeal a grant made by the previous legislature were widely dispersed and discussed. Bills were introduced in Congress to settle the claims of the purchasers, but the vehement vituperation of John Randolph of Roanoke prevented them from passage for years. To resolve this important question of title and of the power of a state to control the disposition of its own territory, a "friendly suit" was finally filed in the federal Circuit Court for the District of Massachusetts.

Involved in the test was a tract of fifteen thousand acres, bought by a man named Fletcher from one Peck for three thousand dollars. The land was part of the Georgia Company's allotment by patent under the Georgia legislature's act of 7 January 1795, and had come to Peck by way of numerous mesne conveyances. Fletcher sued Peck for breach of covenant, alleging that Peck had covenanted in his deed that the State of Georgia had good title to the property and that its legislature had authority to sell it. Briefly summarized, the breaches were alleged in four counts: first, that the legislature had no authority to sell the lands, second, that the passage of the Act of 7 January 1795 was procured by the fraud of the associates of the Georgia Company, who offered members of the legislature part of the land to vote for the bill; third, that on 13 February 1796 the Georgia legislature had repealed and rendered null and void the "usurped act" of 7 January 1795, and had declared all grants and claims of title deriving therefrom "annulled, rendered void, and of no effect"; and fourth, that on 7 January 1795 title to the lands in question was in the United States and that the State of Georgia had no title to convey.

Peck filed four pleas: first, that the governor of Georgia had authority under the act of 7 January to convey, by patent, the property in question; second, that the associates of the Georgia Company had not improperly influenced the Georgia legislature, as alleged, and that in any event neither he nor any of the mesne grantees from the Georgia

Company had any knowledge of such impropriety until after the land had been conveyed from the said company to James Greenleaf on 22 August 1795; third, that the mesne grantees after Greenleaf were citizens of other states than Georgia; and fourth, that on 7 January 1795 Georgia had fee simple title to the lands in question. The plaintiff demurred to the first three pleas, and issue was joined on the last plea, pursuant to which the jury brought in a long, twenty-page special verdict.

Justice Cushing, sitting as judge of the Massachusetts Circuit Court, overruled the plaintiff's demurrers and ruled with the defendant on the fourth issue, finding that the State of Georgia had had good title to the lands in litigation. The plaintiff thereupon appealed to the Supreme Court.[39] On 1 March 1809 the case was called for argument in the Supreme Court, with Luther Martin appearing for Fletcher and John Quincy Adams, with Robert Goodloe Harper, for Peck. Martin's opening argument was as simple as it was decisive: the defendant's pleas were not responsive to the matters alleged. The first count denied the authority of the Georgia legislature to sell the land, but the plea was that Governor Matthews was so empowered. The second count alleged that the State of Georgia's title "was never legally conveyed" to Peck's predecessor in title, but the plea was that Peck had no knowledge of the improper influences upon the members of the legislature. The third plea was dealt with similarly. The next day Adams argued on behalf of Peck for more than five hours. (He himself noted in his diary that he had not been very effective and that his exposition had been "dull and tedious almost beyond endurance."[40])

The following day, Harper continued the argument on Peck's behalf for two or three hours, and Martin began his closing speech. He had not finished when the Court adjourned, and was still going strong the next morning.

One week later, the Court handed down an opinion as brief as it was inconclusive. It agreed with Martin that the defendant's pleadings were defective, and the case was remanded for amendment of the pleadings. However, with the consent of the Court, Martin and Adams agreed upon a short cut, viz., to have the case set down for reargument on "the covenants and the facts appearing upon the record." Accordingly, one year later, at the 1810 term, the case was argued again, with Joseph Story replacing Adams, who had been appointed minister to Russia. Cranch's

[39] Much has been made of the possibility, or even the probability, that the case was "manifestly made up" for the purpose of getting an adjudication of this vexatious matter (see, for example, Beveridge, *Life of John Marshall*, 3:585; Warren, *The Supreme Court*, 1:395; dissenting opinion of Mr. Justice Johnson in 6 Cranch, p. 147). It was undeniably a test case, brought to settle a myriad of like disputes, but no one has been able to show that the sale to Fletcher was anything other than as set forth, upon the covenants set forth, for the purpose of determining title. This, no more than hundreds of other similar test cases—taxpayers' and bondholders' suits and the like—does not make the litigation "feigned," "moot," or nonadversarial.

[40] *Memoirs*, 1:543.

Report does not give even a brief outline of the reargument. Marshall's opinion, however, states that Martin had rested his argument for the plaintiff "on a single proposition": that the proclamation of 1763, in reserving to the crown all the lands on the western waters (including those here in litigation) "for the use of the Indians," had withdrawn them from the territory of Georgia, and that by the Revolution this area had been acquired by the federal government "for the joint benefit of the United States, and not for the benefit of any particular state."[41] In view of Martin's consistent practice of addressing himself at length to every possible point raised by a case, this was probably an oversimplification on Marshall's part to permit, as we shall see, rejection of the argument.[42]

Marshall's opinion held, first, that under the state constitution of 1789 the Georgia legislature had the power to sell its unappropriated lands. Next, Marshall and the majority of the Court ruled that a legislative act of a soverign state may not be attacked collaterally in a suit between two private parties, one of whom is a bona fide purchaser without notice of the fraud. One may ask how else the state could be attacked, as the Eleventh Amendment to the Constitution, the result of *Chisholm* v. *Georgia*,[43] forbade a suit against a state without its consent. Long before the days of declaratory judgments, how could Georgia have had any interest to support a suit by it against either Fletcher or Peck? The latter's defense as a bona fide purchaser, moreover, was unconvincing: he alleged only that he and his predecessors in title had no notice of the fraud "until after the purchase by . . . Greenleaf" from the original grantees. That purchase took place on 22 August 1795, however, while Peck made his purchase from Oliver Phelps over five years later, on 8 December 1800, by which time it is certain that he, along with everyone else in the country, was well aware of the legislative trickery involved. Marshall's broad assertion that Peck "himself and the first purchaser under the original grantees, and all intermediate holders of the property, were purchasers without notice"[44] is quite a different matter.

Marshall's majority opinion then held that a legislature could not validly repeal an earlier statute under which property rights had "vested." Although this would seem to beg the principal question at

<hr/>

[41] 6 Cranch 141–42. Such was the case with the Northwest Territory, comprised of western lands claimed by the colonies of Virginia, Connecticut, Massachusetts, New York, and others, which were ceded for the "common good of the United States" (see, for example, Samuel Eliot Morison and Henry Steele Commager, *The Growth of the American Republic*, 1:255, and Chapter 7 above).

[42] Beveridge's and Magrath's characterization of Martin's reargument as "perfunctory" and their suggestion that Martin's intoxication compelled an adjournment of the Court during the hearing of the case are both unsupported. Beveridge's citation of John Quincy Adams' *Memoirs* (1:115) in support of the first charge is meaningless, as Adams was in Russia at the time. The second assertion rests upon a "tradition" without any source or support given, and nowhere else reported.

[43] 2 Dall. 419 (1793).

[44] 6 Cranch 132.

issue, he moved on to hold that such an action by a state violates art. I, sec. 10, of the Constitution, which provides that "no State shall pass any . . . law impairing the obligation of contracts." Finally, Marshall held that the fee simple title to the Yazoo lands, at the time conveyed by the State of Georgia, was in the latter, despite the proclamation of 1763 reserving the western lands for the use of the Indians and despite the succession of the United States to the title of the English crown following the American Revolution. For this, and for his cavalier dismissal of the Indians' title, Marshall gave no reason other than a bald ipse dixit.

Thus ended the judicial aspect of the great Yazoo lands scandal.[45] By it the Supreme Court first declared a state statute unconstitutional and invalid; and John Marshall, by a tour de force, gave life and a broad national application (quite unintended by its drafters) to the "obligation of contract" clause of the Constitution.

[45] The same result had already been reached by the Supreme Judicial Court of Massachusetts eleven years earlier in Derby v. Blake (1799), belatedly reported in 1918 in 226 Mass. 618, not referred to in Marshall's opinion.

26

Nisi Prius Judge and Again Attorney General, 1811-1818

> [I am] the same Luther Martin; who through life, has
> been, as far as in his power, the sincere friend of distress,
> and the sworn foe of oppression, from whatever quarter
> it may come, in whatever form it may appear.—*Federal
> Republican* (Baltimore), 30 September 1811

Because of the death of Justice Cushing and the delay in finding a successor who was acceptable to the Senate, the Supreme Court could not seat a quorum to hear cases in 1811 at its February term.[1] However, Martin was kept busy with his state practice in the trial courts and in the Court of Appeals. Hosts of clients more interested in the outcome of their lawsuits than in the sobriety of their counsel filled Martin's office with litigation. Perhaps typical of his nisi prius practice was his defense of John Bentley and Isaiah Green, jailer and turnkey, respectively, of the Baltimore County Gaol, who had been cited for contempt of court.[2] The Maryland Insolvent Act of 1805 provided that a person arrested for debt might be released from prison after publishing a notice to his creditors giving a schedule of his assets and the date set by the court for his appearance. Bentley and Green were alleged to have obtained money from insolvent debtors for the publication of notice to creditors over the name of the sitting judge of the Circuit Court without his knowledge.

The defendants' case looked hopeless, but Martin argued with all his customary vigor and learning that his clients had committed no crime and that, in any event, they could only be convicted of criminal contempt by a jury. The court had submitted certain interrogatories to Bentley and Green, which Martin insisted it had no power to require his clients to answer. For the first time in a busy life in the courts, he pointed out, he had a nameless and faceless adversary. The proceedings against his clients were not brought by the state pursuant to a grand jury indictment, nor by any private party. In short, Martin objected,

[1] Warren, *The Supreme Court*, 1:400ff.
[2] See John H. Bentley, *An Inroad upon the Sacred Trial by Jury, passim.*

"I can find no antagonist to oppose . . . and between whom and my clients I can appeal to this court for their decision." Moreover, he boldly told the court, "I have to convince you of the innocence of my clients against . . . strong impressions which you have taken up of their guilt and upon which you have acted." On the merits, Martin insisted that Bentley and Green had "acted as innocently, as free from crime and as inoffensively, as any nurse who ever prepared water gruel or chicken water for her patient."[3]

The court called as witnesses the newspaper editor to show the provenance of the publication and the clerk of the Circuit Court to prove lack of judicial authorization. Martin countered that no one had been injured by the publication and that his clients had done nothing for which a grand jury could indict or for which a petit jury would convict them. It was, accordingly, a "monstrous doctrine" that a court should be allowed to punish persons for matters not even presentable by a grand jury. Moreover, he demonstrated from a formidable line of English cases and texts that his clients could not lawfully be convicted by other than a jury of their peers. The court took the case *sub curia* and, several days later, rendered its opinion. It reasserted the allegation that the prisoners had extorted large sums of money from indigent debtors, as proved by "oral testimony" (presumably ex parte and in chambers), which was not a part of the record of the case, and which was now a difficult matter to prove because of the "dispersion" of witnesses. Despite a scolding from the bench, the prisoners were finally, though grudgingly, discharged, and Luther Martin had won another "impossible" case.

While the above matter was being decided, Martin was engaged in trying another case before Judge Joseph Hopper Nicholson. Nicholson considered Martin's remarks to the bench rude and disrespectful and suspended him from practicing in the Baltimore County court for a year.[4] (The next day the decision in the Bentley-Green case was handed down, and the day following that, Martin won fifteen thousand dollars in a hospital lottery. "How different," noted one observer, "are the Judgments of God from those of Man."[5]) Martin was busy enough in the other courts, however. He had clients from Somerset County on the Atlantic Ocean[6] to Allegany and Washington counties in the Appalachians. A case from Washington County, concerning a property of over two square miles,[7] was of unusual interest because of the persons involved and the eminence of the counsel on both sides. The land in question had descended from Jonathan Hagar the elder to his two children, Jonathan and Rosannah, who had married Daniel Heister. The issue was the validity of a conveyance by a married woman

---

[3] *Ibid.*
[4] *Whig* (Baltimore), 17 April 1811.
[5] Bentley, *Trial by Jury.*
[6] E.g., West's Ex'rx v. Hyland, 3 Harris and Johnson 200 (1811).
[7] Lawrence v. Heister, 3 Harris and Johnson 371 (1813).

whose husband's acknowledgment of the deed was made before one of the justices of the Supreme Court of Pennsylvania rather than before a Maryland officer, as required by statute.

The lower court ruled in favor of the conveyance but was reversed by the Court of Appeals. Martin, William Pinkney, and John Thompson Mason[8] argued for the plaintiff, Lawrence,[9] Francis Scott Key, Arthur Shaaff, and Roger Brooke Taney for Mrs. Heister. The argument of counsel for both parties exhausted the authorities back to Sir Edward Coke, with stops at Blackstone's *Commentaries*, Bacon's *Abridgement*, and other texts along the way. Chief Judge Jeremiah Townley Chase was finally prompted to observe that "This case has been ably and amply discussed by the counsel, and placed in every point of view of which it is susceptible, or which ingenuity, united with profound legal knowledge, could suggest[. A]lthough the Court think the first and important question lies within a narrow compass, and did not seem to admit of that diffusive range of argument in which the counsel have indulged, they have been much gratified by the discussion."[10]

On 21 September 1811, the Baltimore *Federal Republican* carried the following announcement "To the Citizens of Baltimore," above the well-known signature of Luther Martin:

I offer myself, gentlemen, for your suffrages at the ensuing election, to represent you in the house of delegates of this state, and should I obtain them, I will endeavor to serve you in that capacity with zeal and fidelity.

It is now 33 years that I have resided in this city; you have long and intimately known me. You have been witnesses to my conduct through life, and I believe my enemies will admit, that I wear no disguises; and after so long & intimate an acquaintance with me, you must be fully capable by this time to form an opinion whether I have sufficient talents, abilities and information to judge of the true interests of this city and of this state; and whether I have firmness and integrity to pursue them; and unless I meet, in these respects, with your approbation, I neither expect nor desire your votes. . . .

Having thus publicly offered myself to the consideration of my fellow citizens, they will excuse me from calling them together occasionally, to hear from me speeches, either in favor of myself, or to the prejudice of the other candidates— for I have no wish to raise myself by the depression of a rival.—And they will also excuse me if I offer no public dinners, nor open any house for entertainment, for, as I can solemnly assure them that I do not mean to sell them, so I am determined not to attempt, either directly or indirectly, to buy them.

Shortly after this forthright demonstration of his complete innocence of practical politics, the *Whig*, an opposition newspaper which had recalled with editorial amusement the hanging in effigy of Martin, John Marshall, Aaron Burr, and Blennerhasset by torchlight on Hampstead

---

[8] He briefly succeeded Pinkney as attorney general of Maryland in the summer of 1806.

[9] Either the husband of Jonathan Hager's granddaughter or some relation of his.

[10] 3 Harris and Johnson 377.

Hill four years before, published a letter to the editor from a correspondent who signed himself "Self Respect." It suggested that no one
who reflected on *"the moral obligation of the citizen* to exercise aright the
sovereign privilege of suffrage" could vote for Martin.[11] Martin replied:

> By the *Whig* of Saturday last, some information is requested concerning the
> Luther Martin, who is now a candidate, particularly, whether he is the same
> Luther Martin who was concerned for Col. Burr? As it is in my power, gentle-
> men, to answer this question, I frankly acknowledge to you that he is the same
> Luther Martin, who, when Col. Burr's enemies, four years past, would have
> deprived him of counsel in a trial where his life was at stake, had the fortitude
> to render him those services which the Constitution of the United States . . .
> had solemnly guaranteed, not only to *him*, but to the *meanest citizen.*
> He is also the same Luther Martin, who, when he saw what he considered
> an attempt to oppress the lower, though not less useful orders of society, in the
> persons of the Journeyman Shoemakers, successfully advocated their cause, and
> gave them complete triumph over their persecutors. . . . In fine, he is the same
> Luther Martin, who through life, has been, as far as in his power, the sincere
> friend of distress, and the sworn foe of oppression, from whatever quarter it may
> come, in whatever form it may appear. Such, my fellow citizens, is *the* Luther
> Martin, who, with all those deadly sins upon him, has the temerity to stand a
> candidate on the present occasion, & who looks forward, with a pleasing con-
> fidence to obtaining on Monday next, the votes of all such of you, who *really*
> "reflect on the *moral obligation of the citizen* to exercise aright the *sovereign priv-
> ilege of suffrage.*"[12]

The electorate, however, unused to being wooed in such cadenced
measures, and upon such lofty principles, gave Martin only about 30
per cent of the vote.[13]

The criminal court of Oyer and Terminer and Gaol Delivery for
Baltimore City and County was created by Chapter 58 of the Acts of
the General Assembly for 1799. Its first Chief Justice was Walter
Dorsey, succeeded by John Scott in 1808. Scott died in 1813, and
Martin was appointed in his place and served until this court was
abolished by the Acts of 1816, Chapter 193. Certainly no judge had a
wider background and greater experience in the field of criminal law
than Martin. He had defended the accused in scores of cases and had
prosecuted well over five thousand others.[14] Even as prosecutor, his
attitude and conduct toward the accused was scrupulously fair, and he
regularly called the jury's attention to evidence in favor of the defendant, as well as to that incriminating him.

As chief justice of the Criminal Court, Martin continued the old
Federalist practice of stating from the bench his position on the political

---

[11] 28 September 1811.
[12] *Federal Republican* (Baltimore), 30 September 1811.
[13] William Pechin received 1,627 votes, Donaldson 1,599, and Martin 1,143 (*ibid.*,
8 October 1811).
[14] According to his statement in 1805 to the Senate in the course of the Chase
impeachment (see Evans, *Trial of Chase*, p. 187).

and social problems of the day. In a charge to the grand jury made in the fall of 1813, for instance, he delivered a rousing sermon, sounding the themes of theology (man's responsibility arising out of his "freedom of will"), politics (the dangers of Republicanism), economics (the evils of paper money), and morals (the deterioration of "virtue, morality, and religion" since the Revolution). The grand jury, largely Republican in its composition, made a spirited reply in kind.[15]

Martin's accession to the bench does not appear to have materially diminished his state appellate practice. In the three-year period 1813–16 he argued numerous cases before the Court of Appeals.[16] That he was not able to pursue his United States Supreme Court practice is evident from the failure of the reporter to list him among counsel in any case argued before that tribunal in 1814, 1815, and 1816. He did appear, however, in the February term of 1813 to argue half a dozen cases, four in prize law.

Upon his retirement from the bench after the abolition of the Court of Oyer and Terminer, he resumed his heavy load of private practice. He was now nearly seventy years old, his hair gray, his furrowed face fiery red from years of brandy drinking. His considerable income had dribbled away in expensive finishing schools for his daughters (and, later, an expensive private sanitarium for one); constant speculation in real estate, with consequent heavy mortgages on his real property; misplaced generosity to his friends; and his habitual wasteful and extravagant habits. Not only did he have no savings, but he was heavily in debt. However, he was still acknowledged as the outstanding source of legal learning and wisdom in the state. For example, the General Assembly, by Chapter 219 of the Laws of 1816, required every member elected to the legislature, before taking his seat, to take an oath that he had not taken part in a duel, either as a principal or a second. When the legislature convened in December of 1817, a number of the legislators were reluctant to take the oath. Rather than writing to the attorney general or another lawyer in the state, Delegate Benjamin LeCompte wrote to Martin asking his opinion of the constitutionality of the act. Martin's answer was as direct and unequivocal as it was prompt, and marked, as usual, with his rough but relevant and pointed humor: "I certainly would not wish," he wrote,

to throw any obstacles in the way of any legislative provisions for the suppression or prevention of duelling; but so far as the law of last session requires, that the member chosen as a representative shall be obliged to take the oath prescribed by that act, I think there can be no doubt but that the same is unconstitutional.

---

[15] See "Charge Delivered to the Grand Jury on the Fourth of October, 1813 by Luther Martin, Chief Justice of the Court of Oyer and Terminer and Gaol Delivery for Baltimore County," Niles's *Weekly Register*, 5:146, 151.

[16] See 3 Harris and Johnson 302ff., beginning with Partridge v. Dorsey's Lessee, *passim*, and 4 Harris and Johnson 1ff., beginning with Shields's Lessee v. Miller, *passim*.

The Constitution has declared what are the qualifications which shall render a person eligible, and when duly elected, what oaths are to be taken by the member chosen, before he takes his seat. The additional oath required by the aforesaid law, has not the apology of having any relation to the peculiar duties he owes to his country in his legislative character, nor to regulate his conduct while he sustains that character. If such law can be constitutionally passed, the legislature may with as much propriety, enumerate every breach of the decalogue through all the subdivisions of each of the commandments and compel each member, before he can serve his constituents, who have made him their choice, to bind himself by the solemn sanction of an oath, to live thereafter a life of sinless purity. Nor can I think it, even in a moral or religious point of view, correct that such oaths should be taken.[17]

On the strength of Martin's opinion, the taking of this oath was disregarded. The same session of the General Assembly granted him $1,440.31 as additional compensation for his services, presumably for acting as unofficial attorney general after his appointment to the bench.[18]

He had by now become a legend. Niles's *Weekly Register* recalled a story concerning him which was apparently common knowledge, or at least commonly believed. While in the midst of trying a case before the General Court in Annapolis, he discovered, the story went, that he vitally needed a certain paper which at that moment was on file in the Baltimore County Court, thirty miles away. He dispatched an express on horseback for it and meanwhile "undertook to employ the court" until the desired paper could be brought back. Accordingly, he "amused and instructed the court and the bar by a flood of law knowledge, which though it did not always bear on the case, was not sufficiently irrelevant to be checked. He was in the midst of a learned exposition of a great point at the moment that the official copy was put in his hands; and, at once breaking off his argument, he said, 'And please your honors, here is the very thing that I have been speaking *for*!' The paper was read by a junior lawyer; and it must be acknowledged that 'he spoke to some purpose,' for he gained the cause!"[19]

In spite of his fame, however, his personal life was difficult and, in part, tragic. His eldest daughter, Maria, suffered from a religious mania and had had to be confined in Dr. Thomas Parke's private asylum in Philadelphia. She had become obsessed with "the horrid idea," as Martin described her condition, that "the beneficient Creator of the Universe . . . instead of being a God of goodness & mercy, . . . is a cruel tyrant delighting in misery of which he is the Author."[20] Martin's lengthy correspondence with the doctor concerning her condition, treatment, and possible cure are pitiful to read. At

[17] Niles's *Weekly Register*, 13 December 1817.
[18] Resolution No. 4, Dec. Sess., 1816.
[19] 30 August 1817, n.s., 1:1.
[20] Letters to Dr. Parke, 20 and 26 May and 1 July 1815, 14 January 1816, Historical Society of Pennsylvania, Philadelphia, Pa.

the same time, his creditors were pressing him for payment of their claims. Many of his debts had been reduced to judgment, and Martin was constantly fighting for time to avoid the forced sale of his real estate holdings at a great financial sacrifice.

Most onerous of all, perhaps, was his indebtedness arising out of the Burr trial. When Burr stood trial for treason at Chillicothe, following his acquittal at Richmond, Dr. Commins had put up the bond along with Martin.[21] Commins, however, went into bankruptcy, and the whole burden of payment of the bail forfeited by Burr's flight was thrown on Martin. Burr, of course, was never brought to trial, despite the fact that he practiced law openly in New York City for more than twenty years after his return to this country in 1812 from his exile in Europe. Apparently, Martin eventually satisfied this debt, and in turn secured a judgment against Burr for some twenty thousand dollars, either in subrogation of the debt he had paid as Burr's security or for legal fees as Burr's attorney.[22] This judgment was noted as "satisfied" on 28 July 1833, some seven years after Martin's death.

It was at this point in Martin's life, the point at which most lawyers decide to rest on whatever laurels they may have won, that he was once more appointed attorney general of Maryland. The office had been abolished by constitutional amendment in 1817, but on 7 February 1818 the General Assembly nevertheless ruled that it should be filled.[23] Martin was appointed by Gov. Charles Ridgley on 11 February and took the oath of this familiar office on 18 February, exactly forty years from the day in 1778 when he first assumed its duties.

A few months after his reappointment, Martin was involved in a case which caused great excitement in western Maryland.[24] On the evening of Sunday, 16 August 1818, a large Methodist outdoor camp meeting was held on the plantation of Joseph Hogmire in Washington County near Hagerstown. The Reverend Jacob Gruber had been sent down from Pennsylvania to preach the sermon in place of the local minister, who was ill. Some four or five thousand white people were present, along with a few hundred Negroes, mostly slaves, who sat on benches at the rear of the others. With more valor than discretion, Reverend Gruber attacked the institution of slavery as a national sin which would in the end bring on national punishment at the hands of God. He warned that slavery might result in insurrection and the murder of slaveowners; however, he also cautioned the Negroes present that their only hope was to lead godly lives here so that hereafter they might be "happy in heaven forever, while wicked masters are turned into hell and damned forever."[25]

[21] Martin to Aaron Burr, 17 May 1815, Historical Society of Pennsylvania.
[22] Wandell and Minnegerode, *Aaron Burr*, 2:308.
[23] Laws of Maryland, 1817–18, ch. 146.
[24] See *American State Trials*, 1:69ff.; William Peter Strickland, *Life of Jacob Gruber*, p. 248ff.
[25] Strickland, *Life of Jacob Gruber*, p. 139.

Such talk as this, of course, was inflammatory. A group of slave-holders procured an indictment against Gruber, charging him with inciting slaves to mutiny. He was defended by Roger B. Taney, together with an able local attorney named Pigman and a youthful lawyer, trying his first case, whose name was also Martin.[26] The case was prosecuted by Franklin Anderson, the state's attorney for Frederick County, to which the trial had been removed because of the animus against the accused in Washington County. With Anderson sat Luther Martin, whose presence was largely unofficial, since he had no stomach for the case. His closing address to the jury was even more perfunctory than Anderson's: he merely told them that the state had no desire to convict an innocent man and that the verdict should be dictated by their consciences. Despite the ill-concealed bias on the part of the presiding judges (who went so far as to suggest to the clergymen who appeared as witnesses for the accused that they be mindful of their oaths), the jury was out only a few minutes and returned with a verdict of not guilty.

[26] His first name was not reported, but it is very possible that he was Luther Martin's nephew, the son of his brother Lenox, a lawyer and judge in Hagerstown.

27

The Bank Case and Demise, 1819–1826

Died, . . . Luther Martin esq until lately a resident of
Baltimore, and celebrated in the annals of Md. and of the
U.S. as a jurist. He died of old age, and without a groan,
and was respectfully interred.—Niles's *Register,* 15 July
1826

He died so poor that he scarce left money to bury him,
which tho' he had a great wit, did argue no great wisdom. . . . I have read, that it had been the fortunes of all
poets commonly to die beggars; but for an orator, a lawyer, and philosopher, as he was, to die so, 'tis rare.—
James Howell, of Lord Bacon, *Epistolae Ho Elianae* (6
January 1625).

Let not his frailties be remembered; he was a very
great man.—Samuel Johnson, of Oliver Goldsmith

Luther Martin's general practice, despite his age and alcoholism, had
as yet declined very little. Of the cases reported in the fourth volume of
Harris and Johnson's Reports, Martin appeared in over one quarter,
and won over half of them.[1] At its February 1819 term the Supreme
Court decided three great, landmark cases: *Dartmouth College* v. *Wood-
ward, Sturges* v. *Crowninshield,* and *McCulloch* v. *Maryland.*[2] The greatest
of these, and one in which Martin appeared for the state, was the last,
which decided the question of whether a state could constitutionally
tax the notes issued by a federal bank.

The Bank of the United States was incorporated for a twenty-year
period by an act of Congress in 1791. Although the Constitution contains no language explicitly granting such power to the federal government, the enactment of this law was justified as being within the scope
of its "elastic clause,"[3] which empowers Congress to make all laws
necessary and proper to execute the powers specifically granted. The

---

[1] Harris and Johnson report a total of 107 cases, of which Martin argued 27,
winning 15.
[2] Decided 2 February, 17 February, and 7 March, respectively; 4 Wheat. (17
U.S.) 518, 122, 316.
[3] Art. I, sec. 8, par. 18.

strict constructionists viewed the law with alarm, fearing that such a broad interpretation of the "sweeping clause" (as Jefferson called it) would eventually make the states mere vassals of an all-powerful federal government. The controversy on this point grew until it split the country along both sectional and party lines. So vehement was the opposition to the bank that an extension of its charter failed of enactment by Congress in 1811, though by the narrowest of margins.[4]

The War of 1812 and the crisis in both public and private credit, banking, and currency which immediately followed brought about the chartering of the second Bank of the United States in 1816. However, local banks continued to multiply, and the uncertainty, fluctuation, and speculation in and devaluation of their bank notes and bills continued to increase, driving large numbers of property owners into bankruptcy. Many people blamed this situation upon the Bank of the United States, with the result that a number of state legislatures considered or enacted laws to put the bank out of business.[5]

In Maryland, an act of 11 February 1818[6] required that all banks established "without authority from the state" pay a stamp tax on notes issued by them, which tax might be commuted by an annual payment of fifteen thousand dollars. The Baltimore branch of the United States Bank, however, ignored the Maryland statute and continued to issue its notes without payment of the state tax. Accordingly, on 8 May 1818 John James, the treasurer of the Western Shore, filed suit on behalf of the state against William McCulloch, the cashier of the Baltimore branch of the United States Bank, to recover the penalties prescribed by the state law. The Maryland Court of Appeals sustained the judgment against McCulloch in a brief *per curiam* notation[7] without rendering any opinion on the merits of the question. The ostensible reason for this was to hasten the case on its way to the United States Supreme Court, to which tribunal it was immediately taken upon an agreed statement of acts, by a writ of error. It was set down on the Court's docket for argument at its February 1819 term.

For days the press had kept the public advised of the impending argument in "the bank case." Mr. Justice Story's departure from Boston on 21 January was duly noted, as was the arrival of the various justices in Washington.[8] The decisions of the Court in the Dartmouth College case on 2 February and in *Sturges* v. *Crowninshield* on 17 February were reported, as was the argument by Francis Scott Key, Walter

---

[4] The bill failed by one vote in the House of Representatives and by one vote in the Senate; Vice-President Clinton voted against the bill to break a tie vote in the Senate (*Annals of Congress*, 11th Cong., 3rd sess., 1826, 347).

[5] E.g., Illinois, Indiana, Kentucky, Tennessee, and Georgia.

[6] By coincidence, the very day on which Luther Martin was reappointed attorney general of Maryland.

[7] Unreported in Harris and Johnson's Reports.

[8] *Daily National Intelligencer* (Washington), 26 January 1819.

Jones, and Luther Martin in *Bank of Columbia* v. *Okely*.[9] On 20 February it was announced that "the argument in the great case of *McCulloch* against the *State of Maryland* (involving the question of the right of the State governments to tax the Bank of the United States) will be opened by Mr. Webster on Monday next."[10] The interest of the case was heightened by the fact that the House of Representatives was hotly debating a resolution calling for the repeal of the bank's charter at that very time.

When the case was called for argument on the morning of 22 February, the hearing room "was full almost to suffocation, and many went away for want of room."[11] Seated on the bench were Bushrod Washington (nephew of the first president, whom Martin had met as a boy almost half a century before[12]), "a little sharp-faced gentleman with only one eye, and a profusion of snuff distributed over his face"; William Johnson, tall, handsome, with white hair and a florid complexion; Gabriel Duvall, "a patriarch in appearance," his hair "as white as a snowbank, with a long, white cue hanging down to his waist"; Brockholst Livingston, with his "fine Roman face: an aquiline nose, high forehead, and projecting chin"; Thomas Todd, a "dark complexioned good-looking, substantial man";[13] Joseph Story, bald, learned, quick in thought and courtly in manner; and in the center the great Chief Justice, John Marshall, dominating the Court and the occasion.

No less interesting to the crowd of spectators were the counsel assembled to argue the case.[14] For the plaintiff-in-error (the appellant, the United States Bank) sat Daniel Webster, William Wirt, and William Pinkney. The "godlike Daniel," fresh from his victory in the Dartmouth College case, was already famous as an orator and constitutional lawyer. For this, as on other important occasions, he was dressed "in the height of fashion, tight breeches, blue cloth coat cut away squarely at the waist, and adorned with large brass buttons, waistcoat exposing a broad expanse of ruffled shirt with high soft collar surrounded by an elaborate black stock."[15] William Wirt had only recently succeeded Richard Rush as attorney general of the United States. Fifty-two years old, handsome and graceful, with a powerful but pleasant voice, his arguments were noted for their happy allusions, flashing wit, and logical clarity. Most exciting of this trinity, however,

[9] 4 Wheat. (17 U.S.) 235. Martin was only partly through his argument when he "was stopped by the Court," which was persuaded that his client's cause was clearly right.

[10] *Daily National Intelligencer* (Washington), 20 February 1819.

[11] Joseph Story to Stephen White (*Life and Letters of Joseph Story*, 1:325). See the numerous contemporary descriptions of this room collected in Warren, *The Supreme Court*, 1:460ff.

[12] See Chapter 4, p. 32n, above.

[13] George Ticknor, *Life, Letters, and Journals of George Ticknor*, 1:38ff.

[14] The Court dispensed, on this occasion, with its usual rule limiting counsel to two on each side (4 Wheat. 422n).

[15] Beveridge, *Life of John Marshall*, 4:284.

was that eccentric genius, William Pinkney. Although he was a profound lawyer and a busy and successful advocate,[16] he was haughty, vindictive, and vain. A dandy in dress, he wore corsets to reduce his embonpoint, and cosmetics to smooth his skin.[17] He was always aware in court of the women in the audience and often addressed his argument more to them than to the bench.[18] Highly conscious of his ability and success, he had a pontifical air and was often sarcastic (as we shall see), and upon occasion even insulting, to his brothers at the bar.[19]

At the other end of the table sat the counsel for the State of Maryland. Joseph Hopkinson was marked by a quiet, distinguished appearance, a mellifluous voice, and wide erudition. Walter Jones was physically unimpressive, but his arguments were fluent and choice in their language, compelling in presentation, simple in style, and clearly expressed.[20] The third attorney was, of course, the attorney general of Maryland. Now seventy-one years of age, seedy in dress, and his face ravaged by years of alcoholism, he still commanded respect for his learning, his long acquaintance with the men and events of American history, and his undiminished vigor and strength as an advocate.

When the clerk of the Court called the case of *McCulloch* v. *Maryland*, Daniel Webster opened the Bank's argument. He maintained, at great length, that the power of Congress to incorporate a bank could not at that date be seriously questioned: it had been assumed and exercised for almost thirty years as a proper exercise of the elastic clause of the Constitution. He then proceeded to the major issue: does a state government have the power to tax such a federal agency? "An unlimited power to tax," he insisted, "involves necessarily a power to destroy." Throughout the entire day, Webster rang the changes on that theme.[21]

The following day, Joseph Hopkinson, opening for the State of Maryland, immediately picked up the challenge of the "elastic clause." Even if the creation of the United States Bank had been "necessary and proper" under the condition of the country in 1791, it did not follow that a small and selfish group of directors subject to no public control had the right to establish branch banks: that power was reserved for Congress.[22] As the newspapers reported, the debate touched upon "some of the most important principles of constitutional law, which have been discussed with an equal degree of learning and eloquence, and have constantly attracted the attention of a numerous and intelligent auditory."[23]

[16] His income from his practice in 1816 was about $21,000 a year.

[17] See letter from Ticknor to his father, February 1815, *Life, Letters, and Journals*, 1:38-40.

[18] Many instances of this are noted in Warren, *The Supreme Court*, 1:473; Beveridge, *Life of John Marshall*, 4:131-34, 140.

[19] Wirt to Gilmer, 1 April 1816, Kennedy, *Life of William Wirt*, 1:403; William Pinkney, *The Life of William Pinkney*, 100-1.

[20] John Edward Semmes, *John H. B. Latrobe and His Times, 1803-1891*, pp. 369-70.

[21] 4 Wheat. 322ff.

[22] 4 Wheat. 330ff.

[23] E.g., the Washington *Daily National Intelligencer*, 25 February 1819.

On Wednesday morning, William Wirt arose to address the Court on behalf of the Bank. He closed his relatively brief address by insisting that the "supremacy clause" overrode the Tenth Amendment, and that any of the powers otherwise reserved to the states by the latter must yield to an act of Congress passed pursuant to the elastic clause.[24] When Wirt took his seat, Walter Jones rose to make the second argument for the State of Maryland. He maintained that, never having been submitted to judicial decision, the power of Congress to incorporate the bank was necessarily still open, and that a "practice . . . however inveterate" could not sanction a "manifest usurpation." The taxing powers of the sovereign state of Maryland and those of the sovereign federal government are coequal and coextensive, he argued: "This is an anomaly, and perhaps an imperfection in our system of government. But neither Congress, nor this Court, can correct it."[25]

Jones spoke all Wednesday afternoon and Thursday morning. Martin then rose to conclude the argument for the State of Maryland. He began by referring to the deliberations of the federal constitutional convention of 1787 at Philadelphia, "*quorum pars minima fui.*"[26] There and thereafter during the period of ratification by the state conventions, he recalled,

it was maintained, by the enemies of the constitution, that it contained a vast variety of powers, lurking under the generality of its phraseology, which would prove highly dangerous to the liberties of the people, and the rights of the States, unless controlled by some declaratory amendment, which should negative their existence.

This apprehension was treated as a dream of distempered jealousy. The danger was denied to exist; but to provide an assurance against the possibility of its occurrence, the 10th Amendment was added to the Constitution. This, however, could be considered as nothing more than declaratory of the sense of the people, as to the extent of the powers conferred on the new government.

We are now called upon to apply that theory of interpretation which was then rejected by the friends of the new Constitution, and we are asked to engraft upon it powers of vast extent, which were disclaimed by them, and which, if they had been fairly avowed at the time, would have prevented its adoption.[27]

Martin then read a number of extracts from the Federalist Papers in support of his position. Alexander Hamilton, writing as "Publius," had assured the public that

(with the sole exception of duties on imports and exports), [the states] would, under the plan of the convention, retain [the taxing] authority in the most absolute and unqualified sense; and that an attempt on the part of the national

---

[24] 4 Wheat. 352ff.
[25] 4 Wheat. 362.
[26] *Aeneid*, bk. 2, line 6: "in which [proceedings] I played a very small part." Martin modestly changed Virgil's "*pars magna*" to "*pars minima.*"
[27] 4 Wheat. 372ff.

government to abridge them in the exercise of it, would be a violent assumption of power, unwarranted by any article or clause of its constitution.[28]

. . . The inference from the whole is that the individual states would, under the proposed constitution, retain an independent and uncontrolable [*sic*] authority to raise revenue to any extent of which they may stand in need, by every kind of taxation, except duties on imports and exports.[29]

In quoting these and other reassurances of the proponents of the Constitution to its opponents, who had expressed fears of federal restrictions upon state taxation, Martin may have belabored the point excessively, but he did show how diametrically opposed to these expressions was the position of the national government in the McCulloch case. His argument was barely under way by Thursday evening, and on Friday morning he continued: "We insist, that the only safe rule is the plain letter of the Constitution; the rule which the constitutional legislators themselves have prescribed, in the 10th amendment . . . : that the powers not delegated to the United States, nor prohibited to the States, are reserved to the States respectively, or to the people. The power of establishing corporations is not delegated to the United States, nor prohibited to the individual States. It is, therefore, reserved to the States, or to the people.[30]

On Saturday, Martin continued his exposition. For the sake of the argument, he assumed that Congress had the right to incorporate a banking company; however, he insisted upon the states' right to tax it. He scoffed at the suggestion of counsel for the Bank that Maryland claimed the power to tax the public property of the national government, such as its ships, its munitions of war, its treasury, post offices, even its judicial proceedings and customs house papers, as a "straw man" introduced to obscure the issues. These were obviously not the subject of taxation but were the proper instruments of national sovereignty, essential to the exercise of the powers expressly granted to the federal government altogether separate from the taxing powers reserved to the states.

The right of taxation by the State is co-extensive with all private property within the State. The interest of the United States in this bank is private property, though belonging to public persons. It is held by the government, as an undivided interest with private stockholders. . . .

The shares belonging to the United States, or of any other stockholders, are not subjected to direct taxation by the law of Maryland. The tax imposed is a stamp tax upon the notes issued by a banking house within the State of Maryland. Because the United States happen to be partially interested, either as dormant or active partners, in that house, is no reason why the State should refrain from laying a tax which it has, otherwise, a constitutional right to im-

---

[28] *The Federalist*, no. 32.
[29] *The Federalist*, no. 33.
[30] 4 Wheat. 374.

299

pose. The situation is the same as if the United States were to become interested in any other house of trade, which should issue its notes, or bills of exchange, liable to a stamp duty, by the law of a State.

Then, attacking the principal argument put forward by each of the bank's lawyers, Martin began his peroration:

But it is said that a right to *tax*, in this case, implies a right to *destroy*; that it is impossible to draw the line of discrimination between a tax fairly laid for the purposes of revenue, and one imposed for the purpose of prohibition. We answer, that the same objections would equally apply to the right of Congress to tax the State banks. . . .

The whole of this subject of taxation is full of difficulties, which the Convention found it impossible to solve in a manner entirely satisfactory. The first attempt was to divide the subjects of taxation between the State and the national government. This being found impracticable, or inconvenient, the State governments surrendered altogether their right to tax imports and exports, and tonnage, giving the authority to tax all other subjects to Congress, but reserving to the States a concurrent right to tax the same subjects to an unlimited extent. . . .

The debates in the State conventions show that the power of State taxation was understood to be absolutely unlimited, except as to imposts and tonnage duties. The States would not have adopted the Constitution upon any other understanding.[31]

To illustrate this last point by means of an authority which, he submitted, the Court would accept as conclusive, Martin announced that he would read from the reports of the debates in the Virginia ratifying convention of 1788. At this point, Justice Story recalled, he saw John Marshall draw a long breath, as if apprehensive of what was to come.[32] Thirty years earlier, Marshall had been one of the principal proponents of the Constitution at that convention and had denounced as baseless the fears that the new national government would usurp the powers of the states. He had insisted that the federal government had only those powers expressly granted to it, while the states retained all powers not granted to the national government and not denied to them:

The state governments did not derive their powers from the general [federal] government. But each government derived its powers from the people; and each was to act according to the powers given it. Would any gentleman deny this? . . .

The powers not denied to the states are not vested in them by implication, because, being possessed of them antecedent to the adoption of the government, and not being divested of them, by any grant or restriction in the Constitution, the States must be as fully possessed of them as ever they had been. And it could not be said that the states derived any powers from that system, but retained them, though not acknowledged in any part of the Constitution.[33]

---

[31] 4 Wheat. 376.

[32] Richard Malcolm Johnston and William Hand Browne, *Life of Alexander H. Stephens*, p. 183.

[33] John Marshall, in 3 Elliot's Debates 419ff (16 June 1788); David Robertson, *Debates and Other Proceedings of the Convention of Virginia*, p. 298ff.

On this note Martin concluded his astounding two-and-a-half-day performance.[34]

On Monday morning, William Pinkney began the closing argument for the Bank. He opened with his customary flattery of the Court: "I meditate with exultation, not fear, upon the proud spectacle of a peaceful judicial review of these conflicting sovereign claims by this more than amphictyonic council." Amphictyonic leagues or councils in ancient Greek history were legislative bodies whose members represented neighboring states, and not judicial bodies in any sense, but this point was unknown to most members of the Court, who accepted the inappropriate classical allusion as a tribute to their learning and station. Pinkney then entered upon an *argumentum ad homines*, with characteristic sarcasm:

> Our opponents think of the importance of this cause as I do. They have, therefore, put forth their whole power in the argument of it. All the graces of a polished execution within the reach of two of the learned counsel [Hopkinson and Jones]; all that more robust and hardy wit within the reach of the other [Martin] . . . ; all the artifices of a cunning and disciplined logic more or less within the reach of all learned counsel, have been exhausted upon it.
>
> We have had the affecting retrospections of Mr. Martin upon scenes *"quorum pars magna* (or *minima) fuit"* (for I will not object to his amendment lest I should distress the modesty that suggested it), which scenes, luckily for the time of the court, had their commencement at an epoch considerably subsequent to the flood.

(This last was, of course, a reference to the length of Martin's argument, which history has duly ascribed to Martin's habitual verbosity.)

Pinkney then ruefully observed, regarding the issue in the case, "that what was at first only threadbare, has now been worn to tatters; and that consequently very little is left for me but miserable shreds and ragged odds and ends, the *tristes reliquiae* of those who have gone before me."[35] He then proceeded to discuss these "sad remains" for three full days, but because of his skill and powers of elocution (as well as the susceptibility of the Court), the length of his address went unremarked. When it was over, Joseph Story wrote: "I never, in my whole life, heard a greater speech; it was worth a journey from Salem to hear it; his elocution was excessively vehement, but his eloquence was overwhelming. His language, his style, his figures, his arguments were most brilliant and sparkling. He spoke like a great statesman and patriot, and a sound constitutional lawyer. All the cobwebs of sophistry and metaphysics about State rights and State sovereignty he brushed away with a mighty besom."[36]

[34] The Baltimore *Patriot* for 5 March 1819 announced that Martin was "preparing for the press his argument in the highly interesting case of McCulloch v. The State of Maryland . . . ; which will be accompanied by a review of the eloquent and able speech of Mr. Pinkney in reply." It is not known whether this matter was ever published.

[35] Henry Wheaton, *Some Account of the Life, Writings and Speeches of William Pinkney*, p. 163ff.

[36] Letter to Stephen White, 3 March 1819, *Life and Letters of Joseph Story*, 1:325.

Chief Justice Marshall began writing his decision in the case long before the arguments were concluded—probably even before they were begun.[37] His ten-thousand-word opinion was delivered on 6 March 1819, only three days after Pinkney finished his speech. As was his wont, Marshall seized the opportunity presented by the case not so much to decide the rights of the parties put in issue by the facts as to lay down broad principles of government for all future cases in the construction and application of the nation's basic statute, the Constitution. Apparently, his opinion, as originally written, closed with these words: "We are unanimously of opinion, that the law passed by the legislature of Maryland, imposing a tax on the Bank of the United States, is unconstitutional and void."[38] However, Martin's argument compelled the Court to narrow considerably the broad judgment urged so vehemently by Webster, Wirt, and Pinkney, and Marshall added, at the end of his opinion, some important concessions to the State of Maryland and to all other states:

This opinion does not deprive the States of any resources which they originally possessed. It does not extend to a tax paid by the real property of the bank, in common with the other real property within the State, nor to a tax imposed on the interest which the citizens of Maryland may hold in this institution, in common with other property of the same description throughout the State. But this is a tax on the operations of the bank, and is, consequently, a tax on the operation of an instrument employed by the government of the Union to carry its powers into execution. Such a tax must be unconstitutional.[39]

With one exception,[40] this was Luther Martin's last argument before the Supreme Court and one of his last before any court. Five months later, while "zealously engaged in making out 60 presentments against our famous bank gentry,"[41] he suffered a severe paralytic stroke which destroyed his intellectual functioning, although he made some physical recovery.[42] For the remaining seven years of his life he was a derelict, mindless, helpless, and without family or support. Out of sheer habit he would enter the courthouses where he had spent most of his life and wander into the room where court was in session. The presiding judge would tap his gavel and suspend proceedings briefly, while Martin pushed open the gate into the counsels' area, sat down at the trial table, and stared vacantly around the room, nibbling all the while on a

---

[37] Beveridge, *Life of John Marshall*, 4:290.
[38] 4 Wheat. 436.
[39] 4 Wheat. 437.
[40] Sergeant v. Biddle, 4 Wheat. 508.
[41] Mrs. Anna McHenry Boyd to John McHenry, 13 August 1819, Maryland Historical Society Collection, Baltimore, Md. The reference is to the indictments which Martin drew up against James Buchanan, James W. McCulloch (who had been the defendant in McCulloch v. Maryland) and George Williams for conspiracy to defraud the United States Bank of some $1,500,000. See State v. Buchanan 5 Harris and Johnson 317 (1821); *An Exhibit of the Losses Sustained at the Office of Discount and Deposit, passim*. Demurrers to the indictments were sustained by the Harford County Court but were overruled by the Court of Appeals. The defendants were subsequently acquitted (see 5 Harris and Johnson 500).
[42] Mrs. Anna McHenry Boyd to John McHenry, 18 August 1819, Maryland Historical Society.

piece of gingerbread. After a time, he would rise and find his way out of the room, while the judge again suspended proceedings out of respect for the man he had been.[43]

The General Assembly finally took legislative notice of Martin's condition and adopted a measure without parallel in American history. It was first proposed that he be given an army pension, but it was pointed out that he had been an attorney general, not a major general (his service in the Baltimore Light Dragoons during the Virginia campaign against Cornwallis in the summer of 1781 had been forgotten). After further discussion, Martin's old friend, Delegate Levin R. King of Somerset County, introduced a resolution which was adopted without a dissenting vote:

WHEREAS, Luther Martin accepted appointment as Attorney-General at an early period of our glorious Revolution, at the hazard of his life and property; and

WHEREAS, he is now, by an afflicting dispensation of divine Providence, bereaved of his intellectual powers, and is poor, and unable to procure support; Now, therefore, be it

RESOLVED, That each and every practitioner of law in this state shall be and he is hereby compelled . . . to obtain from the clerk of the county court in which he may practice, a license to authorize him so to practice, for which he shall pay annually . . . the sum of five dollars; which said sum is to be deposited by the clerk . . . in the treasury of the western shore, or eastern shore, as the case may be, subject to the order of Thomas Kell and William H. Winder, Esqrs., who are hereby appointed trustees for the appropriation of the proceeds raised by virtue of this resolution, to the use of the said Luther Martin.[44]

Within a year Aaron Burr heard of Martin's plight and brought him to his home in New York City, whereupon the resolution was repealed.[45] Martin lived with Burr for more than three years and is said to have been the last person in New York to persist in wearing the old-fashioned Federalist garb—a white-haired, red-faced, vacant-eyed old gentleman in worn velvet jacket, with clubbed hair, and frayed lace at his wrists, wandering aimlessly in the streets of lower Manhattan. On 10 July 1826, halfway through his seventy-ninth year, Luther Martin died. After a brief, sparsely attended service at St. John's Chapel, he was buried in St. John's burial ground in Trinity Parish.[46] It is doubtful that a tombstone ever marked his grave. Some seventy years later, the area was condemned for a playground, which is now known as James J. Walker Park. Martin's grave has long since been covered over, and today its site is unknown and unmarked.

[43] Semmes, *John H. B. Latrobe*, p. 204.

[44] Resolution No. 60, passed 23 February 1822, session of 1821–22, *House Journal*, p. 145; *Senate Journal*, p. 80.

[45] Resolution No. 16, passed 6 February 1823, *Laws of Maryland*, 1822, p. 141.

[46] Upon hearing of Martin's death, the bench and bar of the City of Baltimore resolved that "as testimony of our regard for his memory and of our great respect for his exalted power and profound learning, we will wear mourning for the space of thirty days" (Report of the Eighth Annual Meeting of the Maryland State Bar Association Held at Ocean City, Maryland, on July 7, 8, and 9, 1903, in *Maryland State Bar Association Reports*, 8:129).

The Tradition of Martin's "Eternal Volubility" at the Constitutional Convention of 1787

Martin's address of 27 and 28 June, spread as it was over three hours of one day and one hour of the next, necessarily constitutes the basis for the tradition of his "eternal volubility"[1] during the convention, as it was the longer of only two speeches of any duration made there by him. William Pierce, a delegate from Georgia, wrote a series of character sketches of most of the delegates, some of which are quoted in the appropriate sections of the text. Even though it is not known when, or for what purpose, Pierce wrote these descriptions, they have generally been accepted as reasonably accurate, apparently for the inadequate reason that there is a dearth of other information on the subject. His brief sketch of Martin was as follows: "Mr. Martin was educated for the Bar, and is Attorney General for Maryland. This Gentleman possesses a good deal of information, but has a very bad delivery, and so extremely prolix, that he never speaks without tiring the patience of all who hear him. He is about 34 years of age."[2]

Martin's "delivery" did lack the graces of Randolph, the brilliance of Hamilton, the pithiness of Sherman, the bookishness of Madison, and the eloquence of King or Rutledge, but there is grave doubt as to Pierce's competence as a witness to his "prolixity." He was at Philadelphia for only thirty-two days of the convention, from 31 May to 1 July,[3] and Martin was present for only twenty-two days of this period. In these twenty-two days he addressed the convention ten times: on six of these occasions he made a simple motion or a brief observation; twice he made long prepared speeches (his only such of the entire convention); and his remaining two addresses could not have exceeded fifteen minutes each. During the same period Madison, for example, spoke more than fifty times, almost always at much greater length than Martin, and the effusive James Wilson spoke more than sixty times. Pierce, however, found Madison "a Gentleman of great modesty" and,

---

[1] The term is Oliver Ellsworth's (see Farrand, *Records of the Federal Convention*, 3:272).

[2] *Ibid.*, p. 93. Martin was actually well over thirty-nine at this time. Pierce's sketches of delegates whom he never saw at the convention (or anywhere else, in all probability)—Langdon, Gilman, Gouverneur Morris, and Daniel Carroll—were as complete as those of the men he knew.

[3] *Ibid.*, p. 589.

"tho' he cannot be called an Orator . . . a most agreeable, eloquent, and convincing Speaker"; Wilson, he said, was "clear, copious, and comprehensive." One can account for this judgment of Martin only on the basis that Pierce was a supporter of Madison's and Wilson's large-state bloc and therefore found Martin's comments "tiring," whatever their length or frequency.[4]

A comparison of Martin's record with that of other delegates is instructive. The most frequent speaker was Gouverneur Morris, who addressed that body on some 173 recorded occasions,[5] this despite an initial handicap of not having arrived until July. Wilson of Pennsylvania spoke 168 times, Madison 161, Sherman 138, Mason 136, and, of particular interest, Ellsworth himself spoke 84 times. Further examination of the record shows that just over half of Martin's total of 53 "speeches" consisted of making or seconding a motion, as recorded in two or three lines each in Madison's and Yates's notes. On 16 occasions he made brief observations on the subject under discussion, the whole of which are reported in less than sixty lines in Farrand's *Records*. On not more than six occasions did he make any address which could conceivably be termed extended.

On this basis Ellsworth later reported that Martin "so exhausted the politeness of the Convention" that it "at length prepared to slumber" whenever he rose.[6] Martin's reply to this, while serious in intention, is characteristically humorous:

If my rising to speak had such a somnific influence on the Convention as the Landholder represents, I have no doubt that time will come, should this system be adopted, when my countrymen will ardently wish I had never left the Convention, but remained there to the last, daily administering to my associates the salutary opiate. Happy, thrice happy, would it have been for my country, if the whole of that time had been devoted to sleep, or been a blank in our lives, rather than employed in forging its chains.[7]

Ellsworth, however, did not limit himself to such generalities but went on to describe in detail an alleged response by Gerry to this very speech:

There needed no other display to fix your character and the rank of your abilities, which the Convention would have confirmed by the most distinguished silence, had not a certain similarity in genius provoked a sarcastic reply from the pleasant Mr. Gerry; in which he admired the strength of your lungs

---

[4] The large amount of error, both direct and collateral, in Ellsworth's account of Martin has been discussed in Chapter 9 above. Seldom in the history of American politics have so many demonstrable misstatements been contained in one short public document (see Ellsworth's anonymous letter to the *Maryland Journal* of 29 February 1788 [*ibid.*, p. 271ff.]).

[5] McMaster, *History of the People of the U.S.*, 1:421n; Warren, *The Making of the Constitution*, p. 125; Beck, *The Constitution of the United States*, p. 125.

[6] "The Landholder," *Maryland Journal*, 29 February 1788 (Farrand, *Records of the Federal Convention*, 3:271ff.).

[7] *Maryland Journal*, 21 March 1788 (*ibid.*, p. 292).

and your profound knowledge in the first principles of government; mixing and illustrating his little remarks with a profusion of hems, that never fail to lengthen out and enliven his oratory. This reply (from your intimate acquaintance), the match being so equal and the contrast so comic, had the happy effect to put the house in good humor, and leave you a prey to the most humiliating reflections.[8]

Under the cover of his anonymity as "The Landholder," Ellsworth placed this fictitious reply after the first part of Martin's speech on 27 June. He was perfectly safe in doing so because, thanks to the secrecy of the convention proceedings, there were no public records to refute him. All the accounts which have since come to light, however, show that Martin was the last to speak on that day and the first to speak on the next. Madison, Yates, King, and Paterson all testify that no such "comic contrast" ever took place, and Gerry himself specifically denied it. He wrote: "This is so remote from the truth, that no such reply was made by Mr. Gerry to Mr. Martin, or to any member of the convention; on the contrary, Mr. Martin, on the first day he spoke, about the time of adjournment, signified to the convention that the heat of the season, and his indisposition prevented his proceeding, and the house adjourned without further debate, or a reply to Mr. Martin from any member whatever."[9] The conclusion is inescapable that, "wordy" as Martin may have seemed to Ellsworth and others on that side, the term "volubility" has been misapplied here, as there were other delegates (including Ellsworth himself) who were many times more voluble than Luther Martin.

[8] *Ibid.*, p. 272.
[9] *New York Journal*, 30 April 1788 (*ibid.*, p. 299).

George Rogers Clark on Logan-Cresap

On 25 March 1798 Thomas Jefferson wrote to Dr. Samuel Browne asking him to interview various people, including George Rogers Clark, with regard to the Yellow Creek massacre (see Jefferson Papers, 103: 17676, Library of Congress, Washington, D.C.). Clark wrote to Browne on 17 June 1798 (Jefferson Papers, 104:17801–4), but for some reason not now known Browne did not forward this letter to Jefferson until 4 September of that year (Jefferson Papers, 104:17861–62). The copy of Clark's letter which appears below is taken from the Clark papers.[1]

June 17, '98

Dear Sir

Your letter of last month honored by Mr. Thurston, was handed me by that gentleman. The matter contained in it and in the inclosed papers was new to me. I felt hurt that Mr. Jefferson should be attacked with so much virulence on account of an error of which I know he was not the author. Except a few mistakes in names of persons, places, etc., the story of Logan, as related by Mr. Jefferson, is substantially true. I was one of the first and last of the active officers who bore the weight of that war; and on perusing some old papers of that date, I find some memoirs. But independent of them, I have a perfect recollection of every transaction relating to Logan's story. The conduct of Cresap I am perfectly acquainted with. He was not the author of that murder, but a family by the name of Greathouse through some transaction that happened under the command of Capt. Cresap a few days previous to the murder of Logan's family gave him sufficient ground to suppose that it was Cresap that had done the injury. To enable you fully to understand the subject of your inquiries, I shall relate the incidents that gave rise to Logan's suspicion and will enable Mr. Jefferson to do justice to himself and the Cresap family by being made fully acquainted with [the] facts.

This country was explored in 1773. A resolution was formed to make a settlement the spring following, and the mouth of the Little Kenaway [sic] was appointed the place of general rendezvous in order to descend the river from thence in a body. Early in the spring the Indians had done some mischief. Reports from their towns were alarming which deterred many. About eighty or ninety men only set out at the appointed rendezvous where we lay some days. A small party of hunters that lay about ten miles below us, were fired upon by the Indians, whom the hunters beat back and returned to camp. This and many other circumstances led us to believe that the Indians were determined on war.

[1] *Papers*, pp. 3–9.

The whole party was enrolled and determined to execute their project of forming a settlement in Kentucky, as we had every necessary store that could be
thought of. An Indian town called Horsehead Bottom on the Sciota and near
its mouth, lay nearly in our way. The determination was to cross the country
and surprise it. Who was to command was the question. There were but few
among us that had experience in Indian warfare and they were such as we did
not choose to be commanded by. We knew of Capt. Cresap being on the river
about fifteen miles above us with some hands settling a plantation; and that
he had concluded to follow us to Kentucky as soon as he had fixed there his
people. We also knew that he had been experienced in a former war. He was
proposed; and it was unanimously agreed to send for him to command the
party. Messengers were despatched and in half an hour returned with Cresap.
He had heard of our resolution by some of his hunters that had fallen in with
ours, and had set out to come to us. We now thought our army, as we called it,
complete, and the destruction of the Indians sure. A council was called and to
our astonishment, our intended commander-in-chief was the person that dis-
suaded us from the enterprise. He said, that appearances were very suspicious,
but there was no certainty of a war. That if we made the attempt proposed, he
had no doubt of our success but a war would at any rate be the result, and that
we should be blamed for it, and perhaps justly. But if we were determined to
proceed, he would lay aside all considerations, send to his camp for his people
and share our fortunes. He was then asked what he would advise. His answer
was that we should return to Wheeling, as a convenient post, to hear what was
going forward. That a few weeks would determine. As it was early in the spring,
if we found the Indians were not disposed for war, we should have full time to
return and make our establishment in Kentucky. This was adopted, and in two
hours the whole were under way. As we ascended the river we met Kill-buck,
an Indian chief with a small party. We had a long conference with him, but
received but little satisfaction as to the disposition of the Indians. It was observed that Cresap did not come to this conference, but kept on the opposite side
of the river. He said he was afraid to trust himself with the Indians. That Kill-
buck had frequently attempted to way-lay his father to kill him—that if he
crossed the river, perhaps, his fortitude might fail him and he might put Kill-
buck to death. On our arrival at Wheeling (the country being pretty well
settled thereabouts) the whole of the inhabitants appeared to be alarmed. They
flocked to our camp from every direction and all we could say would not keep
them from under our wings. We offered to cover their neighborhood with
scouts, until further information, if they would return to their plantations, but
nothing would avail. By this time we had got to be a formidable party. All the
hunters, men without families, etc., in that quarter had joined our party. Our
arrival at Wheeling was soon known at Pittsburg. The whole of that country,
at that time, being under the jurisdiction of Virginia, Dr. Connolly had been
appointed by Dunmore, Capt. Commandant of the district which was called
Waugusta [West Augusta].

He, learning of us sent a message addressed to the party letting us know that
a war was to be apprehended and requesting that we would keep our position
for a few days, as messages had been sent to the Indians, and a few days would
determine the doubt. The answer he got was that we had no inclination to quit
our quarters for sometime. That during our stay we should be careful that the
enemy should not harass the neighborhood that we lay in. But before this answer
could reach Pittsburg, he sent a second express, addressed to Capt. Cresap, as

the most influential man among us, informing him that the message had returned from the Indians that war was inevitable, and begging him to use his influence with the party to get them to cover the country by scouts until the inhabitants could fortify themselves. The reception of this letter was the epoch of open hostilities with the Indians. A new post was planted, a council was called and the letter read by Cresap. All the Indian traders being summoned on so important an occasion, action was had and war declared in the most solemn manner; and the same evening two scalps were brought into camp. The next day some canoes of Indians were discovered on the river keeping the advantage of the island to cover themselves from our view. They were chased fifteen miles down the river and driven ashore. A battle ensued, a few were wounded on both sides, one Indian only taken prisoner. On examining their canoes, we found a considerable quantity of ammunition and other warlike stores. On our return to camp, a resolution was adopted to march the next day and attack Logan's camp on the Ohio about thirty miles above us. We did march about five miles and then halted to take some refreshment. Here the impropriety of executing the projected enterprise was argued. The conversation was brought forward by Cresap himself. It was generally agreed that those Indians had no hostile intentions as they were hunting, and their party was composed of men, women and children with all their stuff with them. This we knew as I myself and others present had been in the camp about four weeks past on our descending the river from Pittsburg. In short, every person seemed to detest the resolution we had set out with. We returned in the evening, decamped and took the road to Redstone. It was two days after this that Logan's family were killed and from the manner in which it was done, it was viewed as a horrid murder. From Logan hearing of Cresap being the head of the party on the river, it is no wonder that he supposed he had a hand in the destruction of his family. Since the reception of your letter, I have procured the "Notes on Virginia." They are now before me. The act was more barbarous than related by Mr. Jefferson. Those Indians used to visit and return visits with the neighboring whites on the opposite side of the river. They were on a visit to a family by the name of Greathouse at the time they were murdered by them and their associates. The war now raged in all its savage fury, until the fall, when a treaty of peace was held at Camp Charlotte, within four miles of Chillicothe, the Indian capital on the Ohio. Logan did not appear. I was acquainted with him and wished to know the reason. The answer was "that he was like a mad dog, his bristles were up and were not quite fallen, but the good talk now going forward might allay them." Logan's speech to Dunmore now came forward, as related by Mr. Jefferson. It was thought to be clever although the army knew it to be wrong as to Cresap. But it only produced a laugh in camp. I saw it displeased Capt. Cresap and told him "that he must be a very great man, that the Indians palmed everything that happened on his shoulders." He smiled and said that he had an inclination to tomahawk Greathouse for the murder. What I have here related is fact. I was intimate with Cresap. Logan I was better acquainted with, at that time, than any other Indian in the Western country. I was perfectly acquainted with the conduct of both parties. Logan was author of the speech, as altered by Mr. Jefferson, and Cresap's conduct was as I have related it.

I am yours, etc,

G. R. Clark

310

Roger Brooke Taney on Luther Martin

Late in life Roger Brooke Taney, then Chief Justice of the United States, began writing his autobiography (printed in Samuel Tyler's *Memoir of Roger Brooke Taney, LL.D.*, which covers the period from his birth to March 1801). His portrayal of Luther Martin is the most intimate, detailed, and objective which has been preserved.

In the enumeration of the great men of the bar, I have placed Luther Martin first. He was not only much older than any of the other gentlemen, but he was the acknowledged and undisputed head of the profession in Maryland. He was so in the eye of the public, he was so admitted by the bar. Nobody disputed it with him until Mr. Pinkney returned from Europe. Yet I confess, when I first heard Mr. Martin, I was disappointed; and, if I had followed the dictates of my own inexperience and unformed judgment, I should have awarded a higher place to some others. Mr. Martin's habits, however, had at that time become bad. He often appeared in Court evidently intoxicated, and perhaps, was not free from the influence of stimulants when I first heard him. His dress was a compound of the fine and the coarse, and appeared never to have felt the brush. He wore ruffles at the wrists, richly edged with lace,—although every other person had long before abandoned them,—and these ruffles, conspicuously broad, were dabbled and soiled, and showed that they had not been changed for a day or more. His voice was not musical, and when much excited it cracked. His argument was full of digressions and irrelevant or unimportant matter, and his points were mixed up together and argued without order, with much repetition, and his speech was consequently unreasonably long. He was an accomplished scholar, and wrote with classical correctness and great strength. But in his speech . . . he seemed to delight in using vulgarisms which were never heard except among the colored servants or the ignorant and uneducated whites. For example, I have heard him say he *cotch* him, instead of *caught* him, and he *sot* down, instead of *sat* down, and many other words and phrases not much better. He seemed to take pleasure in showing his utter disregard of good taste and refinement in his dress and language and his mode of argument. He was as coarse and unseemly at a dinner-table, in his manner of eating, as he was in everything.

But with all these defects, he was a profound lawyer. He never missed the strong points of his case; and, although much might generally have been better omitted, everybody who listened to him would agree that nothing could be added, but, unfortunately for him, he was not always listened to. He introduced so much extraneous matter, or dwelt so long on unimportant points, that the attention was apt to be fatigued and withdrawn, and the logic and force of his argument lost upon the Court or the jury. But these very defects arose in some measure from the fulness of his legal knowledge. He had an iron memory, and forgot nothing that he had read; and he had read a great deal on every branch of the law, and took pleasure in showing it when his case did not require it. His associates at the bar had, as I have said, great respect for his legal learning. Many years after I came to the bar, I remember on one occasion, when I was engaged in an important case on the same side with Mr. Shaaff, and Mr. Martin was opposed to us, Mr. Shaaff and myself went over the case together very carefully; and when we had done with the examination, he said, I think the case is with us, and I see nothing in it to be afraid of; but I am always afraid of Martin. Yet Mr. Shaaff ranked then with the foremost men in Maryland, was resolute and firm in his opinions, and would, I am sure, have felt no apprehension of being taken by surprise by any other member of the bar.

Mr. Martin was Attorney-General of Maryland in the war of the Revolution, and continued so for a great many years. He did not resign until long after I had entered upon the practice. His prosecutions were always conducted with great fairness to the accused, and the attention of the jury called to the evidence which might operate in his favor as well as that against him. Nor was any attempt made to take from it by argument the weight to which it was justly entitled. He was strong in his attachments, and ready to make any sacrifice for his friends. This was proved by the zeal with which he defended Mr. Chase when he was impeached by the House of Representatives of the United States, and still more in the time he devoted, and the money he spent, in defense of Colonel Burr. In both of these cases he was a volunteer.

He certainly received, and would have taken, no fee in the impeachment case; and I doubt whether he received any from Colonel Burr. He became one of his securities for his appearance to answer the charge of misdemeanor after his acquittal for treason. After that recognizance was forfeited, Mr. Martin was harassed with proceedings against him to recover the amount. How it ended, and whether Mr. Martin paid it out of his own means or not, I do not know; but if it was in the end paid by Colonel Burr, no fee, however liberal, could have remunerated him for his sacrifices in behalf of his friend, whom he persisted in believing, in spite of evidence, to be an innocent and persecuted man, and a pure patriot; for the case withdrew him from all other practice, and the cases in the Maryland Courts, in which he was engaged, were tried in his absence by others. He was kind to young members of the profession, and liberal, and indeed profuse, in his charities, and easily imposed upon by unworthy objects. Indeed his unfortunate habits made him reckless in money matters; and after a long life of severe labor and large profits, when late in life he was struck with paralysis, which impaired his intellect and rendered him incapable of business, he was found to be utterly penniless, and dependent upon charity for support. And the only good thing I know of Colonel Burr is, that, soon after this happened, he took Mr. Martin to his house and provided for his wants, and took care of him until his death.

Wilkinson's Affidavits

WILKINSON'S FIRST AFFIDAVIT

I, JAMES WILKINSON, brigadier-general and commander in chief of the army of the United States, to warrant the arrest of doctor Erick Bollman, on a charge of treason, misprision of treason, or such other offense against the government and laws of the United States as the following facts may legally charge him with, on my honor as a soldier, and on the Holy Evangelists of Almighty God, do declare and swear, that on the sixth day of November last, when in command at Natchitoches, I received by the hands of a Frenchman, a stranger to me, a letter from doctor Erick Bollman, of which the following is a correct copy:

> SIR: I have the honor to forward to your excellency the enclosed letters, which I was charged to deliver to you by our mutual friend: I shall remain for some time at this place, and should be glad to learn where and when I may have the pleasure of an interview with you. Have the goodness, to inform me of it, and please to direct your letter to me, care of —————, or enclose it under cover to them.

I have the honor to be,
With great respect, Sir,

Your excellency's most obedient servant,
(Signed) ERICK BOLLMAN.

Gen. Wilkinson.   *New Orleans, September 27, 1806.*

Covering a communication in cipher from Colonel Aaron Burr, of which the following is substantially as fair an interpretation as I have heretofore been able to make, the original of which I hold in my possession:[1]

> I [allegedly Burr] have obtained funds, and have actually commenced the enterprise. Detachments from different points, and under different pretences, will rendezvous on the Ohio, 1st November. Everything internal and external favors views; protection of England is secured. T.[2] is gone to Jamaica to arrange with the admiral of that station, and will meet at the Mississippi—England—navy of the United States are ready to

---

[1] U.S. v. Bollman and Swartwout, 4 Cranch 455, Appendix Note (A). For obvious reasons, Wilkinson omitted the first sentence of Burr's letter, "Your letter, postmarked 13th May, is received" (see p. 233, n. 22, above).
[2] Allegedly Truxton.

join, and final orders are given to my friends and followers; it will be a host of choice spirits. Wilkinson shall be second to Burr only; Wilkinson shall dictate the rank and promotion of his officers. Burr will proceed westward 1st August, never to return; with him go his daughter; the husband will follow in October with a corps of worthies: send forthwith an intelligent and confidential friend, with whom Burr may confer; he shall return immediately with further interesting details: this is essential to concert and harmony of movement; send a list of all persons known to Wilkinson west of the mountains, who could be useful, with a note delineating their characters.

By your messenger send me four or five of the commissions of your officers, which you can borrow under any pretence you please; they shall be returned faithfully; already are orders to the contractor given to forward six months' provisions to points Wilkinson may name; this shall not be used until the last moment, and then under proper injunctions: the project is brought to the point so long desired: Burr guarantees the result with his life and honor, the lives, the honor and fortunes of hundreds, the best blood of our country: Burr's plan of operations is to move down rapidly from the falls on the fifteenth of November, with the first five hundred or one thousand men, in light boats, now constructing for that purpose; to be at Natchez between the fifth and fifteenth of December, then to meet Wilkinson; then to determine whether it will be expedient, in the first instance, to seize on, or pass by Baton Rouge: on receipt of this send Burr an answer; draw on Burr for all expenses, &c. The people of the country to which we are going are prepared to receive us: their agents now with Burr say that if we will protect their religion, and will not subject them to a foreign power, that in three weeks all will be settled. The Gods invite to glory and fortune: it remains to be seen whether we deserve the boon; the bearer of this goes express to you; he will hand a formal letter of introduction to you from Burr, a copy of which is hereunto subjoined; he is a man of inviolable honor and perfect discretion; formed to execute rather than to project; capable of relating facts with fidelity, and incapable of relating them otherwise; he is thoroughly informed of the plans and intentions of ————, and will disclose to you as far as you inquire, and no further; he has imbibed a reverence for your character, and may be embarrassed in your presence; put him at ease and he will satisfy you; doctor Bollman, equally confidential, better informed on the subject, and more intelligent, will hand this duplicate.

29th July.

The day after my arrival at this city, the 26th of November last, I received another letter from the doctor, of which the following is a correct copy:

New Orleans, November 25th, 1806.

Sir: Your letter of the 16th inst. has been duly received; supposing that you will be much engaged this morning, I defer waiting on your excellency till you will be pleased to inform me of the time when it will be convenient for you to see me. I remain with great respect,

Your excellency's most obedient servant,

Erick Bollman.

314

His Excellency Gen. Wilkinson, Fauxbourg.
Marigny, the house between Madame Trevigne and M. Macarty.

On the 30th of the same month I waited in person on doctor E. Bollman, when he informed me that he had not heard from colonel Burr since his arrival here. That he (the said doctor E. Bollman) had sent dispatches to colonel Burr by a lieutenant Spence, of the navy, and that he had been advised of Spence's arrival at Nashville, in the state of Tennessee, and observed that colonel Burr had proceeded too far to retreat; that he (colonel Burr) had numerous and powerful friends in the United States, who stood pledged to support him with their fortunes, and that he must succeed. That he (the said doctor E. Bollman) had written to colonel Burr on the subject of provisions, and that he expected a supply would be sent from New York, and also from Norfolk, where colonel Burr had strong connections. I did not see or hear from the doctor again until the 5th inst., when I called on him the second time. The mail having arrived the day before, I asked him whether he had received any intelligence from colonel Burr; he informed me that he had seen a letter from colonel Burr of the 30th October, in which he (colonel Burr) gave assurances that he should be at Natchez with 2,000 men on the 20th December, inst. where he should wait until he heard from this place; that he would be followed by 4,000 men more; and that he, (colonel Burr,) if he had chosen, could have raised or got 12,000 as easily as 6,000, but that he did not think that number necessary. Confiding fully in this information, I became indifferent about further disguise. I then told the doctor that I should most certainly oppose colonel Burr if he came this way. He replied that they must come here for equipments and shipping, and observed that he did not know what had passed between colonel Burr and myself, obliqued at a sham defence, and waived the subject.

From the documents in my possession, and the several communications, verbal as well as written, from the said doctor Erick Bollman, on this subject, I feel no hesitation in declaring under the solemn obligation of an oath, that he has committed misprision of treason against the government of the United States.

(Signed)   JAMES WILKINSON.

Signed and sworn to this 14th day of December, 1806, before me, one of the justices of the peace of this county.

(Signed)   J. CARRICK.

WILKINSON'S SECOND AFFIDAVIT

I, JAMES WILKINSON, brigadier general and commander in chief of the army of the United States, to warrant the arrest of Samuel Swartwout, James Alexander, Esq., and Peter V. Ogden, on a charge of treason, misprision of treason, or such other offence against the government and laws of the United States as the following facts may legally charge them with, on the honor of a solider, and on the Holy Evangelists of Almighty God, do declare and swear, that in the beginning of the month of October last, when in command at Natchitoches, a stranger was introduced to me by colonel Cushing, by the name of Swartwout, who a few minutes after the colonel retired from the room, slipt into my hand a letter of formal introduction from colonel Burr, of which the following is a correct copy:

DEAR SIR:

Mr. SWARTWOUT, the brother of colonel S., of New York, being on his way down the Mississippi, and presuming that he may pass you at some post on the river, has requested of me a letter of introduction, which I give with pleasure, as he is a most amiable young man, and highly respected from his character and connections. I pray you to afford him any friendly offices which his situation may require, and beg you to pardon the trouble which this may give you.

With entire respect,
Your friend and obedient servant.

(Signed)   A. BURR.

His Excellency General Wilkinson.   *Philadelphia, 25th July, 1806.*

Together with a packet, which, he informed me, he was charged by the same person to deliver me in private, this packet contained a letter in cipher from colonel Burr, of which the following is substantially as fair an interpretation as I have heretofore been able to make, the original of which I hold in my possession [here follows a letter, purportedly from Burr to Wilkinson, with substantially the same wording as the one delivered by Bollman reproduced above].

I instantly resolved to avail myself of the reference made to the bearer, and in the course of some days, drew from him (the said Swartwout) the following disclosure: "That he had been dispatched by colonel Burr from Philadelphia, had passed through the states of Ohio and Kentucky, and proceeded from Louisville for St. Louis, where he expected to find me, but discovering at Kaskaskias that I had descended the river, he procured a skiff, hired hands, and followed me down the Mississippi to Fort Adams, and from thence set out for Natchitoches, in company with captains Sparks and Hooke, under the pretense of a disposition to take part in the campaign against the Spaniards, then depending. That colonel Burr with the support of a powerful association, extending from New York to New Orleans, was levying an armed body of 7,000 men from the state of New York and the western states and territories, with a view to carry an expedition against the Mexican provinces, and that 500 men under colonel Swartwout and a colonel or major Tyler, were to descend the Allegheny, for whose accommodation light boats had been built, and were ready. I inquired what would be their course: he said, "this territory would be revolutionized, where the people were ready to join them, and that there would be some seizing, he supposed, at New Orleans; that they expected to be ready to embark about the first of February, and intended to land at Vera Cruz, and to march from thence to Mexico." I observed that there were several millions of dollars in the bank of this place; to which he replied, "We know it full well;" and on remarking that they certainly did not mean to violate private property, he said they "merely meant to borrow, and would return it; that they must equip themselves in New Orleans; that they expected naval protection from Great Britain; that the capt. _____, and the officers of our navy, were so disgusted with the government that they were ready to join; that similar disgusts prevailed throughout the western country, where the people were zealous in favor of the enterprise, and that pilot boat built schooners were contracted for along our southern coast for their service; that he had been accompanied from the falls of Ohio to Kaskaskias, and from thence to Fort Adams, by a Mr. Ogden, who had proceeded on to New Orleans with letters from colonel Burr to his friends there." Swartwout asked me whether I had heard from doctor Bollman; and on my answering in the negative, he expressed great surprise, and observed, "That the doctor and a Mr. Alexander had left Philadelphia before him, with despatches for me, and that that they were to proceed by sea to New Orleans, where he said they must have arrived."

Though determined to deceive him if possible, I could not refrain telling Mr. Swartwout it was impossible that I could ever dishonor my commission; and I believe I duped him by my admiration of the plan, and by observing, "That although I could not join in the expedition, the engagements which the Spaniards had prepared for me in my front, might prevent my opposing it;" yet I did, the moment I had decyphered the letter, put it into the hands of colonel Cushing, my adjutant and inspector, making the declaration that I should oppose the lawless enterprise with my utmost force. Mr. Swartwout informed me he was under engagements to meet colonel Burr at Nashville the 20th of November, and requested of me to write him, which I declined; and on his leaving Natchitoches, about the 18th of October, I immediately employed lieutenant T. A. Smith to convey the information, in substance, to the President, without the commitment of names; for, from the extraordinary nature of the project, and the more extraordinary appeal to me, I could not but doubt its reality, notwithstanding the testimony before me, and I did not attach solid belief to Mr. Swartwout's reports respecting their intentions on this territory and city, until I received confirmatory advice from St. Louis.

After my return from the Sabine, I crossed the county to Natchez, and on my descent of the Mississippi from that place, I found Swartwout and Peter V. Ogden at Fort Adams; with the latter I held no communication, but was informed by Swartwout, that he (Ogden) had returned so far from New Orleans, on his route to Tennessee, but had been so much alarmed by certain reports in circulation that he was afraid to proceed. I inquired whether he bore letters with him from New Orleans, and was informed by Swartwout that he did not, but that a Mr. Spence had been sent from New Orleans through the country to Nashville, with letters for colonel Burr.

I reached this city the 25th ultimo, and on the next morning James Alexander, esq., visited me; he inquired of me aside whether I had seen doctor Bollman, and on my answering in the negative, he asked me whether I would suffer him to conduct Bollman to me, which I refused. He appeared desirous to communicate something, but I felt no inclination to inculpate this young man, and he left me. A few days after he paid me a second visit, and seemed desirous to communicate, which I avoided until he had risen to take leave; I then raised my finger, and observed, "Take care, you are playing a dangerous game." He answered, "It will succeed." I again observed, "Take care;" and he replied with a strong affirmation, "Burr will be here by the beginning of next month." In addition to these corroborating circumstances against Alexander, I beg leave

317

to refer to the accompanying documents, A. B. From all which I feel no hesitation in declaring, under the solemn obligation of an oath, that I do believe the said Swartwout, Alexander, and Ogden, have been parties to, and have been concerned in, the insurrection formed or forming in the states and territories on the Ohio and Mississippi rivers, against the laws and constitution of the United States.

(Signed)   JAMES WILKINSON.

Sworn to, and subscribed before me, this 26th day of December, in the year of our Lord, 1806.

(Signed)   GEORGE POLLACK.
Justice of the Peace, for the county of Orleans

Bibliography

Abernethy, Thomas Perkins. *Western Lands and the American Revolution*. New York: Appleton-Century Co., 1937.
————. *The Burr Conspiracy*. New York: Oxford University Press, 1954.
Adams, Henry. *History of the United States of America during the Administrations of Jefferson and Madison*. 9 vols. New York: C. Scribner's Sons, 1888–91.
————. *John Randolph*. Boston: Houghton Mifflin, 1882.
Adams, Herbert Baxter. *Maryland's Influence upon Land Cessions to the United States*. Baltimore: N. Murray, 1885.
————, ed. *Life and Writings of Jared Sparks*. 2 vols. Boston: Houghton Mifflin, 1893.
Adams, James Truslow. *Dictionary of American History*. 5 vols. New York: C. Scribner's Sons, 1940.
Adams, John. *Works*. 10 vols. Boston: Little, Brown, 1850–56.
Adams, John Quincy. *Memoirs*. 12 vols. Philadelphia: J. B. Lippincott, 1874–77.
————. *Writings*. 6 vols. New York: Macmillan, 1913–17.
Alexander, Holmes. *Aaron Burr, the Proud Pretender*. New York: Harper and Bros., 1937.
Alford, Clarence W. *The Mississippi Valley in British Politics*. 2 vols. Cleveland, O.: Arthur Clark Co., 1917.
Allen, Max P. "William Pinkney's First Public Service." *Maryland Historical Magazine* 39 (December 1944).
Andrews, Matthew Page. *The Fountain Inn Diary*. New York: Richard R. Smith, 1948.
Aptheker, Herbert. *American Negro Slave Revolts*. Studies in History, Economics and Public Law, no. 501. New York: Columbia University Press, 1943.

Bacon, Thomas, *Laws of Maryland at Large . . . (1637–1763)*. Annapolis, Md.: Jonas Green, 1765.
Bailey, Kenneth P. *The Ohio Company of Virginia and the Westward Movement: A Chapter in the History of the Colonial Frontier*. Glendale, Calif.: Arthur H. Clark, 1939.
————. *Thomas Cresap, Maryland Frontiersman*. Boston: Christopher Publishing House, 1944.
Bailey, Thomas A. *A Diplomatic History of the American People*. 7th ed. New York: Appleton-Century-Crofts, 1964.
Bakeless, John. *Background to Glory, the Life of George Rogers Clark*. Philadelphia: J. B. Lippincott, 1957.
Balch, Thomas, ed. *Papers relating chiefly to the Maryland Line during the Revolution*. Philadelphia: The Seventy-Six Society, 1857.
Bancroft, George. *History of the Formation of the Constitution of the United States of America*. 2 vols. New York: D. Appleton, 1882.

Barker, Charles A. *The Background of the Revolution in Maryland*. New Haven, Conn.: Yale University Press, 1940.

Barstow, George. *The History of New Hampshire, etc.* Concord, N.H.: I. S. Boyd, 1842.

Bass, Robert D. *The Green Dragoon*. New York: Holt, Rinehart and Winston, 1957.

Bassett, John Spencer. *The Federalist System, 1797–1801*. New York: Harper and Bros., 1906.

Bayard, James A. "Papers of James A. Bayard." Edited by Elizabeth Donnan. In *Annual Report of the American Historical Association*. Washington, D.C.: By the Association, 1915.

Beam, Jacob N. *The American Whig Society of Princeton University*. Princeton, N.J.: By the Society, 1933.

Beard, Charles A. *An Economic Interpretation of the Constitution of the United States*. New York: Macmillan, 1913.

Beck, James M. *The Constitution of the United States: Yesterday, Today and Tomorrow*. New York: George H. Doran, 1924.

Behrens, Kathryn L. *Paper Money in Maryland, 1727–1789*. Baltimore: Johns Hopkins Press, 1923.

Beirne, Francis F. *Shout Treason: The Trial of Aaron Burr*. New York: Hastings House, 1959.

Belknap, Jeremy. *The History of New Hampshire*. 3 vols. Boston: Bradford and Read, 1813.

Bemis, Samuel Flagg. *A Diplomatic History of the United States*. 5th ed. New York: Holt, Rinehart and Winston, 1965.

———. *Jay's Treaty, a Study in Commerce and Diplomacy*. New York: Macmillan, 1923.

Bentley, John H. *An Inroad upon the Sacred Trial by Jury*. Baltimore: n.p., 1811.

Beveridge, Albert G. *The Life of John Marshall*. 4 vols. Boston: Houghton Mifflin, 1916–19.

Bill, Alfred Hoyt. *The Campaign of Princeton, 1776–1777*. Princeton, N.J.: Princeton University Press, 1948.

Binkley, Wilfred Ellsworth, and Moos, Malcolm Charles. *A Grammar of American Politics*. New York: Alfred A. Knopf, 1952.

Boardman, Roger Sherman. *Roger Sherman, Signer and Statesman*. Philadelphia: University of Pennsylvania Press, 1938.

Bond, Beverly W., Jr. *State Government in Maryland, 1777–1781*. Johns Hopkins Studies in Historical and Political Science, no. 23. Baltimore: Johns Hopkins Press, 1905.

Bond, Carroll T. *The Court of Appeals of Maryland, a History*. Baltimore: Barton-Gillet Co., 1928.

Borden, Morton. *The Federalism of James A. Bayard*. New York: Columbia University Press, 1955.

———, ed. *The Antifederalist Papers*. East Lansing, Mich.: Michigan State University Press, 1965.

Boyd, George Adams. *Elias Boudinot, Patriot and Statesman*. Princeton, N.J.: Princeton University Press, 1952.

Bozman, John Leeds. *History of Maryland, from Its First Settlement in 1633 to the Restoration in 1660*. 2 vols. Baltimore: James Lucas and E. R. Deaver, 1837.

Brackenridge, Henry Marie. *Recollections of Persons and Places in the West*. 2d ed. Philadelphia: J. Kay and Brother, 1834.

Brackett, Jeffrey R. *The Negro in Maryland.* Johns Hopkins Studies in Historical and Political Science, extra vol. 6. Baltimore: Johns Hopkins Press, 1889.

Brant, Irving. *James Madison.* 6 vols. Vol. 1, *The Virginia Revolutionist;* vol. 2, *The Nationalist, 1780–1787;* vol. 3, *Father of the Constitution, 1787–1800;* vol. 4, *Secretary of State, 1800–1809;* vol. 5, *The President, 1809–1812;* vol. 6, *The Commander in Chief, 1812–1836.* Indianapolis, Ind.: Bobbs-Merrill, 1941.

Brown, Edwin H., Jr. "First Free School in Queen Anne's County." *Maryland Historical Magazine* 6 (March 1911).

Brown, R. E. *Charles Beard and the Constitution.* Princeton, N.J.: Princeton University Press, 1956.

Bryan, James Wallace. *The Development of the English Law of Conspiracy.* Baltimore: Johns Hopkins Press, 1909.

Buckmaster, Henrietta. *Let My People Go.* New York: Harper and Bros., 1941.

Burnaby, Andrew. *Travels through the Middle Settlements in North America in the Years 1759 and 1760.* Edited by Rufus Beckwell Wilson. Reprinted from the 3d ed. of 1778. New York: A. Wessels, 1904.

Burnett, Edmund Cody. *Letters of Members of the Continental Congress.* 8 vols. Washington, D. C.: Carnegie Institution, 1921.

Calendar of Maryland State Papers, No. 3, The Brown Books. Publication of the Hall of Records Commission, no. 6. Annapolis, Md.: By the Commission, 1948.

Calendar of Maryland State Papers, No. 4, The Red Books. Publication of the Hall of Records Commission, no. 8. Annapolis, Md.: By the Commission, 1953.

Carpenter, Thomas. *The Trial of Col. Aaron Burr on an Indictment for Treason.* 3 vols. Washington City, D.C.: Westcott and Co., 1807–8.

Carter, John H. "Shikellamy." *Northumberland County Historical Society Proceedings* 3 (March 1930).

Catterall, Helen Honor. *Judicial Cases concerning American Slavery and the Negro.* 4 vols. Washington, D.C.: Carnegie Institution, 1926–36.

Chafee, Zechariah, Jr. *Free Speech in the United States.* Cambridge, Mass.: Harvard University Press, 1941.

Chapin, Bradley. *The American Law of Treason: Revolutionary and Early National Origins.* Seattle: University of Washington Press, 1964.

Clark, Allen C. *Greenleaf and Law in the Federal City.* Washington, D.C.: W. F. Roberts, 1901.

Clark, Bennett Champ. *John Quincy Adams, "Old Man Eloquent."* Boston: Little, Brown, 1932.

Clark, Charles Branch. *The Eastern Shore of Maryland and Virginia.* 3 vols. New York: Lewis Historical Publishing Co., 1950.

Clark, George Rogers. *Papers of George Rogers Clark, 1771–1781.* Edited by James Alton James. Springfield: Illinois State Historical Library, 1912.

Columbian Eloquence, Being the Speeches of the Most Celebrated American Orators, as Delivered in the Late Interesting Trial of the Hon. Samuel Chase. 3 vols. Baltimore: S. Butler and S. Coler, 1806.

Commons, John R., et al., eds. *A Documentary History of American Industrial Society.* New York: Russell and Russell, 1958.

Cooke, John Esten. "Logan and Cresap." *New Eclectic Magazine* 6 (February 1870).

Coombs, J. J. *The Trial of Aaron Burr for High Treason.* Washington, D.C.: W. H. and O. H. Morrison, 1864.

321

Corwin, Edward S. *John Marshall and the Constitution*. New Haven, Conn.: Yale University Press, 1921.

Cox, I. J. "General Wilkinson and His Later Intrigues with the Spaniards." *American Historical Review* 19 (July, 1914).

Cresap, Joseph Orr, and Cresap, Bernarr. *The History of the Cresaps*. McComb, Miss.: Cresap Society, 1937.

Crowl, Philip A. "Antifederalism in Maryland, 1787–1788." *William and Mary Quarterly*, 3d ser., 4, no. 4 (October 1947).

————. *Maryland during and after the Revolution: A Political and Economic Study*. Baltimore: Johns Hopkins Press, 1943.

Cutler, Julia Perkins. *Life, Journals and Correspondence of Rev. Manasseh Cutler, LL.D.* 2 vols. Cincinnati, O.: R. Clarke, 1888.

Dale, Edward Everett, ed. *Letters of Lafayette to Washington, 1777–1779*. Oklahoma City, Okla.: Harlow Publishing Co., 1925.

Daniels, Jonathan. *They Will Be Heard*. New York: McGraw-Hill, 1965.

Davis, Matthew L. *Memoirs of Aaron Burr, 1756–1836*. 2 vols. New York: Harper and Bros., 1836–37.

Delaplaine, Edward Schley. *Thomas Johnson, Maryland and the Constitution*. Maryland State Bar Association 30th Annual Meeting, 1925, Atlantic City, N.J. Annapolis, Md.: *Capital Gazette, 1925*.

Dillon, John Brown. *A History of Indiana*. Indianapolis, Ind.: Bingham and Doughty, 1859.

Documentary History of the Constitution of the United States of America, 1787–1870. 5 vols. Washington, D.C.: Department of State, 1894–1905.

Dodd, William E. *Life of Nathaniel Macon*. Raleigh, N.C.: Edwards and Broughton, 1908.

Dos Passos, John. *The Head and Heart of Thomas Jefferson*. Garden City, N.Y.: Doubleday, 1954.

Drewry, William S. *Slave Insurrections in Virginia (1830–1865)*. Washington, D.C.: Neale Co., 1900.

Eddis, William. *Letters from America, Historical and Descriptive*. London: For the author, 1792.

Emory, Frederic. *Queen Anne's County, Maryland, Its Early History, and Development*. Baltimore: Maryland Historical Society, 1950.

Esarey, Logan. *A History of Indiana*. New York: Harcourt, Brace, 1922.

Evans, Charles. *Report of the Trial of the Honorable Samuel Chase*. Baltimore: Samuel Butler and George Keatinge, 1805.

[President and Directors of the Office at Baltimore]. *Exhibit of the Losses Sustained at the Office of Discount and Deposit, An*. Baltimore: Thomas Murphy, 1823.

Farrand, Max. *The Fathers of the Constitution*. New Haven, Conn.: Yale University Press, 1921.

————. *The Framing of the Constitution of the United States*. New Haven, Conn.: Yale University Press, 1913.

————. *The Records of the Federal Convention of 1787*. 4 vols. New Haven, Conn.: Yale University Press, 1911–37.

Faulkner, Robert K. "John Marshall and the Burr Trial." *Journal of American History* 53 (September 1966).

Fithian, Philip Vickers. *Journal and Letters of Philip Vickers Fithian, 1773–1774.* Edited by Hunter Dickinson Farish. Williamsburg, Va.: Colonial Williamsburg, 1943.

Force, Peter, ed. *American Archives—1790–1868.* 9 vols. Washington, D.C.: U.S. Government Printing Office, 1837–53.

Ford, Paul Leicester, ed. *Essays on the Constitution of the United States.* Brooklyn, N.Y.: Historical Printing Club, 1892.

———. *Pamphlets on the Constitution.* Brooklyn, N.Y.: n.p., 1888.

Ford, Worthington Chauncey, ed. *Journals of the Continental Congress.* 34 vols. Washington, D.C.: U.S. Government Printing Office, 1904–37.

———. *Some Papers of Aaron Burr.* Worcester, Mass.: American Antiquarian Society, 1920.

Freeman, Douglas Southall. *George Washington.* 7 vols. New York: Charles Scribner's Sons, 1948.

Furnas, J. C. *The Road to Harpers Ferry.* New York: William Sloane, 1959.

Geiger, Sister Mary Virginia. *Daniel Carroll, a Framer of the Constitution.* Washington, D.C.: Catholic University of America, 1943.

Giddens, Paul H. "Land Policies and Administration in Colonial Maryland, 1753–1769." *Maryland Historical Magazine* 28 (June 1933).

Giger, George M. *The Cliosophic Society.* Princeton, N.J.: Princeton University Press, 1916.

Gilmor, Robert. "Recollections of Baltimore." *Maryland Historical Magazine* 7 (September 1912).

Glocker, T. W. "Trade Unionism in Baltimore before the War of 1812." *Johns Hopkins University Circular,* no. 196 (April 1907).

Goodell, William. *The American Slave Code in Theory and Practice: Its Distinctive Features Shown by Its Statutes, Judicial Decisions, and Illustrative Facts.* New York: American and Foreign Anti-Slavery Society, 1853.

Gordon, Thomas Francis. *The History of New Jersey from Its Discovery by Europeans to the Adoption of the Federal Constitution.* Trenton, N.J.: D. Fenton, 1834.

Gottschalk, Louis. *La Fayette and the Close of the American Revolution.* Chicago: University of Chicago Press, 1942.

Gould, C. P. *The Land System in Maryland, 1720–1765.* Baltimore: Johns Hopkins Press, 1913.

Graham, James. *The Life of General Daniel Morgan of the Virginia Line.* New York: Derby and Jackson, 1856.

Gray, Lewis Cecil. *History of Agriculture in the Southern United States to 1860.* 2 vols. Washington, D.C.: Carnegie Institution, 1933.

Griffith, Thomas W. *Sketches of the Early History of Maryland.* Baltimore: W. Wooddy, 1824.

Hagan, Horace H. *Eight Great American Lawyers.* Oklahoma City, Okla.: Harlow Publishing Co., 1923.

Haines, Charles Grove. *The American Doctrine of Judicial Supremacy.* Berkeley: University of California Press, 1932.

Hamilton, Alexander. *Works of Alexander Hamilton.* Edited by John C. Hamilton. 7 vols. New York: J. F. Trow, 1850–51.

Harding, Samuel Bannister. *The Contest over the Ratification of the Federal Constitution in the State of Massachusetts.* New York: Longmans, Green, 1896.

Harrell, Isaac. *Loyalism in Virginia.* Durham, N.C.: Duke University Press, 1926.

Harrison, Samuel A. *A Memoir of John Leeds Bozman—The First Historian of*

Maryland. Maryland Historical Society Fund Publication no. 26. Baltimore: By the Society, 1888.

Hay, Thomas R., and Werner, M. R. *The Admirable Trumpeter.* Garden City, N.Y.: Doubleday, Doran, 1941.

High, James. "A Facet of Sovereignty: The Proprietary Governor and the Maryland Charter." *Maryland Historical Magazine* 55 (June 1960).

Hill, F. A. *The Mystery Solved: Facts Relating to Lawrence-Townley–Townley–Chase Marriage and Estate Question.* Boston: Rand Avery Co., 1888.

Hurd, J. C. *The Law of Freedom and Bondage in the United States.* 2 vols. Boston: Little, Brown, 1858–62.

Hurst, Willard. "Treason in the United States." *Harvard Law Review* 58 (December 1944): 226–72, (February 1945):395–444, (July 1945):806–57.

Irving, Washington. *Life and Letters of Washington Irving.* Edited by Pierre Munroe Irving. 4 vols. New York: G. P. Putnam's Sons, 1862–64.

Jacob, Rev. John J. *A Biographical Sketch of the Late Captain Michael Cresap.* Reprinted from the 1826 ed. Cincinnati, O.: n.p., 1886.

Jacobs, James Ripley. *Tarnished Warrior: Major-General James Wilkinson.* New York: Macmillan, 1938.

James, James Alton. *The Life of George Rogers Clark.* Chicago: University of Chicago Press, 1928.

Jefferson, Thomas. *The Complete Anas of Thomas Jefferson.* Edited by Franklin B. Sawvel. New York: Round Table Press, 1903.

———. *Notes on the State of Virginia.* Edited by William Peden. Chapel Hill: University of North Carolina Press, 1955.

———. *The Papers of Thomas Jefferson.* 17 vols. to date. Edited by Julian P. Boyd. Princeton, N.J.: Princeton University Press, 1950–.

———. *The Works of Thomas Jefferson.* 12 vols. Edited by Paul Leicester Ford. New York: G. P. Putnam's Sons, 1904–5.

———. *The Writings of Thomas Jefferson.* 20 vols. Definitive ed. Edited by Andrew A. Lipscomb. Washington, D.C.: Thomas Jefferson Memorial Association, 1905.

———. *The Writings of Thomas Jefferson.* 9 vols. Edited by H. A. Washington. Washington, D.C.: Taylor and Maury, 1853–54.

Jensen, Merrill. *The Articles of Confederation.* Madison: University of Wisconsin Press, 1940.

———. *The New Nation, a History of the United States during the Confederation, 1781–1789.* New York: Alfred A. Knopf, 1950.

Johnson, Janet Bassett. *Robert Alexander, Maryland Loyalist.* New York: G. P. Putnam's Sons, 1942.

Johnston, Richard Malcolm, and Browne, William Hand. *Life of Alexander H. Stephens.* Philadelphia: J. B. Lippincott, 1878.

Journal of the Constitutional Convention. Reprinted in Max Farrand, *The Records of the Federal Convention of 1787,* vol. 3. New Haven, Conn.: Yale University Press, 1911.

Keene, Richard Reynal. *A Letter from Richard Reynal Keene to Luther Martin, Esq. . . . upon the Subject of His "Modern Gratitude."* Baltimore: Prentiss and Cole, 1802.

Kelly, A. H., and Harbison, W. A. *The American Constitution, Its Origins and Development.* Rev. ed. New York: W. W. Norton, 1955.

324

Kennedy, John Pendleton. *Memoirs of the Life of William Wirt*. 2 vols. Philadelphia: Lea and Blanchard, 1849.

Kenyon, Cecelia M., ed. *The Antifederalists*. Indianapolis, Ind.: Bobbs-Merrill, 1966.

Kilty, John. *The Land-Holder's Assistant and Land-Office Guide*. Baltimore: G. Dobbin and Murphy, 1808.

———. *Laws*. Annapolis, Md.: John Chandler, 1811.

Knapp, Samuel L. *The Life of Aaron Burr*. New York: Wiley and Long, 1835.

Leopold, R. W., and Link, A. S. *Problems in American History*. New York: Prentice-Hall, 1952.

Lewis, William Draper. *Great American Lawyers*. 8 vols. Philadelphia: John C. Winston, 1907–9.

Livermore, Shaw. *Early American Land Companies*. New York: Commonwealth Fund, 1939.

Lynch, William O. *Fifty Years of Party Warfare*. Indianapolis, Ind.: Bobbs-Merrill, 1931.

McCaleb, Walter F. *The Aaron Burr Conspiracy*. New York: Dodd, Mead, 1903.

McDonald, Forrest. *We, the People*. Chicago: University of Chicago Press, 1958.

McLaughlin, Andrew C. *A Constitutional History of the United States*. New York: Appleton-Century Co., 1935.

Maclean, John. *History of the College of New Jersey, from Its Origin in 1746 to the Commencement of 1854*. 2 vols. Philadelphia: J. B. Lippincott, 1877.

McMaster, John Bach. *A History of the People of the U.S. from the Revolution to the Civil War*. 8 vols. New York: D. Appleton and Co., 1883–1913.

McMaster, John Bach, and Stone, Frederick D. *Pennsylvania and the Federal Constitution, 1787–1788*. Philadelphia: Lancaster, Pennsylvania, Inquirer Printing and Publishing Co., 1888.

McRee, Griffith John. *Life and Correspondence of James Iredell, 1750–1799*. 2 vols. New York: D. Appleton and Co., 1857–58.

McWhorter, Lucullus Virgil. *The Border Settlers of Northwestern Virginia from 1768 to 1795*. Hamilton, O.: Republican Publishing Co., 1915.

Madison, James. *Letters and Other Writings*. 4 vols. Edited by Gaillard Hunt. Philadelphia: J. B. Lippincott, 1865.

———. *Writings*. 9 vols. Edited by Gaillard Hunt. New York: G. P. Putnam's Sons, 1900–10.

Magrath, C. Peter. *Yazoo: Law and Politics in the New Republic*. Providence, R.I.: Brown University Press, 1966.

Main, Jackson Turner. *The Antifederalists, Critics of the Constitution 1781–1788*. Chapel Hill: University of North Carolina Press, 1961.

Malone, Dumas. *Jefferson and His Time*. 2 vols. Boston: Little, Brown, 1948.

Marshall, John A. *American Bastille*. Philadelphia: J. W. Hartley, 1876.

Martin, Luther. *The Genuine Information*. Reprinted in Max Farrand, *Records of the Federal Convention of 1787*, vol. 3. New Haven, Conn.: Yale University Press, 1911.

———. *Modern Gratitude*. Baltimore: Privately printed, 1801.

———. "Queries, addressed to Robert Lemmon, Esq." In Miscellaneous Broadside Volume, Maryland Historical Society, Baltimore, Md.

Maryland State Bar Association, *Report of the Fourth Annual Meeting of the Maryland State Bar Association*. Ocean City, Md.: Hanzsche and Co., 1899.

325

Mathews, John Mabry, and Berdahl, Clarence A. *Documents and Readings in American Government*. New York: Macmillan, 1940.

Mayer, Brantz. *Tah-gah-jute; or, Logan and Cresap*. Albany, N.Y.: Joel Munsel, 1867.

Miller, Alice E. *Cecil County, Maryland, a Study in Local History*. Elkton, Md.: C and L Print and Specialty Co., 1949.

Minutes of the Proceedings of a Convention of Delegates from the Abolition Societies Established in Different Parts of the United States. Philadelphia: Zachariah Poulson, 1794–1801.

Mish, Mary V. *Jonathan Hager, Founder*. Hagerstown, Md.: Hagerstown Book Binding and Printing Co., 1937.

Mitchell, Broadus. *Alexander Hamilton*. 2 vols. Vol. 1, *Youth to Maturity, 1753–1788*; vol. 2, *The National Adventure, 1788–1804*. New York: Macmillan, 1957–62.

Monaghan, Frank. *John Jay*. Indianapolis, Ind.: Bobbs-Merrill, 1935.

Monnette, Ora Eugene. *First Letters of Ye Plantations of Piscataway and Woodbridge Olde East, New Jersey, 1664–1714*. Los Angeles, Calif.: Leroy Carman Press, 1930.

Montross, Lynn. *Rag, Tag and Bobtail*. New York: Harper and Bros., 1952.

Moore, John Bassett. *International Adjudications. Modern Series*. New York: Oxford University Press, 1931. Vol. 3, *Arbitration of Claims for Losses and Damages Resulting from Lawful Impediments to the Recovery of Pre-War Debts*.

Morgan, Donald G. *Justice William Johnson, the First Dissenter*. Columbia: University of South Carolina Press, 1954.

Morison, Samuel Eliot, and Commager, Henry Steele. *The Growth of the American Republic*. New York: Oxford University Press, 1942.

Morris, Richard B. *John Jay, the Nation, and the Court*. Boston: Boston University Press, 1967.

Mott, Frank Luther. *Jefferson and the Press*. Baton Rouge: Louisiana State University Press, 1943.

Mullin, John. *The Baltimore Directory for 1799*. Baltimore: Warner and Hanna, 1799.

Murray, Sir James. *Letters from America 1773–1780*. Edited by Eric Robson. Manchester: Manchester University Press, 1951.

Owings, Donnell M. *His Lordship's Patronage—Officers of Profit in Colonial Maryland*. Maryland Historical Society Studies in Maryland History, no. 1. Baltimore: Maryland Historical Society, 1953

Paterson, William. *Glimpses of Colonial Society, and the Life at Princeton College*. Edited by Wayne Jay Mills. Philadelphia: J. B. Lippincott, 1903.

Pinkney, William. *The Life of William Pinkney*. New York: D. Appleton, 1853.

———. *Speech of William Pinkney, Esq. in the House of Delegates of Maryland, at their Session in November, 1789*. Philadelphia: Joseph Crukshank, 1790.

Plumer, William. *William Plumer's Memorandum of Proceedings in the United States Senate, 1803–1807*. Edited by Everett Somerville Brown. New York: Macmillan, 1923.

Plumer, William, Jr. *Life of William Plumer*. Edited by A. P. Peabody. Boston: Phillips, Sampson, 1857.

Poole, William Frederick. *Anti-Slavery Opinions before the Year 1800*. Cincinnati, O.: R. Clarke, 1873.

Prentiss, Charles. *Life of the Late General William Eaton.* Brookfield, Mass.: E. Merriam, 1813.

Prescott, Arthur Taylor. *Drafting the Federal Constitution.* Baton Rouge: Louisiana State University Press, 1941.

Preston, Walter W. *History of Harford County, Maryland.* Baltimore: Sun Book Office, 1901.

Proceedings of the conventions of the Province of Maryland Held at the City of Annapolis, in 1774, 1775, & 1776. Baltimore: Lucas and Deaver, 1836.

Queen Anne's School Minute Book. Maryland Historical Society, Baltimore, Md.

Quynn, Dorothy Mackay. "The Loyalist Plot in Frederick." *Maryland Historical Magazine* 40 (September 1945).

Raffensperger, Rev. E. B. "Who Killed the Logan Family?" *Potter's American Monthly* 11 (July 1878).

Report of the Committee of Grievances. Baltimore: W. Goddard and J. Angell, 1792.

Rich, Wesley E. *History of the United States Post Office in the Year 1829.* Cambridge, Mass.: Harvard University Press, 1924.

Richardson, James Daniel. *A Compilation of the Messages and Papers of the Presidents 1789–1897.* 10 vols. Washington, D.C.: U.S. Government Printing Office, 1896–99.

Robertson, David. *Debates and Other Proceedings of the Convention of Virginia.* 2d ed. Richmond, Va.: Ritchie and Worsby and H. Davis, 1805.

———. *Trials of Aaron Burr.* 2 vols. Philadelphia: Hopkins and Earl, 1808.

Robertson, J. M. *Louisiana under the Rule of Spain, 1789–1807.* 2 vols. Cleveland, O.: Arthur H. Clark, 1911.

Robinson, Blackwell P. *William R. Davie.* Chapel Hill: University of North Carolina Press, 1957.

Rodd, Francis Rennell. *General William Eaton, the Failure of an Idea.* New York: Menton, Balch and Co., 1932.

Roddy, Edward G. "Maryland and the Presidential Election of 1800." *Maryland Historical Magazine* 56 (September 1961).

Roosevelt, Theodore. *The Winning of the West.* 4 vols. New York: G. P. Putnam's Sons, 1886–96.

Rowland, Kate Mason. *The Life of Charles Carroll of Carrollton, 1737–1832.* 2 vols. New York: G. P. Putnam's Sons, 1898.

———. *The Life of George Mason.* 2 vols. New York: G. P. Putnam's Sons, 1892.

Rutland, Robert Allen. *The Ordeal of the Constitution: The Antifederalists and the Ratification Struggle of 1787–1788.* Norman: University of Oklahoma Press, 1965.

Schachner, Nathan. *Aaron Burr, a Biography.* New York: Frederick A. Stokes, 1937.

———. *Thomas Jefferson, a Biography.* New York: Thomas Yoseloff, 1960.

Scharf, John Thomas. *The Chronicles of Baltimore.* Baltimore: Turnbull Bros., 1874.

———. *History of Baltimore City and County.* Philadelphia: L. H. Everts, 1881.

———. *History of Western Maryland.* 2 vols. Philadelphia: L. H. Everts, 1882.

Schlesinger, A. M. *The Colonial Merchants and the American Revolution, 1763–1776.* New York: Columbia University Press, 1917.

Semmes, John Edward. *John H. B. Latrobe and His Times, 1803–1891.* Baltimore: Norman Remington Co., 1917.

Semmes, Raphael. *Baltimore As Seen by Visitors, 1783–1860.* Baltimore: Maryland Historical Society, 1953.

Shepherd, William R. "Wilkinson and the Beginning of the Spanish Conspiracy." *American Historical Review* 9 (April 1904).

Shreve, Royal. *The Finished Scoundrel.* Indianapolis, Ind.: Bobbs-Merrill, 1933.

Shriver, J. Alexis. *Lafayette in Harford County.* Baltimore: By the author, 1931.

Silver, John Archer. *The Provisional Government of Maryland (1774–1777).* Johns Hopkins Studies in Historical and Political Science, no. 13. Baltimore: Johns Hopkins Press, 1895.

Sioussat, Annie Middleton. *Old Baltimore.* New York: Macmillan, 1931.

Slaybaugh, J. Paul. *Private (Independent) Secondary Education in Maryland.* Washington, D.C.: U.S. Government Printing Office, n.d.

Smith, A. E. *James Madison: Builder.* New York: Wilson-Erickson, 1937.

Smith, Edward P. "The Movement towards a Second Constitutional Convention in 1788." In *Essays in the Constitutional History of the United States in the Formative Period 1775–1789 by Graduates and Former Members of The Johns Hopkins University.* Edited by John Franklin Jameson. Boston: Houghton Mifflin, 1889.

Smith, James Morton. *Freedom's Fetters: The Alien and Sedition Laws and American Civil Liberties.* Ithaca, N.Y.: Cornell University Press, 1956.

Smith, Samuel H., and Lloyd, Thomas. *Trial of Samuel Chase.* 2 vols. Washington, D.C.: U.S. Government Printing Office, 1805.

Sowerby, E. Millicent, comp. *Catalogue of the Library of Thomas Jefferson.* 5 vols. Washington, D.C.: Library of Congress, 1952–59.

Stampp, Kenneth M. *The Peculiar Institution: Slavery in the Ante-Bellum South.* New York: Alfred A. Knopf, 1956.

Steiner, Bernard Christian. *History of Education in Maryland.* Washington, D.C.: U.S. Government Printing Office, 1894.

———. *The Life and Correspondence of James McHenry.* Cleveland, O.: Burrows Bros., 1907.

———. "Maryland's Adoption of the Constitution." *American Historical Review* 5 (October 1899).

Still, William. *The Underground Railroad.* Philadelphia: Porter and Coates, 1872.

Story, William Wetmore. *Life and Letters of Joseph Story, Associate Justice of the Supreme Court of the United States.* 2 vols. Boston: C. C. Little and J. Brown, 1851.

Strayer, Joseph Reese. *The Delegate from New York.* Princeton, N.J.: Princeton University Press, 1939.

Strickland, William Peter. *Life of Jacob Gruber.* New York: Carlton and Porter, 1866.

Sullivan, Kathryn. *Maryland and France 1774–1789.* Philadelphia: University of Pennsylvania Press, 1936.

Suppressed Book about Slavery, The. New York: Carleton, 1864.

Tansill, Charles C., ed. *Documents Illustrative of the Formation of the Union of the American States.* Washington, D.C.: U.S. Government Printing Office, 1927.

Thwaites, Reuben Gold, and Kellogg, Louise Phelps, eds. *Documentary History of Dunmore's War, 1774.* Madison: Wisconsin Historical Society, 1905.

Ticknor, George. *Life, Letters, and Journals of George Ticknor.* Boston: J. R. Osgood, 1876.

Tower, Charlemagne. *The Marquis de LaFayette in the American Revolution.* 2 vols. Philadelphia: J. B. Lippincott, 1895.

Turner, Kathryn. "The Midnight Judges." *University of Pennsylvania Law Review* 109 (February 1961).

Tyler, Samuel. *Memoir of Roger Brooke Taney, LL.D.* Baltimore: John Murphy, 1872.

Van Doren, Carl. *Secret History of the American Revolution.* New York: Viking Press, 1941.

Wallace, Paul. *Princeton Sketches, the Story of Nassau Hall.* New York: G. P. Putnam's Sons, 1893.

Wallace, Paul A. W. *Conrad Weiser.* Philadelphia: University of Pennsylvania Press, 1945.

———. *The Muhlenbergs of Pennsylvania.* Philadelphia: University of Pennsylvania Press, 1950.

Wallace, Willard M. *Appeal to Arms: A Military History of the American Revolution.* New York: Harper and Bros., 1951.

Wambaugh, Eugene. *A Selection of Cases on Constitutional Law.* Cambridge, Mass.: Harvard University Press, 1914–15.

Wandell, Samuel H., and Minnegerode, Meade. *Aaron Burr.* 2 vols. New York: G. P. Putnam's Sons, 1925.

Ward, Christopher. *The War of the Revolution.* 2 vols. New York: Macmillan, 1932.

Warren, Charles. *A History of the American Bar.* Boston: Little, Brown, 1911.

———. *The Making of the Constitution.* Boston: Little, Brown, 1929.

———. *The Supreme Court in United States History.* New rev. ed. 2 vols. Boston: Little, Brown, 1926.

Wertenbaker, Thomas Jefferson. *Princeton, 1746–1896.* Princeton, N.J.: Princeton University Press, 1946.

Wheaton, Henry. *Some Account of the Life, Writings and Speeches of William Pinkney.* New York: J. W. Palmer, 1826.

Whitehead, William A. *East Jersey under the Proprietary Governments.* [New York]: New-Jersey Historical Society, 1846.

———, ed. *Documents Relating to the Colonial History of the State of New Jersey.* Reprinted in *New Jersey Archives*, 1st ser., edited by Frederick W. Record. Newark, N.J.: Daily Advertiser Printing House, 1888.

Wilkinson, James. *Memoirs of My Own Times.* 3 vols. Philadelphia: Abraham Small, 1816.

Willcox, William B. *The American Rebellion—Sir Henry Clinton's Narrative.* New Haven, Conn.: Yale University Press, 1954.

Williams, T. J. C. *History of Frederick County.* 2 vols. Frederick, Md.: L. R. Litsworth, 1910.

———. *History of Washington County.* Chambersburg, Pa., and Hagerstown, Md. J. M. Runtz and L. R. Litsworth, 1906.

Winsor, Justin. *Narrative and Critical History of America.* 6 vols. Boston: Houghton Mifflin, 1884–89.

Wissler, Clark. *Indians of the U.S.* American Museum of Natural History Science Series. Garden City, N.Y.: Doubleday, 1953.

Withers, Alexander Scott. *Chronicles of Border Warfare.* Edited and annotated by Reuben Gold Thwaites. Cincinnati, O.: Stewart and Kidd, 1895.

329

Index

335

THE JOHNS HOPKINS PRESS

Designed by James C. Wageman

Composed in Monotype Baskerville
by Baltimore Type and Composition Corporation,
with display type in Perpetua Bold
by Emil P. Popp & Son
and hand lettering by James Wageman

Printed on 60 lb. P&S R
by Universal Lithographers, Inc.

Bound in Holliston Payko
by Moore and Company, Inc.